NOT

THIS
BOOK
IS
[NOT]
REQUIRED

To my dear one and my inspiration, Rupa, and to my beloved
daughter, my one and only Melanie.

—Bernard McGrane

To Dan and Jack, Thank you for making my life better every day with
your imagination, laughter, and smiles. You are the greatest gifts
in my life and I'm so proud of you both. I love you
more than you can ever know.

—John Gunderson

To my students, who make it all worthwhile.

—Terri L. Anderson

Brief Contents

Detailed Contents

Preface to the First Edition

The years which a student spends in a school must leave behind in him a fragrance and delight.

—Krishnamurti (1974)

In Horse Feathers, Groucho Marx plays Professor Wagstaff, president of Huxley College. As a money-saving move, he suggests tearing down the dormitories. "But, Professor," says the dean, "Where will the students sleep?" "Where they always sleep—in the classroom!"

This is a book that invites you to look at your college education: what it could be and what, alas, it often is. It is a book that suggests to you what you can make of this opportunity, given the resources at your disposal. If you want to become truly educated, you will have to educate yourself, and at times you will have to do it in spite of the academy. Perhaps this is good because knowledge that comes too easily doesn't train one to be an independent thinker, and only an independent thinker is ever truly intelligent.

We will not look at these four years merely in terms of the formal world of classes and professors. We want to look at the larger experience—at your whole environment and your whole life during these four years—because some of the most important learning is done outside the classroom.

I have tried to make this a survival manual for undergraduates: emotional survival and intellectual survival. I will even say that it speaks to the issues of spiritual survival, if by "spiritual" we mean the capacity to live in harmony with oneself and with the universe.

You will undoubtedly disagree with parts of this book. It is only one person's view. But if it connects with your life at any important point, I shall feel that it has served its purpose for you. I have tried to give you the broadest possible picture of your position as a student in the academic world and in the larger society of which you are a part. To do this, I have had to use a large brush, and I have undoubtedly made mistakes. But I have always considered this broad perspective more important than the fine attention to detail given by the academic specialists.

This is not an academic or scholarly work. It is a very critical look at academia by one who has been through it, from freshman to full professor. Occasionally, I will suggest a book that I think you will like. But you will not find an *ibid.* or an *op. cit.* littering these pages.

In my years as a college teacher, I succeeded in what was ever the chief ambition of my career: to keep my students awake. Of course, there were always a comatose few who hadn't gotten to bed until four in the morning, or had mononucleosis, or were merely in love. But on the whole, I succeeded because I discovered that students always came awake when I laid aside academic sociology and talked to them about their lives as students—about the academic institutions in which they labored and how and why those institutions functioned; about the competition and anxiety created by grades; about their ambitions and their difficult choices of major and career; about the travail of those who came from minority or working-class families; yes, even about their love affairs and their loneliness. We talked about how you find out what you want to do in life and about how you can keep your integrity and your sanity in this very difficult society.

Eventually, drawing on sociology and Eastern philosophy, I developed a course devoted solely to these questions. I shall describe that to you in the chapter "Adventures in Desocialization" and give you some of the exercises and "walking meditations" that I used to help students gain insight into their own functioning. As I discussed life in the academy with my students, I also listened and learned a lot. It is, therefore, to all my former students that I dedicate this little book because much of what I have written here I learned from them.

It is, perhaps, ironic that after writing a chapter called "Everybody Hates to Write," I found myself hugely enjoying the process of writing this book. After the writing I had done in the usual, stilted language of social science, it was a huge relief to write in good English. I always loved to write, and I think I did pretty well at it until I got to graduate school and had all the style knocked out of me by the demands of academic sociologese. I always resisted a little. I remember my dissertation chairman asking me sadly whether I had "turned against sociology" because I used too much plain English. In writing this book, I felt that I had regained my writing voice after 30 years.

Acknowledgments

I hope you will bear with me for a moment while I thank the good friends who helped me write this book. My thanks to Glenn Goodwin of Pitzer College who helped me, as he has helped so many students and colleagues through the years, by commenting on and improving the manuscript. Above all, he has given me constant inspiration and encouragement. Glenn struggled mightily with me to provide more documentation and to give credit to more of the sociologists whose insights I have used. I resisted because I didn't want this to be a scholarly book. But I should say here that most of what I know has come to me through the great sociologists

I have studied, as well as the writers of Eastern thought. Probably the only original thing about the book is its focus on undergraduate life.

My thanks equally to Ellin Ringler Henderson of Pitzer College, who made many useful suggestions and whose careful, loving red pencil brought elegance and clarity to my prose. I would also like to thank Barney McGrane for using the book in his teaching long before it was published. Barney sent me much valuable student feedback and encouraged me greatly in the writing of the book. My thanks also to Dawn Hassett, who suggested the title.

Finally, of course, my warmest thanks to Ted Hoffman, who helped with the writing. His confidence in me and my work has been my mainstay. Needless to say, the errors and shortcomings of the book are entirely my own. My thanks also to my former colleagues and to the staff and faculty of Pitzer College for creating an environment in which innovative teaching was not only permitted but rewarded.

—Inge Bell

Preface to the Fifth Edition

This, the fifth edition of *This Book Is Not Required,* has again been a student-centered, student-powered, collaborative, and participatory process. Our aim, as ever, is to keep *This Book* a living document, relevant and immediate for each new generation of college students. Team Bell, under the leadership of Dr. Bernard McGrane, a sociology professor at Chapman University, Dr. John Gunderson, a high school teacher at Dana Hills High School and adjunct professor at Chapman University, and Dr. Terri Anderson, a sociology professor at UCLA, met and went through the text trying to find that special balance of keeping the classical core ideas from Inge Bell and updating the work on issues pertinent to today's college students everywhere. Each generation of college students enters the almost timeless organism of "the university" but is greeted with new, unique, and interesting challenges and changes.

The fifth edition has expanded the chapters "Technology and Learning" and "Survival Skills." In addition, numerous and diverse new student contributions have been grafted on to many of the other chapters. This current version of Team Bell continued its exciting method of collaboration via the Internet. We met in person but also posted our writings on a common site and were able to co-create, share, collaborate, and critique via technology. This method allows for much more sharing of ideas and critiquing than with the earlier editions.

We hope this new process will inspire student readers from all over the country or the world to get involved in co-creating the next edition of *This Book Is Not Required* and to participate in Team Bell 2016. Our goal, as always, is that *This Book* can offer you insight and inspiration on your educational experience. We hope this will make you passionate enough to want to share what you learn with the next (4-year) generation of college students.

Our heartfelt gratitude goes out to the members of Team Bell, listed at the end of this book. We would also like to thank the reviewers over the successive editions of *This Book Is Not Required:*

Glenn A. Goodwin, University of La Verne

Karen Monique Gregg, University of Notre Dame

Douglas W. Hume, Northern Kentucky University

Natalie Miller, Ramapo College of New Jersey

Laura Nathan, Mills College

Jane Penny, Eastfield College

Gina Petonito, Western Illinois University

Ed Sbarbaro, Colorado College

Rik Scarce, Montana State University/Skidmore College

Michael Weinstein, University of Hawaii, Manoa

Alan Willis, Northern Michigan University

—*Barney McGrane, mcgrane@chapman.edu*
—*John Gunderson, gunderson@chapman.edu*
—*Terri L. Anderson, doctorta@gmail.com*

PART I

Academics and Learning

Welcome to College

In Chapter 1, we explore the phenomenon of being a stranger in a strange new land and attempt to encourage you to really listen to what some already established, well experienced "natives" pointedly suggest, coming from their own experience. In particular, we will explore the following topics:

- The transition from high school to college.
- Opportunities and challenges that students typically face as they enter the academy and face the unknown.
- Some remarkably effective strategies to personally consider.
- Some ways students can discover and uncover their own personal academic passions.
- The special opportunities and strategies faced by nontraditional students.

"Welcome to" is a message we are all familiar with. Most of us see these words on signposts around our hometowns and don't pay much attention. However, when we embark on a journey, these signs take on new meaning and indicate we are entering a foreign land filled with new culture, new customs, new ideas, and new vocabulary. As most travelers know, even the most ordinary necessities can be hard to find in a new location if you don't know how to ask or where to look. These disconcerting situations can range from silly and embarrassing to dangerous or life threatening. Luckily, most of them can be avoided with a little help or guidance.

College is also a destination to which we travel. For most new students, it's like traveling to a foreign land. The same problems that afflict most new travelers in a foreign land can be seen in the experiences of new students on campus. Unfamiliar terrain, foreign culture, and unknown rules and customs can make a new student stand out on a campus like a stereotypical backpack-wearing, camera-holding tourist in a foreign city. Even the most confident educational travelers need a guidebook to help make sense of this new world they are entering.

Unfortunately, most colleges don't have a simple guidebook that explains the real "do's and taboos" of college life. New students are left to fend for themselves as they are immersed in this new world. Sometimes lack of information can get new students into trouble that could have been avoided if they'd had a little help. One saving grace for most new students is their numerous fellow students; they are not alone in their struggles.

The plight of the new student is not hidden from view or unknown; even the words used to describe them illuminate their situation: "freshmen," "underclassmen." These anxious new educational travelers are fresh and ripe for picking if someone wants to take advantage of them, just like a traveler in a foreign land. For many of us who have experienced this awkward vulnerability, it is like a rite of passage. We tell ourselves that we went through it ourselves, so it can't be that bad.

A little help and guidance can go a long way to make your transition to this new land a much happier, safer, and more successful journey. Ask for help from some of the "locals," who always are good guides, and after asking, don't forget to listen. A description of the terrain is much different from the experience of the culture, but seasoned educational travelers have already paved the way.

This book is an attempt to give you some useful suggestions and advice from people just like you who are experiencing college for the wonderful, trying, and transformative part of life that it is. Listen to some of these "travel guides" in the pages that follow, and then map a course for yourself.

Transition

A Senior's Advice

Before I graduated from high school, I had this sudden realization: In a couple of short months, I will be in college! What will it be like? Will I make new friends? Will the classes be too hard? I had a million questions that, it seemed, no one could answer. I had a few friends who were already in college, so I decided to ask for some advice. The best advice came from one of my best friends, who was attending UCI's undergraduate school at the time. He told me not to be afraid or intimidated by anything. He opened my eyes to the fact that each of us was in the same boat, especially as incoming freshmen. It doesn't matter if you were valedictorian or a mediocre student in your high school, when you get to college, you start from square one. Professors don't know whether you were a stellar student in high school or not. Their opinions of you are based entirely on your performance from the first day of class onward.

Also, my friend told me to be aggressive and ask a lot of questions. Sometimes it can be intimidating to raise your hand in a room of 100 students in order to clarify a point.

Am I asking a dumb question? Are people going to laugh at me and think I am stupid? No way. He told me that what I had to say was important and that, most likely, the people sitting next to me had the same questions on the tips of their tongues; they were just too scared to ask. I found this to be true as I dove headfirst into my freshman year. It was amazing. I could almost see neighboring students thanking me with their eyes as I asked the professor to reiterate a point. Plus, I built my confidence and my communication skills and ensured that I fully understood the lesson being taught.

Friendships come with time if you embrace them. Chances are, your two best buddies in high school are off to life in the real world or college in another city. For probably the first time in your life, you are removed from your comfort zone and submerged in a world of strangers. This can be scary, but before you make friends with anybody, you need to make friends with yourself. This time of independence encourages a lot of soul searching and testing of your morals. If you were an angel in high school, you can rebel at any moment and explore a whole new world of trouble (or vice versa). Because you're not assigned to a set of required classes, you might find yourself spending a lot of time alone. This alone time may be a first for you, and it can be weird initially. Even if you live on campus with a roommate, you won't have a 24-hour companion. During these times, it is great to look inside yourself and get to know who you are. All kinds of questions come up if you allow yourself to embrace these thoughts. What makes you happy? What do you look for in a friend? What kind of food do you like? What is God? You never stop learning about yourself, but college is a great place to start this healthy habit. Once this exploration had begun, I became much more comfortable with myself; as a result, I became more comfortable around others. It was only natural that I later made some great friendships that have brought me much happiness.

I really feel that my friend's words of advice were what gave me the confidence to begin the journey through college that had intimidated me for so long. Now I am about to graduate, and I find that I have grown in so many ways and made so many new friends. College was a wonderful experience during which I learned a lot about people, the world, and most important, myself.

—Sara Kalawi

The False Image High School Gives You of College

I can honestly say that I must have been blind when I entered college, or at least tremendously naïve. My take on life was that I would graduate from high school, go on to pursue higher education in college for about 4 years, graduate, and then start working and have a family. Let's just say that I was in for a rude awakening. Somewhere in the middle of my freshman year, I was informed that it would be very difficult for me to make a "decent living" (whatever that may be) with only a BA in psychology. My belief was that I would get my BA and begin practicing clinical psychology. Little did I know.

I realize how foolish I was now that I look back on all this, but the truth is that most college students enter college with a completely distorted picture of where their lives are headed. High schools today are more or less prep schools to get you into college, but that's about it. They don't bother teaching students to step back from the high school and college bubbles and look at where they want to be in the end. High schools paint a picture of college as the end of your education, but the truth is that it is only the beginning. It is only after you enter college that you realize you are doing this for you and nobody else (at least, if you're lucky enough).

I believe that this is when you should realize the worth of your education. Everything just begins to make more sense after you enter college: why you were in school to begin with, why you're taking the classes you are taking, and how you see yourself applying your education to your life in the future. I now understand that I will have to go to grad school for about another two to four years after I finish college, but this is not something that I dread. To be honest, I do not feel as though I would be even remotely prepared to go out and practice psychology once I graduate with my BA I actually want to go on and learn as much as I possibly can so that I may one day be the best psychologist that I am capable of being. However, when I compare the way I am thinking now to the way I was thinking 2 years ago when I was a senior in high school, my point of view has made a 180-degree turn. Don't get me wrong, I still want to graduate soon so that I can go on with the rest of my life, but I have now realized that learning psychology is more or less what I will be doing with my life, so there is no need to rush through it. Many students want a college degree more than a college education. I suggest you understand your relationship to your education and what you are doing and don't just do it for the sake of getting the degree and getting out.

So basically, my advice is that you should be open to new things when you enter college. The impression that you get of life when you are in high school is not a very accurate one, so you have to be willing to be open-minded when you enter college.

—Sheyda Bogosyan with John Chuidian

Rejected by a College

One of the hardest reality checks that I have ever had to deal with was receiving a letter of denial from the college that I had dreamed of attending since I was in junior high. Everything that had constituted my reality for such a long period of time had suddenly come crashing down, and I had no clue what to do. For all of my high school life, my hope of getting into that university was what gave me the drive to push harder and take one more AP course, but now it seemed as though all that I had based my motivation upon had been stolen from me. I had reached the end of the rainbow and the pot of gold that I had hoped to find there was missing. The unexpected rejection I faced at the end of my senior year of high school forced me to reevaluate my entire reality: the present, my future, and everything that I had endured in the past.

I had attended private school all my life, and whether we liked it or not, the whole class knew everything about each other because we were a group of about 45 students who had been together for 12 years. We all had expectations for one another, and we more or less knew what we would do with our lives (or at least we thought we did). Even our teachers knew us on a one-to-one basis and had certain expectations for each of us. Basically, if one of us screwed up, there were a lot of people there to let us know, from our parents, to our teachers, to our friends. For this reason, when I got rejected by the school that I was hoping to get into, I felt that everyone was really disappointed in me. This might have been a complete distortion of reality. However, I had put so much emphasis on getting into that school that I had let it define who I was, and once I was rejected, I was afraid that everyone would be disappointed in me. I interpreted people's actions as negatively as possible and felt as though I didn't matter anymore. I was a failure. That one letter of rejection made me reevaluate myself from head to toe. I began to wonder whether I really deserved to go to that school or whether I had what it takes. Maybe I really wasn't good enough for them. Was it that my grades weren't good enough? Or maybe it was my SAT score. But that wouldn't make sense because I had friends from other schools who had lower scores than I but had gotten in.

I knew that I had to pick another school, so I chose the University of California, Irvine and enrolled there in the fall. I was closing one chapter in the book of my life and opening another. All I could hope for was that this new chapter wouldn't be as disappointing as the previous one.

No matter how much I told myself that this was a whole new beginning for me, the rejection I had faced had been embedded in the back of my mind. I felt as though I wasn't good enough and that everyone was much smarter than I. Also, I had lost a great deal of confidence in my writing abilities because I was convinced that my personal statement was the main reason I hadn't gotten into my first choice school. Regardless of all this, I gave my schoolwork my all. I took the hardest classes that I could and was determined to get A's in them, even if it meant that I had to be in my TA's office every other day. I was determined to make the admissions committee that had rejected me kick themselves later on for doing so.

A few quarters passed and I began getting used to UC Irvine. Although I had not really wanted to attend the school, it grew on me. I felt as though I was in a different world when I was there. I was away from home and did not have to explain myself to anyone. This gave me a sense of responsibility that I probably would not have attained had I stayed home and gone to that other school. On the flip side, though, I really missed home. I have always been attached to my family, so moving away was, and still is, a very difficult process for me. But this was positive for me because it kept me motivated to get through school faster so that I could move back home as soon as possible.

I was very focused and knew exactly what I had to do to get where I wanted to be. My bitterness slowly faded, and I realized that I was no longer doing all this to show the other school what a mistake they had made, but I was doing it for me. I had declared a major in psychology and really loved what I was studying. I was at a school where I actually had the opportunity to go and could talk to my professors and get their opinions about certain issues or even have discussions with them. I could actually get the classes that I wanted to take, instead of having to wait until my senior year because there was no room. Even the little things, like being able to find parking in a matter of 15 minutes, made my life a lot easier than that of my friends who were going to the school that I had hoped to get into. I felt as though I had my life under control and I knew what I was doing with it. Because going to school was not as big an ordeal for me as it was for my friends who were in the other school, I even had time to get a job that was directly related to my field and that I loved doing. Everything just seemed to fit together, and I felt as though I was one step ahead of everyone else, even though my original plans had been disrupted. It was a great feeling to know, for the first time in my life, that I was doing all this for myself and not to satisfy everyone else or to meet everyone else's expectations for me.

Although the rejection that I had to face after high school was a very difficult thing for me to deal with, it worked out for the best. I cannot say that I am completely over it and that it doesn't bother me at all. The truth is that I do not think I will ever forget how I felt after receiving that letter and during the months that followed, but the important thing is now I see the big picture. The main solution for me was time. There was nothing anyone could have told me at the time that would have made me feel it wasn't my fault that I didn't get in. I had to prove it to myself.

However, some of the questions that I asked myself made me feel better about all this. Why am I in school? If I'm here because I am truly interested in the field that I'm pursuing, does it matter which school I'm in? I could get the same education in any school as long as I make the effort and I keep in close contact with my professors. Also, will I go to graduate school, and if I do, isn't learning the material my priority? As long as you truly have a passion for what you are doing, you will be the best at it regardless of any obstacles that you may face in life.

You can't let one rejection keep you from being what you want to be. Instead, let it make you a stronger person. Do everything you can to make it work in your favor. Never let anyone or any institution tell you who you are or what you can achieve.

—*Sheyda Bogosyan*

Facing the Unknown

We Earn a Master's in Doing While Forgetting to Master Living

We could compile an endless list of everything that you could experience after you graduate from high school. You will go on vacation, say good-bye to friends, leave family behind, shop for new clothes, buy supplies for the dorm, and hope that you will be ready by the time school starts. The problem is that we all too often forget the changes around us. We will make new friends, but we will leave others.

Perhaps we will attend a relative's wedding over the summer, only to resume packing the next day. We are so busy getting ready that we miss and fail to deal with the deep, profound change that we are about to experience.

Universities will not offer classes in slowing down and being present to change, but it is the change that we undergo that will have the greatest impact on our lives. Marriage and divorce. New friends made, others to whom we bid farewell. Excitement for something new, sadness over leaving the "known" of our life behind. Birth and death. Indeed, our diploma marks a completion and a stepping stone to that which lies ahead. But our diploma in life details something more profound: We shed the high school self and awaken to the college self. The body remains static; the person subconsciously adapts to change.

Some of the changes will be wonderful; others will be painful. You might fall in love and find a soul mate. The next day, a beloved grandfather may die. You'll party the night away with new-found college friends in pure, unadulterated excitement because finals are over, then awaken to the reality that alcohol really does cause hangovers. You cannot fully prepare for change, but you can welcome it when it comes by being fully present to it. You can learn to live and not merely to do.

After 4, 5, or maybe even 6 years, you might earn a diploma for your efforts. But you will never receive an award for the most important classes you take in your college career. The classes in life, learned by waking up each day, will teach you more about yourself and about others than any novel or scientific proof ever can. Mark Twain said, "I never let my schooling get in the way of my education." Before graduating as a master of your discipline, graduate first with a mastery of the self.

—Christopher Patrick King

First College Experience

It was the first Saturday of the quarter before classes started, and I was still adjusting to living in the dorms. As I was walking down the hall, I overheard some of my floormates talking about the biggest frat party of the year. It was going to happen on

Sunday. I took this into consideration but kept walking. The frat party didn't particularly interest me. I didn't think it would be too much fun going someplace with a bunch of strangers and lots of alcohol. But as the day progressed, the idea seemed to get even more popular among my floormates until everyone was talking about going. Even my roommate, a biochemistry major addicted to studying, was planning to go, so this convinced me.

With the biggest party of the year only a night away, people from my floor decided to go to a frat party on Saturday to see what it would be like. So we gathered our new acquaintances and headed down to frat row to find a party. Soon we were on a patio looking onto a dance floor in a room filled with black light. Before we began dancing, my new friends headed over to the bar and were greeted with hard liquor; apparently, the frat had run out of beer. My roommate and I didn't get anything, but there was one in our group who seemed determined to get drunk as soon as possible.

After alcohol was obtained, we danced until we became tired. Then we went out onto the patio for some fresh air, where we were greeted by a frat boy trying to give us more alcohol. We already had some and refused his request to give us more, but I couldn't help thinking how desperately they wanted us drunk.

A couple of our floormates weren't having a good time and decided to leave, and my roommate and I followed them after a couple of hours. We danced for the remainder of the time, in a pretty mellow atmosphere of glowing objects and music. We headed back up the large hill to our dorms with our drunken colleagues in hand, literally. To keep them from falling into the gutter, we had to hold them. We went back up to our rooms, where two drunken boys climbed up to my roommate's bed and stayed there for a couple more hours, talking with us about college and high school and general getting-to-know-you things. My roommate talked about our experience.

She liked the party and was glad we went in a group because she felt safer, even though our group was a bunch of strangers who lived on our floor. She told me she drank, and I asked her when because I had never seen her with a drink, and she said she drank from someone else's drink because she didn't want an entire drink to herself. I couldn't believe what I was hearing. What a dangerous decision, but she didn't know it was dangerous. She was new to the party scene and had no idea what precautions to take. Luckily, her friend's drink wasn't laced with anything. I proceeded to tell her the rules of safe partying so that I wouldn't have to worry about her on Sunday.

On the morning of the big day, I was excited about what the biggest party of the year could hold, but I was a little scared at first because I had heard rumors of fraternity life, and I didn't want to get myself into a situation that I couldn't escape from. If the previous night's party was only a fraction of what was to come, then I might be in trouble. Rumors were floating around that the police would have to shut it down and fire hoses would drench spectators. Every frat would participate in the event, there would be an overwhelming crowd, and we would have to arrive early to get in. And so we did.

Before we even reached the party, the visual we got was insane: All of the frats were filled to the brim and long lines of students snaked through the streets, with large crowds just wandering around looking for a potential frat. Frat brothers were shouting for us to leave so that they wouldn't be shut down. That didn't stop us. We had been thinking about this party for 2 days, and we weren't about to leave without a fight. So we pushed and shoved to get to the front of the line of a frat that would let our guy friends in. Apparently they aren't too strict about girls, but they don't want a lot of guys. Maybe they think they have a better chance if the male to female ratio is tampered with. This is rather ironic anyway because they are supposed to be recruiting for their frats.

Finally we found a suitable party and waited in line with the rest of the freshmen to try to get in. But there was a list, and apparently we weren't on it. Still determined, we pushed our way through the crowd and somehow past security into the party. Three floors of dancing and drinking! Oh joy! But the pushing didn't stop there. It was really crowded and disorienting. Loud music shook the floors as we worked our way to the top of the stairs. We made it, and I found myself again among strangers. I didn't feel comfortable, and after all the work we did to get in the frat, I left and went back to the dorm.

As I entered my floor, I saw people playing cards in the study lounge. One of them was a fellow partier from the night before. I regaled him with a tale of the chaos I had just seen, and he seemed really eager to go. Being easily swayed, I went back for the second time, to see whether we could get into a party. I thought maybe I could find one I liked better. A huge mass of people had accumulated in that short time, and now it was impossible to get in. So we sat down on a giant university sign and watched havoc ensue. The people were all in the middle of the street, which had to be shut down. This tightly packed group swayed back and forth as if trying to get somewhere. Pushing and bottle throwing started, and we watched from a safe distance, remarking on how crazy it all was. Tomorrow everyone would go back to their normal lives, but some would end up in the hospital instead. Firefighters and police were waiting on the edge of the mass for a cue that they should exercise their authority.

As midnight struck, they shut the party down. With fire hoses in hand, the firefighters threatened the crowd as loudspeakers announced the end of the party. We would all have to go home. The crowd wasn't happy, but my friend and I didn't stick around to get hosed. We went back up to our dorm and told everyone we had been to the biggest party of the year and survived.

What happened to my roommate, you ask? She ended up freak dancing with a guy on our floor and felt guilty about it afterward. Later on, she was in a long line with him for the bathroom, and someone asked whether they were together. She said they weren't, and he asked whether she was drunk. She said no and asked why. The stranger said he wanted her to go in the bathroom with her freak-dancing partner to make the line go faster. Go figure. What a wonderful way to start your first year of college!

This is what many of us face when we go to college. Books and tests will follow, but partying will always be there for us, even when we least expect it. We all hear about college parties, but not all of us expect to go to one of this magnitude as soon as we move in!

—Shawna Wood

Instructions and Suggestions

Orientation Is Required

I highly recommend going to orientations. This is where I met some of the most interesting people who are now my friends; one has been my roommate for 2 years. When I first stepped into the big university in the big city I was scared. I had no friends. I didn't know my way around. After orientation I knew my way around this large campus almost as well as I know the town I grew up in. Next, living in the dorms is awesome. If you live near campus, you should still live in the dorms. This place helped me socially and intellectually. Everything was there! First, I became friends with my roommates, then neighbors, and soon the whole floor. It helps to leave the room door open, and also living in front of the elevators helps. You should also participate in floor activities organized by the floor's Program Assistant or Residential Advisors. I'm not saying it's a must to go to all of the events, but go to as many as you can, at least for the first 5 weeks. Networking is very important in college, not to mention essential for life once you're out of school. Clubs and fraternities or sororities are also good places to meet people. But beware; don't fall into the segregated cliques or groups.

I opted to stay out of the fraternity system, but this doesn't mean I can never communicate or party with them. You just need to know one or two of the members in the Greek house to reap the benefits. This includes getting into parties with those long lines that don't seem to move because only the girls are being let in. Basically, the strategy is to start with whatever you feel comfortable with; start small. I started small and branched out; it's better that way, and plus, it feels good to know people almost everywhere you go.

—*Kenneth W. Chow Jr.*

Top 10 Things to Do Before You Get Out of College

1. *Live in the dorms.*   You may have to live in a room the size of a closet, and you may have to live with a terrible roommate, but the dorms are still one of the best places to meet the student population.
2. *Meet with a counselor.*   A counselor will help you plan your classes, inform you about programs you may be interested in, and let you in on some wisdom. Counselors are here to help, and you may not know it yet, but you do need the help.
3. *Study abroad.*   Escape the familiar and explore the unknown. You'll discover so much about the world and yourself.
4. *Commit to community service.*   Whether you volunteer to build houses for the underserved or become an activist, your community needs your energy, talent, enthusiasm, and fresh perspective.

5. *Find a part-time job.* College doesn't have to be vocational training. Find a part-time job that will help you gain the experience and build the skills necessary for a career so that you can also major in something you truly love studying. Plus, it doesn't hurt to have some extra spending money!

6. *Go to office hours.* Get to know a professor. This is important to your understanding of the material and your grade in the class, and it will make it easier to get the recommendation letters you may need in the future. Professors can give you internships, open up opportunities for academic and scholarly growth, and let you in on some priceless wisdom that you definitely need. Be nice to them because whether you believe it or not, they were once in your shoes.

7. *Attend a school rally.* Whether you're a biology major, mathematics major, or performing arts major, everybody comes together as one at a school rally. It's a powerful experience to share in the spirit, excitement, and energy of the student body during a school cheer. So put on your school colors and wear them proudly!

8. *Have your heart broken.* "'Tis better to have loved and lost than never to have loved at all." Don't neglect your heart in college. It is just as important to experience the joys and pains of love as it is to study. Take a risk, follow your heart, and fall in love!

9. *Explore your spiritual self.* College will overwhelm you. Your friends will upset you. And life will challenge you. Taking a step outside your everyday routine and exploring the spiritual realm through yoga or meditation can serve as an outlet for your stress. Slow down, calm your mind, and take a deep breath.

10. *Take a class outside of your requirements.* You may learn to love it.

—*Steven Truong, Neil Poria, Aggie Wong*

Grocery Store Analogy

You are about to register for classes. Imagine that the university is like a large grocery store. You walk in, and because you are a biology major or sociology major or a computer engineering major or are undeclared, you are guided to a particular aisle. You wheel your cart over to that aisle and you begin walking down it. You see this item is "required," that you can select one of these three items, two of these 12 items are necessary, and over there is a shelf of electives. So you methodically go down the aisle taking all the items you are supposed to take.

You get to the end of the aisle and you stop. You stop and you turn around and you leave. Of course you stop at the cash register and you pay. And then you leave. You *leave*! All this while you have been subconsciously operating on the high school model of "have to" behavior, the conveyer belt model of education.

Meanwhile, one aisle over there was a class that would have rocked your mind and changed your life. One aisle. Or two aisles over there was a professor who you would have profoundly connected with. But you missed it! And you missed it because you didn't look! You didn't look because you thought you were just "supposed to" go down your aisle and select. The point of this analogy is to get you to increase your freedom and awareness regarding this university education you are about to undertake for many years. Be a smart consumer. Go down all the aisles. See what is in this giant supermarket.

I have often asked my classes, "How many of you have had the experience of being in a class in third week, fifth week, or sixth week and had the sinking feeling, 'Oh shit . . . I hate this class!'" Usually many hands go up. It is an all-too-common experience. Being a smart shopper in advance can almost eliminate this depressing experience. So go down the aisles. Practically speaking, this may mean first going to the bookstore to see which books are being used by different courses. See which ones excite and interest you. Look at the teacher evaluations that are often publicized at many universities. Above all, that first week of classes, go and sit in on as many classes as you possibly can. Go shop down all the aisles. No one knows who's who or what is going on the first week or two of classes. No one is going to throw you out for not being officially registered. It is, after all, your education. You have the right—and responsibility—to shop and see which courses appeal to you.

I've worked at approximately 12 universities in my career, and every one of them was very good at processing students. As a professor, and hence part of the university system, I too have become skilled at processing students. Cha-ching, cha-ching, cha-ching. No problem. A factory, a post office, a line of customers at the movie theater. Ba-boom, ba-boom, ba-boom. Unless you take some creative control of your education, some personal, energetic co-creative stances, you will be processed. That is just the nature of institutions.

—Bernard McGrane

Discovering Your Passion

Passion

In the philosophy of existentialism, to exist is to be passionate. Passion gives us the motivation to take control of our lives and gives us a reason to live. According to this philosophy, no matter how many oppressive forces we have in our lives holding us back, we all ultimately have the power to make our own decisions in our lives. College is the first time in your life that you become mentally and physically independent from your parents. When you move into the dorms, nobody constantly looks after you, telling you what to do. You get to choose whether you want to wake up in the mornings and go to your lectures, whether you want to study or hang out with your friends, and even what time you go to sleep. You are endowed with this freedom to do all of these things without the constant nagging of your parents.

In college, you are also allowed to choose what classes you want to take and what majors you want to study. This freedom empowers you to shape the context of your own education, but it can also create stress. Although you may not live with your parents while you are in school, there can be constant family pressure to pursue a certain major or field of study. You are often told to choose a practical major that will give you a high-paying, prestigious job, such as medicine, law, or engineering.

However, you must choose a major that you are passionate about. You cannot let your parents dictate what you study. When I started college, my parents wanted me to be a doctor. I chose biology as my major, but only a few weeks into the curriculum, I found that I genuinely despised the material and didn't feel that I was getting anything fulfilling from it. I told my parents, but they told me to simply "suck it up" and continue. I tried to stick it out, but the further I delved into the subject material, the more depressed I became. I knew that I had to switch to another major that I was truly passionate about to find meaning and satisfaction.

I soon stumbled upon sociology, which sounded interesting, as it addressed many aspects of society. With my interest piqued, I made the plunge, took a leap of faith, and changed my major. After a quarter of studying sociology, I knew that I had made the right decision. For the first time in my life, I actually wanted to go to class, and I enthusiastically immersed myself in the class materials and readings. Empowered by the knowledge that I was learning, my world view started to change. I started to see things for the way they truly were, rather than what I was taught to believe by society. Three years later, I find myself wanting to continue my passion for sociology with a master's and a PhD in the field.

Family pressure can often be a very difficult obstacle to overcome, but you must realize that in the end, you are the only one who can make the ultimate decision. Regardless of how much pressure you face, you are the only one able to choose your major. Sure, your parents may even threaten to disown you if you decide not to become that world-famous doctor they wanted you to be, but don't worry; those are all bluffs. Your parents have dedicated the last 18 years or so raising you with love and support, and they will continue to support you regardless of your academic decisions.

Pursue what you are truly passionate about, not just what makes a lot of money or sounds practical. College is not job training; it is life training. In college, you learn about the world around you, and you learn how to see it in a different way while developing the critical skills of an independent thinker. You will also learn how to better interact with other people and create some of the deepest bonds in your life. You have only one life to live, so live it to the fullest without regrets. After all, if you fail to pursue your passion, you will always feel empty and longing for more. And, so the existentialist would say, when you fail to pursue your passion, you fail to even exist.

—Eric Kim

Be Available for Change

For many, college will be a time and place where you will find out who you are—or who you are not. The college experience is not cookie cutter, but due to the pressures of society and the media's portrayal of college, freshmen enter with unrealistic, limitless expectations.

I entered college right after high school with an undeniable faith that I was taking my first steps to becoming an oncologist. I was sure that taking life science courses and partaking in all of the medical school preparation activities would gain me an advantage over others pursuing medicine. But after living this life for more than 2 years, my passion for becoming a doctor faded. My introduction to internships, volunteer work, and science courses should have reinforced my faith, but it instead pulled me away. My body shuddered every time I inhaled the air of the medical center at the start of my hospital shifts. The classroom environment didn't help either. I was often surrounded by people who were viciously inhospitable and many whom I would never want as a personal physician. Exposure to medicine gave me reason to focus elsewhere.

When junior year rolled around, I was still denying my disinterest in medicine. Becoming an oncologist had been the only option I gave myself. At last, I opened up to other choices, and it was like a breath of fresh air that I had been longing for. As painful as it was to admit that I was no longer going to be an oncologist, I found the reason I had initially wanted to pursue oncology: to serve others.

Despite society's teachings of quick and easy fixes to things, my personal experience proved that college does not always guarantee a set and narrow path for the rest of your life. Frustrations and doubt will always be a part of the agenda, something that is largely neglected by the media.

Although I am still in the process of finding a brighter path, progressively achieving peace with myself has slowly produced genuine joy for others and their successes. Most of the successful people that I admire in my life have struggled over imperfections and have learned to appreciate the things that they have gained and let go of the things that have been lost.

Sights should still be set high in college. If things don't meet your expectations, don't be too hard on yourself. College and the rest of your life can be a process of discovering who you are and what you can offer yourself and the rest of society.

—Moo Young Kim

Nontraditional Students

Don't Give Up

In every student's life, there comes a time when he or she says, "Why am I doing this? A college degree doesn't really matter, and I have a job offer anyway." You become tired of the schedule, papers, and midterms. You begin to think the grass is greener on the "working side." At that point, it is so easy to just drop out of school and say, "I'll take a quarter off and come back in the fall," or "I'll just work this quarter and save some money to come back." Most of us, once we're out of the habit of taking classes, do not come back. Time goes by so quickly that we suddenly realize, years down the road, that we were so close but didn't cross the finish line. We forget that we were tired, broke, or just sick of the routine. All we remember is that we were close to fulfilling the degree but gave up.

I made that mistake 25 years ago, and it has bothered me constantly since I left college. I left college because I had a great job offer. I had convinced myself to just earn some money for a year, at which point I could easily go back. That job led to another one, which led to a great career, marriage, and children. Time moved quickly by. Suddenly, 25 years later, as I was preparing my oldest son to go to college, I realized it still haunted me that I hadn't finished the last year of my undergraduate degree and was still considered "a high school graduate." All my friends and associates had degrees, and although they did not judge me by my lack of a degree, I judged myself by that measure. Once I left college, my schedule became so busy that I couldn't see how I could go back for even one class.

It took an immense amount of work and commitment to finally go back to college and finish what I started 25 years ago. How would I fit in? How would the other students accept me since I was the age of their mothers? These fears were unfounded once I just jumped in and did it. I found that the classes are much more meaningful to me after living the very topics I only studied years ago. But I can see that finishing the work is indeed more demanding now because I have the added responsibilities of family and work. Do not give up, no matter how difficult you find the work or what else sounds interesting. Finish the college degree and do whatever it takes to make it happen at this stage in your life, while you can devote all your energy to achieving that goal.

—*Christine Hazy*

The Student Athlete Experience

Ask college students to list their favorite experiences at school, and college sports are likely to make an appearance somewhere. Who doesn't love cheering their team on to victory? Marveling at the athletes on the field or court, it's easy to think of them as professionals there to provide that night's entertainment. But this isn't the case. Those athletes, who are so good at what they do, are also students just like their peers in the stands; they're student athletes. Why is it so difficult to envision them as both? Maybe it's because this part of college sports is seldom publicized.

How many times do you see the whole student-athlete story told on ESPN? Not too often, I'm afraid, which brings me to why I'm here. I am a student athlete, a senior guard on the UCLA women's basketball team.

Although getting used to the physical rigors of being on the basketball team as a freshman was difficult, the totality of my life as a student athlete presented a slew of unanticipated challenges. Being an athlete is quite an honor, and I began college looking forward to walking around campus looking the part. During my first week in class, however, I was rudely awakened by the reality that living life as a student athlete was not going to be as glamorous as it seemed.

The first incident occurred when I attended one of my professor's office hours to simply introduce myself. "Hi, my name is Allison..." I began, entering his office. My professor took one look at me before cutting me off. "Hello Allison," he said. "Well, let's just get this over with, shall we? I don't accept late homework or do make-up tests. If you can't handle these requirements, then I suggest you find another class because you probably won't succeed otherwise." I stared at him incredulously, wondering, "What is he talking about?" Glancing down at what I was wearing, I had my answer. I was dressed head to toe in my issued athletic gear, which boldly proclaimed my membership on the UCLA basketball team. My professor had automatically assumed that I was there to try to sidestep some of his class rules or get special treatment because of my athlete status. This was the first of many incidents when I realized that being an athlete was not looked upon fondly in the classroom.

I was also introduced to the stereotype that many regular students held about athletes being dumb. In a heated classroom debate about UCLA's acceptance process, one student shouted out, "So many people are being turned down who deserve to get in. I mean, look at all these athletes who get in just because they can run around a field or something. It's not fair that they get a free pass when they don't deserve it." Most of the class nodded their heads and murmured their agreement. I was shocked and a little embarrassed. "Do people really think I'm a dumb jock too, just because I'm on the basketball team?" I wondered. I sank in my chair as I tried to nonchalantly remove my bright blue athletic jacket.

Being a part of the athletics program was something I was proud of, but I also took great pride in my academics. Once I realized that being an athlete actually put me at a disadvantage in the classroom, I did my best to rid myself of that image. I stopped wearing my athletic gear around campus and tried to blend in as a regular student as much as I could, thinking that it would give me a better chance of getting good grades and being respected by my classmates. I was almost ashamed of who I was and what I loved to do.

I've learned how to cope with these things over the years. Not all professors are anti-athlete, and not all of the student body thinks that we're incompetent. And if I encounter those who do think this way, I just smile and enjoy proving them wrong. I wear my UCLA athletic gear proudly now, and I don't care what others think. You think I'm a dumb jock,

Professor so-and-so? That's okay. I'll let my grades and my play on the court speak for themselves.

Trouble with professors and classmates was not the only challenge I faced in my freshman year. During this time, I also went through a crash course about the importance of time management skills. I entered college confident in my time management skills, thinking that I was ready to tackle everything. I was going to excel in my sport, get good grades, and experience the once-in-a-lifetime college student life. Right away, though, I found out that this was not going to be as easy as I had thought. From the start I was overwhelmed with everything that was thrown at me. We had 3 hours of practice 6 days a week, an hour of weight training 3 days a week, a full load of classes, and mandatory tutoring sessions, not to mention hours upon hours spent playing games at home and traveling to play at different colleges all over the country. This left me with very little free time. I began my first quarter devoting every single free minute to studying, which earned me the reputation of being the "nerd" on our team. Shutting myself in my dorm room right after practice resulted in great grades but basically left me with no life outside of basketball. Wanting to prevent "loner" from joining my nerd label, I decided to use my free time the next quarter to go to events on campus and hang out with friends. I loved living the college life, but I became so involved in these activities that I was left with no time to study or put in extra basketball practice.

Since that disastrous freshman year, I've come to learn that it is possible to get the best of both worlds if I just prioritize and manage my time wisely. This means giving up some things in order to accomplish the things that absolutely must get done. As a student athlete, I have an obligation to my teammates and coaches to show up every day ready to give them my all. I definitely have to put aside extra time for shooting and ball handling practice to ensure that I am at my best, but I also have obligations to myself to do well in school and have fun outside of basketball. I have to make time for studying, going out to group meetings, and hanging out with friends. Sacrifices have to be made, such as giving up watching the television shows I like and shortening the extra hours I spend in the gym to perfect my game, but the result is a well-rounded, enjoyable college experience.

Being a student athlete is more than throwing a ball in a hoop and going to take a test in class. It isn't the easiest way to live your college life; you have a lot more on your plate than most other people. With everything that is being asked of you—to be an excellent student, a top athlete, a son or daughter, and a good friend—it is easy to feel overwhelmed. I admit that there are times when I wish that I could just be a normal college student, leading a normal college life. But those moments are fleeting and have become fewer as I have completed each year of school. I have come to appreciate the unique situation that I have been fortunate enough to live. As a student athlete, I have been able to experience things that only an athlete can, in addition to also being able to take part in a few things outside of the athletic world. It's like I have had two different lives in college, each amazing in its own way, and it's something that I will always cherish and never forget.

—Allison Taka

The Real College Experience: What Every Transfer Should Know

If freshman students have worries, woe to the transfer student; the minute students transfer in they already have to start thinking about leaving. One minute we are at our community college stressing to finish our university application and revise our personal statements, and the next minute we need to repeat the same laborious task for grad school. Grad school deadlines start dropping on us like ten-ton bricks by the end of our first year in the university system. In addition, it wasn't too long ago that we decided on a major, and now we have to decide on a career! There are several obstacles and disadvantages that transfer students encounter that faculty may attempt to help with, yet cannot give any solutions for. The typical response I receive from faculty is, "Yes, I know it's hard," followed by a sympathetic face. I'm left thinking, "Yes, it's hard, so what can I do about it?" Universities are not transfer friendly; transfer students must fend for themselves. Perhaps universities don't see the obstacles that transfer students confront, or maybe we're second-class citizens in a land that doesn't care to accommodate us.

The problem that most would-be transfer students encounter is that all we've known for the past 2, maybe 3, years in community college is that higher education has been somehow out of reach. Community college students have one major goal: to transfer out of there as soon as possible and move on with our lives. The problem is that in our hurried state we become so overwhelmed by fulfilling requirements and starting the paperwork for the next level that we forget that there will be new priorities, requirements, and deadlines awaiting us on the other side. Making the transition from community college student to university student is a gradual process; it takes time to get the hang of it.

Whether this transition is a smooth one or not depends on the institution that you transfer into; for instance, private universities may have fewer students, which means intimate class settings and more interaction with professors. Another advantage to attending a small university is that counselors, TAs, and other personnel will not be so overwhelmed and constantly in a rush to move you along. Information also travels quicker in smaller universities, making it easier to be aware of upcoming events and deadlines. Of course, not all private universities offer these advantages, so it's important to research potential universities.

This is not to say that transferring into a public university is a horrific experience. It isn't. I am at UCLA, which I love. It does, however, require more effort on your part. Public universities usually have a large student body, which makes it nearly impossible to have intimate class settings. In addition, the possibility of getting to know your professors is also pretty slim, unless you make the effort to see them during office hours and try to stand out in class by frequently asking questions and sitting in the front rows. It may sound corny, but in huge lecture halls, students can become faceless numbers; therefore, sitting in the front in the professors' sight and asking questions can get them to eventually notice you.

As transfer students, we already have a lot of experience taking charge of our education; we wouldn't be able to transfer if not for a lot of hard work and vigilance on our part. The effort required is worth mentioning because in university, the workload increases substantially within a shorter period of time. It can become difficult to keep up with papers, readings, and exams while at the same time trying to keep an eye on the road ahead.

With such a fast pace, it is easy to get caught up in the moment and never notice deadlines flying right by you: "Oops, I was supposed to start applying for grad school when?" Time is a transfer student's worst enemy. The majority of community colleges use the semester system, but once you transfer, you need to adapt, and fast, to the quarter system. At a community college, procrastination doesn't have consequences as severe as in a university that uses the quarter system. We had 5 long months in which to get things done; therefore, the workload was manageable. In contrast, in the 10-week quarter system, we are given more work and less time. How's that fair? You once had to worry about reading three or four chapters, and you now have to worry about reading three or four books, and actually I'm being kind in this example. Now, before we work ourselves into a frenzy, the situation isn't as dim as it appears. After all, everything's possible if we manage our time properly. Only by managing our time and avoiding procrastination can we reach our goals and fulfill our expectations.

Time also works against transfer students because in order to finish in 2 years, we miss out on the opportunity to take courses for the mere enjoyment of learning something outside of our major. When time is of the essence, transfer students need to hurry and complete their major's requirements, so there is no time for exploring other classes, especially if we're planning to go to grad school.

The way in which transfer students experience university life is also very different than the way traditional students do. The "college experience" is something that every student often fantasizes about. It is true that we all transferred from colleges; however, most transfers don't consider community college experience to be the "real college experience." Community college was merely the stepping stone that was needed to get us closer to the real thing. Therefore, we have illusions based on preconceptions about student life in a 4-year university. Trying to cram 4 years of "experience" into 2 is not an easy task. Living either on or near campus is the best bet for students who set out on this mission. Most universities guarantee housing for a year to transfers; where you choose to live is another factor that shapes your college experience. Usually, the dorms are located on campus; the dorms are where the vast majority of first- and second-year students reside. Then there is "transfer housing," which are off-campus apartments. Choosing between the two isn't too difficult. Dorms are more expensive and are usually the size of a shoebox; in addition, because most transfers are older than first- and second-year students, living off campus might be the better way to go.

When I transferred to UCLA, I decided to live off campus at the university housing for transfers. Everyone in my building was a transfer student. For most of the students living there, this was the first time they had moved out of their parents' home and lived with strangers. I'll be the first to say that living on your own for the first time feels liberating; we had a real sense of independence. Although living in your own apartment does entail responsibility; you have to try to get along with your roommates, clean, cook, grocery shop, and pay bills. This is a small price to pay for living on cloud nine. No curfews; no one looking over our shoulder. Yes, we were on our own, but as great as this was, we all felt left out. We felt segregated. We didn't know the campus very well or what activities were going on. We had no information about anything, and worst of all, we didn't know anyone who could guide us.

In this situation, dorms do offer some advantages over apartments. Students who live in dorms get the benefit of resident advisors or program advisors. Resident advisors are those wonderful people who also live in the dorms. Students can seek not only information but counseling from their resident advisors. Some dorms will even provide one resident advisor per floor. Resident advisors are also responsible for enforcing the rules and regulations of the dorms; they restore order if students are getting too crazy. In other words, they are there to hold a student's hand. Well, I wanted someone to hold my hand, too. If that isn't enough assistance to students who live in the dorms, there are also program advisors who sometimes live in the dorms as well. These people are even more wonderful; they coordinate special events and activities for the residents of their dorms. They put together picnics, little field trips, and so on, so not only are students being provided with entertainment but they are also getting a chance to meet other students who live in their building. These are definitely a few things that students need to consider when the time comes to decide where to live.

Getting to know your new surroundings is also a crucial part of your college experience; when students know their campus, they have a sense of belonging. As we all know, most large universities can be very intimidating. These campuses are huge; therefore, new transfers should make an effort to explore their campus and the campus resources. Now in my senior year, I have yet to explore the entire campus and am considering going on a tour before I graduate. It's no joke; I would get a formal tour by a guide along with some history of the university. Besides exploring one's university, it's also a good idea to explore the neighboring cities and their establishments. Venturing out into the new town can be fruitful when it's time to unwind.

Unfortunately, there are other things that transfers won't get to check off their "real college experience" list due to time restrictions. Membership in fraternities or sororities might be out of the question. Rumor has it that some sororities won't accept transfer pledges: certain fraternities might. Taking the time to research organizations that fit our needs or ideologies might also be too time consuming. Being part of your school's sports department is also hard to juggle when you have deadlines to meet in your education and future career decisions. Then there's the experience that every student should have: traveling abroad. The classes we actually need for our major are not always offered to upper division students. Therefore, if we decide to travel abroad, the classes that we would take would only count as electives and would not fulfill the requirements for our major. Transfer students need to get a lot done in a limited time, so traveling would mean delays, and we can't afford that. Because freshmen and sophomores are still taking their general education requirements, they have more to choose from; they could live abroad for a whole year and not worry about running out of required courses. However, if traveling abroad is a "must," it can be done after graduation; speaking to an advisor early in the year can set you on the right path.

In sum, transfer students can feel like second-class citizens, foreigners in a new land. Often transfers, like foreigners, will arrive at their destination and be disappointed when they realize that their expectations will never fully be met. But there is hope; it doesn't have to be this way. In retrospect, I am now able to recognize where I, among other transfers, have gone wrong. You see, it was when I first opened my acceptance letter from UCLA; at this point, I should have already started to think about life after undergraduate school. Instead, I succumbed to the overwhelming demands of being an undergrad, balancing my sanity with schoolwork, oblivious to anything else. I figured that I would gradually find things out when I needed to, but before I knew it, one whole year was gone. "Time waits for no one."

So as a word of advice for would-be transfers who are about to embark on the next journey, give yourself plenty of time to look into what lies ahead. Find out what resources your school has available for transfers. Some schools offer programs that are specifically designed for transfer students, such as workshops on how to adapt and "transfer counselors." The Career Center is also another place a student can go to seek guidance on placement exams, graduate schools, and jobs. Ultimately, however, it's important for you to know yourself; know what it is that you want to get out of your time as an undergrad. In order to get the most out of this 2-year experience, transfers need to take the initiative to do their own research. At times, I felt like a detective following leads to get the right information I needed. Now, in my second and last year, I finally feel that I have gotten the hang of undergraduate school and the quarter system.

Hopefully, by providing you with my experience I have given you a glimpse into what obstacles may lie ahead for transfers and ways to ease this transition. There will be times when you will feel overwhelmed and discouraged, but you must remember that you have made it this far for a reason: You have earned this.

—Veronica Fematt

Grades

Can You Perform Without the Pressure?

The universal cry of every student is, "I want an A." Really? Do you want an A because you genuinely and authentically want an A or because you've been programmed and conditioned to want an A? In Chapter 2, we critically reconsider our deep training and socialization in the institution of "school" and our unconscious, acquired, emotional relationship to "grades." Am I me, or am I my grade? We will look at the following dimensions:

- The destructive psychology of grades—the institution of grades.
- The vital difference between *internalizing* versus *understanding* the rules.
- The possibility of experimenting with some of your school work "without grades."
- How to consider alternatives if you just can't stand it anymore.

The only thing that will give you as much heartache in college as love is the grading system, with its exams, papers, and attendant complexities. I want you to understand the vital difference between operating within a set of rules and internalizing those rules. The cardinal point here is that what you don't internalize can't really hurt you, while what you do internalize can destroy you very rapidly, and this goes for the high-scoring student as much as for the lower-scoring student.

Let me use military service as an example. Obviously, when you're in the army, the army has got you by the ass. To survive intact, you had better know the rules.[1] We all know, however, that obeying the rules is a far cry from actually believing that the army is a wise and just institution that will "make a man out of you."

---

[1] I don't mean, by using this example, to imply that everybody should lie down in front of an unjust system. Some very wise and brave people will take the system on. But they had better understand clearly what to expect.

Those who fall for this version of reality are doing what people frequently do when confronted by power: They are internalizing the rules. In one way, this is a safe reaction because it will suppress any internal rebellion that might crop up and get us in trouble. However, we also feel, instinctively, that this path can destroy our integrity as human beings. So the healthier of us will do the minimum to survive without, for a moment, caring whether or not we are "good soldiers." This is the attitude that the Bible recommends when it says that you should be "in the world but not of it." Robert Fried (1995) explains this in *The Passionate Teacher*.[2]

A game is both a microcosm and a parody of life. It is like life: it brings forth the same energies and the same feelings, but, in the end, it is not *real*. It is a charade of something real. We may be absorbed by it and be willing to play along. But a voice within us is there to say, "Take it easy. It doesn't really matter. *It's only a game.*"

The particular offense of playing the Game of School lies in the disengagement of our intellect and our feelings from tasks that deserve to be taken seriously: tasks like writing, reading, thinking, planning, listening, researching, analyzing, performing, applying, and evaluating. We do harm when we reduce these acts of intellect, creativity, and judgment to rote exercises, perfunctory deeds, or meaningless gestures. Faced with the stresses of daily life in school, it can seem easier, at times, to pretend to believe rather than to truly believe in the value of what we are about. Despite the positive aspects of going to school that many children and adults experience, the temptation is always there to cope with school by going through the motions. (p. 95)

The Destructive Psychology of Grades

But what has all this to do with the seemingly more benign institution of university education? I would like to suggest to you that the competition for grades, which you have already experienced for 12 years and will experience for at least 4 more, is a very dehumanizing and damaging system that has its roots deep in the injustices of our society. Since early childhood, it has set you against your peers and filled you with intermittent anxieties about your worth as a person. One student, Stephanie Pappas, wrote the following when she reflected on her schooling:

Children are programmed even as young as first grade that grades are the most important aspect of school. I clearly remember being in the third grade and having a chart with stars in our classroom, which indicated who knew their multiplication tables. As an 8-year-old child, I recall feeling humiliated that all my friends had more stars than I did. My motivation for studying my multiplication tables was no longer to learn them per se but to gain more gold stars. Learning was not my reward. It was the grade and praise I desired.

---

[2]I'd like to recommend Fried's *The Passionate Teacher* (1995), *The Passionate Learner* (2001), and *The Game of School* (2005) to anyone interested in looking at teaching and learning from a humanistic perspective.

Throughout our school years, society teaches us to believe that grades demonstrate our intelligence. Because of this, our motivation, learning, and personal growth are subordinate to attaining the ultimate goal—the grade. Society first teaches us about societal norms and codes, yet it is in the school system that we are ultimately taught to imitate. We are programmed to imitate what the teacher wants. If we don't, we get a bad grade. This imitation is so strong because it is reinforced through schooling for a minimum of 12 years. Imitation, competition, and fear of grades hinder our discovery. Lawrence Lu, a college senior, reflects on his school career below.

Two children scribble images that remotely resemble their names. They receive praises with perhaps chocolate rewards. The children smile, beaming at the accomplishment and relishing the encouraging warmth of the chocolate giver. Next year, they are asked to include their name in a sentence and are given a gold star. The years continue as the praises and gold stars become fewer. Somehow, they have now mystically transformed into numbers and letters. Even more interesting is that the numbers and letters have curiously become more valuable than any chocolate treat on the planet. We speed forward another few years.

Relief was the word of the hour as my friend and I finished finals for the umpteenth time as college seniors. . . . Long gone were the kids who looked forward to school and thirsted for knowledge. Long gone were the praises, the stars, and the chocolate. In their places stood statistically skewed numbers and harsh comments about not following so-and-so format. What had happened and, more important, why hadn't anyone stopped it from happening?

We are scared of being at the tail end of a curve, of receiving lower than average marks, of expressing how we truly feel to the TA because he or she might grade us with unchecked bias, of not writing down on the test what they want us to write even though we couldn't disagree with it more, of making one wrong move that would result in a smudge on our platinum resumes, and of not getting that big job so society can feed us approval and positive reinforcements like little freakin' lab rats. We are scared to death of everything. No one cares that they don't remember what they learned last quarter because they are relieved they kept up their GPAs. They don't have time to care because they are worried again about the same thing in the present quarter. Learning? Who the hell has time for that? I'm too busy trying to pass the bar and become a lawyer to worry about negligible trinkets like ethics. The worst part is that no one talks about it. Everyone sucks it up and accepts it as "the way it is."

In high school, the teachers did not teach for knowledge. They taught us what we had to know to pass the advanced placement tests. The notion of developing young, curious, scientific minds was a luxury that no one had time for. The SAT followed and encouraged students to spend hundreds of dollars on learning the tricks of how to best guess the correct answer. Of course, we students disregarded that the test did not reflect anything worthwhile about anyone. Why should we have cared? Every other test was like that.

Thankfully, the pain for most ended here. The average students had already been accepted by whatever college would take them, and, more important, they had adapted to working inside the system that did not care an ounce about intellectual curiosity or expansion. If you still believe that quality learning and learning for the test can occur simultaneously, then good for you. I do not. The bottom line is that I was a kid who had smiled when the magnetism lesson was the next day. I was a willing sponge to soak in anything and everything. *Then one day it wasn't about being curious. It was about the grades.* There was no room for anything else. With the grades came pressure that systematically builds. And the only emotion appropriate for describing the brief moments when we don't have to worry is relief. That is the way it just is. Period. For what grandiose treasure did we trade our souls?

—Lawrence Lu

If the system has not totally destroyed your love of learning, it is only because a parent or an occasional teacher has rescued you or, perhaps, because of your own natural resilience. Almost everybody I know, including most college professors, hates and fears writing because their writing has always been judged. If you have made it to college, you aren't among those who also failed to learn to read because of the anxiety school induces. Actually, the plight of nonreaders is a perfect case in point. Any child who has learned to speak can learn to read.[3] Learning to speak is actually harder because it requires the child to grasp symbolism and grammatical structure. That anybody should fail to read in a society where signs and labels surround us everywhere is a profound indictment of the traumatizing effects of school. If speaking were taught in school, we would have a nation of stutterers.

Anxiety doesn't help people to learn. On the contrary, anxiety causes most people to withdraw. Research indicates that negative sanctions (punishments) are particularly destructive to motivation. Yet, year after year, schools continue to create anxiety in their students:

> Children simply do not learn better when education is transformed into a competitive struggle. To be sure, a teacher may want to turn a lesson into a competitive game to attract and hold students' attention. But the real appeal of this strategy is that it makes teaching easier, not more effective. . . . Competition does not generally promote excellence because trying to do well and trying to beat others simply are two different things. (Kohn, 1986, p. 22)

In my classes, I have sometimes asked students to jot down the thing they remember most vividly from their elementary school education. You may want to try this exercise before you read on.

---

[3]I'd like to recommend a very interesting book to you: *If You Can Talk, You Can Write*, by Joe Salzman (1993).

Ninety-eight percent of the incidents my students listed were negative experiences: times when students felt humiliated, punished, harassed, and so on (remember, these were the "academic successes" I was asking for, not the "failures"). The only students who didn't describe negative experiences were students who went to private schools.

One student, Alex Hayden, wrote about his experience in a grade-free private elementary school:

> The idea of goal seeking is illustrated by the use of grades. The question is whether or not students would work as hard or learn as much if grades were eliminated. I feel that if grades were eliminated, I would learn just as much. When I was in elementary school, I attended a private school that did not have the formal grading system. I worked hard on my studies and enjoyed knowledge. However, when grades were introduced to me in junior high school, I no longer concentrated so much on the actual subjects; it became more of a game. I now had to learn how to please my professors, with their various styles, to receive a good grade. To me, school has become much more stressful since the grading system was introduced to me. I have been trying to tell myself that I am getting my grades for me, but am I really? Or, rather, am I getting the knowledge for myself and my grades for society so that I may be judged or rated for a future socially accepted activity?

Another student, Phillip Nichols, had similar insights when he reflected on his socialization into the student role:

> If an individual has grown up in an environment where that which was desired was nurtured for its own sake, and then the same individual is placed in our educational institutions, where his or her natural desires are replaced by artificial ones, the entire process of acquiring knowledge is twisted. High marks replace the desire to learn. . . . The traditional grading system motivates students through fear. It trains them to avoid failure at all costs, and, by whatsoever means possible, the student learns that he or she must receive high marks regardless of whether or not they are deserved. This system allows the student to prostitute his or her way through the halls of higher education, and, ironically, even the honest students contribute to the perpetuation of this blatant disregard of humanity.

My experience as a teacher has been that *high achievement is closely related to self-confidence.* Think about it. If you are afraid of failure in a certain class, don't you find yourself procrastinating and cutting class more often—in short, avoiding the cause of your anxiety? These behaviors will, of course, cause you to do even more poorly. Sometimes, in the case of a student who was doing poorly for such reasons, I have simply slipped him or her a high grade to see what would happen. Usually, by the end of the term, the student was earning those higher grades. *Our expectations become self-fulfilling prophecies.* Yet the anxiety approach to education continues right through college, and even though the teachers will no longer keep you after school, they seem to find other ways to make you feel like a fool.

We are so used to the system that it seems inevitable. Most people have to admit to themselves that, if grades were to disappear tomorrow, they might never learn another set of irregular verbs and might, indeed, just lie down and not move for a very long time. Naturally! This is a *result* of the system, not a *reason* for it. Having been bullied all your life into learning things you didn't much want to know, you would, indeed, quit if you could and so, perhaps, would most of your professors. I suspect, though, that in a few months you would get up, look around, and begin to take an altogether different sort of interest in altogether different kinds of knowledge.

Why do our schools function in this way? Why is intellectual curiosity regularly killed in order to teach discipline? Why do our schools give even 7-year-old children failing grades? Whenever sociologists see a system continually operating in "dysfunctional" ways, they suggest that perhaps we have not discovered the "real" function of the system. A hint is given us here in that the only schools that don't beat up their students emotionally are a few private and public schools that serve the rich. The real purpose of school is to make people obedient to authority. The mindlessness of school is meant to prepare people for unquestioning acceptance of the mindlessness of most jobs. Perhaps most important, it is the job of schools to convince those who will have lousy jobs and low wages that their fate is their own fault, that they just weren't smart enough (translate, deserving enough) to do any better.

Our system exaggerates intellectual differences between people because the concept of IQ is used to justify wide disparities in income and, in general, chances for a satisfying life. This is why intelligence and academic performance are measured not in the spirit of helping children to grow but in the spirit of instilling in certain children basic doubts about their self-worth as human beings.

Why are small children made to stand in line and at attention in school? So they will stand in line and at attention in the army! Schools are quite open about their aim of producing "good citizens." In an old cowboy movie, there was a scene in which a small-town bank had just been robbed, and the banker was out on the street exhorting the young men of the town to join the posse to go after the robbers. One young man next to him asked coolly, "Why? I didn't have any money in the bank." It is just such "poor citizenship" that the school system is dedicated to expunging.

College is a little different. Here, you are now among the prospective winners and at least the middle-range future leaders. (If you are at an Ivy League school, you are among the high-range future leaders.) These folk will not function correctly if they are simply browbeaten. Because they have independent responsibilities, it is necessary that they have the confidence to act independently; therefore, the intimidation is much more subtle, and the inducement to internalize the system is subtle, self-deceptive, and more insidious. Of course, the sorting machine of the system is still in high gear. Only some will become leaders; others still have to be convinced of at least their relative worthlessness. Otherwise, could we count on teachers to obey principals and junior accountants to obey senior executives? In particular, could we count on everybody down the line to carry out orders that are often nonsensical, self-serving, and not infrequently catastrophic? Would social workers, for example, agree to hound their clients off the welfare rolls because they have a man living with them? During wartime, would college professors forward failing grades to draft boards? Would nurses continue to tolerate gross underpayment while doctors get rich?

I have gone on at some length about the grading system because I think it is only by getting a broader perspective on it that you can put this system in its proper place—which is not inside your gut. One undergraduate wrote perceptively about this internalization.

Another student compares how this internalization/socialization takes place in countries outside the United States.

My mother raised me to be the best that I could. She always told me that as long as I tried my hardest, I could be proud of myself. This may seem like great advice, but it has cost me years of self-torment. I have never tried my hardest, and I beat myself up over it. Even if I spent 60 hours doing research for a 10-page paper that my professor loves and gives me an A for, I am not satisfied. I know I could have tried harder. I know that I could have gone to bed a little later on a few nights and done 70 or 80 hours of research. I could have written a better paper, more concise with more insight, if I had not gone out with my friends that Thursday night. I would have impressed the professor more if I had actually found that perfect quotation that I spent 3 hours looking for before giving up. I could have tried harder. I chose not to. Does this mean I shouldn't be proud of myself? I don't think that my mother intended to instill such pressure with her standard. I took her too literally. What she meant was that if I set aside a certain amount of time to work on a paper or project, and I stick to it, and if I put in some thought and effort, then I did what was expected, and I should be content with the result. She wasn't trying to tell me that I had to go above and beyond the call of duty and push myself to the limit and beyond on every occasion. I created that demand myself. I wasn't content with doing what was expected and being "just average." I wanted more. For years I sacrificed time with friends and family so that I could be not just above average but excellent. I learned, though, that it's no fun to be the best if you're all alone when you get there. I've finally learned the benefits of being average. I've learned that I can do well in school and still have healthy relationships with others. I learned to balance academia and friendship, stress and frivolity; I'm at peace because I made that decision myself. I am finally trying my hardest to do something . . . to be happy and enjoy my life. I am proud of that decision.

—*Kristin Rydberg*

I completed 7th through 11th grade in Australia, and returning to American high school in South Orange County, California, was a little more than a culture shock. I went from a public school in St. Ives with a uniform code and an emphasis on discipline to a public school in "the O.C." with a "fashion code" and an emphasis on social hierarchy. Nothing could have prepared me for entry into such a foreign institution.

St. Ives High School ran from 7th grade to 12th grade, and I had a mere 100 students in my class. The atmosphere of the school was one of discipline until students hit the 9th grade—after a seasoned 2 years, many had learned their way around all the rules, regulations, and faculty. There is no GPA in Australia or any A's, B's, or C's—only excellent, good, satisfactory, unsatisfactory, and failing. Your report card would consist of checkmarks in these areas regarding behavior, assignments, and so on as well as a percentage for your overall grade in the class and the number you rank among your peers. The latter score is the most interesting because to get first in the year held great social significance. In fact, this little number caused intense emotions between my best friend and me, both perfectionists striving to be the best. Yet to be ranked high in the year also held the stigma of being a nerd, dork, or something similar. At the same time, being ranked against one's peers created a sense of unity among the mature students—many held the perception that this ranking system was a necessary evil that the faculty and administration insisted on, and, therefore, students paid little attention to this number as they got older, and slowly its significance faded.

While the Australian grading system seems as if it would pit students against one another, I feel that the American system, by far, is worse. Students attach so much worth to their GPA, and the fact that they are not flat-out ranked among their peers makes students inquisitive as to where they stand. In Australian high school, it is a loaded question to inquire about another's grades. An example would be when an assignment is returned and a general murmur invades the classroom: "What did you get?" Students who pretty much failed the assignment, as well as students who excelled in it, are stigmatized. It appears that the "proper" grades to achieve in high school are C's and B's. One might think that ranking students would create a lot of competition, but, when these numbers aren't presented obviously, students compare themselves anyway in a much more vicious atmosphere.

Another interesting aspect regarding grades is how American college students continue to internalize the grading system and how Australian students seem to abandon this mindset. I ventured back to Sydney to study abroad and attend university for one semester. The way Australian universities grade is with High Distinction, Distinction, Credit, Pass, and No Pass. According to my fellow Australian students, a Pass was satisfactory and a Credit deserved congratulations. A Pass translates into a C and a Credit translates into a B. Getting a High Distinction was not of much importance and was definitely not worth tailoring your life to achieve. As you can imagine, none of my Aussie friends could understand why I was stressing about getting top grades—to them passing was enough. Once I tried explaining to them that my grades made up my GPA, that my scholarship funds relied on me keeping a high GPA, and that I needed high scores to get into a good graduate school. They just looked at me and said point blank, "You Americans are crazy."

School worldwide is a socialization tool, a place for youth to learn the dos and don'ts, the haves and have nots, as well as the role they are assigned in this mini version of the overall social hierarchy. Yet even though this is a common denominator for all education, I believe that American schools are the most brutal in this socialization process.

At St. Ives High School, the socialization that took place was very subtle. Perhaps this was due to a combination of grade size and culture. As a result of having about 100 students per grade (and having the majority of these kids attend elementary school together), students interacted with the group as a whole, even if there were little cliques defined at recess and lunch. These cliques were loosely formed and permitted people to network between groups rather than be shut out by firm boundaries. Consequently, students knew the majority of their peers and had at least acknowledged acquaintances within the entire grade. Even those students who were not popular at all were acknowledged and fit into the social framework. Culturally, high school was not considered the stepping-stone to the rest of your life. Australian students have so many avenues that can lead to careers that the possibilities are nearly overwhelming. First of all, students can opt to drop out at 10th grade with their Lower School Certificate. From here they can either apprentice in a field of their choice or attend TAFE (which is a type of junior college that allows students to tailor their classes to fit a certain profession). Or students can choose to remain in school for 11th and 12th grade and complete their HSC (Higher School Certificate). This is a series of assessments throughout the 2 years, culminating in exams in subjects of their own choice—these scores are then weighted and combined, giving the student one overall score. This educational path is by far the most stressful and demanding because that single score determines which programs of study and universities you are eligible for.

In fact, it should be noted that several students have actually committed suicide during this time in their life from the pressure of having the scores published in the *Sydney Morning Herald* for all to see. However, not all students take it that seriously, and once high school is complete, it is culturally encouraged for students to take a year off to travel around the world. If you have ever traveled, it might make sense now that you always seem to meet Australians. Travel is considered to be essential, and many students save money throughout high school if their parents haven't already started a fund for them. Or students can begin a university course, and then at any point during their education, they can defer their program for 6 months to travel. Looking at the array of paths one can take in this culture shows that high school is not a crucial element in the path to one's success in life, as they make it out to be in our culture.

For me, transitioning from the situation described earlier into an institution known among students in the district as the "snobbiest" school was an experience, to say the least. At this school, there were approximately 600 kids in my class, and since I was entering at 11th grade, it goes without saying that everyone had already established their own niche within the social hierarchy. I soon learned that I would be judged, acknowledged, and discarded solely due to my appearance and material possessions. Students were ruthless, and I never fit in to any clique. So I became a wanderer, an observer, and early on I decided I hated my school. Apart from feeling isolated, I rapidly began to see the system for what it was—an institution for learning the social boundaries by being thrown together and forced to survive daily. Any type of education in this system to me seemed a joke, and I was even in the honors program, a place for the accelerated students! Yet I soon realized that to work the system all I had to do was exercise by rote memory

(I can confidently tell you that I remember nothing from my history class) and finesse my assignments to suit each professor's style to ensure I got that A.

Our society leads its youth to believe that a successful life will be obtained by 110% effort to be the very best of the best. Not only do we have to be on the ball and driven to succeed at every venture, but also we must know exactly where we are heading from the ripe old age of 17. Every day, high school seniors walk into their career counselor's office and are asked to decide what they want to do for a career. We expect these kids to have given proper thought to their future and to commit to it by applying to colleges that have a good program for the major that they will need for their future careers. How are kids that age supposed to know what is really out there and available to them if they have spent the last 4 years memorizing information that they suspect they really aren't going to need? College graduates often still don't know what they want to do into their second or third year of school, let alone graduating high school students.

This push for our youth to decide now, now, now is what I like to call the Inevitable Inertia of our lives—we live in a culture that is obsessed with preparing for the future. A common question asked of children in our society is "What do you want to be when you grow up?" I am sure every one of us has been asked this at some point (if not repeatedly) during our childhood. As soon as a child can articulate a sentence, we put thoughts of the future into her or his head. Then it merely escalates; in junior high, we work hard to get into the honors program at high school. In high school, we strive for the GPA (let alone extracurricular activities) to gain entry into a good undergraduate college. In college, we push ourselves to get into a good graduate school. In graduate school, we go the extra mile to ensure a good career and a high income, and in our career we work overtime so that we can retire comfortably. Therefore, we are 60 years of age (if we are lucky) when we finally stop, breathe, and enjoy our days. Our society shapes our minds so that we are continuously living for tomorrow—a tomorrow that may arrive too late.

—Andrea Crane

Andrea's concluding remarks about how we are conditioned to keep our eyes on the ever-receding future brings to mind similar thoughts by a great translator and explorer of the Eastern paths of liberation, Alan Watts. In his classic work, *The Book: On the Taboo Against Knowing Who You Are* (1966), he states,

> We are thus breeding a type of human being incapable of living in the present—that is, of really living. For unless one is able to live fully in the present, the future is a hoax. There is no point whatever in making plans for a future you will never be able to enjoy. When your plans mature, you will still be living for some other future beyond. You will never, never be able to sit back with full contentment and say, "Now, I've arrived!" Your entire education has deprived you of this capacity because it was preparing you for the future,

instead of showing you how to be alive now. In other words, you have been hypnotized or conditioned by an educational processing system arranged in grades or steps, supposedly leading to some ultimate Success. (p. 80)

Whether you are an excellent, poor, or average grade earner is beside the point and may not even be relevant to whether you are a good student—that is, one who really questions and perhaps even enjoys the material. You must, in any case, be absolutely clear within yourself that *the grading system is not a measure of your worth as a human being.* This is hardest for those who do well because there is usually a temptation to believe in a system that ranks you highly. If you feel this way, notice the good feeling is never there permanently. Every time you are tested, you are on the line again. Internalizing leads to addiction. Indeed, John Holt (1982), in his classic work *How Children Fail,* said that school makes some people into failures and others into "praise junkies." The latter can get pretty wretched if they don't get their regular "fix" of A's. Alfie Kohn's (1993) work *Punished by Rewards, The Trouble with Gold Stars, Incentive Plans, A's, Praise, and Other Bribes* also perceptively addresses this issue.

Grades "R" Us

Students have a labeling system that defines their status. This is the label of grades. Grades define their reality. Grading, this process of placing a letter on our knowledge, has reduced each of us to a mere letter. Our GPA determines our status. The honored elite few who have received A's are equivalent to the upper class of society. They both have one thing in common: They have learned to chase the grade (or the dollar) by allowing the system to degrade them. It degrades them because they are not being evaluated on who they are but rather on what they have become by following the selfish mode of society.

Students have internalized the grading system to such a point that their health is dependent on the grades. It was not until recently that I realized how I allowed grades to control my life. I had two midterms back to back, and I literally became ill from stressing over the grade I might receive on the midterms. *I put the grade before my health.* I was blown away by that realization. A mere letter of the alphabet became more important than my health. I cannot understand when I stopped being the individual that I thought I was and started becoming the robot trained to chase the grade. At that moment, I realized that I had given someone else control of my life.

Someone else holds the key to my life. This person decides whether my future will be one of joy or pain. This person decides whether I am competent or not and whether my parents will be proud of me or lecture me on the importance of receiving that A. I have no control over my life as long as I am a student and grades continue to exist. Now, I understand that grades are supposed to be simple feedback on our work and a way for us to learn. However, we have been trained to value grades more than the knowledge itself. In all my courses, it does not matter how much I learn; it only matters that I receive an A.

That is so sad. The knowledge means nothing; the chosen letters of the alphabet are what define our reality. The worst part is that I am a prisoner to this system, and I do not know how to free myself. It is almost as if I would cease to exist if grades stopped defining my reality. This is the world I know, and I cannot get away from it.

The funny thing is that I have become so dependent on grades that I actually receive some psychotic pleasure from having grades structure my life. They keep me from having to decide for myself. There would be utter chaos if grades were eliminated from our educational system. Students would have mental breakdowns; their entire identity would disappear. They would lose their status and their label and their role. They might as well not exist.

—Gagendeep Sandhu

The type of intelligence measured in college is a very narrow range of the total spectrum of abilities that determines your success and happiness in life. Practical knowledge is not tested in university courses because it is not taught. There is precious little relationship between people's grades and how successful they actually are at future jobs. Many skills, particularly skills in human interaction, are relevant to one's success. Unfortunately, professors will seldom admit this. To illustrate an extreme case, we have the sad spectacle of graduate schools in clinical psychology choosing applicants on the basis of grade point alone, when all the evidence on the success of therapists points to emotional traits as key elements. Remember that your professors exaggerate the importance of academic learning because that is where they were able to make their mark.

As for your chances of happiness in your human relationships, academic excellence will help you here not at all. As a matter of fact, it will probably stand in your way, particularly if you have taken seriously the idea that you are better than other people because you can outshine them on an exam. If this has happened to you, school has made you a foolish person, which is not at all unusual.

If you want to see whether you have internalized the grading system, just observe how you feel when you are waiting to get back an exam or a paper. Are you perfectly at ease, secure in the knowledge that you are sitting in a comfortable room, safe from any physical danger? If so, you're all right. But to the extent that you feel discomfort at these moments, you have internalized the system.

Understanding Versus Internalizing the Rules

Let us now go back to the distinction between *understanding* the rules and *internalizing* them. If you want to stay in college and perhaps go on to graduate school, you will have to perform according to the rules. You must know what they are and not kid yourself about them. But you will work more easily and competently if you refuse to let grades represent who you are. If you have fears about who you are—and most young people do—these fears must be dealt with on an altogether different level. You must simply make direct contact with yourself, not the indirect contact and indirect self-approval given in the grading system. If you wish to check who you are directly at this moment, sit still for 10 minutes with your eyes closed and just pay attention to what the different parts of your body are telling you. Is your stomach feeling jumpy? Then that is who you are at the moment. Is there tension in your neck and shoulders? Make friends with the tension. Don't evaluate or pass judgment on yourself. Just feel yourself directly. This is the beginning of becoming your own friend. It is absolutely direct, and you can do it for yourself without anybody else's approval. When you have become friends with your body and your emotions, you will begin to know who you are. It isn't easy, and it isn't quick, but it beats basing your sense of self on grades.

You may now be tempted to say, "But if I don't aim for certain grades, how will I control my efforts sufficiently to keep from flunking out?" The answer is that you must learn to organize your life so as to give a reasonable and steady amount of time to your studies. Do this sensibly and then accept whatever grade result it produces.

Students develop a particular lifestyle, and, as a student, you will get caught up in it to some degree. It will be more intense if you live in a dormitory than if you live at home. With regard to schoolwork, the student lifestyle is a hysterical alternation between feast and famine, indolence and cramming. About three weeks before the end of every semester, the college atmosphere becomes noticeably more harried. Eyes become bloodshot, and dark circles appear under them. Hands get shaky. People begin gulping down caffeine and other artificial stimulants as they stay up all night typing papers that they have put off for the whole semester and studying material that they should have read weeks ago. By the last week, many are in the campus clinic suffering from exhaustion and a variety of physical ills stemming from the same causes.

Yet this pattern of squeezing everything into a few weeks at the end of the term does not make the average undergraduate carefree and elated during the first 13 weeks of the semester. On the contrary, students are feeling guilty all along about their indolence. In one class where I ask people to make a list of their favorite self-accusations, laziness is on everybody's list. One undergraduate wrote the following:

In college, laziness is like a disease, one that I am deathly afraid of. While some people wallow in laziness, I spend every waking moment trying to avoid it. I finish class readings weeks before I have to, and I write papers long before they're due. I get so worried that I won't get it all done that I do a semester's worth of work in the first 3 months. I fear laziness so much that I literally breed stress within myself. That's not the worst of it, though. I don't relax once the work is done. I keep pushing. If I relaxed, that would be lazy. I feel that, since I have so much free time, I should be using it wisely. I should be rewriting all of my papers and rereading the assignments. I should do more research and maybe some fieldwork. If I don't, I'm just being lazy. I fear laziness so much that I won't even enjoy the free time that I've earned.

—*Kristin Rydberg*

The student who does not suspect himself or herself of laziness doesn't exist. A pattern of nervous procrastination has nearly everybody in its grip. Indeed, if we look at the college culture as a structure of time, we can see that it breeds procrastination almost like certain bacteria breed yogurt culture.

But if you are perceptive and look around, you will notice that there are always a few people who don't fall into this deadly cycle of indolence, guilt, and harried labor. They are not noticeably worse off during the last 3 weeks than during any others. If you investigate these folks, you will probably discover that they also do pretty successful work. They have discovered what I am about to tell you.

It is perfectly possible to do well in school without having to get hysterical at any point if you set aside approximately 15 to 30 hours a week, as best you can, of study time, in addition to your class meetings. A reasonable schedule, for example, might be 3 to 4 hours a day, Monday through Saturday. If you put these hours in early in the day, your evenings, Saturday afternoons, and Sundays should be totally free. If you are a night worker, you might wish to plan a very different schedule. The important thing is—like an athlete in training—*to keep your schedule pretty much without fail from the very first week of the semester*. The schedule will be tougher if you also work, as most students do, but in that case, it is even more essential. Barring emergencies, just put in the time. Just sit at your desk or in the library as a daily practice. Don't make any elaborate demands on yourself. Just put in your hours. Beyond this, be satisfied regardless of your grade.

Procrastination and Russian Roulette

If you're like me, you probably have something else you are supposed to be doing at the moment. So let's put that stuff aside and talk about procrastination. There are many lessons in life about things you shouldn't do that you can't learn until you've done them. College is a great time to experiment and learn those things you cannot glean from a textbook. Procrastination is an indispensable tool that is crucial in enabling us to learn many of these lessons. That being said, procrastination is an art form. If you never put off work and are always getting ahead, you could miss out on all the fun in life. The world could end tomorrow, and what a shame it would be if you spent the last 24 hours of your life doing homework. On the other hand, if you put off work past its deadline, your world could very well end tomorrow when you flunk out.

Like all things, procrastination requires moderation. College is a big adjustment after high school. Depending on who you are and where you went to high school, you may find college easier or harder; you may have less work or more. Regardless, you definitely have more freedom. The key to having both a successful academic career and enjoying life is to know yourself and your own capacities. Know how much time you need to get something done comfortably and how much you need when the situation requires you to crank out work as fast as possible, print, and sprint to class. Take it slow while you figure this out, and err on the side of caution. Once you've learned this, always give yourself some extra time in case you get stuck or your professor throws you a curveball.

Deadlines don't disappear because you want them to. You need to understand that the joy of a party is offset by the pains of the all-nighter you may have to pull to meet the deadline. When you push things close to the deadline and make yourself short for time, you play a very dangerous game of Russian roulette. If you want to survive, you have to stay flexible. When you have a major assignment due or have more on your plate than normal, you are going to have to spend less time having fun and more time working. You also may have to cut into time you would otherwise spend sleeping.

At some point during our college careers, we are all going to get hit with the perfect storm. When you do, prioritizing is the key to staying afloat; otherwise, you will drown. Procrastinating is a lot like barbequing. It takes a lot of care and attention, and if you do it right, it can taste great, but if you are not careful or just unlucky, you can wind up burned.

—Michael Creim

If you are worried by some piece of work you have to do, do that first. Don't procrastinate to avoid it. *Procrastination inevitably increases the anxiety,* whereas tackling the work will get you past the chore and leave you feeling better for the rest of the day. What I am suggesting here is that you replace self-laceration with self-discipline. It is so much easier.

If your schedule seems to demand a much heavier investment of time, then take a close look at how you are choosing classes. Always diversify. Take some easy courses along with the hard ones. Try to work in a "fun" course every time—something like music or dance, which doesn't require much homework. Unfortunately, many professors seem to think that it is reasonable to expect students to put in 50 or 60 hours a week—a figure vastly in excess of anything required of the workforce. You have the right of self-protection here.

Of course, nervous procrastination and unreasonable professors are not the only reasons students run into disaster with their schedules. Another common reason is overinvestment in college activities. Every college prides itself on having lots of organizations and events. For students, this means that the college world is often aglitter with things to become involved in, to delight in, and to learn from. We are a greedy society, so it is not surprising that we are greedy individuals. Perhaps you thought that greed only meant desiring material possessions. But it is much more subtle than that. We are also greedy for learning, for experience, for participation, and sometimes just for things to list on our future job applications. We forget that we have only a finite amount of time and energy to expend. So we have to face this greed and recognize it for what it is. The question is, would you rather try to grab it all and have a harried schedule, or would you prefer to be more modest and have a serene and reasonable schedule?

Helping to Reduce Pressure to Achieve

It is only human to feel pressure, and it is no surprise that everyone feels pressure often in his or her life. The situations and environment we place ourselves in create pressure. The pressure to succeed is fomented in a student's life by his or her environment: class, competitive student body, monetary issues, familial opinions, and image self-consciousness all contribute to the pervading presence of pressure.

My professor always swore by the edict of pressure. He said pressure makes diamonds. Pressure can also make a wreck. The right amount of pressure in the right atmosphere could produce diamonds; however, any miscalculation may leave you with a weaker lump of coal.

The pressure to achieve is one of the many pressures a student will experience while in college. The permanence of this pressure is no doubt a result of a college student's thought processes about his or her ability to achieve and personal yearning to succeed. It is important to not run from this pressure; instead, embrace it so that you are able to tackle the feelings of uneasiness and fear that go hand in hand with the "ivory tower goals" of your collegiate endeavors.

To begin, let us look at the idea of pressure. Pressure, in many circumstances, is a product of your mind. It does not exist in the tangible state. One cannot touch, hear, smell, taste, or see pressure. However, one can be under pressure, metaphorically feel pressure, and be stressed by pressures, which all leave evidence in the tangible world. One can see the stress caused by pressure, but one cannot see the perpetrator pressure itself. Ideally, in order to take control of pressure, one must take control of the mind.

Orient your mind toward reducing that pressure. Before going to the big party, instead of studying for your midterm, you should think to yourself, "Is this going to cause me more or less pressure?" Though going to the party may be rewarding in the short term, it can be damaging in the long run. Similarly, studying may not be rewarding in the present but will be helpful in the future. You do not want to increase your pressure with your actions. Be aware of the pressure-reducing or pressure-inducing properties of your actions. The more aware you are of the repercussions of your actions, the better you will be able to combat pressures later on in your life.

Don't panic. There will be times that pressure will be unavoidable. If you find yourself caught in a situation and feel a tremendous amount of pressure, just remember to breathe. It is important to stay grounded at all times and to not get carried away with your emotions. Maintaining a calm and relaxed state during times of pressure will help you alleviate the pressure and find possible remedies. If you have to turn in an assignment in an hour and you haven't started yet, remember to breathe. Or if what's causing your pressure is a looming test date such as a final exam, the MCAT, or LSAT, remember to breathe. When breathing and remaining placid, one allows the body to distribute the stress caused by pressure in a more efficient and orderly fashion. Once the body is able to distribute stress, your brain is more adept at reasoning a remedy or working extra hard to meet a deadline.

—Neil Poria

The quality of your learning and maturing during these 4 or more years means infinitely more than the mere quantity of what you learn and do.

Having read this far, some students have objected, "Your attitude toward grades is all very well and good, but what if you have to make grades to get into medical school or law school or some other graduate training?" My answer to that is this: If you have put in steady time and are getting poor results, you should find out whether your basic study and writing skills can be improved. Talk to your advisor and other professors and ask them to recommend writing courses or other ways to improve study skills. Check into any tutoring programs your college provides. This is especially important if your high school background is weak.

If you have done all this and you are still not making the grades for graduate school, you must accept the results—because they indicate that you are heading for the wrong profession. *Reevaluate your goals.* I say this because if you have to stay up all night and wear yourself to a frazzle to get grades for graduate school, imagine how difficult it will be for you once you get there—and perhaps also how difficult and burdensome the profession will be once you get into it.

Usually there are alternatives you can explore in the same general field to which you were heading. If your grades suggest that you cannot become a physician, how about opting for physical therapy or dentistry? Or perhaps you are heading for the wrong field altogether. This is a time to go to the career counseling center and widen your horizons on the great variety of careers that are available. If your school doesn't have good career counseling, try a professor in the general field in which you might be interested. Career possibilities in most fields are quite complex. In the field of primary and secondary teaching, for example, there are many specialties for which one can train: Besides classroom teachers, there are reading teachers, speech therapists, special education teachers (for disabilities of various kinds), school counselors, and educational administrators. Each specialty requires a different kind of graduate training. The complexity is so great that you really need to become rather familiar with a field before you can see where it might lead you. Therefore, don't make up your mind and close off all options. Proceed one step at a time, guided by the subjects you like and feel good at (plus, if possible, some direct looks at the jobs themselves). That your father wants you to be a lawyer or one of your childhood heroes was a wonderful doctor should not dictate your own outcomes prematurely.

Another word of advice about choosing a career: If you have any very strong preferences about where you want to live, you would do well to research the situation to see whether you can find employment in your chosen location. College teaching, for example, offers very little choice of location because the job openings are so specialized. On the other hand, a skill such as nursing can take you almost anywhere. If you long to live in the country, you shouldn't aspire to become a television executive. Some specialties are in great oversupply in certain desirable urban areas. Research these questions through your campus job counseling service or by contacting practitioners and institutions in the area in which you are interested.

Experimenting

When we were kids and had bicycles, we used to love to coast down hills with our hands dangling nonchalantly at our sides. If you would like to get some of that "Look Ma! No hands!" feeling about the grading system, try doing some work without grades. If your campus permits it, you might take some courses on a pass/fail basis. Or you might ask the professor to give you comments, but no grades, during the semester. When it is time to pick up your final grades, ask a friend to remove the "ungraded" course grade, so you won't see it. Or if you want to take a real flyer, take a whole quarter or semester this way. See whether you experience a change in the educational process. Students who have tried this report very encouraging results, and two excellent books to help you develop your skills are John Gardner and Jerome Jewler's (1992) *College Is Only the Beginning* and David B. Ellis's (1984) *Becoming a Master Student.*

Pass/No Pass Experimentation

"Should I take it pass/no pass?" This familiar question is normally reserved for those killer classes in which you have no hope of getting a shining A. However, the true benefit of gradeless classes—and the reason they were first implemented in the 1960s—is to allow for freedom within a pressurized academic environment. By taking a "normal" class without being graded, it is possible to escape (partially, at least) from the stress and paranoia surrounding the dreaded grade. If you commit to taking a class based on pass/no pass, you must decide also to commit to the work. Professors don't like lazy students who opt out of being responsible by avoiding a grade, but they do tend to favor those students who proclaim that they do not wish to be graded but will be doing the work, taking the tests, and showing up to class. One wonderful anthropology professor at the University of California at Irvine (UCI), who actually dared to fill his lecture time by asking his students to discuss topics he introduced to them, spoke individually to students who wished to take his class without the grading hierarchy, to make sure that they would be involved and would put the same amount of energy and effort into his class as they would if they were being graded.

Now, certainly the first pass/no pass class you ever take will instill some aspect of laziness (due to the freedom), but if you take yourself and your education seriously, you will come to the realization that classes are indeed much more interesting and provocative when you include yourself in them.

According to many people, grades are the motivation behind success. Another perspective, however, is that such assessments of your worth restrict your actual growth by confining you to worrying over five little letters. Should you be concerned with grades? The answer is, of course, yes. Should you let this concern consume most of your waking moments? This is harder to answer. You have to decide early on whether the grading system ought to have the right to run your life, determine your schedule, and support (or more likely deflate) your ego.

The point of taking classes on a pass/no pass basis is not to avoid learning or to avoid grades. Rather, the purpose is just the opposite: By realizing how strong a grip the grading system has over you, you will be able to loosen the grip and enjoy your courses more. Most schools limit the number of such classes you can take, so it's not to your benefit to load up on them. Still, an entire term (quarter or semester) without grades could make a big difference in the way you view school.

Now, you may be stuck in a field that presents academic competition as a prerequisite to success. For instance, most premed programs don't allow for pass/no pass and, worse, tend to weed out those who can't study all day or won't sabotage their classmates (tales of flag switching on anatomy specimens are quite common). Obviously, if you choose this curriculum, you won't be able to implement the changes I've mentioned. However, you are not at a total loss, either. You can still take elective classes without the pressure of grades, to offset your required classes that thrive on competition and one-upsmanship.

—Tatian Greenleaf

If You Just Can't Stand It Anymore

I realize that in the remainder of this book I have been fairly easy on the academy. I have not dwelled on the teachers who humiliate students in class or the ones who spring a paper on you just before vacation. I have not mentioned the frustrating difficulty of getting into required courses in certain fields. I have not really said anything about the pitfalls of dealing with the administration in many of our huge institutions.[4] Paulo Freire (1970) in his *Pedagogy of the Oppressed* boldly stated the following:

> Education must begin with the solution of the teacher-student contradiction, by reconciling the poles of the contradiction so that both are simultaneously teachers *and* students. This solution is not (nor can it be) found in the banking concept. On the contrary, banking education maintains and even stimulates the contradiction through the following attitudes and practices, which mirror oppressive society as a whole:
>
> a. the teacher teaches and the students are taught;
> b. the teacher knows everything and the students know nothing;
> c. the teacher thinks and the students are thought about;
> d. the teacher talks and the students listen—meekly;
> e. the teacher disciplines and the students are disciplined;
> f. the teacher chooses and enforces his choice, and the students comply;
> g. the teacher acts and the students have the illusion of acting through the action of the teacher;
> h. the teacher chooses the program content, and the students (who were not consulted) adapt to it;
> i. the teacher confuses the authority of knowledge with his own professional authority, which he sets in opposition to the students;
> j. the teacher is the subject of the learning process, while the pupils are mere objects. (p. 59)

If there has been little bitterness in my tone, it is probably because it has been many years since I was a student. I would like, therefore, to quote at some length from a paper sent to me by a University of California at Los Angeles student. What she has to say is very incisive.

Confessions of a Student Slave

To a large extent, we are graded in school on our ability to memorize trivial things and, even more, on our endurance at memorizing. The more items a student gets right on an exam,

---

[4]For a scathing (but not undeserved) criticism of the American professoriate, read Charles Sykes's (1989) *PROFSCAM: Professors and the Demise of Higher Education.*

the more he or she is credited with knowing. From years of this kind of reinforcement, it is not unnatural for students to develop the conviction that knowledge consists of the accumulation of hard facts by hard work. Unfortunately, students are being conditioned to falsely associate persistence and a good memory that can readily recall information for exams with being a bright and knowledgeable person. It is not *what* students are taught that does the harm but *how* they are taught. Teachers think providing substance to students is force-feeding their minds with a goodly store of general ideas, available on demand. Students are robbed of their will and sense of power and made into apathetic slaves of authority. Teachers encourage students to spend a considerable amount of time memorizing facts, theories, and definitions to do well on exams. They reinforce this activity with good grades and praise, which are of utmost importance to students. At first, this process seems very useless and demeaning, but as time goes by and it is continually reinforced, it becomes very appealing to most students. They adopt and identify with the system and thereby become a slave to it. What this system does to students is where the real danger lies.

This system traps us and stifles our minds by reinforcing us to not think. Our own ideas and thoughts are suppressed, while the regurgitation of other people's ideas and thoughts is reinforced. The consequence of this is put very succinctly by Schopenhauer (1960), who says, "The safest way of having no thoughts of one's own is to take up a book every moment one has nothing else to do. It is this practice which explains why erudition makes most men more stupid and silly than they are by nature." This system discourages thinking and learning to the point where we actually choose to pass up learning experiences and seek to suppress our own ideas and thoughts. The students' view of what knowledge is becomes distorted by how teachers go about measuring it. It is much harder to develop one's own ideas than it is to memorize and regurgitate those of others. The system reinforces the latter, which is not only much easier but also highly unproductive. Students' desire to suppress their own ideas is clearly shown in their choice of classes: Mickey Mouse courses and classes that have multiple-choice exams and no papers are highly relished. Students have an overwhelming dislike for writing papers, especially those that require some individual expression. They dread expressing their own ideas and strongly prefer to work with other people's because this activity has been reinforced to such a great degree in the past.

One of the most damaging effects of this system is that we are conditioned to seek reinforcement from others rather than from ourselves. We tend to avoid learning experiences and opportunities for creative thinking that do not lead to external rewards (i.e., grades) because these kinds of thought processes have not been reinforced in the past. Internal rewards are seen as foreign and are not recognized as being important. A pathetic condition exists where we learn for others and not for ourselves. This is illustrated in students' reluctance to put forth any extra effort that is not required for a course. If it is not on the test or we are not going to be graded on it, "forget it" is the prevalent attitude. Extra nongraded assignments for learning purposes (i.e., experiments) and voluntary readings are quickly dismissed. What makes this effect even more damaging is that it does not stop once one graduates; it tends to prevail throughout one's life. Knowledge for its own sake is not seen as a valid and valuable goal.

Another detrimental effect of the system is that we get used to *not* thinking and become afraid of it. The thought or act of thinking and developing our own ideas becomes very frightening. Thinking is an activity that is not reinforced in the system, and therefore we have little practice at it. Thinking is an ability that does need training; it is extremely difficult to develop and impart ideas. Initially, we are all lousy at it, but this is a shock to most people. It is not until one has to think that one realizes to what a great extent he or she has relied on other people's thoughts. Blinded by the fact that thinking does require training, it is hard for us to face the fact that thinking is a very difficult process, at least initially. The most common response is avoidance because we are afraid of failure. "What if I can't think?" is a prevalent fear that haunts us. But fortunately for us, we are saved by the system that does not reinforce thinking, only regurgitation of other people's thoughts. As a result, we don't think, and we don't learn.

—*Lorraine Feldman*

If college has brought you to the point where you just can't stand it anymore, you should at least know that you have some alternatives to just continuing to drag yourself through. Many students interrupt their schooling at some point to work for a while or to travel or even to spend a semester or year at another institution. I have always encouraged students to take these bypaths because I know how much it can enrich their education. Any professor who has taught older, returning students will tell you that it is a special joy to teach people who have been out in the world for a while because they bring so much sense of purpose to their education. They have a much clearer idea of what they are looking for, and their experience of the world greatly augments the book learning of college courses. *It is, in fact, a grave mistake to process people through college directly from high school. It would be better if everyone had to spend at least a year or two working between high school and college.* Time off in the middle of college can serve the same purpose. Ideally, you will come back to college refreshed by your "time off."

Parents often oppose such a move because they are afraid you might get lost and never finish and thus doom yourself to a low income. I think that these fears, though genuine and heartfelt, are misplaced. Often, they arise from the parent's own sense of inadequacy in dealing with the world. It may be necessary for you to oppose your parents on this score.

There is yet another possibility: You may decide that you just do not want a college degree or the type of career to which it normally leads. There are alternative ways of life out there. I have known quite a few craftsmen and craftswomen who like what they do and are perfectly happy without a college degree. You can become a carpenter or even a master cabinetmaker, an electrician, gardener, plumber, tile setter, or auto mechanic. Not all trades are manual in nature. Some combine manual and intellectual skills, and some are purely intellectual. A look at a community college catalogue tells me that they give 2-year degrees in animal science, ornamental horticulture, business information systems, commercial art, photography, marketing, drafting, electronics, musical instrument repair, aviation service, welding, and preschool administration, to take only a small sample.

You will not get rich in these occupations, but you may find satisfying work and make enough to survive quite well. Many of these skills have the added advantage of giving you some freedom to live where you please. It is sometimes cheaper and more pleasant to live in rural areas than in cities. Of course, you should check out whether opportunities for a given trade exist in the location of your choice.

In northern California, where I live, as in rural areas throughout the United States, there are even a lot of people who are surviving on the land by raising their own food and taking occasional jobs in town. Many worked for a number of years before they were able to put together a down payment on a plot of land. These folks are not prosperous by the usual standards. They face many hardships, but they are some of the happiest and most satisfied young people I have met.

If you are considering such a drastically different lifestyle, you should proceed with some caution. When you have decided on an area in which you would like to settle, spend at least a year there, picking up whatever jobs you can and getting to know people who are working the land. Such a way of life involves very serious sacrifices and changes, and you should not commit yourself without investigating these thoroughly.

Unfortunately, society uses the invidious phrase *dropping out* for people who take up a rural way of life. I can assure you, though, that most people who do it feel neither "dropped" nor "out." I don't know any who would trade their situation for an urban lifestyle. Not getting a bachelor's degree does not automatically mean failure and unhappiness any more than a bachelor's degree ensures success and satisfaction.

Throughout your educational journey, keep in mind that certain subjects generally, and academics broadly, may not play to your personal strengths. A parable by George H. Reeves highlights this crucial idea:

> Once upon a time, the animals decided that their lives and their society would be improved by setting up a school. The basics identified as necessary for survival in the animal world were swimming, running, climbing, jumping, and flying. Instructors were hired to teach these activities, and it was agreed that all the animals would take all the courses. This worked out well for the administrators, but it caused some problems for the students.
>
> The squirrel, for example, was an A student in running, jumping, and climbing but had trouble in flying class, not because of an inability to fly, for she could sail from the top of one tree to another with ease, but because the flying curriculum called for taking off from the ground. The squirrel was drilled in ground-to-air take-offs until she was exhausted and developed charley horses from overexertion. This caused her to perform poorly in her other classes, and her grades dropped to D's.
>
> The duck was outstanding in swimming class—even better than the teacher. But she did so poorly in running that she was transferred to remedial

class. There she practiced running until her webbed feet were so badly damaged that she was only an average swimmer. But since average was acceptable, nobody saw this as a problem—except the duck.

In contrast, the rabbit was excellent in running, but, being terrified of water, he was an extremely poor swimmer. Despite a lot of makeup work in swimming class, he never could stay afloat. He soon became frustrated and uncooperative and was eventually expelled because of behavior problems.

The eagle naturally enough was a brilliant student in flying class and even did well in running and jumping. He had to be severely disciplined in climbing class, however, because he insisted that his way of getting to the top of the tree was faster and easier.

It should be noted that the parents of the groundhog pulled him out of school because the administration would not add classes in digging and burrowing. The groundhogs, along with the gophers and badgers, got a prairie dog to start a private school. They all have become strong opponents of school taxes and proponents of voucher systems.

By graduation time, the student with the best grades in the animal school was a compulsive ostrich who could run superbly and also swim, fly, and climb a little. She, of course, was made class valedictorian and received scholarship offers from all the best universities.

CHAPTER 3

Technology and Learning

In Chapter 3, we examine the subtle and bludgeoning love/hate effects of our digital technologies upon us and upon the very structure of our consciousness, as well as the dangerous and unintended consequences on our ability to learn and even perhaps on our ability to engage in human relationships. We will in particular explore technology in the classroom.

We have spent time discussing the impact of the pressures and situations that make college a new, exciting, and challenging social landscape for everyone. Yet we have not addressed an area that many of you take for granted and consider part of your everyday life and reality: technology—particularly the electronic interconnective technologies.

College is much more than just a new set of material or courses to take and digest. Learning is at the heart of the college experience, whether we are learning about our personal or academic life. Recently our relationship with learning has changed, and this change is having an impact on all aspects of society. Technology has become so much a part of our self and our reality we rarely think about its impact or even its existence until it is not around. Many students we come in contact with even sleep with their phones so they don't miss anything and stay connected to everyone. As you have grown, you have traded in your security blankets for a technological security blanket and feel strange without it.

For your entire life, you have been immersed in and occupied with technology, from TV to computers, from video games to cell phones. Most of you have combined all of these technologies into one device and now interface with the world and your friends via technology. The question is not *whether* technology is changing the experience and meaning of education and college but *how*. In what ways is technology impacting your education and college life? We wish, in this chapter, to become more reflexively aware of these momentous changes. We are not saying that this change is bad, but without being aware of how technology has changed the way we access, interpret, understand, and learn information about ourselves and our academic life, we have no control over its power. As many of you found out in Chapter 2, your relationship with grades *has been deeply internalized* and has altered your educational life. Not realizing the power grades have had over our education and learning has very deep psychological consequences; we believe that the use of technology has psychological consequences, too.

Technology has revolutionized the way we access information. Going to a library to do research is something many of you will never do without a computer. You can find out about almost any topic in seconds with a search on Google and even see streaming video of the concept in the process. You can keep track of your friends and family in real time and communicate with them in various modes: phone, e-mail, social networking, and Skype, to name a few. You can check on assignments or ask teachers questions remotely and get feedback almost immediately. In class, you have the ability to use your computer to take notes and record and check what the professor says. But with all this technology there does seem to be a very human cost.

Turn Off, Tune Off, Drop In

It is hard for most students to envision a life without phones, computers, or being wired to the Internet. A life of electronic connections to friends, classmates, and information is as normal as the air we breathe. But what is the cost of this electronic connection? Does it impact the way we interact with ourselves and others and even impact our learning and education? Unfortunately these are questions that are not being really addressed enough. Sherry Turkle in her TED Talk (Turkle, 2012) and book *Alone Together* (Turkle, 2011) is taking the time to expose and inform all of us about some of the costs our electronic life is having. It is important to be aware of these costs so we are not taken by surprise. She warns us all that our inability to be away from our phones and technology divides our attention toward life. Instead of giving attention to the world, we go *into* our phones and technology. As a result, both the idea and the phenomenological experience of communication have changed, thus changing how we interact and know each other.

Texts, tweets, and e-mails are, on one level, very controlled forms of communication. They are not susceptible to the unpredictable openness, risk, and vulnerability of authentic face to face conversations. Turkle claims we have been *sacrificing conversations for connection.* This is a very important distinction. Without authentic conversations, we don't get to know each other, and not knowing others keeps us from knowing ourselves. Our obsession with being connected to our friends has actually made us more alone. As students in a university, being part of the conversation is essential. Just being connected is not going to help with your growth and development as an individual and your education will suffer as well. Education is a human endeavor that takes place together in shared space—not chat rooms. Being in the room with your professors and classmates creates a shared experience that can't be replicated by Internet technology. By sacrificing conversation for connection, we are losing more than we know.

As professors, we notice that this has had a big impact on how actual discussions are occurring in our classes. We have seen it become tougher to get students to talk in class. Talking in class (like talking in person) is risky without the ability to pre-edit our thoughts. But by not sharing and talking, we miss the ability to learn from each other in the dynamic exchange of conversations. It is inherently different to communicate by text or e-mail than to feel the energy of a discussion about ideas in a classroom. The sterile companion of technology is never going to replace the human experience of a conversation about ideas. We have almost come to the opposite end of the 60's mantra of "Turn On, Tune In, and Drop Out." We now need to "Turn Off, Tune Off, and Drop In." To get the most out of education or life, we need to re-engage in conversations with people and not let technology make us Alone Together.

—John Gunderson

The Library

Dearest Library,

There is something I have been meaning to confess for a long time. I have been unfaithful. At first I thought it was just a fling, but after my first quarter in college, I realized the strong emotional and physical attachment I have developed for the Internet. It's not that the Internet is better, per se, or could ever replace the physical interaction I experience with you. It's just, sadly, the Internet has the ability to satisfy my needs in ways you never could. Being a college student, I have a demanding schedule and the Web is just more resourceful and practical; I can do twice the amount of research in half the time. Please understand, it's not you; it's me. I'm just at a point in my life when I have so much going on that I cannot give you the time and attention you deserve. I'll be seeing you around.

Yours truly,

Library card number 1111650246931

Sitting in the study room of our university's undergraduate library, I look over to my left, through the glass windows that enclose the thousands of untouched books that continue to collect dust on the shelves. Going to the library, referencing authors, researching, and checking out books all seem to be a thing of the past—the library is more like a museum now. What happened? Technology has caused a rift in our relationship. The means by which students experience college has shifted from traditional to technological. It has shifted from a bookish, literate, scholarly relationship to knowledge to a screened, Internet-based, electronic, digital-graphic relationship. Yes, many students still use the library, but not to research and read the actual books; rather, students use the library as a study environment, to go online and conduct research via Google, article databases, and e-resources. Students are no longer trained to physically refer to books; instead, students learn to refer to books using electronic library catalogs, article databases, Google Scholar, interactive tutorials, and digital libraries.

Because America thrives on consumerism and ownership of personal possessions, we insist on purchasing our media: books, magazines, movies, and music. Consequently, we are forgetting about the simple joys that our college and local community libraries offer. Considering that the vast majority of college students are broke and we are in the midst of an economic crisis in which money is tight and unemployment rates are high, we should be taking advantage of simple luxuries such as the library. Individuals feel the need to buy personal copies of books from Amazon or Barnes and Noble, which, on average, will only be read once or twice. The library is free, open to the public, and provides an environment that helps build a sense of community and camaraderie between individuals and groups. We must stop this hyper-love affair with the Internet and bring a vital part of our education back to the basics. Therefore, I encourage everyone to turn off the computer. Go to your local library, check out a book, and take a moment to sit down and enjoy it!

—*Steffany Strain*

Education, whether formal or informal, has always been the most human exchange. We learn from our families, our friends, our significant others, and our teachers. Being in the presence of human beings talking, discussing, and observing others has always been central to learning to be human. Now that technology has become part of our very intimate selves, a new dimension seems to have created an unforeseen virtual barrier. We still learn by talking, discussing, and watching, but now often there is a technological screen and buffer between us. We seem to be using the same words to describe what we are doing, but there is a qualitative difference between interacting in person and interacting with technology.

Is a discussion over the Internet or via Skype the same as interacting with a teacher and a class or your peers? Are the notes you buy the same as the ones you take in class? Can you really pay attention and learn as you text or check Facebook during your lecture? Does your campus or personal social networking site integrate you into your campus and undergraduate life as much as physically going to places would?

Facebook Versus Face Time

Facebook: What a great invention! It's an online social networking site that lets you keep up with friends and classmates without actually talking to them in person. It comes in handy when you don't have the time or energy to leave the comfort of your home. This seems like a wonderful resource for students—they're able to find classmates online, send them a "friend request," and use them as an extra aid when it comes to their education. So what if someone needs some quick homework help? It's pretty simple, really; he or she can just type a question and classmates respond. Problem solved. Although now anyone can sign up for Facebook, it was initially only available to students (their e-mail addresses had to end in.edu). However, as with all things, it must be used in moderation. Facebook should not completely take the place of face-to-face interaction because the social aspect of college is something that needs to be lived and experienced for oneself. There are some things that you can't learn from a book, or a Web site, and a college social life is one of them.

I have been guilty of depending too much on Facebook for interaction. I'm a shy person at times, and Facebook has been great for me because it is much easier to be outgoing online. Conversations can be started effortlessly when there is a computer to hide behind. So I can contact classmates and ask them for their opinions on certain topics without actually having an awkward face-to-face interaction. It gives me a virtual veil of security. Facebook enables students to communicate with each other and ask for help when they otherwise would not have the courage to ask because Facebook gives users total control of who they appear to be.

Facebook is a very convenient tool for students; it allows them to connect with others easily and instantly. However, this can become problematic once an individual starts to replace all face-to-face interaction with virtual contact. There comes a point when one must realize the impersonal aspect of Facebook—individuals may be able to have online friends and colleagues, but be careful to consider them just virtual sources of information and not actual human beings. Once a person looks to Facebook as his or her sole source of social contact, it's possible that the opposite actually happens—users may feel isolated and withdrawn from others.

Nothing can replace the social experience of college. There's something to actually getting a group of college kids together for a study group: have pizza, stay up all night, and maybe even get some studying done. Students must find a balance between the convenience of instant virtual communication and actual face time with other students and professors. Try to find a balance between taking advantage of technological developments and experiencing in-person interaction. So go ahead and add friends to your Facebook account and resort to online sources for homework help, but keep in mind that some day when you're looking back on your life as a college student, you may not remember how many friend requests you received or which of your friends sent you virtual gifts, but those late nights hanging out with friends will somehow always make you smile.

—Daniella Reynoso Graves

Facebook Deactivating and Reactivating

At the beginning of my senior year in college, I decided to deactivate my Facebook. Much to my surprise, it proved to be an extremely difficult decision. In the process of making this decision, I reflected on the hard work and hours spent creating this version of myself. I felt silly when I thought of the time I pressured my then-boyfriend to update his profile so that it showed he was "In a Relationship" with me. (Because if it is not on Facebook, it must not be true in real life, right?) I debated long and hard about whether I wanted to save my Facebook photos to my hard drive. I updated my status notifying my friends of my departure. I wondered if anyone would notice my absence.

When I deactivated, Facebook tempted, "Are you sure? Your friends will miss you."

I surveyed the random assortment of "friends" that Facebook included on the good-bye page. *Thump-thump... Thump-thump... Thump-thump.* I clicked the "YES" button. I received the cold confirmation e-mail. I followed the link and clicked "YES" once again.

And then I thought to myself: *Now, what?*

I already felt withdrawals within the first few hours. I was anxious thinking about what I was missing out on in my virtual cocoon. My palms were actually sweaty. In the next few days, I reminded my fingers to forget the reflex of typing "f-a-c-e" into the search bar when I was bored. I was forced to think of other things to do since I could no longer log onto Facebook. Then, over the next few weeks, I actually finished reading entire novels. I caught up on world news. I went on long hikes. I painted. I slept longer. I dedicated more time to school and work.

Without Facebook, however, I realized that I severed a crucial line of communication with my friends. I called, texted, or e-mailed my friends to tell them about a funny link, a good song, or an interesting Web site. I rarely received these calls, texts, or e-mails in return. Instead, I received texts saying, "where's ur fbook??" or "i wanted to show u this but ur not there anymore," and "y weren't u there last night? didn't u get my fbook invite?" *Although I felt a profound sense of freedom upon deactivation, I also developed a profound sense of isolation.* In addition to losing touch with my close friends, I missed birthdays, went unaware of a friend's engagement, and missed invites for winter break trips to Vegas and Tahoe.

I surrendered and reactivated Facebook within 2 months. Whether I like it or not, changing times and advances in technology require me to be plugged in to connect with others. I realized, however, that being plugged in only becomes a problem when it negatively affects my personality, inhibits my mental processes, or hinders my real-life sociability. Deactivation was a good "cleansing" exercise because it reminded me that I was capable of doing other things besides surfing the Web and that I was a more substantial person when the concern over maintaining my profile was eliminated. *I highly recommend temporary deactivation to anyone who feels that Facebook monopolizes his or her time on the computer.*

—*Samantha St. Laurent*

The moral of the story is this: Make time to do the things you wouldn't normally do because of time spent on Facebook. Make a point of only logging on once or twice a day. Use Facebook for its intended purpose. Connect with people, but don't use it as a mental escape. All it takes is moderation and a little bit of discipline.

As educators, we have all witnessed a disturbing change. We are concerned that some of the most important lessons in life are being mediated through technology and not through personal exchange. We believe that this technology-mediated learning has consequences, perhaps in a similar way that the chained prisoners in Plato's famous parable of the cave experienced the consequences of learning only through shadows cast on the wall of their cave.

In college, you have the opportunity to learn and discover knowledge at every turn. Whether in the dorm, at coffee, or in class, college life is a nonstop learning experience. However, we need to be aware and not let technology infringe on this arena too much. We like to believe technology has made us more efficient, but don't let that hurt your effectiveness. Even if your class is wired, try to break that connection and not text or check Facebook for that lecture. If you are immersed in technology land, you miss the experience of the human exchange between teacher and student that has gone on for thousands of years unmediated. Great teaching and learning is transformative and powerful and can be felt in ways that technology has a hard time transmitting or recording. Although powerful teaching and learning can be seen and heard in the media in multiple formats, it is not the same as the interaction between teacher/student, friend/friend, boyfriend/girlfriend. That human exchange is the most powerful connection you can have. Remember, to truly be connected you need human interface, not a 3G/4G network or Wi-Fi. Don't miss your chance for an education in college because you are afraid to miss an incoming text.

Technology and Loss of Focus

It's the night before your 10-page paper is due, and the blank Word document stares you in the face. The high brightness of the monitor starts to become somewhat intimidating, making you consider changing its settings just so that you don't burn a hole in the back of your retina. As the blank page lies before you, you keep telling yourself that all you need is the first few lines to give yourself the momentum necessary to finish. Eventually, a few coherent sentences manage to end up on the Word document, and you're in business. Turns out you were right. All you needed was that initial push. After all, it's not the first time that you stressed yourself out by leaving your work for the last minute. Unfortunately, you have experienced this type of stressful situation too many times before, each time reinforcing the idea that those first few lines were the key to your success. If it truly is the case that a few short sentences is all one needs in order to finish a paper, then why didn't you start writing those few sentences before? If you had written those initial sentences earlier, doesn't that mean you would have finished earlier as well? Perhaps watching that film was more important than getting important work done. Evidently, *productivity and success seem to be more dependent on focus rather than momentum.* It's focus that gives you the correct mentality to start your work, and it's focus that gives you the momentum required to finish. In the internal struggle to gain focus, technology has become the one thing that consistently proves to be a person's worst enemy and a person's best friend. Looking carefully, the influence that technology has on us becomes as clear as day. For example, advances in technology gave way to the television set which has the potential to render us into screen fixated zombies instead of productive humans. On the other side of the spectrum, advances in technology have allowed us to type an entire essay without needing to replace the ink in our typewriter—making us more productive. So is technology a friend or foe? I found my answer in school.

During college, I sometimes struggled with maintaining a healthy balance regarding the use of all my technological assets. I knew that there was a very thick line between utilizing technology as a resource for my work and using technology to satisfy my mindless cravings. Regardless of how thick this line was, I crossed it many times. Unlike making the mistake of giving your mom an apron as a mother's day gift, simply having good intentions isn't going to alleviate your problems when it comes to school work. I remember times when I would open up my textbook or my word processing software with the intention of working, but I would often feel the need to simultaneously populate my head with some carefully chosen music. Eventually, I would spend more time looking for good music than actually being productive. This type of behavior wasn't uncommon for me. For one class, I had to find movie clips that reflected important values within our society. Using YouTube, I was able to quickly find the movie clips that I was looking for. When it came time to write my analysis of the videos, I started with good intentions but managed to get myself into a nonstop video watching rampage. It's amazing how many "funny cat" videos one can watch without getting bored.

The most interesting aspect of all this was that many of my classmates had similar experiences (not the part about the cat videos but about video watching sessions in general). This could be because schools often emphasize the importance of technology, but rarely do they emphasize the negatives of it. Moreover, *students aren't taught how to overcome the harmful effect that technology has on focus. You have to teach yourself, and you have to win the battle on your own.* Today, I still see many struggling with this. Students sometimes try to obtain reputable information online and get stuck in an endless loop of Internet surfing. They might also use social networking Web sites to get school help from classmates, only to end up spending long periods of time chatting with each other about nonsense. Other times, students use their laptops in class, with the good intention of taking notes, but they ultimately veer towards playing a game of solitaire. *It's not that students don't know how to use technology efficiently; they actually know very well. The problem is the lack of focus that arises from all this technology.* For example, students are able to use their smartphones effectively when they want to meet up with members of a group project. Then, during the meeting, they might spend their entire time playing Tetris on their $200 smartphones. That is not to say that you can't have fun with technology, it's just important to remember that your smartphone is only as smart as the end user. In fact, that's true with all technology.

The main dilemma comes about when trying to rectify this issue. How does one gain focus? This shouldn't even be a problem in college as it is something that should have been dealt with earlier in life. Having focus is an integral part of one's study habits, and it's a misfortune for those that haven't learned how to control their focus prior to entering college. Thus, it is up to the students to figure out the best way to deal with this. It's a difficult journey that many embark on, but its payoff is of fundamental importance. Luckily, there are numerous people and businesses that are aware of this issue. Thus, many companies have developed programs that forcefully limit Internet use and cell phone use. If that isn't helpful enough, there are countless online forums that deal with this very subject. It's somewhat paradoxical that technology is one of the most useful ways in combating the problems that arise from technology itself. It personally took me the first year of college to learn how to control my focus, but it facilitated the rest of my college career. It's important to understand that, just like many other things in this world, there needs to be a balance when using technology. It's a tough battle, but winning it is a sign of great discipline. More importantly, having focus is an incredible stress reliever for the purposes of school.

—Soheil Shahri

A Memoir of Distraction: "Oh Look, a Cat Photo!"

It started with a desk encyclopedia. My dad received it free with a computer game in the 1980s, but despite the outdated Soviet-era information, I was captivated by its concise summation of all the world's knowledge. Elementary school homework that should have taken minutes stretched past dinner time and into precious hours of prime time television. But it didn't last; junior high brought me a hand-me-down PC computer and thus, the Internet. I abandoned my small blue brick of a Broderbund desk encyclopedia for the clean black and white pastures of Wikipedia. The oceans of my curiosity broke upon Wikipedia's marginally trustworthy shores. Anything that popped into my head that I might want to learn about was there, free of charge, whenever I wanted it.

With high school graduation came several farewells and a need to stay connected. Wikipedia was relegated to the same lonely place in my heart as the desk encyclopedia, for Facebook was the new obsession. It was like Wikipedia, but for people! I could be the passive-aggressive shut-in socialite, clicking through photos and reading people's information without having to ask for it. I thought I had stumbled upon the ultimate safeguard—social interaction's answer to caller ID. With the right amount of observation and critical thinking, I thought I could extrapolate people's personalities by how they represented themselves. It was all the joy of discovery with none of the talking and awkward pauses and missed social cues. And so I would lose hours of sleep or productivity to the task of doing nothing in particular: clicking through wall posts and albums or leaving the perfect quip on someone's wall. I fancied myself a cultured man about town without going anywhere or doing anything.

I realize now that I was falling into what video gamers call "grinding." Certain games are designed not with any creativity or fun involved but rather the provision of a minimum amount of gratification to keep you playing. You don't *want* to kill that last troll, but if you do, you level up and light explodes out of your eyeballs. Facebook was the same way. Mulling through my newsfeed is as mundane as a task can be, but just often enough, there would be some amusing link or adorable cat photo that would reward my drowsy attention.

My hours on the Internet grew, and the time I spent on school work shrank. I became the master of procrastination. The only thing that could pull me away from the slow-burning thrill of social networking to write a paper was the intensity of finishing it in a single evening. I'd park myself somewhere on campus and work until the night janitors needed to vacuum. After popping over to the 24-hour taqueria, I'd hunker down for the home stretch and try to avoid falling asleep.

I can't say I ever really learned my lesson. In a twisted way, this process worked for me. But I must have spent many months' worth of time clicking aimlessly through meaningless information. One of my biggest deathbed regrets will undoubtedly be spending so much precious time doing something so numbingly dull. Since college, I've developed some strategies to mitigate these behaviors, like checking e-mail and Facebook 10 minutes before I absolutely have to leave to go somewhere. And saving certain sites and Web comics for weekends helps make my time on the Internet something I can look forward to rather than an onerous vice. Also, finding locations with no wireless is a good way of forcing myself to work.

I'll admit that I still lose sleep to the Almighty Book of Faces. It probably won't fall to the wayside like the desk encyclopedia and Wikipedia until something even more ensnaring takes its place. *But the key to handling Internet addiction is knowing yourself and acting upon that self-knowledge.* Cultivate the little voice in your head that speaks up when you are pointlessly Facebooking. Hopefully over time, you can log in, log out, and avoid the disorienting and disappointing feeling of having unwittingly traveled an hour into the future.

—Daniel Bulone

On Real-World Social Isolation in the Cyber-Community

I don't have a Facebook account. I don't use Myspace. I don't have an instant messaging account. I don't have a Twitter or a YouTube account or any Internet username besides my e-mail (which I maintain a bit grudgingly, to be honest).

I do have a cell phone, and I do occasionally send and receive text messages, but on the whole, it vibrates rather infrequently. So what I'm trying to say here is that I am disconnected from many of the social networking advances of the 21st century, the mechanisms of human globalization.

I admit the title of this essay is unfair. The new social cyber-community is as much a part of the "real world" as the nebulous concept of a "real world" is. This is not meant to be the vitriolic scripture-thumping of a delusional preacher touting the glories of relics and archaic systems. This is not an attack on modernity or "progress." I could really care less, at least for the sake of this writing.

What I mean to address here is the social isolation that comes with being like me. I am in no way a unique individual. There are countless others like me who just don't want to hit the "enter" button and be absorbed.

What does it mean to not be "connected"? What does it mean to come home to a computer that isn't storing dozens of messages from friends while you were offline, some of whom you see daily, some of whom you haven't heard from in ages? What does it mean to know that you're not always accessible to the general public, that there are times when you are out of reach (or at the very least, a phone call away)?

The great majority of your friends will inevitably be online, especially if you're in college. Doubtless, you will miss out on many of the constant back-and-forth conversations and inside jokes. You will miss out on e-vites to social gatherings and parties and occasions of festivity. You will inevitably miss out on the day-to-day happenings of the 50, 100, 300, 500, 1,000 people you know and care about. You'll probably forget the faces of those friends who weren't really friends but were more like acquaintances you met at that party that one night. It will likely be harder to learn about/spy on/ogle/brood over the ones you like, have crushes on, have left (or who have left you). You certainly won't have their pictures and the pictures of their assorted parties or motley crews to sift through. You'll have a harder time figuring out how people are really doing, as opposed to how they'd like everyone to think they're doing.

Probably worst of all, you'll have too many hours in the day to kill. You'll have to come home and probably confront those endless hours you have at your disposal. You'll have to develop interests that range beyond the temporary, transient fleeting pleasures of glowing rectangles, or god knows how soon it will be before you lose your sanity.

This is not addressed to everyone. I know I said before that this was not going to be an attack on modernity and "progress," but we've all lied before. I know I said before that I don't care, but I do care! It's sad to see so many of my generation disappearing behind laptop screens instead of books. Please pardon the tongue-in-cheek approach employed above. Let me clarify the purpose of this article.

Like most everything else, moderation is key. If you use these new social networking tools in moderation—responsibly, if you will—then fine. Ignore me. This article is directed, in earnest plea, to those out there who find themselves increasingly absorbed in 24-hour connectedness. To those who spend the better portion of their days cloaked by a binary world. To those whose conversation seems inevitably directed back to "who wrote what on whose wall." To those with a growing irrational fear that if they don't check their Internet treasure troves weekly, daily, hourly, or every other minute, the floor below them will fall out.

People say that the ability to always be connected with old friends you don't see is a wonderful thing. Relationships have the potential for infinite expansion. Strangers from two countries can now learn each other's intimate details. But what about the stranger down the street you've never introduced yourself to? What about that boy you see getting on the bus with you every day who you've never said hello to? What about the girl who drinks coffee in the same seat every day before class?

Don't forget that there is a soft beauty to the transience of the disconnected world. There is only a finite amount of time you will have to share with each person you meet. Not every emotion and moment can be experienced with every individual in your life. Someday soon, all you'll have is the memory of the person and relationship to contemplate; to remember; to laugh, smile, or cringe at. Doesn't that make it all the more interesting, all the more powerful, all the more beautiful? Doesn't permanent electronic connectivity detract at least a little from the natural temporary, momentary state our fathers, their fathers, and their fathers lived in? Yes, it's a little sadder. Yes, it's a little lonelier. But it's an invaluable experience, and an inimitable lesson—nothing in this life is forever.

Do yourself a favor. Break free for one, tiny moment. Take a walk. Learn the landscape; the beauties and flaws; the odors and aromas; the feels, tastes, and powers of your city or town. Meet with a friend randomly on the street. Have no plans for one night. Explore. Find a nice place to sit and do nothing for a while. People-watch in the "outside" world, instead of an online gallery. Meet people you will never see again. Reclaim yourself. Don't just be who you are in cyber text and HTML. Be more. Or be less. If you keep giving yourself up, piece by piece, to the insatiable connectedness, you may soon find yourself completely lost to that virtual-image you. It's okay to be alone for some time, to think, do nothing, and "defragment."

Disconnect. That is all.

—Rohan Shamapant

Technology in the Classroom

"Technology in the classroom" today means students have laptops and iPhones (or some equivalent). As professors, what is the issue with this? How should we best frame the issue?

Many students say these new electronic technologies expand their freedom to learn. We say they strengthen your freedom to ignore the class you are in. For us, as professors, the biggest concern is that this form of technology reduces presence. By this we mean that it essentially promotes and invites a fractured, distracted consciousness. Students take classroom presence less seriously. It does not aid, help, or empower the learning process in the classroom. "But," our students often respond, "what if our Blackberry, iPhone, laptop, and so on is properly used?" Cigarettes, if properly used, will kill you. The cost here is obviously not as high, but these devices will kill an ancient and deep style of attention and learning. If you're on the surgeon's operating table and she or he is in the midst of surgery on you, would you be OK with her or him multitasking? Would it be OK for her to have her cell phone on? Consider that the significance of presence in the classroom, in the "learning environment," has consequences for all later situations in life—whether you're the patient on the table or the surgeon operating.

A Faceless Age

While college students walk around with their heads buried in their Blackberry, they are missing out not only on their interaction with their peers, but also their interaction with their professors. Many students use their laptops or text during class, causing disengagement between students and professors. This not only distracts the student from learning the material they paid thousands of dollars to obtain, it also impairs them from developing a relationship with the professor. Without said relationship, it is often difficult for the student to acquire what they will beg for from their professor at the end of their college career: a letter of recommendation.

Technology has enhanced relations and daily interactions so that students are able to be "connected" at all times. However, if you do not go offline and have nonvirtual interactions, you may find yourself eating alone in the dining hall, having to go shopping alone, or failing to notice that cute football player in your sociology class. Once you're willing to turn off that computer and put away the iPhone, you will find that the real world requires no extra devices for you to enjoy it. So put on a smile and meet someone in your class, have lunch with the people in your dorm, or introduce yourself to that cute girl in the yellow dress (whom you would not have noticed if you were staring at your phone this entire time).

—Aggie Wong

Let's look at the distinction between the urgent and the important. We think this distinction is, today, central to our relationship to accomplishment, productivity, success, and stress in our modern lives. During the ordinary course of the ordinary day, most of us need to steer a course, hopefully a skillful course, in addressing our tasks. All the modern surveys that address the sense of accomplishment, success, and satisfaction in our lives—and in particular our work lives—speak about the feeling of "not enough time" and of "being overwhelmed." We live in the age of stress and of time poverty rather than time affluence. Consider, to put it simply, that one of the chief causes of this feeling in our lives is "lack of accomplishment." At the end of the day (or week or month), we can say we've been very busy—yet we haven't really accomplished much. We have been dealing with the urgent rather than the important.

What is the distinction? The important are the things you—the deepest, most enlightened dimension of you—want to accomplish, that you want to spend your time on: The things that you value. The urgent are the things that must be done immediately. One often-cited example is that you value reading and wish you could read more or even just read. In a nutshell, one of the reasons we don't read more is that, during the course of the ordinary day, books don't "ring." Phones ring. E-mails chime. There is a summoning quality to our electronic technology. From this perspective, it is overwhelmingly easy and constantly reinforced to all day be at the mercy of the urgent, to be in the presence of the urgent, and present to the urgent rather than in the presence of the important and present to the important. Think of the often-used example of personal relationships. Today's surveys show again and again that when consciously asked, people put "time with their significant relationships" on the top of the list of the important things in their life—yet when actually measured, many executives, for example, found to their shock and amazement that they only spent 7–10 minutes per week in a focused, present relationship with their child.

Technology's Power to Connect and Isolate Us

Right about the time I was getting ready to head off to college, Facebook was about to take off and steadily carve its way into the lives of college students across the globe. I consider myself to be part of the first generation of Facebook, back in the day when Facebook was exclusively for college students, and even then, it was only set up for a small number of universities. This was a time when profiles consisted of a picture and basic demographic and contact information. There was no such thing as "applications," so just about all you could do on Facebook was search for people, request to be their friends, and send them messages. Currently, I have 108 requests on Facebook to do things such as discover my hero ability, join my friend's wagon on the Oregon Trail, race a car, find out which Disney Princess I am most like, join a mob war, catch a snowball, accept a blue-eyed grass plant, play dodge ball—the list goes on and on. Even though it's easy to scoff at how seemingly ridiculous Facebook has become, I cannot deny the fact that I'm on it nearly every day and it has impacted my life in considerable ways.

My first college friend also happens to be my first Facebook friend. She found me on Facebook because I was enrolled in one of her classes, and after instant messaging each other over the summer, we decided to meet in person. Before we ever set foot on campus as students, we began a friendship that continues today both in the real and virtual world. This is simply one of many ways in which technology has given me the means to connect with others. I remember losing my cell phone while I was in college, and it took about a week before I could replace it. My primary vehicle for communication had disappeared, and with this loss, I felt a frightening effect on my way of life. I found it difficult to meet up with friends because our plans would often change at the last minute and I had no way to be notified. I was frustrated that I could not make calls or send text messages; how was I supposed to tell anyone something important or manage the logistics of my life? Worst of all was my fear that no one could reach me in the event of an emergency. I felt completely helpless and isolated. In addition, technology has revolutionized what it means to maintain a long distance relationship. I have witnessed a number of couples who spend an absurd amount of time every day talking over their Webcams. If it were not for Skype, I would be very limited in my ability to stay in touch with my best friend, who is currently living in New Zealand. These are only a few examples of how technology allows us to draw nearer to others. Consider, for a moment, how your relationships might be affected if you did not have a computer or phone.

Yet technology also provides a way to alienate oneself from the world, and this can have particularly harmful consequences for a college student. I was amazed when I would walk to class and nearly every student I passed was either listening to an iPod or talking on a cell phone. Countless students, myself included, could spend hours in a dorm room glued to their computers. Many students burn through hours at a time playing video games and watching television, with mind numbing effects. College is rich with opportunities to engage with one's community and to discover what lies beyond the classroom, but with all the latest technology at hand, college could simply pass one by like a dream. Studies have shown that the less involved a college student is in campus life, the more likely it is that he or she will fail to graduate. Technology should be used as a supplement, not a substitute, for face-to-face interactions. Instead of throwing a sheep at someone on Facebook, create an event to go play hide-and-go-seek on campus at night with a group of friends. Utilize technology to stay in contact with the people you care about, but don't neglect the ones who live next door to you.

—*Kristen Hammel*

As classroom teachers, we find that cultivating the practice of being present is at the very foundation of the enterprise of formal education. We emphasize the word *practice* as much as the word *presence*. If you are not present, not here and now, consciously and alertly here and now, then you cannot make contact with learning. You will be (a) stuck in the brain network circuitry of your own narrative daydreaming or (b) distracted by your electronic network circuitry.

Thinking is, according to recent investigations into brain circuitry, painful and to be avoided. We are, as it were, wired to think the same thoughts over and over again (Rock, 2009). We are highly predisposed to dwell in the already known, the familiar. The "aha moments" in true learning and discovery only occur when we are present to not-knowing, to the puzzling uncertainty of enigma. We crave familiarity because the uncertain is threatening. All our ancient, all-too-human evolutionary wiring is heavily weighted to avoid danger, uncertainty, and pain. Paradoxically, we must somehow go against this ancient survival wiring and remain in the presence of uncertainty and not-knowing to experience the breakthrough of creativity. Our technologically distracted benumbment with our laptops and iPhones does not lead us into the presence of uncertainty, though there are, of course, exceptions. Being truly and radically present does lead us into the presence of uncertainty.

Screened electronic tools detract from the practice of presence in the classroom in a way that paper and pen do not. Screened electronic tools invite somnambulant distractedness in a way paper and pencil do not. A blank sheet of paper and pen usually make us uncomfortable and invite us to the challenge of thinking. A television or computer screen does not.

Outside the Lecture Halls

When I was a child, every summer our local library had a read-a-thon, and every week I would choose a new book to read. I looked forward to walking through the aisles with the smell of old books all around, amazed at the vast quantity of knowledge around me. Now I have the World Wide Web, the vastest knowledge base of all, at my fingertips. Books, articles, organizational Web sites, data—an immense amount of information available, always. It doesn't smell as good, but, let's face it, it's a lot more convenient.

Technology has changed both how we learn and how we are taught. We are no longer geographically bound by the necessity of having the library near us or our reference books at hand. Now we take our work with us wherever we go—on a flash drive or a laptop—and can access an immense amount of research on the Internet. In fact, sometimes we don't even go to class because we have all the resources we need, we think, to learn the material without attending class. But technology has made it simultaneously easier and harder to carry out our daily activities.

I can look online for the article I need to read for class, so I have no need to go to the library. Perfect; that will save me some time. And while I am searching Google Scholar for that article, I can also search for those shoes I've been meaning to buy. And while waiting for the article to load, I can check my e-mail. And when my e-mail application opens, my instant messenger program pops up and my friend messages me. And so the hours go . . . and go . . . and go.

The overstimulation we are programmed to accept as normal throughout our daily lives has affected our ability to be still. To listen. To just be. We are constantly searching for stimulation. As a result, in the classroom, a simple lecture is not enough to keep the interest of most students. No PowerPoint presentation? No Web site to download the slides from? No entertainment, so to speak? Well, then, my attention will only last for so long (which won't be very long). A marketing professor at Pace University recently said in a television interview, "Companies must tailor their marketing efforts to our shrinking attention spans. Whoever delivers the most concise and compact information wins the consumer over."

Is this what education has become? A marketing scheme in which teachers attempt to win the attention of students by diluting the information they present? And worse, are we, as students, looking for sound bites?

Some argue that the key to success in life—I mean tangible, real success, not the fleeting and myopic idea of success as having money—is focus. Daniel-san did not become the Karate Kid by filtering out Mr. Miyagi's pearls of wisdom through his headphones. Obi Wan didn't become a bad-ass Jedi by having one hand on his light saber and the other on his cell phone during Yoda's lessons. We must, as part of the college experience, learn about ourselves, and we can only do that by simplifying, by introducing silence into our daily routines, by focusing.

Perhaps some of the most important lessons in college are not academic lessons. Perhaps developing as a person is just as important. Technology will keep evolving. Teachers will turn off wireless access in classrooms, and students will find a way around it. The onus is on us, as students and members of society, to decide how and when to use technology.

—*Georgiana Bostean*

My Love-Hate Relationship

Technology. I must confess—I have a love-hate relationship with it—which has often teetered toward dislike lately. How, one might ask, could anyone hate technology? It's the best thing since sliced bread, right? Well, yes and no. Simply put, I think, in the recent years, technology has aggravated an already impatient society where immediate gratification is a must and, when achieved, is inadequate. Think of the cell phone ads where a couple of friends "one up" everyone else with the latest news, criticizing others' news by saying "that's so 10 seconds ago." Wow. . . really? I didn't realize that knowing the latest gossip 10 seconds before someone else could be so crucial.

No one looks forward when they walk (or drive for that matter) because they are forever looking down at a device to which they have become a slave–texting, e-mailing, playing words with friends. If Freud were still around, he would be horrified to find the domination of the "id" in society. With the likes of Facebook and Twitter, not only is it about now, now, now, it's also all about me, me, me—what I ate for lunch, what I'm doing at any given moment, look at all these pictures I took of myself as I faced the bathroom mirror making a duck face or sticking my tongue out, ad nauseam. I am astounded that people really think others care about this type of information. I am equally astounded, if not more, by those who care enough about this triviality to make inane comments! I don't have a Facebook account (if you haven't figured that out already), and I feel (just a wee bit) like I am alienating myself because many of my friends (I am referring to real friends now—not the 1,000+ friends some Facebookers boast to have) use Facebook. They urge me to join, but I have not relented and do not foresee my doing so in the near future. I am just "old school" you could say. I like having real conversations where people talk to one another on a one-on-one basis, where people can hear and see happiness, excitement, sadness, irritation, or some other emotion in my voice rather than reading emoticons that can't begin to convey a true emotion. What's also great is having a private conversation where others can't just horn in by posting comments!

All this social media makes me wonder how it will affect the development of future generations' social skills. With increasing time being spent communicating via the Web, I wonder if kids will develop the requisite social skills for in-person interactions. It also makes me wonder about the development of their verbal and written skills. I will occasionally read comments in response to articles on Yahoo, and am consistently floored by the number of comments that contain ill-structured sentences and are fraught with spelling errors.

But enough of my disenchantment. There are certainly many aspects of technology for which I will be eternally grateful. The Internet is easily in my top 10 of the most amazing technological developments. I am enamored with the various search engines that allow me to research topics and receive results at the drop of a hat (here's more of that immediate gratification, but I like this one). The Internet has spawned the likes of match.com and other dating services that allow people the capability to meet (and potentially fall in love) with people they probably would have never met. The advent, too, of wireless connection is truly a blessing for me. I work full-time, and when I decided to go back to school, I was concerned about how I was going to get it all done—not to worry, Internet and wireless connection to the rescue. I could work from home, attend on-line courses, and listen to lecture podcasts, anytime day or night. I also can't ignore the numerous medical advancements achieved through technology. Laser surgeries that can repair vision, skin cell guns that can repair second degree burns in a matter of days, and bionic legs that will help disabled people stand and walk. Wow. . . really? Said, this time, with awe and appreciation.

—Rose DeLeon Carter

The nature of distractedness due to the use of technology in the classroom is, as we see it, close to the distractedness that we call "watching television." It appears to us that students with computers or iPhones in the classroom are very much akin to an individual in a room with a television and a remote control; the phenomenon that they most often manifest is the phenomenon of "channel surfing." This habit of mind is the opposite of sustained focused attentiveness. There is the sustained, disciplined focus that one struggles with in the practice of mindfulness meditation—wherein the meditator works to notice when his or her mind wanders and then comes back to the present moment. There is the sustained, disciplined focus of reading—wherein the reader is attentive to one word after another, one sentence after another, one paragraph, one page, and so on. This is a discursive attentiveness. There is the sustained, attentive focus of writing—wherein the writer focuses on creating one word after another, one sentence, one paragraph, one page, and so on. All these forms of focused attentiveness are at the opposite ends of the spectrum of "monkey mind distractedness," wherein the person simply jumps haphazardly, yanked about by the nose ring of an anxious technology attachment.

The classroom student with the technology is the same as the channel surfing television watcher. Practicing this form of mental activity weakens our sustained attentiveness muscles and strengthens our jumpy distractedness muscles. Imagine listening to a friend who is in real distress expressing her concerns to you. You are present, you are there, you are focused attentiveness, focused listening—you are not busy, in the sense of preoccupied, planning what you will say in the future, nor reviewing what you might have done in the past, nor judging whether what she is saying is true or valid. During that time, you are present attentiveness in all its dimensions. William Stringfellow perhaps put it best:

> Listening is a rare habit among human beings. You cannot listen to the word another is speaking if you are preoccupied with your appearance or with impressing the other, or are trying to decide what you are going to say when the other stops talking, or are debating about whether or not what is being said is true or relevant or agreeable. Such matters have their place, but only after listening to the word as the word is being uttered. Listening is a primitive art of love in which a person gives himself to another's words, making himself accessible and vulnerable to that word. (Wylie-Kellerman, 1994, p. 34)

We consider that type of listening presence the optimum state of mind, the mental condition to aspire to in the classroom environment. Imagine listening to that friend while you are simultaneously channel surfing and texting. How do you think that would turn out?

Cell Phones

Although computers, phones, and other gadgets seem to keep us connected to friends and family, in reality, the contrary is occurring. Technology is an addiction, and I admit to being addicted myself. I became aware of my addiction when I forgot my phone at home for the first time and felt naked and uncomfortable, like something was missing. I'm sure you have had a similar experience.

Here is something to think about regarding cell phones: Most of the features that attract you to them, such as Internet, e-mail, and other applications, are not necessities; you probably just wanted them or were tricked into adding these applications for a few additional dollars.

Do you really need to check your e-mail while you're having dinner? Next time you go out to dinner, observe how many people set their phone next to them and look down at it while someone is sitting right in front of them. I see this at student restaurants quite often. Someone tries to enjoy time and a meal with a friend, but the friend seems to be stuck inside his phone.

Do you really need to update your Facebook, Twitter, and Myspace while you are actually having a face-to-face conversation? Do you really need to post your frustrations, highlight of the day, or a nonsensical status update every single day, sometimes multiple times a day? Why not call a good friend instead and tell her about it? What? Did you say you don't have a friend to call, even though you have hundreds of Facebook friends? Though we have more "friends" than we can remember, we have disconnected ourselves from them so much that we are afraid to call them and simply talk. Every call nowadays seems to have a purpose; we no longer call just to say "hi" or see how someone is doing.

Consider what you are actually missing out on when throughout the day most of your attention is trapped in technology. Yes, it helps us to communicate and does help us stay connected, especially with friends and family who do not live nearby, but also think about how much technology is isolating us from one another.

Try this: Next time you go out to dinner, put your cell on silent or put it in another room where you will not hear it vibrate or see it light up. It takes practice, but after a while you will notice how much more satisfying your meal is. And here is the best part: You probably won't miss a call. If it's urgent, they'll leave a voicemail; if it's a text, it will still be there after you finish eating. Eventually, try this with every activity you do. This includes working out, reading, driving, and so on. You do not want to one day realize you don't have anyone to have dinner with because you were too busy checking your phone; besides, it's rude, and you know that.

—*Fabiola Santiago*

Technology is a tool and always will be—though it does have a Jekyll and Hyde, or perhaps Frankenstein, curse to it. The amazing new technological tools that enable us to "connect and interface" with our friends, family, and school are still only tools. It is easy to let these tools, with their sleek efficiency and promise of doing things in "real time" in "lifelike" useful environments, distract us from the complicated and messy process of living through human exchanges. We often see people using a mediated form of interaction with friends, family, and classes. How many of our human relationships and exchanges have suffered as this technological buffer and distraction has changed our human interactions? Growing up in a technological world has changed our relationship to our family, our friends, our education, and most important, ourselves. Remember, technology is a tool and not a replacement for living. Tools are there to enhance, not replace. Becoming aware of the hypnotic pull and power that technology and the media have over us gives us the ability to use this incredible tool instead of being used by it. (For a much more thorough discussion on the power media has over us all, see McGrane & Gunderson, 2010.)

Often science fiction writers see more clearly and intimately the actual consequences of the technological directions we are heading in. In this vein, we strongly urge the reader to take a look at the vision of the future of education written by the renowned Isaac Asimov in 1951 for a syndicated newspaper. Titled "The Fun They Had," it begins, "Margie even wrote about it that night in her diary. On the page headed May 17, 2157, she wrote, 'Today, Tommy found a real book!'" (http://users .aber.ac.uk/dgc/funtheyhad.html).

Everybody Hates to Write

In Chapter 4, we begin by honestly acknowledging that nearly everyone at the university, including professors, hates and fears the process of writing. Why? Judgment! Consider, as an image, that our school training has been our "civilized" version of the Roman gladiatorial arena: We've all grown up doing "mortal combat" with the harsh, omnipresent, ever-grading RED PEN! We also address new and healthy ways of overcoming these traumas and possibly rediscovering and freeing our "inner writer." We also address the following:

- The oral report as a "Chinese Opera."
- Blue books/green books and other sadistic measures.

I would like to begin this chapter's discussion on writing by quoting from one of my students' papers.

Challenge the System

After 4 years of high school and three semesters of college, I was sick of writing boring term papers. There are only so many ways that you can regurgitate the same dry facts. I decided I wasn't going to do it anymore. I was going to enjoy writing papers, even if it meant being uncouth in the eyes of my professors. I wrote one paper as a purely fictional past life regression that included diary entries of the life of a historical person. Through fiction I was able to present my research clearly, while actually enjoying the writing process. Another time I opted to do field research rather than book research. The assignment was to explore the origin of a cultural symbol or practice and learn what it meant to different people. I went around to local tattoo and body piercing parlors conducting interviews and taking pictures of people who indulged in body art. It was the most amazing and enlightening project I had ever done. Another time I was assigned to explore the differences between men and women as presented through the media. I decided to do a video presentation. I took clips from movies, commercials, and television shows from the past and present and arranged them on two 1-hour videos. The videos depicted stereotypical and progressive roles of men and women in the media. My editing method was crude: I hooked up two VCRs in my bedroom and copied from tape to tape. Sometimes two clips overlapped, and sometimes there was a 2-minute break between clips, but I did what I could with my lack of film editing knowledge. And I got an A. My professor loved my ingenuity and creativity. In college, you don't always have to stick to the rules. Professors like it when you break the mold. When I tackle an assignment, I make sure that I am doing something that will entertain me and that I will grow from. That's why I came to college, to challenge myself and to grow. I won't settle for less.

—Kristin Rydberg

Nearly everybody I know, including professors, hates and fears the process of writing, and small wonder. Since we were in grammar school, we have been forced to commit our precious thoughts to paper, where a red pencil might, at any moment, attack them. When we tried to develop intelligent ideas, we were regularly hassled about spelling, commas, and semicolons. Our labors were usually returned to us crawling with corrections and a few well-chosen insulting remarks. When we did really well, however, we usually just got back a terse "good" and nothing more. When I first began teaching, I fell into the same thoughtless habit of giving more negative than positive feedback on papers. I had a feeling that if I gave a good grade, I didn't need to defend my position, whereas a low grade had to be accompanied by a lot of explanation.

Then I had a very salutary experience. I taught a section of remedial writing. Here I discovered how utterly crushing and traumatizing our practices were, particularly for students who came to school speaking an ethnic or class-based dialect slightly different from the "King's English" (an interesting term, indicating the class snobbery involved in our notions of "proper" language). If you are Black, for instance, you probably grew up hearing a somewhat different language from academic English. Yours is a beautiful language full of imagery and rhyme and poetry. One has only to listen to the words of gospel music to see how vividly and with what wit Black poets illumined the King James version of the Bible. Yet most English teachers see it as their duty to expunge all traces of this native tongue in their Black students.

What I discovered from my remedial writing students was that they so much hated writing that the old avoidance mechanism always set in. They resisted working on papers. When they did finally write them, they dashed them off quickly and never edited them. What really hurt these students was that they weren't properly enamored of their own creations. They weren't willing to read their papers to friends and relatives, to read them over and over, embellishing and correcting (and even looking up an occasional spelling) as they went. In our class, we began to take one person's paper each week, editing it as a group. We made it a habit to give praise to every piece as well as correction. We tried to show each person the strong points of his or her writing. From this experience, I learned to give positive feedback. If I marked one paragraph "confusing," I would mark a better one "clearly written. Do you see the difference?" Gradually, the students warmed to the task until, by the end of the semester, I had at least induced most of them to exchange editing services with a friend. Somebody else can always see your errors more clearly than you can yourself. Reading your work out loud to yourself also helps you to catch clumsy phrasing.

In an interesting article on writing problems, one professor makes the essential point that time pressures in school force students to write only one draft. This runs counter to all good writing practices. Famous writers generally write many revisions of their original drafts. Not only do the drafts improve, but rewriting is perhaps the best way to improve writing skills. Be advised, then, to knock out a first draft (it should not be perfect at this point) in time to revise, preferably with the help of a friend.

There are several common problems in student writing. By remembering the kinds of comments you have received on your writing, you may be able to diagnose your own ills and take the advice that applies. Some students get lost in the earliest phase of the paper by beginning work before they thoroughly understand the professor's assignment. If the topic is unclear, you must talk to the professor. If you have a choice of topics, pick carefully to find a topic you like and one that offers the chance to use material with which you are already familiar from personal experience or from other courses. If your topic is simply given as, say, "juvenile delinquency in urban areas," try to develop a hypothesis or a theme. For example, your hypothesis might be that low-income youngsters have higher rates of delinquency than higher-income youths. Your title might then be "The Correlation Between Income and Juvenile Delinquency." Or, if you would rather use a theme, it might be "the influence of mass media on juvenile violence." Developing a hypothesis or theme helps you to narrow down the topic and give direction to your research.

The most frequent and grade-lowering problem with writing is lack of clarity. This is really not a writing problem but results from a failure to think the issues you are writing about through to the point where they are clear to you. Sometimes it may require you to ingest more information than you now have; sometimes you may need to discuss your confusion with a sympathetic friend. When I am in deep water, I may just drop the work for a few days, but if the going continues to be boggy when I return to it, I generally talk it out with someone. An outsider can frequently see the forest when you are lost in the trees.

Rewriting is also crucial here. First drafts generally contain some confusion, but *the act of writing the confusion down is a major step in clarification.* Often, you do not even know you are confused until you try to submit your thoughts to paper.

What is most troubling to me is that *many students don't seem to know when they are confused.* I think this is because they have been confused so often at school that they have come to accept this mental state as natural. Because we teach people in batches of 30 to 40, with widely varying experience and ability, only the quickest and best prepared can insist on clarity (i.e., keep questioning the teacher until they really understand). Everybody else is going along pretending to understand until, finally, the line between understanding and confusion begins to blur and the student has lost the ability to practice self-correction. If this rings a bell with you, begin to make it a regular practice to insist on clarity in class. *Keep asking questions until you understand.* If you have to let something go, mark it clearly in the margin of your notes as "confusing." When you edit your writing, mark suspect sections in a similar way and then work them over with the professor or friends if you can corner them. In other words, either refuse to settle for confusion or at least mark off your confusions so you can keep them from contaminating your whole thought process. Remember that something that is perfectly clear to you will come out clearly on paper. One of the reasons why writing is hard is that it is really thinking. Improving your writing also improves your thinking, which is why it is well worth laboring over.

A related, but slightly different, problem concerns students who have fallen whole hog for one of the many "secret languages" used in the academy. These students usually don't think much of their own abilities and hope to rescue themselves by learning to write in the jargon of a discipline before the jargon is at all clear to them. These unfortunate folk are catching a disease that is so rampant in academia that many professors will even reward this type of behavior. I will discuss the function of secret languages in Chapter 6. Here, I can only say, stay away from any jargon you don't feel completely at home with. Don't use long, complicated words and sentences when simpler ones will do. Good writing is simple writing. Academic writing is often lousy writing.

Another writing disease directly fostered in school is padding. Anyone who really knows literature will tell you that brevity is the very soul of poetry and prose. Yet we continue to demand certain quantities of writing ("Write a 10-page paper," etc.). Of course, this is an invitation to pad. I tell my students, "Write as if you were wording a telegram, as if each and every word cost you money." When you edit your first draft, edit for brevity. If that results in too short a paper, according to your professor's lights, maybe you need to develop some additional ideas. If you just can't, take your chances with the shorter paper. Don't become a poor writer just to please your professors.

I want to tell you how not to write a lengthy term paper—from years of personal experience. I used to go at this type of assignment by proceeding to do all the research first. I would take voluminous notes just right: on an 8-inch by 5-inch card or half sheets of paper with the citation and subject at the top for easier sorting—one main item to a half sheet. This was fine, but I would invariably find myself nearing the end of the semester with a huge pile of unorganized notes, a loose collection of ideas, and a lot of anxiety about how the thing was ever going to come together. Before I could overcome my mounting fears and actually sit down to organize a paper, I would practice a ritual of self-torture. This took the form of a 3- or 4-day vigil in the college coffee shop, where I would sit from morning until late afternoon consuming coffee and cigarettes while commiserating with my fellows in the same predicament until I was quite physically ill. Only then, when my discomfort became patent and physical, would I overcome my avoidance mechanism and sit down to the dreaded task. Such rituals of self-torture are, I discovered, quite common among students before they undertake a heavy assignment. You may have your own variation. Suddenly, we enlightened, modern folk find ourselves practicing a primitive rite to appease the angry academic gods. It is really hard for us to see that the ritual adds nothing whatsoever to our efforts. The only way I know to cure yourself of these rituals is just to dare it—just once—without the ritual. It's worth it, even if you chance a low grade. What will happen, of course, is that you will come out about as usual. It may take several such leaps of daring to overcome the ritual entirely, but it can be done. (It might be fun to do a study of such rituals, exploring the great variety of forms they take in different students.)

You can develop positive as well as negative rituals. In one of my writing courses, I had a student who told us that, before she sat down to write a paper, she always imagined herself to be a great expert on the subject under consideration. She imagined the many people who were waiting for enlightenment from her pen. In this way, she jollied herself into a positive rather than a fearful frame of mind. She was, in fact, a very successful student, although she had to come from behind in terms of her earlier education. Perhaps you can develop your own variant of this fantasy. Imagining yourself to be a teacher may help. In fact, an interesting and subtle process sets in when one changes from the role of student to that of teacher. It is still the same process of mastering material, but now you are no longer the judged but are among the judges. You feel very responsible to your class to give them a straight and clear rendition. But you are working from a position of power, and this adds wings to your word processor. Another type of positive ritual would be anything you can do to loosen up and relax your body and mind. Perhaps some exercise and meditation would work well for you. It may be easier to replace rituals of self-torture with positive rituals than just to give them up altogether. It's worth trying.

If you find that you will be doing library research for a paper, avoid the experience of going into the library cold. Most college and university libraries have huge collections in which you can easily lose your way. If at all possible, get some recommendations for sources from your professor. Sometimes you may have a topic on which your professor is not too knowledgeable. In that case, try to find another professor who knows the area. It is quite usual for students to ask for help from someone other than the professor teaching the course. Two sources of advice are always better than one. In some cases, librarians will also be helpful. Another valuable source of reference is the Internet. It is a modern luxury abounding with information, allowing you access to virtually any information, all with the ease of a simple finger click. Here you may also find the most recent publications and updates on all subjects.

If none of these methods has yielded a list of sources, you can sometimes use one or two current textbooks in the subject and begin by reading the relevant section and then following the footnotes. With all these methods, you are getting the benefit of advice from people who have already sifted through the mass of writing on the subject, thus saving yourself hours of frustration.

I also learned some other ways to ease the burden of a research paper. I would strongly recommend that you write little bits of your paper while you are in the research phase. Even if you don't yet know where—or even whether—the little section will eventually land, write it down as it occurs to you. By the time you finish your research and turn to your collection of little sections, you may find that you have your paper nearly half written. It is also the case that the process of writing forces you to clarify your ideas. You may discover, for example, that you are lacking a piece of information without which you cannot really make your point. Thus, your ongoing writing will add direction and precision to your research.

Finally, I would like to give you some advice about writing social science papers. (I cannot speak with authority in other areas.) Good social science writing has a lot in common with good fiction: It is the telling, concrete detail or example that makes a theory or generalization come to life. Never nurture, much less put down, a generalization that you don't understand well enough to translate into a specific case. Make it a mental practice to approach every theory with the question, "How would this work in one individual's experience?" For example, voting studies show that husbands and wives who have opposite voting choices vote less frequently than couples who agree. How would this actually look if you were peering into their living room? Perhaps you can imagine that, having just had some heated words with his spouse about the comparative venality of two candidates, Mr. A decides, "This isn't worth quarreling about; the less said about it, the better." Henceforth, he avoids listening to the evening news and eventually conveniently forgets Election Day.

Or let us say that you have just made the assertion that poor people have higher rates of mental illness than richer people. Here you want to throw in a few nice, startling statistics on rates of schizophrenia found in the latest study. There you have the illuminating fact. Now, can you see exactly why the poor might become ill more frequently and stay ill longer? You can see from your source material that the richer and better educated people are, the more likely they are to rush to a psychiatrist with the first symptoms, whereas poorer, less educated people might not know what was wrong or whom to go to until the symptoms become so severe that they come to the attention of some public agency, such as the schools or the police. Now, you can see the process in a little more detail.

Or, again, poor children who attend predominantly middle-class schools are more likely to go to college than similar poor children who go to schools where everybody is poor. Just what is the mechanism involved here? One is that the intellectually successful poor child may be excluded from his or her peer group, which wishes to punish the child for being more successful: *Teacher's pet* might be the colloquial expression of this sentiment. In a school where everybody is poor, the friendless child will usually respond to this exclusion by giving up the intellectual success to regain the acceptance of his or her peers, whereas in a more mixed school, the child may begin to attach himself or herself to a higher-class, higher-scoring peer group, take on their aspiration level, and make it to college. Once you can picture this youngster in the halls and at lunchtime, you have understood the mechanism behind the generalization. Now you have the picture.

At times, a telling quotation or anecdote will illuminate the point. On this particular subject, I sometimes tell my students about a friend I had who had come from a very poor background to become a professor. When he was a young teenager and unusually studious for his group, his worried mother once placed a newspaper article on his bed that said that homosexuals hang out in libraries. Wow! Now you really sense what it means to break with the accepted working-class role for males. If I were writing this up, I would make a direct quotation—have my friend tell it in his own words. While you never want to let a paper become a collection of quotes, you do want to collect some nice, juicy ones as you research your subject, like ripe, plump raisins you can put in the final pudding. Don't hesitate to use examples from your own experience. Only a very pedantic professor will fail to appreciate this. Thus, your exposition in social science should always be brightened and sharpened with a concrete example (or even a hypothetical example); a nice, crisp fact and a telling quotation. If you have trouble doing this for a particular generalization, then you don't yet understand it.

If your college offers writing courses, it will be worth your time to see whether they have a good reputation and take one early in your college career. In most non-scientific fields, writing is crucial to successful work. Writing courses are definitely not just for the weak student. If the course is at all well taught, even the A student can learn a great deal from it.[1]

Writing Is Required

As some of you might have already noticed, writing is an essential part of life. Whether you like writing or not, you have already realized that writing is required. For many people, writing can be a dreadful experience; for me, writing went from a frightful encounter to one that became gratifying and, ultimately, my career path.

In high school, writing papers was nowhere near a satisfying experience. When it came to writing, my goal was to just get through it. In-class writing exams (as well as in-class assignments) were the worst. The pressure created while writing during a limited period of time resulted in my worst writing. Although I would study hard for my exams, the pressure of writing four to five short answers and essays would always take me to my breaking point. For some reason, I could never portray the knowledge that I had in my head through my writing. All of my thoughts were cluttered and disorganized. Instead of using my writing to exhibit my knowledge on the exam, I would do the opposite and hand over a muddled piece of work. As a result, I tried to avoid the act of writing during my high school career. However, this soon changed when I went to college.

In my first year at a university, I did not have many writing assignments because I took mostly general education courses. However, in my second year, I faced the task of having to write five to eight papers in one quarter. During that year, someone suggested that I take an upper-division English course—English 100W. I hesitated at first but decided to take it because it satisfied one of my writing requirements. My goal for the

---

[1] For unusual, creative ways to enhance your writing skills, see Rico (1983) and Goldberg (1986).

course was just to get through it, but somehow the class served as a life-changing experience for me. My feelings toward writing went from hesitation to welcome.

One may wonder how a change like that can occur. Well, it all began with the arrangement of the course. The class was set up in a format that allowed the students to work on one research paper throughout the whole quarter. In addition, all the required reading assignments were not novels; rather, they were reading assignments that dealt with the art of writing and how to break through its difficulties. As a result, I essentially spent 10 weeks working on improving my writing. Because I was working on only one 15-page research paper, I was able to constantly revise my work and identify my key writing faults. The class structure also allowed me to consult with my professor on a weekly basis about any difficulties I was having. During this process, my skills soared, and by the end of the quarter I was able to identify my writing weaknesses and strengthen them.

In addition to the English 100W course, I also acquired a writing mentor that same quarter. She assisted me by reading my papers, and she influenced me to become an even better writer. Thus, she helped me to gain not only more confidence in my writing but also more insight into it.

I really did not notice that my writing had improved so dramatically until I began to take writing exams in other courses and excelled in them without feeling the pressure I felt in the past. Somehow, my thoughts became clearer, and it was exhibited through my writing. Or, rather, my writing became cleaner, and that echoed back and made my thoughts clearer. I was no longer scrambling through random ideas or trying to endure a scattered exam. Writing became a battle that I conquered. During my studying, I was able to develop various techniques and strategies for myself that would improve my performance on in-class exams as well as take-home writing assignments:

1. For in-class writing exams, make sure you find out in advance the number of questions you are going to be given as well as the time allotted for the exam. This is important because it enables you to calculate the amount of time you have for each question before the exam. In addition, always make sure you allow more time for long essays and less time for short answer questions. Set aside time for yourself to think about what you want to write about, and don't hesitate to jot down any of your ideas on the side or back of your paper. Most important, bring some type of watch to keep track of time; do not rely on your professor to update you on the time remaining.

2. Start early on papers. If a paper is assigned 2 weeks before its due date, make sure you start as soon as possible. One of the worst habits to practice is procrastination because, in most cases, it ends up causing your worst writing. You do not have to write your entire paper the first day you are given the assignment, but developing an outline of some sort can be one of the best things you could do. An outline enables you to plan what you want to write and the topics you would like to discuss. More important, it allocates time for you to develop a well-formulated thesis, giving you ample time to consult your professor with any difficulties you are having early in the process.

3. Once you have written your paper, do not make the mistake of only reading it on the computer. Print out a hard copy and read it aloud to yourself. Using both methods will enable you to catch mistakes you could have missed by only reading it straight from the computer. Also, by reading your paper aloud, you are able to hear the flow of your writing.

4. After reading your paper, make sure you give it to someone else to read. This is an important aspect of writing because, in most cases, you cannot discover all of your mistakes on your own. By letting someone else critically analyze your paper, you can gain more insight into your writing style and further improve it.
5. Last, make sure you give yourself enough time to revise because, more often than not, you can always develop a much better draft than your first.

By using these techniques, I guarantee clarity in my writing and avoid costly mistakes. As an experienced news magazine editor and script writer, I know writing can sometimes be stressful. However, by developing certain strategies and techniques for yourself, you can learn to transform that anxiety into encouragement while steadily developing your writing.

—*Nkemdilim Nwosu*

The Oral Report as a Chinese Opera

Almost everybody hates to give an oral report. I believe this is because students fear each other's opinions even more than they fear the teacher's. You do not want to make an ass of yourself in front of your peers. In fact, many students never speak up in class for the same reason. It may help you a bit if you realize that everybody in the class probably shares your fears. Occasionally, I ask students to jot down on a piece of paper what people will think of them if they take part in the class discussion. Everybody fears disapproval from their fellows. Perhaps the most damning thing about education by coercion is the way it sets you against your peers. When we were younger and less socialized, we used to all gang up on the teacher—remember? But as some of us began to see that we could rise in the system by pleasing teachers, we also had to cut ourselves off from the body of our peers and begin competing with them instead. This is a fundamental betrayal that our fiercely competitive society exacts from each of us: We must break faith, must sell out our friends. From the day this process begins, fear of retribution grows in us. I used to try dealing with this by kidding around a little bit in class about oral reports and by letting everybody give immediate pro and con feedback on a report. This helped, but unfortunately most professors will not go this far. What they want from you is a coolly executed, highly professional performance.

It will help you to see the oral report for what it really is: as highly stylized a performance as a Chinese opera. It doesn't follow the usual rules of daily communication, and your ability to execute it properly may have very little to do with your ability in ordinary conversation. A judgment on your report is in no way a judgment on your personality and mind.

A small, positive ritual is recommended here. Before you start, you need to spend about 10 minutes slowing down your physical and mental processes and lowering your tension level. This will help in every way but is particularly good for the most common of mistakes: overly fast presentation. If you are inclined to be very nervous, the best thing you can do is just to sit quietly with your eyes closed and get in complete touch with the physical sensations of nervousness. This is not at all a pleasant process, but you may be surprised at what can develop from it. If your anxieties are rather vague, you may wish to do some slow, deep breathing and some good physical stretching. Again, as you are about to begin your report in the classroom, allow yourself 30 seconds of quiet to collect your scattered self before you begin. Perhaps you can imagine yourself to be a famous professor, about to give the word to a collection of grateful, alert students (pure fantasy, under any circumstances).

Never read an oral report or PowerPoint presentation verbatim. You will lose your audience instantly. Rather, prepare a fairly detailed outline. I find that, for a 50-minute lecture, I need anywhere from 4 to 10 pages of detailed outline. The outline has a cue phrase for each major idea; it is marked off so that I can see at a glance whether I am in Part 1 or Part 3. If I plan to use quotes, I type them out verbatim. Nothing creates more anxiety than having to shuffle around in a huge sheaf of papers and books looking for a quotation or a statistic, while your listeners are waiting for you to continue.

A very effective way to break up the pace of your report and make a good impression all around is to have some handouts. Sometimes an outline of your report may be in order, though more usually a set of statistics or some graphs or diagrams or maps may be better. Occasionally a dull subject may be made more lively by using good illustrations. If you are working on some aspect of parent-child relations, for instance, it may be interesting to bring in some examples of the way these relationships are treated in advertising: "Have your mommy buy you a box of Super Sugar Bombs." Rare is the professor who doesn't appreciate these signs of extra effort.

If possible, practice your report formally before an audience of your friends, and always practice your report once or twice, timing yourself in the process. Students almost universally overestimate what can be said in a given length of time. Nothing is so exasperating as having two students scheduled for a given date and having the first one take up three quarters of the allotted time. This situation can be easily prevented, and you will have the added boon of discovering that you don't need as much material as you thought.

Now, let us assume that you have prepared your outline well, given out your handouts, and gone through your preparatory ritual. You have given yourself a few seconds to become centered and are about to begin. Here, precisely, is where most people blow half a grade. They begin with a little self-deprecating giggle, pull at their hair and say, "Well... I don't really know too much about this, but...."

That is not the way this particular Chinese opera is played. You don't have to apologize or appease anybody. Instead, you look at your audience for a moment and then dive in crisply and clearly: "My topic today is the influence of foundations on the direction of medical research." Does it sound too daring? Do you fear that you can't deliver on the promise of such an opening? Be assured! The opening itself is worth half a grade. Your opener could be more original. I remember with particular pleasure the student who began his report on the Krupp family (the powerful owners of Germany's steel industry) with a picture of the Kaiser's whole family, which included a Krupp placed strategically just at the Kaiser's right hand. It was a beautiful opener and the picture was worth a lot of words.

If your professor permits it, tell the class at the beginning of your presentation that you will welcome questions during your report. This helps vary the pace and keeps your audience involved and awake. Don't be terrified by the prospect of questions you can't answer. A simple "I'm sorry; I don't know that" is always permissible. Delivered in an unruffled, calm way, it can even raise your stock with the audience and the professor. People who calmly admit they don't know seem, somehow, to be in special command of themselves and their subject matter. (Look for professors who are not afraid to say, "I don't know.") If you do wish to allow questions, allocate time for them when you time your presentation.

Bluebooks/Greenbooks and Other Sadistic Measures

Unfortunately, most of you will spend more time taking short-answer tests and writing 3-hour bluebook exams than you will spend on writing term papers or giving oral reports. The latter at least have the virtue that they prepare you for much of the writing and speaking that you will probably have to do in the course of your professional work. Short-answer tests and 3-hour writing marathons, on the other hand, find no parallel in life outside the academy. In real situations, you will always have more flexible time schedules, a word processor, and access to books and notes.

It is difficult for me to write on these subjects because I discontinued these methods very early in my teaching career. I quit using short-answer tests after I allowed students to defend their answers in writing and discovered that half the right answers were right for entirely wrong reasons. Three-hour bluebooks disappeared as soon as I found that most students' handwriting undergoes drastic collapse after 2 hours of writing. I could never figure out the last third of the effort. Since then, I have used only term papers and take-home exams.

Anyone who has suffered through a 3-hour writing marathon must have suspected that there is a definite sadistic harassment factor in most education. It really becomes extreme when you hit graduate school. In the sociology department at Berkeley, where I did my graduate work, we had at one time an examination program that required 5 hours of writing per day for 5 consecutive days. It was truly dreadful to run into a friend in the middle of this exam week and see the stubble of beard, the red-rimmed eyes with their wild look, and the general demeanor of exhaustion and suffering. Perhaps such measures are meant to ensure that only the physically toughest survive. More probably, our professors were merely repeating the treatment they themselves had received. Adults have an awful tendency to believe that whatever their youthful sufferings, surely the next generation must benefit from their repetition.

If ever I write a final chapter to this book titled "Academic Chickenshit," the 3-hour bluebook exam will surely be granted center stage. I cannot really offer you a way out. You can but know that, in this instance, you are victims of collective idiocy.

The only positive advice I can give you is slight. Some professors very much like bluebooks, which have an outline at the beginning. If you go in for this idea, leave the first page of your bluebook blank and compose the outline at the end of writing—when you know what, in fact, you have said. It helps to write from an outline, but keep this one on the side to be thrown away.

When taking a bluebook exam, read the question very carefully and make sure your paper speaks directly to each part of the question. Take time to read through the entire exam and plan your answering schedule. Try to stick to your schedule. In general, the same advice applies as for term papers: Use as many facts and examples as you can, but don't pad.

My other advice is tongue-in-cheek, though it may be useful. Very early in my undergraduate career I discovered *Weltanschauung*. This German word—one of those "untranslatables"—means "worldview" or "ideology." I took to throwing one *Weltanschauung* (correctly spelled) into nearly every bluebook I ever wrote. I don't know for sure, but I always suspected that it raised my mark by half a grade.

PART II

Navigating the Institution

CHAPTER 5

Support Your Local Teacher

Or the Care and Feeding of Professors

In this chapter, we explore how the central figure in you formal college education will be the professor. It is important for you to know what professors are all about, not only so that you can choose among them and approach them with skill and wisdom but also to understand why a college education is structured in the peculiar way that it is. We address in particular the following:

- Why teaching, strangely enough, has been relegated to a peculiar position of unimportance.
- Skillful suggestions regarding the care and feeding of professors.

The central figure in your formal college education will be the professor. If you are attending a small liberal arts college or community college, you may get to know a few of these worthies quite well. If you are at a large university, they may remain figures on the podium, and your immediate contacts will be with young aspiring professors called teaching assistants. The latter are usually in some advanced phase of study for a doctorate and, therefore, will share the general orientations and values of the professors. It is important for you to know what professors are all about, not only so you can choose them and approach them wisely but also to understand why a college education is structured in the peculiar way that it is.

As you might expect, most professors are people who were outstanding in the academic competition from childhood. Most were the stars of their respective classrooms, from kindergarten on. For many, this intellectual superiority became the basis of what might otherwise have been a shaky self-image. Hence, it is hardly surprising that they consider the academic intellect to be the highest form of human expression. They are also people who succeeded in the academic game, which makes them highly competitive. Luckily, their competition is mainly directed against each other rather than at you. You are an element in that competition only in the sense that in some liberal arts colleges and community colleges, popularity as a teacher may win faculty some points in the competitive game, though it is more likely that having a few very bright students who go on to graduate schools will win them more points. In large universities, however, it is a mark of status to do as little teaching as possible. In these institutions, professors specialize in getting research grants, which can free them from contaminating contact with undergraduates. In many of these research and publication institutes thinly disguised as universities, undergraduates are seen as a necessary evil. Even graduate students may be treated with some contempt and condescension in these settings. From this angle, we can see that educational suppression is committed by the institution itself—the very system that seeks to educate.

The arena of important competition for most professors is the nationwide network of fellow professors in their particular discipline, rather than the local campus where they happen to teach. In this network, often referred to simply as "the discipline," "the profession," or "the field," teaching does not count.[1] In fact, the professor's skill as a teacher is not part of his or her reputation at all. Here, it is publication of research that counts, and quantity of publication often counts for more than quality.

Once when I was teaching at a campus of a major university, my colleagues and I were to consider hiring a rather well-known professor for our department. A couple of us, who were greenhorns, did the unusual and actually read some of the books and articles on this man's lengthy list of publications. They were terrible. But when we brought this fact up at the department meeting, the chairman regarded us with some annoyance and said, "But look at the length of his list." We were silenced.

The academic professional associations in the various disciplines have a variety of annual meetings at which exceedingly dull papers are usually read, and very important personal contacts are made. Personal contacts are the name of the game. Without them, no academic could land a job, and few would get their work published.

What all this means to you is that you must realize that you are a side issue in your professor's career. At Pitzer College, where I taught for many years, this tendency was counteracted by our procedure for promotion and job tenure. For these reviews, we actually interviewed large numbers of our undergraduate students about a professor's teaching, and this evidence was weighted quite heavily, though there was a continuing battle between those who wanted to emphasize teaching and those who wished to emphasize publishing. However, even in a small college that values teaching, professors know that should they find themselves back on the job market, their publications would be their major selling point. At the other end of the scale, on large university campuses, popularity as a teacher may even be somewhat suspect, like spending too much time on your golf game.

---

[1]There are minority movements in some disciplines to strengthen teaching, but these forces are still very small voices in the wilderness of "publish or perish."

Why Has Teaching Been Relegated to This Position of Unimportance?

One reason teaching has been relegated to unimportance is professors are elitists in an elitist profession. They are much better informed than most people, and the degree of their expertise is partly measured by the sophistication of their students. As college education has become available to larger and larger numbers of people, professors have felt their status threatened by the requirement that they teach "run-of-the-mill" students. Many sociologists, for example, really want to teach students who are going to get doctorates in sociology. They would rather ignore the obvious fact that most of their undergraduate students will go into middle-rung occupations, such as teaching in public schools or doing social work. They do not really want to be bothered with such students.

Another reason teaching is devalued is that too much good teaching might encourage freely questioning, heretical minds. Sacred cows such as "free enterprise," "the free world," or the "happy consumer society" might then be called into question. Should such questions lead to action, universities stand to lose their federal grants, while trustees and their political friends bring unpleasant pressures to bear. The intellect is always a danger to those in power. Hence, it is necessary to curb a too free and stimulating exchange of ideas. Professors are cordoned off by the requirement that they publish exclusively for their fellow professionals and generally in a secret language, which is unintelligible to the layman.

Professors who write best sellers are looked down on as "popularizers." Good teachers are also frequently suspected of this sin. As long as professors only talk to each other, the general public will not be the wiser.

One of the things that happened on campuses during the 1960s that mightily alarmed trustees and university presidents was that students and some professors started communicating in class and elsewhere about the state of the university and the world. This turned out to be extremely "disruptive." Even though some reforms were pushed through during the 1960s to make teaching more rewarding and relevant, few of these innovations survived the 1970s, and now professors are safely back in their own corrals.

During the past 10 years, at a time when there has been an oversupply of professors, academic institutions have taken advantage of the weak bargaining position of young faculty by setting up a two-class system within the professoriat. Young scholars are hired as visiting lecturers (titles may vary) who are never eligible for advancement or tenure and who are generally kept on for only 2 or 3 years, so tenure can be avoided. Persons hired into such positions cannot advance into the regular faculty no matter how well they perform. Their pay is usually dramatically lower than that received by the tenured faculty, whose salaries may run more than twice as high. The worst aspect of this new system is that young professors are forced to tear up their roots, disrupt their personal lives, and move every few years. Increasingly, this army of migrant professors is generally used to cover a large proportion of the teaching load.

I would like to quote from a memorandum by Bernard McGrane and J. William Gibson, two tremendously popular University of California, Los Angeles, instructors, whose temporary contracts were not renewed despite considerable protest by students:

> We believe the "Visiting Lecturer" position (as primarily teaching load coverage) has the exploitation and devaluation of teaching structurally built into it. It seems to be somewhat of a migrant farm worker position to be filled with disposable, throwaway lecturers. If you go quarter by quarter (we have 10 weeks in our quarter system) for roughly the last 2 years (we have data on 5 quarters), Bill and Barney have taught 22%, 23%, 24%, 13%, and 29% of the total undergraduate sociology student enrollment. Hence, 5% of the sociology faculty (using 40 faculty members as a base) has taught 23% of the undergraduate students. (These figures would probably be more dramatic if we asked, "What percentage of the sociology student body is taught by all of the Visiting Lecturers? How much of the overall UCLA student body is taught by Visiting Lecturers?") As migrant workers, we receive lower wages (Barney, $21,000 1st year, $23,000 2nd year; Bill, $18,000 1st year, $22,500 2nd year) for higher teaching work, thereby embodying an implicit institutional devaluation of teaching. If we do well as teachers, we get larger and larger student enrollments . . . without ever getting any proportionate increase in resources (e.g., always just one Teaching Assistant), thereby the department institutionally penalizes good teaching. We "process" more and more students, inspire more and more students to become sociology majors; we produce the body count that enables the department to get more resources and more tenure track positions. As migrant lecturers, we're subsidizing other people's research in the department. In turn, our own research becomes more difficult.

That social scientists should take part in the creation of such a class system within the academy or that they are powerless in the face of it is evidence, I often feel, that they have learned nothing from their own disciplines. If there is one clear phenomenon in the comparison of societies, it is that wider class differences invariably produce greater social pathology. Such differences inflict great pain on the oppressed, while destroying the integrity of those at the top.

As students, you have a real stake in such developments. Very simply, you must speak out to retain good teachers. In so doing, you should be aware of your power as students. Even the threat of boycott (taking either the form of students transferring out of the affected department or transferring to other schools) will make senior faculty and administrators sit up and take notice. Their budgets are based on the number of students they serve, and nobody is ever indifferent to budget questions.

Understanding the institutional structure governing the professor's career will explain to you the widespread phenomenon of poor teaching and indifference to your needs as a student. You can deal with this by judicious selection of classes. Whenever your requirements allow some choice, you should choose your classes by finding the best teachers, rather than choosing them by subject matter. The most fascinating subject can be made dull by an indifferent teacher, whereas the most obscure material may, in the hands of a gifted teacher, become a vehicle for teaching the art of disciplined thinking. Your academic advisor will not usually clue you in to which teachers are good or bad because they are your advisor's colleagues. You must pick this information up from more experienced students on your campus. Some campuses even publish student ratings of professors, and there are a number of online teacher rating sites.

Try the occasional campus radical—indeed, any instructor with an unusual perspective. Because such folks are generally interested in persuading people, they are motivated to teach well. Luckily, you will find, on almost any faculty, a few wonderful characters who are original people and well worth knowing because the academy has always been a haven for nonconformists. Despite the real pressures toward conformity, teaching college still remains one of the very few jobs in which no one can tell you to wear a tie to work.

When you find a professor with a good reputation for teaching, remember that you are this person's main incentive for teaching. Such deviants in the academic scene must get their emotional rewards from their interaction with students. You can become a rewarding person for your professors. Giving emotional support is also important in the case of poor teachers because, despite the irrelevance of student opinions to career, it is still pretty unpleasant to get up 12 hours a week in front of a patently uninterested audience. Even the poor teacher is grateful for a supportive student. It goes without saying that the supportive student will be rewarded with personal attention and even, perhaps, friendship and will often get a better deal when grading time comes around.

Support your professors during class. All of you know how hard it is to get up in front of a class and give an oral report, yet most of you quite wrongly assume that professors do not suffer the same anxieties. Not so! Professors have egos as sensitive as anybody's. The student who dozes off during class is a very depressing sight indeed to the hapless lecturer. In one of the first classes I ever taught, a large young man regularly sat in the front row and dozed off. At times, he would lurch forward so dangerously in his seat that I would nearly reach out to catch him. Yet, he always woke up just in time to pull himself back into his chair. He was not my favorite student. But, oh, for that rare individual who actually makes eye contact with me during class and whose expression tells me that I have occasionally brought home a point! That is the student whose name I will remember. In line with this, it stands to reason that the professor will never notice you if you sit in the last row nearest the door. Strut right up to the front of the class.

Ask questions whenever the size and format of the class permit it. Nothing is more discouraging than a mute audience. Don't worry about whether your questions are sophisticated. Don't worry whether your questions will make you look ignorant to your fellow students. It is the professor you are trying to contact, and for the professor, any question indicates the stirrings of the intellectual fire he or she is hoping to kindle. The only type of question to avoid is one that is too directly utilitarian. Never ask, "Will that be required on the exam?" This is an oft-repeated question that professors disparage noisily among themselves. In this process of questioning, you must, of course, use reasonable restraint. Remember that others also want to ask questions or hear the instructor.

Ask questions during class, after class, and in the professor's office during office hours. What professors love is genuine curiosity about their subject matter. You cannot fake genuine curiosity nor should you try. It is easy to become a fake, even a successful fake, but fakery will make you a poor human being. What I am suggesting is, rather, that you allow yourself some genuine intellectual curiosity. Ask yourself how what you are studying relates to your own life or to other subjects you have taken. If the Greeks believed in the golden mean, how did they justify slavery, which is rather an extreme institution? What would they have thought of our tendency to put all our efforts into succeeding competitively? As you read your assignments, jot down a question or two for the next class. It will stimulate you to approach your reading actively rather than passively. An added bonus of asking questions is that you will learn more. You will get specific information that is of more interest to you than the general material. You may even experience an occasional "aha!" And remember that your "aha!" is your professor's "ahhhh!" Good teachers live for those "aha!" moments in their students. Again, don't fake this, but remain always open to it.

Everybody knows that most classes are boring. We have experienced this since kindergarten. As children, we screamed with undisguised delight whenever we were released from the boredom of the classroom. When I was in grammar school, on that last day of class in early summer, we would wait expectantly for the final moment when we were directed to place our chairs on our desks for the last time of the year. At that moment, a wild, collective shriek of joy went up and rang from room to room.

By the time we reach college, the shriek of delight has been internalized. We are running from class to make a date rather than to climb trees, but the general feeling remains. Class is something to be suffered through. This is not inevitable or even normal. Private schools exist in which children are given enough freedom and offered enough truly relevant, interesting subject matter to make learning a delightful experience. But, unfortunately, 99% of our educational institutions, from kindergarten to graduate school, are pretty dull and really designed to discipline you rather than to stimulate and delight your intellect. The very format of school works to ensure boredom. At 9:00 a.m. three times a week, you are supposed to become engrossed by medieval history. Never mind that you broke up with your boyfriend last night or that your parents are on your back for not majoring in business administration; at 9:00 a.m., it's medieval history. Our education has, all along, been answering questions we never asked. When we were in high school, we needed to know why we weren't popular or why our parent came home drunk, but these subjects could not be brought up in class. At the same time, we were expected to show genuine interest in the causes of the Civil War.

All this is merely to say that, yes, classes are often boring. How can you cope with this while being a supportive student? Believe it or not, the best way to deal with this situation when it is unavoidable is to concentrate on the material being offered. The time will actually go faster than if you dream of last night's party or doodle elaborately in your margins. I have always been immensely bored by meetings (and, believe me, there are lots of meetings one has to attend as a professor). I used to enrage my fellow academics by doing needlepoint during meetings in an attempt to escape the boredom. But I made an interesting discovery. The time went faster if I concentrated on the business at hand. Since then, I have always volunteered to be recording secretary. For this job, one must keep one's mind intensely focused on the discussion, so the time passes much more easily. Try this tactic in your classes, and I think you will see that it works. It is also a cardinal lesson in attaining the wisdom talked about in Buddhist philosophy. The Buddhist masters always tell us to be alert, alert, alert. In short, don't drift off or daydream.

The following is a beautiful story recounted in Schiller (1994, p. 17):[2]

> *One day a man approached Ikkyu and asked,*
>
> *"Master, will you please write for me some maxims of the highest wisdom?"*
>
> *Ikkyu took his brush and wrote: "Attention."*
>
> *"Is that all?" asked the man.*
>
> *Ikkyu then wrote: "Attention. Attention."*
>
> *"Well," said the man, "I really don't see much depth in what you have written."*
>
> *Then Ikkyu wrote the same word three times: "Attention. Attention. Attention."*
>
> *Half-angered, the man demanded, "What does that word 'Attention' mean anyway?"*
>
> *Ikkyu gently responded, "Attention means attention."*

The Care and Feeding of Professors

The care and feeding of professors extend beyond the classroom. Pay a visit to your professors or teaching assistants during office hours. Go with questions, maybe questions having to do with mastery of the material. If you are at all worried about an upcoming exam or paper, always go and discuss it. Professors, being human, will generally be more tolerant of the student who cares enough to come in and get help. If the material gives you no trouble, think about the larger questions it raises in your mind and go in for a more general talk. If you can possibly resist it, don't ask about your grade. Don't monopolize the professor's time. Very few professors will make you feel absolutely unwanted. Most will generally clue you in to how much time they have available for you. Be sensitive to this.

---

[2]As the renowned educator William Glasser once said, "We learn . . .
   10% of what we read,
   20% of what we hear,
   30% of what we see,
   50% of what we see and hear,
   70% of what we discuss with others,
   80% of what we experience,
   95% of what we teach to someone else."

10 Tips on Asking for Letters of Recommendation

Letters of recommendation play a critical role in getting into graduate or professional school or obtaining your first job. Here are some tips for getting effective letters of recommendation from your professors.

1. *Be certain to request letters from faculty who know you well.*   Think about how the letters you are requesting "fit" together. You may want your letter writers to focus on different aspects of you. Telling each writer what you would like him or her to emphasize is helpful.

2. *Give the writers lead time.*   Do not wait until the day before to ask for a letter of recommendation. Ask 3 to 4 weeks in advance, 2 weeks minimum.

3. *Make your request first orally, and then follow up with a written request.*   "Dear Dr. X, Thank you for agreeing to write a letter of recommendation for law school for me. . . ." Don't expect your professors to remember a request that was shouted to them in the hall.

4. *Provide talking points.*   We care about all of our students, but sometimes we forget all the wonderful things they have done. In your written request, include talking points to jog our memory, such as, "I took the following courses with you and earned the following grades." "I wrote the paper on 'The Debates of 1976,' which you said was the greatest thing you'd ever read on the subject." "I wrote the paper 'Using Marx's Concept of Alienation in Contemporary White Collar Work,' which you said was an outstanding application of a classic sociological concept to contemporary issues." When telling us what you've accomplished, don't forget to mention travel courses, study abroad, internships, and things you might have done to help out around the department or school.

5. *If the program to which you are applying requires a personal statement, please provide it for us.* It tells a great deal about how you are presenting yourself to the program and will aid us in writing a targeted letter for you.

6. *Get help with your personal statement before drafting it and sending it off.*   Often, your academic advisor can provide good input with respect to the substance of the statement and the programs to which you are applying. In addition, have several really good writers proof the document and help you edit. You want to send the best looking personal statement you can write. When we work on your letter, it helps us to know that you've written a quality document.

7. *Provide all the necessary forms.*   We receive many requests each semester for letters of recommendation. (It seems they all come in the same week!) Make it as easy as possible for us to write your letter. Provide us with the necessary forms, due dates, addressed envelopes, and other pertinent information, for example, "It is important for you to put the letter in the envelope, seal it, and then write your name across the seal." If you are requesting a letter for a program that does not have a form, please be kind enough to type out the exact name of the program and the address of the school. Include the name of the graduate advisor. This helps us to know to whom to address the letter. Type in the information at the top of the forms. This looks better than your printing it by hand and will be one more positive detail on your application file. The graduate program will be able to read it more easily.

8. *It is OK for you to (politely) bug us.*   A gentle reminder will always be appreciated. We are busy, and sometimes we need to be reminded of an upcoming due date.

9. *Have a backup.*   Professors occasionally promise more than they can deliver, so it is a good idea to have a backup you can go to in case your first choice letter writer doesn't come through.

10. *Thank-you notes are really appreciated.*   Writing a good letter of recommendation takes time and effort, so it is nice to write a thank-you note to those who have written on your behalf. And later, once you hear from the places you've applied, we want to hear from you. We want to know how it all turned out. Where are you going to graduate school? Where did you end up working? Please send us an e-mail and tell us.

—*Fred Smoller and Roberta Lessor*

Pitzer College in California is admittedly atypical in its concern for students, but some of the things that delighted me with students there can be tried in other environments. I always enjoyed the student who would bring an occasional relevant newspaper clipping or magazine article to class or to me for my perusal. I also enjoyed suggestions for things the class might do, such as inviting guest speakers or having a film or going on a field trip. I taught several classes solely at the request of a student or a small group of students. Of course, your suggestions should not imply that the course is lacking in appeal. It may even be good to preface suggestions with a good word about the class, but only the most neurotic professor will resent a show of interest or initiative.

Always remember that professors who care about teaching are going counter to the official system of career rewards and punishments. They need the student feedback to keep them going. It is in your interest to provide some of that feedback. Everybody will be better off for it.

How personal should your relationship with professors be? In this regard, you must proceed with hope and caution. It is distinctly unwise to discuss your personal emotional problems with most of your professors, even though these problems may sometimes greatly affect your academic performance. Most professors consider it unprofessional to deal with students as emotional creatures. Indeed, those who are willing to do so are frequently accused by their peers of coddling students. In fact, of course, the claim of professionalism is a convenient way to hide from the acute fear many professors have of their own and other people's emotions. Intellectuality is often used to keep threatening emotions at a distance. Young women who cry in professors' offices are particularly dreaded. Those professors who are open to emotional issues are usually known by reputation or will communicate where they stand during your conversations with them.

However, any professor whose ideas interest you may be cultivated as an intellectual friend on that level. If the atmosphere of your school allows for informal interactions with professors, you would be wise to nurture a few such contacts. Professors, as I have said before, may often turn out to be very interesting people. It is also the case that they are generally a whole lot nicer off the job than on. Unfortunately, the social role of professors brings out the worst in people. I have often been pleasantly surprised by the way particularly stiff-necked colleagues change into warm human beings around their children or while doing their hobbies.

Outside the Lecture Halls

Like most college students, I find getting to know a professor a task. It's not easy. There is a haunting fear of rejection. This fear peaked my freshman year when I approached one of my professors and lost all ability to speak. Due to my intense nervousness, I stuttered my speech as my face turned hot and fiery red. I was unfortunately too slow, and he quickly wrapped up the conversation.

Regardless of this first negative experience, I was blessed to have gotten to know a number of professors throughout my undergraduate years. Many students will automatically assume that they know their professors because they attend their lectures a few times a week throughout a term. This, however, does not create any real relationship with the professor.

My opportunities came largely due to my love of traveling. Many students do not take advantage of travel opportunities or getting to know their professors while in college and regret the lost opportunities when it is too late. I was able to accomplish both through travel study experiences. During my first study abroad, my professor was accompanied by his wife and daughter. I naturally befriended his daughter because I was comfortable working with high school students. This brief friendship enabled me to get to know my professor as well as his wife and inevitably allowed me to view my professor as a professor, a father, a friend, and a human being. The intimidation was really all in my head. My professor was very much available to his students, and travel study was an opportunity for him to get to know them. Traveling enabled me to communicate with my professor in a different dynamic and a different environment while fulfilling my graduation requirements.

—*Moo Young Kim*

Let me also say a word about social class and personal contact. Professors are, by definition, upper-middle-class people, regardless of their social origins. Hence, children of similarly placed parents will find it much easier making friends with professors than those of you whose parents were not so highly educated or highly placed. Such class-based cultural differences are very real barriers to human contact. It helps to be aware of them, so you can make a little extra effort to overcome them. Most professors are not consciously snobbish about their class position and will bend over backward for an interested student from any background. When encountering class and ethnic barriers within the academy, remember that it is only ethnocentrism that causes us to look on some people's cultures as more valuable or of higher status than other people's. (More about this can be found in Chapter 15.)

A word should be said about the opposite sort of problem: the professor who wants to know you more personally than you wish to be known. This applies mainly to male professors who pursue their young female students, though, increasingly, female professors are also guilty. If the professor is young, attractive, and unmarried, this may not seem like a problem. But you would be well advised to postpone the relationship until you have finished the class. Imagine the consequences of a broken affair while class is still underway.

When the professor is older or just not attractive to you, you can be put in a very delicate situation. High-status males in our society generally assume that they deserve physical access to the young and sexually appealing, and society is much more accepting of older man–younger woman combinations than their reverse. Secretaries, flight attendants, waitresses, and similar folk have long had to deal with this problem, and female students are in the same boat. Sometimes the approach is so oblique and indirect that you really don't know how to cope with it. The professor may come across as fatherly, for example, or assure you that his only concern is to free you from psychological inhibitions. If this happens, you should promptly withdraw from the class and, if appropriate, report it. If there are grading problems or other academic issues at stake, talk to your advisor or someone you trust in the culprit's own discipline. Faculty members usually know each other's reputations on this score. Remember that you have an absolute right to protect yourself from sexual exploitation. Indeed, we have laws that forbid sexual harassment on the job or in schools. Female faculty will probably help you with these difficulties, and so will any feminist groups on your campus.

Finding Your Local Professor

The key to succeeding in college is to take a personal stance on your education. Too many students follow the requirements and never stray to find their passion. Students need to realize that they have the right to change their education. In high school, I rejected teachers I didn't believe had my best interest at heart by switching classes. The administration was set against this, so I had to put a little muscle behind my wishes. I complained of poor teachers, but I also did something to rectify the situation. The gym teacher lecturing on history wasn't going to cut it for me.

Every school has teachers who are decidedly better than others. The beauty of college is that there are many more teachers available, with a medley of styles and personalities. Find teachers who inspire you and light a fire beneath you. And once you do, hold on tight. I realized that the course titles didn't matter as much as the instructors. A course on artificial intelligence could be as dry as sand, whereas a lecture on sand could be as exciting as artificial intelligence should be, if delivered by a dynamic professor.

Getting to know your professors is another step in personalizing your education. Many students feel intimidated by these landlords of academia, and rightly so, because professors are likely to exude an impression of intellectual superiority.

As a student, your education is in your possession. Instead of sopping up the good with the bad in an attempt to be a productive sponge, why not demand a worthy response from your teachers? Involve yourself.

One common misunderstanding that students have about professors is that faculty is synonymous with *administration*. Although their union does exist at some level (otherwise, how would the university function?), it is rarely the case that professors agree with administrators' disregard for students.

Keep on the lookout for visiting professors and guest lecturers so that you may take advantage of good teachers. Most new (nontenured) professors are there to teach, especially if they have been to several schools before yours. These are often the people to search for and take classes with. They may be the only people at the university who have not drowned in the publish-or-perish sea and are there because of their desire to help you learn.

—*Tatian Greenleaf*

Support Your Local Teaching Assistant

Get to Know Your Teaching Assistants

If you attend a large public university, you will likely encounter at least a handful of Teaching Assistants, or TAs, during the course of your college career. TAs work with professors who teach lecture classes of hundreds or even thousands of students. TAs lead small "discussion sections" of about 15 to 30 students that are designed to supplement lectures. Sometimes sections are very casual, a time to get clarification from your TA about concepts the professor introduced in the lecture. Sometimes TAs present new course material in discussion sections. Sometimes attending sections is optional, other times section attendance is mandatory and TAs require you to meet additional course requirements. Every discussion section you are a part of will be different. Before the quarter/semester begins, it's important to take charge and find out whether the classes you're enrolled in have accompanying discussion sections. If they do, you should find out whether you need to sign up for the sections yourself, separately from the lectures, or whether you're automatically enrolled in them when you enroll for lectures. You'll find out what your particular discussion sections will entail when classes begin. I realized that when I was in college, I didn't have any idea who my TAs actually were or how they had come to be TAs for my classes. Here is some (hopefully) helpful information about those fearless workhorses of the academy, your humble TAs.

Five Things You Should Know About Your TAs

1. *Teaching Assistants are full-time graduate students.* They are college graduates who have decided to pursue a master's degree and/or PhD in the field you're taking university classes in. Most often, graduate students become TAs in their own departments, but occasionally TAs teach outside their home departments.

2. *Most Teaching Assistants have limited choice of classes they teach.* They are usually given several classes to choose from, and they must rank their preferences based on their research and course commitments. An administrator then assigns TAs to classes based on their preferences, schedules, and professors' requests.

3. *In most courses that have TAs, the TAs grade the majority, if not all, of the work you turn in.* Therefore, it is important to get to know your TA's grading style and what he or she is looking for in your assignments. Go to his or her office hours and find out. If you don't understand why a TA gave you a B instead of an A on a paper or exam, ask him or her about it. He or she would probably be happy to go over your paper with you and point out areas that could have been improved. Furthermore, if there is a participation component to your final grade in the class, the professor will probably ask the TA whether you came to his or her office hours and how much you spoke in discussion section. This is especially the case in large lecture classes. The professor is probably not going to remember that you asked him or her a question once in lecture during the quarter/semester, but your TA will almost certainly remember whether you participated in your section.

4. *Be nice to your TAs.* They work very hard. However, don't buy them gifts and don't ask them on dates. Before becoming TAs at UCLA (and I'd assume at other universities as well), all graduate students have to attend a seminar on pedagogy and ethics in the university. During the one I participated in, we were admonished not to accept gifts from or dates with our students.

5. *Teaching Assistants can be great resources, and you should take advantage of what they offer.* Teaching Assistants will also write you letters of recommendation for jobs or graduate school if you get to know them and do well in their classes. Make the most of your discussion. Participate!

—Sarah J. Morando

Reflections on the TA Role

In the search for good professors, the TA is often overlooked. These are folks you do not choose, and they can either make or break a class. A positive, creative, dynamic TA can bring out the best in his or her students, while a slumbering, patronizing one can stomp on students' desire to learn. Teaching assistants are the workhorses of the academy. Some large schools even use TAs to teach small lectures, thereby increasing the strain on them. In spite of their heavy time commitment, teaching assistants are a wonderful resource for undergrads who have even the slightest glimmer of curiosity about graduate school or, better yet, about the educational system they are currently swimming in. Graduate students, if picked when ripe, can make wonderful mentors and often are more giving of their advice than professors.

One of the most empowering experiences I ever had at college was student teaching. If you are lucky enough to get to know a professor well enough to find out what he or she is up to around the campus and to have taken a few classes with him or her, find out whether the professor will allow you to become an undergraduate teaching assistant or at least to facilitate discussions among classmates. The key is that you become both a student and a teacher at the same time. This in-between state is a wonderful place to be.

—Tatian Greenleaf

CHAPTER 6

An Academic Question

In this chapter, we explore how in many of the social sciences, overly academic jargon serves to obscure reality and stifle dissent. Here we delve into these issues:

- Excessive specialization.
- The unusual meanings of "scholarly" objectivity.
- The back-stage functioning of upper-class control.
- The peculiar inaccessibility of "scholarly" publications.

"We call it 'academic freedom,'" said the queen, "because everybody is free to be completely academic."

—Lewis Carroll (1865/1960)

An *academic question,* as we all know, is a question about such an obscure fine point that only an academician would bother with it. Thus, our very language informs us that there is something a little bit weird about the kind of knowledge offered at the academy. In this section, I would like to talk primarily about the social or behavioral sciences because from these fields we would normally expect a lucid explanation of how our society works. Further, these fields have, in large part, sold out the goal of seeing social reality clearly.

The first thing that strikes anyone entering the province of social science is that there are several different secret languages. Sociologists cannot really speak psychologese, psychologists cannot decipher articles in the *American Anthropologist,* and economists are stumped by sociologese. The ordinary layperson encounters a deafening babble of tongues. Looking down the table of contents of a few prestigious social science journals, we encounter such puzzling titles as the following:

"A Spatial Autocorrelation Model of the Effects of Population Density on Fertility"

"A Quantitative Analysis of Temporal Symmetry in Microsocial Relations"

"Paradoxical Consequences of Excess in Structural Complexity: A Study of a State Children's Psychiatric Hospital"

"Analyzing the Instrumental Use of Relations in the Context of Social Structure"

"Additive Clusterings: Representation of Similarities as Combinations of Discrete Overlapping Properties"

This is enough to send most people running for cover. However, earnest students who applied themselves to making sense of the contents of these articles would discover that after reading, let us say, *The American Sociological Review* for a whole year, they still would not have the faintest idea that the United States has the most severe poverty problem of any industrialized country, that we have a greater percentage of our population in prison than any country except South Africa and China, that big money controls the nomination processes of both major parties, or that the leadership of this country is perfectly willing to trade in total annihilation to gain its ends in the world—in short, reading *The American Sociological Review* tells you almost nothing about the important things going on in our society.

In the 1950s, there was a radical sociologist named C. Wright Mills who wanted to use social science knowledge to change society. He wrote in plain English to persuade as many people as possible. He also had the temerity to attack the secret language of sociology, particularly as it was written by an eminent Harvard sociologist named Talcott Parsons. No one, to my knowledge, has ever unmasked the secret language more dramatically than Mills does in *The Sociological Imagination* (1959), where he offers the following "translation" of a passage from Parsons (1951). To get the full benefit, really try hard to understand Parsons in this passage before you go on to the translation by Mills:

Talcott Parsons: An element of a shared symbolic system which serves as a criterion or standard for selection among the alternatives of orientation which are intrinsically open in a situation may be called a value. . . . But from this motivational orientation aspect of the totality of action it is, in view of the role of symbolic systems, necessary to distinguish a "value orientation" aspect. This aspect concerns, not the meaning of the expected state of affairs to the actor in terms of his gratification-deprivation balance, but the content of the selective standards themselves. The concept of value orientations in this sense is thus the logical device for formulating one central aspect of the articulation of cultural traditions into the action system.

It follows from the derivation of normative orientation and the role of values in action as stated above, that all values involve what may be called a social reference. . . . It is inherent in an action system that action is, to use one phrase, "normatively orientated." This follows, as was shown, from the concept of expectations and its place in action theory, especially in the "active" phase in which the actor pursues goals. Expectations then, in combination with the "double contingency" of the process of interaction as it has been called, create a crucially imperative problem of order. Two aspects of this problem of order may in turn be distinguished, order in the symbolic systems which make communication possible, and order in the mutuality of motivational orientation to the normative aspect of expectations, the "Hobbesian" problem of order.

The problem of order, and thus of the nature of the integration of stable systems of social interaction, that is, of social structure, thus focuses on the integration of the motivation of actors with the normative cultural standards which integrate the action system, in our context interpersonally. These standards are, in the terms used in the preceding chapter, patterns of value-orientation, and as such are a particularly crucial part of the cultural tradition of social systems. (Parsons, 1951, pp. 12, 36–37)

Mills's translation: People often share standards and expect one another to stick to them. Insofar as they do, their society may be orderly. (Mills, 1959, pp. 25–27)

Interestingly, Talcott Parsons was the leading theorist in sociology, whereas Mills was, during his lifetime, considered "unsound" by most establishment sociologists.[1] The 1960s generation rediscovered Mills, and he briefly attained the wide audience he always deserved.

I do not mean to say that nobody should ever make up a new word. In studying any subject, we come across phenomena for which the language has no word readily available. We cannot use our discovery unless we give it a name, so any field will necessarily require you to learn a certain amount of vocabulary. In learning new words, you are really discovering and pinpointing new phenomena. But obviously, the secret language of the social sciences has gone far beyond these modest necessities. The secret language is obscure, nothing more. It is meant to block communication with the outside world.

Now, we have to ask ourselves, why would scholars do this? What purpose does it serve? Secretive writing is not novel in our century. Many medieval writers wrote for a very limited audience in a cryptic style that only the very dedicated and intelligent could decipher. They did so because they feared offending the Catholic Church, which occasionally burned unwanted scholars at the stake. Do our scholars also fear reprisal? Not only is this the case, but also the pressure to become obscure is so great that it is completely internalized by most social scientists. That is, they are not just hiding the real picture from the public, they actually manage to become so confused about reality that they no longer know what it is themselves.

---

[1]A postscript about Talcott Parsons: In the winter of 1989, Charles O'Connell, a graduate student at the University of California at Los Angeles studying the history of the Harvard Russian Research Center, discovered something interesting. After World War II, Parsons had worked with Army Intelligence, the CIA, and the State Department in an operation to smuggle Nazi collaborators into the United States as Soviet studies experts. The most important of these "experts" was Nicholas Poppe, a Russian academician who went over to the Germans and helped the Nazis search out the Jewish communities in Russia for extermination. Although Poppe was wanted for war crimes by the Russians, Parsons was instrumental in having him appointed to the faculty of the University of Washington. Other of Parsons's Nazi protégés also joined the Russian Research Center at Harvard. In view of Parsons's long-standing association with the CIA, it is interesting to note that his brand of "value free" sociology undercut sociology's function of critical assessment of American society for a whole generation.

This is the situation that threatens them: We live in a society whose official ideology is so utterly different from its actual practice that people who look around and plainly state what they see are bound to stir up the most profound doubts about the legitimacy of the group in power and the reasonableness, and even the sanity, of the policies they pursue. The danger lies not in that there is poverty, racial discrimination, costly but poor medical service, and a deteriorating environment for all but the well-to-do. Societies have existed for centuries with inequality, injustice, and neglect of citizens. But most societies of the past had an official ideology that supported this state of affairs. In the Middle Ages, people believed that nobles and peasants were two separate species, destined by God to their respective positions. It is only when you juxtapose an egalitarian, humanistic philosophy with conditions of inequality that you are in peril. "All men are created equal" is tough to live up to. But we were all forced to memorize it in grammar school.

Surprisingly, we shared this dilemma with Communist pre-Gorbachev Russia (USSR). They also had an official policy of human equality and, in reality, a class system not too different from our own. They also had to keep their social scientists from speaking clearly about reality. Many of the devices they used to curb their scholars are identical to those used in the United States. Let us look at these devices in our own society to see how it is possible for people to spend their entire lives studying society without ever telling the truth loudly or lucidly enough to be heard. This is actually quite a difficult trick.

Excessive Specialization

One method used in both countries is extreme specialization. To be a proper scholar, one has to become highly specialized. I recall a job applicant for a position in sociology whose entire career had been spent on the phenomenon of adolescent fighting gangs. He had written a dozen articles on the subject, and he clearly intended to teach nothing else, regardless of the names he gave to his courses.

Now, why should this specialization be a block to learning—especially when it seems to work so well in the natural sciences? The problem is that when social scientists confine themselves to such narrow phenomena, they will probably overlook important influences from outside their field of vision. This social scientist may become very good at telling us what delinquency rates are for rich and poor teenagers, but if he lacks knowledge of societies other than ours, he may miss the crucial fact that most western European countries have very little resembling our violent gang activity. He thus misses the vital point that different national economic policies might solve our gang problem.

If our scholar is not familiar with the sociology of political radicalism, he might not know that during the urban insurrections of the late 1960s and early 1970s, gang fighting in the ghettos diminished dramatically. Whole gangs suddenly became highly politicized and turned their aggression against the system, rather than fighting one another. Clearly, the authorities prefer gang fighting and the conditions that make for it. This can be seen by the absolute ruthlessness with which police murdered members of a newly formed, grassroots, political party that dramatically advocated Black power: the Black Panther Party. This community-based, social-movement organization took on Marxist beliefs and instituted public service in their communities and commonly opposed police brutality. The police response to them was almost one of annihilation.

Highly specialized scholars usually buy the idea that they should never say anything outside their field of expertise. Hence, they are in no danger of seeing an overall view of society with its glaring contradictions between the ideal and reality. Highly specialized scholars are also hampered in their teaching. I have said that our specialist clearly intended to teach his own subject in all his classes. This is a very common phenomenon. Feeling that teaching is less important than research anyway, scholars make little effort to help their students get an overall picture of the world and their place in it. A dozen courses in such highly specialized subjects as adolescent suicide or the culture of the Northwest Native Americans are likely to leave the student with a smattering of isolated details that he or she cannot forge together into any comprehensible view of society.

"Scholarly" Objectivity

Another theme taken from natural science and misused in social science is the rule of scholarly objectivity. According to this rule, scholars should never express their value judgments (this rule itself is a value judgment that favors the status quo). Thus, for example, scholars may study the systematic degradation of minority races in our society, but they may not express their feeling that this is evil. Indeed, the very term would bring down criticism on their head from calmer, wiser souls. Anything that cries out against cruelty or madness in our society is considered "shrill."

Objectivity has enormous value, and we can train ourselves to be systematic and careful and to follow certain methods that help us to see clearly. But the most important method for overcoming egoistic prejudice is seldom recommended or assigned to students—or scholars for that matter. This would be to leave your own niche in society for a while and go to live with people of a different social class. (This is not the same as study abroad.)

The glaring failure of the objectivity practiced by most scholars can be seen in the overwhelming extent to which our knowledge is upper-middle-class knowledge. Scholars and, of course, writers, journalists, and publishers are by definition holders of middle- to upper-middle-class income and status. Almost everything we know of the world through the written word and through film, television, and the Internet has been written by upper-middle-class minds and sifted, edited, and judged by other upper-middle-class minds, generally working in institutions that are ultimately controlled by upper-class money. (The complex division of labor that made industrial society possible would never have had half so good a press had not the commentators been the folks who ended up talking for a living.)

The occasional exception to this is the writer or scholar who comes from a different group in society and who has managed to retain his or her loyalties and insights through the whole difficult process of socialization into the intelligentsia. Thus, the Black writer James Baldwin predicted the Black urban uprisings of the

1960s and 1970s long before most White sociologists had the slightest idea they were coming, simply because he remained in touch with poor, urban Blacks. Those of you who come from groups other than the White middle class may have long suspected this. (We will talk more about this in Chapter 15.)

Scholars are also controlled by the large foundations that, together with the federal government, provide most of the prestigious fellowships for which they compete. A sociologist who is on retainer from the U.S. Department of Defense will hardly tell us the truth about the military. The Rockefeller-funded Social Science Research Council is very unlikely to fund an investigation into the political power of the Rockefellers; the Ford Foundation is unlikely to fund someone who wishes to study the alienation and exploitation of workers in auto factories. However, a work on the evils of communism, almost anywhere in the world, is quickly funded. Ambitious scholars (and, you can be sure, they will be socialized to be very ambitious) are thus lured in certain directions and blocked from others.

Upper-Class Control

Another difficulty in understanding society is simply access: Although it is easy to invade the haunts of the poor to study their problems, it is quite impossible to get access to the doings of the rich and powerful. In a society in which power is exercised in secrecy, social scientists really need spies more than they need researchers.[2] Spying, however, is a dangerous business, so scholars confine themselves to what is easily accessible. There have been innumerable studies of voting behavior, but very little good has been done on the real power trading at the higher levels. Meanwhile, the social scientist's emphasis on voting behavior really becomes a piece of propaganda because it implies that voting is terribly crucial to political outcomes. By their silence about the real power centers, scholars help to make these shadowy realms disappear altogether.

Scholars also want to get jobs and keep them. So we have to look at who ultimately controls their job situations: Colleges and universities are controlled by boards (boards of trustees in the case of private colleges; boards of regents in the case of public colleges and universities), which are composed largely of wealthy businessmen. The regents of the University of California (UC) are typical of the nationwide pattern: An early study showed that of the 20 regents, 10 were millionaires, and all were extremely well off.[3] The 20 regents sat on 60 different corporate boards. There were two women, one who was appointed after her husband's death. The median age was 60 years. The only non-White regent was Wilson Riles, who was an ex officio member of the board because he was state superintendent of instruction. He was the first minority person on the board. Over the years, the regents have refused to include representatives of the faculty or students. Most of the regents were

---

[2]For a case where spying paid off, see Domhoff (1975). All of his books are worth reading. Begin with the most recent and work back.

[3]Data given in this chapter from the study, as well as information about the history of business's documentation of higher education, are from Smith (1974).

politically conservative. Several were listed in the Social Register. The majority were Protestants. Like most such boards, the UC regents represent the interests of the top 10th of 1% of the American income distribution—that is, they represent the corporate upper class. Such businesspeople frequently have little sympathy for values such as academic freedom. In another national survey of college trustees, 33% expressed disapproval of full academic freedom in political matters.

These boards remain in the background much of the time, but they have very definite veto power. At the Claremont Colleges during the 1970s, we hired Angela Davis to teach one course on our campus. Dr. Davis had a PhD in philosophy, but she was a Marxist scholar and had also spent the 1960s working closely with the Black Panthers. This political activism put her beyond the academic pale. When our trustees discovered that she had been hired, there was such a fuss that, under the guise of protecting Dr. Davis, the class was limited in number, closed to auditors, and was held in a location that was only announced to the enrolled few just before the class actually began. Seeing this, it was clear that we could never have offered her a job as a full-time faculty member. I would like to stress that the Claremont Colleges is one of the freer institutions around. At the University of California, Dr. Davis was fired by the board of regents, despite the support of faculty, students, and administration. It only takes one Angela Davis to convince most scholars that they cannot stick their necks out very far in any controversial direction. Unfortunately, hers is by no means an isolated case.

While I am on the subject of upper-class control, I must go off on a short historical tangent. It may surprise you to realize that the very shape of your college education was the work of industrial magnates. Before the Civil War, there were a great variety of colleges, largely denominational, which emphasized the classical disciplines and theology. After the war, businesspeople began giving to colleges to create programs in science and business administration. But it was not until John D. Rockefeller and Andrew Carnegie took American higher education in hand during the first three decades of the 20th century that the modern college and university emerged.

These two tycoons, followed by numerous other corporate heads, set out to standardize higher education. They picked a small number of the best schools and gave them enormous grants, thus making them into elite institutions. They demanded secularization of the schools to which they gave money, and most gave up their denominational ties. They brought about the standardized 4-year curriculum, with its grading and unit system and its departmentalization. Standardization is a great thing for industry; it is a terrible thing for education. Not all human beings fit easily into the lockstep of requirements and grading methods that are now nearly universal. Needless to say, Rockefeller and Carnegie used their influence to oust scholars who were critical of the way they wielded power.

Since the beginning of World War II, the government, particularly the U.S. Department of Defense, has taken the place of wealthy donors as the primary source of funds for higher education. From two thirds to three quarters of all money spent on academic research comes from the government. Government influence has been the main push for the emphasis on research and graduate study, which has left so many undergraduates orphaned in our big universities. Like the earlier captains of industry, government has used its power position to ensure that untenured professors whose ideas do not mesh with those of the corporate-state establishment have great difficulty maintaining academic jobs.

Scholars are rewarded to the degree that they write only for a small in-group. As I mentioned in Chapter 5, those who write books that attract a large audience are quickly denigrated as popularizers. (A *popularizer* is somebody who makes knowledge available to the populace.) A scholar who acts as consultant to the management of a corporation or police department gets career credits for doing so, but a scholar who helps a poor community fight for better housing is very unlikely to list that fact in his vita.

Inaccessible "Scholarly" Publications

Finally, scholars are kept so busy by outrageous publication requirements that they have very little time to speak truth to their students and their communities. Most of them are running very scared in a tight job market. The fastest way to publish a lot is to be highly specialized. It is also interesting to look at the form in which work must be cast for publication. Scholarly journals insist on a highly stylized format, without which it is extremely difficult to be published but within which it is impossible to be heard.

First of all, a research article on any subject must begin with a "review of the literature," which shows that you have read everything ever published on the subject you have chosen. Because everyone is publishing for dear life, there is an overwhelming and usually repetitive amount to digest, and even the specialists can barely keep up with it. This makes it nearly impossible for a generalist to write on most topics. It also ensures that we won't hear anything terribly new because the process of digesting the existing verbiage is so exhausting that it will drive any wayward originality out.

It is extremely difficult to pronounce a new idea in a scholarly journal. If you do not cast it in the form of an existing idea, the editors will ask, "On whose authority are you speaking?" I had the droll experience of writing an article on human relations within academic sociology departments. I noted that these relations were very poor and fraught with hostility. The editors simply refused to print this until I put it into the words of another writer, whom I quoted at length. Then it was accepted.

Establishment professors act as gatekeepers to the world of knowledge. Most journals send a submitted article to several academic editors, and the article must pass muster with all of them. It is extremely difficult to please four or five such august persons when you are putting forth a controversial idea. In short, there is a very subtle, complex, but powerful process of censorship by which the academic establishment protects itself against what it deems heresy.

But things are not totally hopeless. In contrast to the situation of scholars in the Middle Ages, we have both greater access to heresy and greater physical safety for heretics. Just about everything you need to know has been published in a book somewhere. This freedom is threatened by publishing houses being gobbled up by multinational corporations. But at present, the freedom still exists. There are still dissident publishing houses. This much freedom of information on the level of scholarly books is perfectly safe for the establishment because only 1 person in 10,000 ever reads such books, and he or she can hardly hold out against the 9,999

who only know what they hear on the evening news. So there is no political consequence to allowing such books to be published. In Russia, too, specialized scholars
were allowed access to forbidden books, but the process was much more tightly
guarded.

Luckily for you, the dissident books that talk about what is going on are written
in plain English because their writers want to reach a large public. Thus, we have
two kinds of material in social science: the scholarly stuff, which is indecipherable,
and the popular stuff, which is worth reading. Some of your professors will favor
one style, some the other. Before you sign up for a course, get a reading list from
the professor; then go to the book store or library and peruse the assignments. Are
these books or articles that speak to you and tell you something new? If they are,
take the course. If not, avoid it.

What I am saying in this chapter is that the scholars have been silenced. They
have been bought. There are exceptions to this rule, but you will have to look for
them. You may be surprised to hear me say this because at times, colleges and universities seem to be the most radical institutions in our society. Opposition to the
Vietnam War, for example, came largely from academic institutions. The situation
is simply this: Yes, colleges and universities are among the very few institutions in
our society that ever criticize the policies of the powerful. The great majority of
scholars, however, never take part in such criticism. As with the current wars and
aggressive gestures, during Vietnam, only a small minority of professors spoke out.
Because opposition is so rare, colleges seem very visible in their critical role, despite
the fact that this role is played only intermittently and by a small minority.

Questions of Academic Integrity

Plagiarism has become an enormous issue of concern in academia, particularly since the rise of the Internet. The clarity of the act and meaning of plagiarism in the age of print has been eclipsed by the fog of plagiarism in the Internet age, as downloading from the Internet has become a fundamental and commonplace part of ordinary school education. In Chapter 7, we

- address a clarifying exercise called "Please Plagiarize,"
- enhance the clarity of our understanding of plagiarism, and
- try to honestly uncover what in fact is the big deal about cheating.

Johnny, Janey, and the Little Search Engine That Could: A Childish Story

As the story goes, Janey and Johnny were having fun being best friends at college. They were in classes, sure, but they much preferred the games and toys the other boys and girls had to play with, so they spent too much time playing in the other kids' rooms, even when they knew they needed to write their reports for class.

One evening, Janey and Johnny looked at their homework and realized everything was due the following day. Imagine how surprised they were! Johnny sat down and cried and cried. He certainly wished his mother were here now—she'd know just what to do. Janey, on the other hand, handed Johnny a clean handkerchief. Janey knew just what to do because friends of hers told her how to beat homework deadlines when they crept up on you. She told Johnny "I think I can. . . . I think I can . . . I think I can get us out of this mess."

Janey sat at the computer. She called up the Little Search Engine That Could—Yahoo! It went all over, looking for other people's writing. Then it stopped to show Janey what it found.

Janey needed one page for her literature class. Because she had so many other things to get done, she didn't think anyone would notice when she downloaded some text to use. But Johnny needed much more than one page, so he began to cry all over again. Janey sent the Little Search Engine off once again, this time for Johnny. She told him to stop crying and reassured him that his homework would be done in a flash.

Yahoo! went the Little Search Engine. It found something especially for Johnny. Neither Janey nor Johnny wanted to think they had done anything wrong. After all, they didn't copy from a book or a magazine! Instead, they had simply plucked some text right out of the virtual world so that they could use it in the real world to meet a really important deadline.

Here is a sample of Johnny's report:

> "Rulings on ADA-related cases made by the Supreme Court have reduced the ADA from civil rights law to entitlement policy. Case law demonstrates that the bulk of decisions have been concerned with who qualifies for ADA protections, rather than offering support and guidance toward its enforcement."

Johnny and Janey were both happy. Janey told Johnny that the report made him sound much smarter than he really was, too!

—Paula Apodaca

Please Plagiarize

Plagiarism has become an enormous issue of concern in academia over the past 5 or so years. Many professors feel it is like a cavity, a corruption eating away at the integrity of academic intellectual life, and I agree. I think it is worthwhile to present the issue of plagiarism at the beginning of each course as an exercise in critical awareness. I try to address my concerns with plagiarism as a political rather than a moral issue. I avoid bringing it up moralistically, as in, "I am suspicious of you; I don't trust you; I am paranoid that you are going to try to get away with plagiarism." That approach runs the risk of poisoning the atmosphere of the classroom and the teacher-student relationship. As we point out in so many of the chapters of this book, we already are embedded in the dialectics of suspicion by virtue of being in a classroom and a part of the institution of school. To approach plagiarism in any way that further reinforces that distrust and suspicion between students and teachers really does not serve any educational purpose. Hence, I think it is more effective and valuable to raise the issue of plagiarism in a political and educational context: "I and my university colleagues across the country are engaged in fighting for the integrity of academic and intellectual work. The issue of plagiarism is a vital threat to that integrity." One of my lectures begins as follows:

> Most of you, if you walked by a very pretty red sports car that happened to have the keys in it, would not simply jump in and steal it. You are already aware of all the rules and regulations regarding ownership and stealing. If you did decide to steal it, you would know that there are consequences for this act. The issue of plagiarism is not this clear. Ownership of words, sentences, and ideas is not as clear and concrete as ownership of automobiles.

I have found that asking students to consciously engage in plagiarism, as an exercise, increases their awareness of plagiarism. The plagiarism problem in higher education today is overwhelmingly the result of ignorance, confusion, and the fog of the Internet. It has been my direct experience that many students today are not clear about the meaning of plagiarism. Downloading from the Internet has been such a fundamental and ordinary part of their education for so long that there is deep confusion whether this is a legitimate part of composing school papers or not. I have students, as a formal homework assignment, define in one sentence what plagiarism is (in their own words—they're not allowed to plagiarize the definition) and then plagiarize someone's writing, preferably using the Internet. I do this so that at the end of the assignment I know that they are clear about precisely what plagiarism is. After completing the assignment and bringing it to class, we have an in-depth discussion clarifying what we know about plagiarism. I also request that, if they are comfortable, they write on their homework paper, in their own handwriting, "I promise not to plagiarize in this class" (or any variation of this statement that they are willing to consciously commit to).

—Bernard McGrane

Plagiarism

Plagiarism is the presentation of another's words or ideas as your own. It is a *bad* thing. Don't do it.

Turning in a paper actually written by your roommate and saying "I wrote this" would be a flagrant example of plagiarism. The same would be true if you were to buy a term paper from a "paper mill." The lightest punishment for plagiarism of this sort would be a grade of zero for the paper. Other common punishments are failing the course or even expulsion from school. As you can see, plagiarism is a very serious offense in academia.

Plagiarism is wrong for several reasons. First, it is *lying*. If you have been asked to write something as evidence that you have grasped the materials of the course you are taking, offering someone else's work as evidence is a lie. It is no different from having someone else take an examination in your name.

Second, it is an *insult* to your fellow students. When you plagiarize, just as when you cheat on an exam, you treat unfairly those who play by the rules. You seek an unfair advantage over them, and, inevitably, you will find yourself looking down on those who devote their time and energy to the task that you have cheated on.

Third, when you use other people's words and ideas without their permission, it is *stealing.* It would be wrong to sneak into a factory and steal the products manufactured there during the day, and in the academy words, ideas, paintings, compositions, sculptures, inventions, and other creations are what we produce. It is wrong to steal them and claim them as your own.

Plagiarism is a big deal in the academy.

There are many forms of plagiarism, some less flagrant than the examples I began with. However, you need to understand and avoid all forms of plagiarism. Presenting someone else's words or ideas as your own—in any form—constitutes plagiarism. Some forms of plagiarism are probably not obvious to you, so I want to spell them out in detail. I think much plagiarism is inadvertent and unknowing. I want to help you avoid that potential embarrassment.

Let's suppose you were assigned to write a book review of Theodore M. Porter's book, *Trust in Numbers: The Pursuit of Objectivity in Science and Public Life* (Princeton, NJ: Princeton University Press, 1995). In preparing to write your paper, you come across a book review by Lisa R. Staffen, published in *Contemporary Sociology* (March, 1996, Vol. 25, No. 2, pp. 154–156).

Staffen's review begins as follows: "It has become fashionable to reject the notion of absolute objectivity on the grounds that objectivity is simply unattainable or, even if attainable, is undesirable."

Staffen's opening is good, active prose. Let's suppose you like it. More important, you imagine that your instructor would like it *a lot.* You decide to start your paper as follows: "I feel it has become fashionable to reject the notion of absolute objectivity on the grounds that objectivity is simply unattainable."

This would be a clear case of plagiarism and therefore unacceptable. Adding "I feel" at the beginning is a nice, personal touch, but it doesn't change anything. Let's tell the truth: You have probably not spent a lot of your waking hours agonizing over "the notion of absolute objectivity," much less worrying about whether others would reject the notion or embrace it with passion.

Plagiarism: "I feel it has become stylish to reject the idea of absolute objectivity on the grounds that objectivity cannot be achieved."

Even this edited passage constitutes plagiarism. While you have changed some of the words—*stylish* for *fashionable, idea* for *notion*—the idea being expressed, along with many of the phrases, have been taken from someone else, without acknowledgment.

Leaving off "I feel," by the way, wouldn't absolve the sin. Anything you write in a term paper, unless you indicate otherwise, is assumed to be your own, original thought. It's fine to have original thoughts, incidentally. In fact, we encourage it. We're happiest when your thoughts and opinions are based in evidence and reasoning rather than rumor and belief, but don't feel that your professors are somehow perversely thrilled by the mindless parroting of ideas they already know about. (I know it sometimes seems like that.)

Plagiarism: "Many people today have rejected the idea that there is such a thing as absolute objectivity since they do not believe that it can be achieved."

Even though few of the original words remain in the passage, the thought expressed has been taken from another writer and offered as your own. Even if you found a way to express Staffen's idea without using *any* of her original words, that would still constitute plagiarism. Sorry. If you're going to use someone else's words or ideas, you have to give them due credit.

Use someone else's words and ideas, go to jail. Well, it's not quite that bad, but academics don't have much sense of humor about cheating. I'll admit, I kind of enjoyed the student who turned in a paper his friend had written for the same course the preceding semester. He just used white out to cover his friend's name and typed his own over it, and you could read the original name from the back of the page. He took the course again.

There is nothing wrong with presenting someone else's words and ideas in a term paper or in a published, scholarly work. In fact, any field of thought evolves as people read each other's ideas, learn from, and build on those ideas. The key to doing this properly lies in *acknowledgment* and *citation.*

When we borrow words and ideas from others, we acknowledge that we are doing so, and we give our readers a full bibliographic reference so they will be able to locate and read the original.

It might be useful for you to leaf through some academic journal articles. It will be clear that academics think it's fine to use other people's words and ideas. It's just important to use them appropriately. Use them as resources for building your own unique contribution to the ongoing conversation of ideas.

You might want to create a sculpture of an elephant. No problem. Get a block of granite and chip away everything that doesn't look like an elephant. Just don't pretend that you created the granite. (Unless you did, in which case I *really* apologize.)

Here's an example of how you might properly include Staffen's comment in your term paper, with a bibliographic entry at the end of the paper:

Proper use: Lisa Staffen (1996) begins her review of Porter's book by suggesting "it has become fashionable to reject the notion of absolute objectivity on the grounds that objectivity is simply unattainable or, even if attainable, is undesirable" (p. 154).

This gets the information out for the reader, and it would be accompanied by an appropriate bibliographic citation at the end of your paper:

Staffen, L. R. (1996). Featured essays. *Contemporary Sociology, 25*(2), 154–156.

Here are some other acceptable ways to use Staffen's passage. Each would be accompanied with a bibliographic entry at the end of the paper.

Proper use: In her review of Porter's book, Lisa Staffen (1996) says the idea of absolute objectivity is now commonly rejected as "simply unattainable or, even if attainable, [as] undesirable" (p. 154).

Proper use: According to Lisa Staffen (1996), it has become fashionable to reject the idea of absolute objectivity altogether (p. 154).

In summary, it is quite acceptable—even desirable—to include the ideas of others in your term paper. This can be a sign of good scholarship, as well as assuring your instructor that you've done some of the reading for the course. (We like to think you read some of it.)

However, it's important that you acknowledge and cite materials properly. The key is that your readers know what you are borrowing and how to look up the original materials.

By the way, if your instructor asks you to write a report on plagiarism, don't copy what you've just read here unless you cite it properly.

—Earl Babbie[1]

What's the Big Deal About Cheating?

What's the big deal about cheating? Isn't it an accepted part of school, even though every student has been told that cheating is not permitted? Schools and instructors have rules and punishments that explain the consequences of breaking these standards. But when researchers ask students whether they engage in serious cheating, the results are always a bit surprising to some. (Serious cheating is defined as copying another's work, using a cheat sheet, plagiarizing, turning in another's work as your own, helping someone cheat on a test, cheating on a test.) In a well-known poll, 80% of high school students, according to *Who's Who Among American High School Students,* admit to cheating.

These statistics immediately sound alarming to most instructors and administrators— little do they suspect. I share these statistics with the classes I teach and ask them to tell me honestly whether they are accurate. The response is always a resounding, "No!" They reply with a smile that the other 20% lied. Is it possible that everyone cheats?

---

[1]This text is excerpted from Earl Babbie's 1998 article (see http://www.csubak.edu/ssric/Modules/Other/plagiarism.htm).

While discussing this moral dilemma with my classes, I'm surprised at the answers they give as to why cheating is so rampant. First came the easy justifications of too much homework or irrelevant assignments. The deeply entrenched belief of the classes I have talked with is that cheating isn't wrong. When pushed, students usually crack and say blatant copying of a test or plagiarism is not right, but copying homework or comparing your answer on a test is just part of being a good student. In the background, what I think is happening here is that the pressure to succeed is more important than the implications of cheating.

In an era of downloading music and information, fudging on personal taxes, and corporate malfeasance, should we be surprised that students think cheating is a normal way to act? Whatever your answer to this question, the important fact is that cheating is moving from a moral and character choice to one of opportunity and success. This is something that needs to be examined more closely by us all.

So what's the big deal? Few things in our lives are truly our own. When you get right down to it, besides your thoughts and ideas, not much is uniquely personal. I know we can argue about appearance and style, but usually even these are takeoffs of others' designs that we adapt to how we want to be perceived or how we want to fit in. Our thoughts, however, although also influenced, are the inner core of our selves.

We have to ask, then, what are homework, tests, and projects in a classroom? Are they arbitrary institutional checkpoints, meritocracy markers, measurement of learning, or wastes of time? Again, the answer to these questions will vary by one's experiences, but no matter what the answer, if you turn in someone else's work, you give away the only thing that you really own—yourself. Claiming another's work as your own or copying someone's work is giving away your voice and self for a few points in a class; that is the big deal. It's a form of educational prostitution.

It might sound like I'm making too much of a small thing in your life, but think of the consequences. In college, there are few things that will get you kicked out of school, but one is academic dishonesty. Students are removed from school for failing and other incidents all the time and get second chances. However, if your academic integrity has been called into question, why should any institution believe that you are now honest and brimming with integrity? Plus, your whole academic record is now in question because if you were caught cheating, you probably cheated in the past. It is hard to gain back the integrity and trust that were once given freely.

Are our thoughts and integrity worth a few points on a test or an assignment? Do we value ourselves so little now that presenting others' work as our own doesn't even make us think twice? The one thing in life that we can be assured of besides taxes and death is that we are unique and have our own thoughts. So why give away so cheaply the one thing that makes us distinctive? Stealing others' property on the Internet is a different moral choice; selling others' thoughts as your own is self-destructive. Internally, it will affect how you view yourself, and externally, institutionally, it won't be just a slap on the hand when you get caught; it might also be a devaluing of your character.

I think we need to look at cheating as a question of character and integrity and not just as a way to achieve a prize in a competitive situation. Schools are competitive, and the pressure can be very high. However, do these pressures outweigh the costs of devaluing your character? I hope not. I believe a better choice is to turn in your own work and relish that no matter what the outcome, at least your ideas and thoughts are being evaluated. Of course grades matter, so study. Can a grade that isn't a representation of your work be more important than your integrity? So what's the big deal? You still have to look at yourself in the mirror and take ownership of your actions. So think about it before you start that next assignment or take that next test. (Of course that won't be until you finish downloading a pirated new song or movie from the Internet.)

—John Gunderson

Wisdom and Knowledge

In Chapter 8, we distinguish between scholarly learning and thinking and the wisdom traditions. Specifically we look at the following:

- Wisdom rather than knowledge and the value of that distinction.
- Where in the university to look for wisdom.
- The immense value of "unlearning" and moving beyond "thinking and ideas."

In college, when you are in the world of your professors and their classes, you are awash in a sea of knowledge. Occasionally, you are drowning in it—so much knowledge, so many facts and names and dates and theories, so many books and articles and handouts. Research indicates that the average college graduate, interviewed several years after graduation, remembers very little of all this. Few can even remember the names of any of the courses they took.

Just exactly what is useful in all this? What is expendable? I want to invite you to sit back for a long moment, away from the things you "must know" by next Tuesday, and consider what kinds of learning you really want and need so that you can choose and absorb and forget with a little sense of direction, rather than merely reacting to each new deadline.

First, *we must differentiate between the knowledge you will actually need in your future profession and the knowledge that is served up to broaden you as a human being.* This latter part of the curriculum is usually referred to as *distribution requirements* or, in reverent tones, as a *liberal arts education.* How much of your chosen major contributes directly to your future occupation differs greatly according to your concentration. In the natural sciences, much of what you learn will be directly usable. In the social sciences, arts, and humanities, it may be very little. A Bachelor of Arts in these subjects seldom leads to a specialized job. Students with degrees in sociology or English or economics may end up waiting tables, doing secretarial work, working for the phone company, or processing unemployment insurance applications. A few luckier ones may squeeze in on the bottom rung of a publishing house or land a good job organizing recreation for the city parks system. Those who go on to graduate schools usually find that it doesn't matter very much exactly what they majored in as undergraduates. There is a kind of pretense that this is not so. But when push comes to shove, the only job for which these majors directly train you is a job teaching somebody else social science, humanities, or art.

The claims of higher education are not limited to preparing you for a job. In small liberal arts colleges, there is a point of pride involved in the idea that these 4 years are not primarily directed toward utilitarian pursuits. These schools still wear the mantle of preparing the children of the rich. It is assumed that these folks have 4 years to spend on broadening themselves before they go on to some more definitely focused graduate education. Even though big universities and state and junior colleges proclaim less about the liberal arts, their undergraduate curriculum is largely indistinguishable from that of the small college.

In this section, I am not concerned with the occupational part of your training. What interests me here is the liberal arts portion of your studies: that portion of your education that is supposed to give you breadth and depth, to make you an "educated person," to acquaint you with the body of knowledge this culture has at its disposal so that you will not wander as a lost stranger in your culture but will be able to direct your future development with some discernment.

The first thing we must consider is that we live in a society whose store of specialized knowledge is so staggering that, confronted by it, any single individual, no matter how educated, is like a person wandering into the United Nations and trying to understand all the languages being spoken. On this score, we differ dramatically from earlier societies. One hundred fifty years ago, a college education could acquaint you with most of the general knowledge available in science, history, philosophy—in all fields. Today, 4 years of higher education cannot even acquaint you thoroughly with a single discipline. Obviously, then, we must be sophisticated in our approach to this huge forest of knowledge. What do we really need to become successful human beings? And, on the other hand, what can we leave aside, knowing that we can always dig it out of a book if we really need it?

Wisdom Rather Than Knowledge

I would like to suggest to you that what is essential is not knowledge at all but something else—something that has become almost unmentionable in the modern college or university: *wisdom*. We all know roughly what knowledge consists of. But what is wisdom? What I mean by this word is the ability to keep your emotional and mental balance in life, to understand yourself well enough to live comfortably with yourself. Thus, *wisdom is essentially self-knowledge*. But it also involves understanding the world you live in well enough to get where you want to go or to see danger coming before it hits you. Wisdom cannot be wholly self-centered, however. It must always include making contributions to other people and the natural world around you. There is wisdom in the old Jewish saying, "If I am not for myself, who will be for me? But if I am only for myself, what am I?" Self-knowledge is one aspect of wisdom; another is the emphasis on direct, experiential knowledge, for books are the tools of knowledge but experience is the tool of wisdom.

The academic version of knowledge involves a strict separation between pure, disembodied intellect on the one hand and the emotional/experiential life of the scholar on the other. These are two very different kinds of knowing. Let me illustrate the difference with an example. I taught a course in race relations during the stormy era of the early 1960s, when the civil rights movement was at its height and the Black urban uprisings were just around the corner. I had assigned my students some very angry writings by the Black author James Baldwin. But White students seemed unable to take Baldwin's message in and respond to it. Then I invited a local Black activist to speak to the class. He turned out to be a young man who was so angry that it was difficult for him to express the extent of his emotion in words. But one could feel it in the tone of his voice and the look on his face. After his talk, several students came up to me and said, "Hey, they are really mad, aren't they?" and "Now I suddenly understand what Baldwin was trying to say." The experience of the human contact broke through where the written word could not. Intellect alone could not fathom the phenomenon of Black anger. *The word is not the thing.*

Students seem, for the most part, to accept the separation between life and scholarship, which is considered good form by most of the faculty. This was often very frustrating to me as a teacher. For example, I used to teach the sociology of social movements. Each student studied a living movement and presented his or her findings in class. Throughout, I emphasized the ideological side of movements. The establishment has its own crazy ideology, of course, but movements show the craziness of belief systems more because they are likely to run counter to the established beliefs and are therefore more easily perceived as bizarre. Here is a group that preaches the advent of the savior in South Korea; here is another in which members speak in tongues to attain salvation; here is a little group clinging to the teachings of Leon Trotsky, one of the leaders of the Russian Revolution of 1918, later exiled and killed by Stalin. Over here are people who believe they can be cured of all the symptoms of aging through an all-vegetable diet; here is another group that believes that communists have taken over the United States. What we learn, of course, is that there is no belief so fantastic that some group of people will not adopt it, if doing so makes them feel better. The mind is endlessly inventive, and the mind is the servant of our emotional needs and wishes.

I did not suspect that I was throwing a curveball when I asked my students to comment on what the course had suggested to them about their own personal ideologies. To my great surprise, nobody had made that vital link; the students hadn't asked themselves, "If this is how other people's minds operate, what might this imply about my own beliefs?" This kind of separation in learning produces learned fools—people who can rattle off the ideologies of countless groups but still naively trust that their own version of truth is immutable and not to be questioned. I have said that wisdom is an unmentionable in the academy. Anyone claiming to offer it would be considered arrogant, opinionated, and unprofessional. Worst of all, such a one would be branded unscientific. Yet there is always the unspoken assumption that a lot of history will give you something called perspective, that literature will provide "insight," that social science will enliven you as a citizen, or that psychology will make you a little saner. The academy has not altogether given up on wisdom but has left it glimmering vaguely on the horizon without daring to approach it too closely.

To understand this state of affairs, it helps to take a look at the history of the modern academy to see how it got this way. The earliest Western universities were schools of theology designed to train priests. The Bible and Catholic theology were medieval Europe's version of wisdom. At the same time, it was their cosmology and included all the knowledge considered important. When modern science began, it developed in the shadow of this body of belief (though not entirely within the universities). Gradually, over several centuries, the various scientific disciplines developed and gained a foothold in the academy. At first, they were squeezed in under the general heading of "philosophy." Only in the 19th century were they given a separate status.

As the astounding power of science developed, the new fields broke off great chunks of the subject matter previously included in theology and philosophy. By the beginning of the 20th century, they already towered above all other subjects. Science was the goose that laid the golden eggs of medicine, industrial technology, and weaponry. In our century, all other subjects have existed only in the shadow of natural science. Theology was kicked out and permitted only a limited existence in graduate schools designed to train priests and ministers. To survive at all, social science, literature, and philosophy took on at least the outer trappings of the scientific method. To appear scientific (and, as I have suggested, to avoid conflicts with power), these subjects abandoned the claim to wisdom and gave themselves over wholeheartedly to the gathering and ordering of knowledge. Philosophy increasingly abandoned "value-laden" subjects like ethics for the more mathematical and scientific, and hence more respectable, areas of symbolic logic and philosophy of science. *Objectivity* became the watch-word. Scholars were told to completely separate themselves as human beings and citizens from their role as social scientists and to drop forever the questions that have always haunted the human race: questions of justice and injustice, avarice and generosity, enlightenment and stupidity.

Of course, there were always those who fought a rear guard action against these tendencies. The humanities, particularly, became the preserve of those who still wished to investigate values, yet even they were heavily contaminated. In every field, scholars had to become specialists to be respectable. Specialization had worked so well in science that now the historian had to be an expert on a single century; the professor of English had to lay claim to a single writer or period. Quantification invaded even fields like literature. Computers were drawn into service to analyze the use of adverbs and conjunctions in Shakespeare. Since highly specialized research was adding up to enormous breakthroughs in science, it was also posited that all the specialized, well-ordered research of social scientists and professors of the humanities would somehow, somewhere add up to a kind of knowledge that would serve us in the same dramatic way that science has served us. Students of these subjects were to benefit by becoming acquainted with the scientific methods applicable to their chosen fields and by studying examples of the many specialized fragments of knowledge that were becoming available. They were permitted to stand by and watch the research process, which might eventually lay another golden egg. As part of this process, students, like their teachers, were to separate themselves as human beings from their role as apprentices of research.

It is, of course, a tall order to evaluate the outcome of some 50 to 80 years of development in the social sciences and humanities, but we cannot wait forever. So far, the golden egg has not hatched. We have lots of psychologists but continue to run enormously high rates of mental illness. We have sociologists galore, but the social fabric continues to disintegrate at an alarming rate. We do not lack for historians, yet our national policies do not even take the next generation into consideration.

Social science has not achieved any real amelioration of our serious social problems. This is not because leaders do not know how to lessen these problems. They know! The problem is that the necessary changes require a commitment of resources and a willingness to break with established ways of doing things. Our leaders are unwilling to do either. This leaves social scientists exactly where the astronomers and engineers would be if there were no commitment to the space program. In light of this situation, it would behoove the social scientists to go over the leaders' heads and educate the public. Unfortunately, most do not even try to educate the public nearest them, that is, the students who pass through their classes.

More damning than this is that these disciplines do not even seem to enlighten the very people who specialize in them. It is an old joke that the psychologists are the craziest people on campus. This is perhaps untrue, but they are certainly not noticeably saner than their colleagues in math or physics. Sociologists, who specialize in forms of human organization and who have studied the inner workings of every major academic discipline, organize themselves exactly as badly as every other discipline. Nor are they known for their superior human relationships. Historians do not seem to have more perspective than other people, specialists in marriage get divorced at the same rate as other people, economists seldom get rich, and political scientists are as subservient to power as anybody. In fact, sad to say, academicians live no more wisely than other people. They are every bit as arrogant, competitive, and quarrelsome as corporation executives.

We would be suspicious of a physician who could not cure his or her own ill health, and we would think twice about depending on a safety engineer who burned his or her own house down. But we accept without much thought the overwhelming evidence that "physician, heal thyself" does not seem to apply to the experts who study human beings and their cultural creations. We cannot believe that all this expertise doesn't work. That is partly because in one way it certainly does work: It provides a good living for the experts. It may even provide you with a job someday. But if you wish to become wise, you must demand a little more than this.

Perhaps what I have said so far leaves you with the feeling that the situation is hopeless—that college will speak to your real human needs no more than high school did—even, perhaps, that wisdom is unattainable or must fall on a lucky few from out of the sky. Things are not entirely this bleak. The academy offers greater diversity and greater freedom of choice than high school. If you know what you are looking for, quite a lot can be found.

Choosing a Major for the Career-Minded Student

One of my most valuable college reads was Michael Lewis's *Liar's Poker*, his autobiography of his work as a trader at Salomon Brothers in the 1980s. What I took away was primarily his famous statement that there is no self-indulgence in the economics major. The book reminded me that liberal arts colleges are not intended to be trade schools. College is a place to "learn new things," but not because learning is mandatory like it was in high school, where everything is standardized. Rather, college is a place to indulge specialized curiosity and refine knowledge—hence, "liberal," as in an array of knowledge pools from which to draw information. Whether or not this information has any practical application to a career is, for the most part within a liberal arts framework, irrelevant. This is one thing I wish had really sunk in when I was just starting college.

—Sarah Nagy

Where to Look for Wisdom

Before we look for sources of wisdom in the academy, we had better zero in more closely on wisdom in its pure, concentrated form. It would not have surprised your grandparents, but it might surprise you, that wisdom is essentially to be found in the great religious traditions of the human race. We must discuss Christianity because we live in a culture that is heir to this religious tradition. But our modern culture has so twisted and obscured the real import of the New Testament that most of us have stopped looking in this direction for guidance in living our lives. It is, indeed, a little difficult to imagine the average suburban church as a vehicle of wisdom. This is not to say that there aren't some wise people among the clergy, but you have to look hard for them, just as you have to look hard among your professors.

In their pure and original form, all religions, including Christianity, are really operating in the area we now call psychology. That is, they are a body of practices and teachings that enable followers to be happy, effective people. They teach us how to meet life's difficulties with equanimity. They provide us with practices that teach us how to handle our mind and our emotions. Most of modern Christianity, however, has lost the psychological insights and has become a historical belief—for example, believing that about 2,000 years ago a certain person was born. This is history, not psychology.

Christian doctrine also contained a critique of established society, including the established church of that time. These are referred to as "the world," whose values we must shun if we are to have a happy life. But Christianity has long since made its peace with the world. To the extent that it survives, it generally sells out to the values of this world.

The supposed Christianity of our civilization has not kept us, as a nation, from stockpiling weapons to fry our enemies wholesale. Indeed, it is not an exaggeration to say that the modern consumer-oriented culture in which we live is, in many ways, the very antithesis of a religion that once advised us not to lay up treasures on earth. Under capitalism, the meek don't inherit the earth but end up tilling it at wretchedly low wages while the landowners ride around in luxury cars. In short, we have lost the wisdom of our religious tradition. It isn't at all difficult to imagine that perhaps, in a few decades, everybody will look upon December 25th as a commercial festival, quite forgetting that it ever had anything to do with a person named Jesus.

This is not at all unusual. Belief systems are seldom discarded by societies; rather, they are frequently reworked into their opposites, so that the very words that originally carried the kernels of wisdom become opaque and incomprehensible, even while they are dutifully repeated once a week. Indeed, there is a sense in which the core of religious teachings brought to us by some saint or prophet is already corrupted the moment it becomes institutionalized into the almost inevitable hierarchy and respectability of a church.

The Christian religion is, of course, only one among several great religious traditions in the world. In each of these, there is a body of teachings that purport to guide human beings in living their lives. The people who brought these teachings were what our society calls mystics. We have chosen to designate them with a word that indicates mystery because from the standpoint of our modern culture these people are, indeed, a mystery to us. What can Madison Avenue or Main Street make of a Buddha who spent years sitting quietly under a tree, not even thinking? We have a pretty good idea where they would put a modern Jesus who tried to drive the moneychangers out of Wall Street. Mystics are, to us, impractical people who don't know how to make a buck and might even end up on food stamps.

Let us look a little more closely at mystics and mysticism. Perhaps we shall find that they dispel mystery. Mystics are people who have their own direct experience of enlightenment. They are not theologians; indeed, they may advise their followers to throw away written tradition: "It is written, but I say unto you. . . ." They usually also make short work of religious institutions and their hierarchies. They are those rare souls who have broken free of inherited belief systems. In the realm of life, they are the explorers, the spiritual adventurers, the experimenters. They are closely akin to poets and revolutionaries, vagrants and saints. People hang around them because just being in their presence is joyful. (There are always more false mystics than real ones. And, since both kinds attract a following, much of what is taken for enlightenment is really just a group high.)

In every religious tradition, there are small groups of people who keep the essential wisdom alive. Unfortunately, they are difficult to locate in our society. In the Catholic Church, some of the religious orders perform this function. In Protestantism, the Quakers are notable for preserving the tradition. In Judaism, the Hasidic sects are close to the spirit of things. If you have access to any such groups, you are fortunate. But it will be difficult for you to judge when you are getting the "right stuff." Put it to the test and ask yourself, do the teachings provide you with joy and balance? Are the teachers themselves joyful, balanced, alert, and effective?

Strangely enough, the most powerful and pure modern representatives of religious mysticism among us are the Buddhists. This is not to say that Buddhism cannot also become institutionalized and go sour: It has done so in many of its home countries. Yet, for a variety of reasons, we currently have, in the United States, a fairly large number of genuine interpreters and teachers of Buddhism. I would like to tell you how I came to study them.

Fifteen years ago, I found myself utterly dissatisfied with the knowledge I had accumulated during many years of studying the most sophisticated modern behavioral sciences. I had ranged widely, over all the main fields of social science, and still I felt I had no real answers for myself or for my students. True, sociology enabled me to point out those features of society that make people unhappy. I could suggest changes in social organization that would ameliorate mental illness and crime. I could probably design a school that would make children creative rather than anxious. But the society in which I lived had no intention of permitting these changes to be made.

In the meantime, I and my students were stuck with the problem of how to live successfully in the world as it is. I looked around me at the college where I taught and saw that students were up to their ears in every kind of knowledge, yet most were feeling very lost. They couldn't handle their parents. They didn't know how to discover what work they were suited for. Every love affair sent them into paroxysms, first of joy and then of bitter anxiety. They lacked for friends among their peers and for role models among the adults around them. In short, their lives were out of balance. We were all, students and faculty, caught in harried schedules and making ourselves physically and mentally ill trying to keep up with each other. In classes, students feared the judgment of their peers and professors. Professors, on the other hand, labored in fear of their peers on the faculty and faced their students with various combinations of fear and contempt. True, we were making a living and getting our students certified to make a living, but the enterprise just didn't seem to be going anywhere. The more words we read and wrote and corrected, the further we seemed to be from peace of mind.

I had been acquainted with Protestant Christianity in adolescence but never really understood it. Most of our earnest discussions seemed to be about trying not to swear. Later, I read Western philosophy and decided to become an atheist because I couldn't imagine a God who actually assented to the injustice and brutality of life. When life became unmanageable for me, I frequented psychotherapists who helped me get over some of my more obvious madness. But, still, I felt that perhaps the problem of the meaning of life was just too deep. Nobody had the answer. I studied sociology in the vague hope of getting a larger perspective. It never seemed to come. Instead, sociology always circled back on itself with this theorist commenting on that theorist, who was trying to make sense of yet somebody else's theories: footnotes upon footnotes.

In the course of my studies and political activities, I came across mysticism. The Quakers appealed to me first because of their energetic and highly successful social programs. Yet, I also found that I liked their form of worship, which was, essentially, just sitting in silence. Silence made more sense to me than all the words swirling endlessly in my head. At least it had a healing quality and dignity. People are frequently charlatans with words, but it is hard to be a charlatan with silence.

I also became interested in the writings of Mahatma Gandhi, who led the Indian independence movement against the British armed only with his philosophy of nonviolence. Gandhi, too, I found, valued silence. In fact, he shocked my scholarly soul by suggesting that "the great principle of nonpossession" extended to the possession of ideas as well as worldly goods. My God! My whole life consisted of collecting ideas. I was paid for my collection of ideas. I put his view down as anti-intellectual and stored it away in the "useless" cubbyhole of my brain. And yet, it haunted me. Gandhi advised his followers to avoid needless talk because that would help them avoid needless thought. Could one really be better off without thought? It ran counter to my whole mode of life.

There was another direction from which my respect for systems of thought was being undermined even as I mastered more of them. Within sociology, there is a field that is seldom taught and even considered somewhat obscure: the field called sociology of knowledge. It is the study of how one's social position influences what one thinks. Karl Marx was the modern founder of this field. He pointed out that every social class has its own particular idea system (he called these systems ideologies). He showed that the ideology of a class always functions to buttress its own power position. If you were rich, you would believe in a whole philosophy that justified the survival of the fittest and proclaimed the ultimate good that comes to the community from the competition of rich people. If you were poor, you would believe that the rich are all corrupt and only the working class could govern in a just way if it took power. I was very intrigued by this type of analysis. As I studied the ideologies of various social movements, it did indeed seem to me that the human mind can believe anything that justifies its own ambitions and desires. The subtlety of this mind and its power of justification and invention are phenomenal. People can believe that the world is coming to an end next Thursday or that aliens have taken over the world banking system. People can believe that they should never see themselves in the mirror naked or that only in becoming nudists can they attain mental health.

But, still, I was a scholar. Didn't scholars have some kind of inside track on interpreting reality? About that time, I studied a book called *Ideology and Utopia* (1936) by a very famous German sociologist named Karl Mannheim. In it, he took off from Marx and showed how even the time sense of human beings was tied to their social position. If you were oppressed, you saw the past and present as leading to an inevitable future revolution followed by paradise. If you were powerful, the present seemed immutable to you. If you were in a group whose power was declining, you saw everything in terms of how the present had degenerated from an idyllic past. There it was again, the treacherous, self-serving human mind. And then Mannheim pulled a whopper. He said that the only people who could make sense of the world were the scholars because scholars didn't really have their roots in any of the economic classes. He called them the floating intelligentsia and proclaimed them the only source of wisdom. But wait a minute: Isn't this just the ideology one would predict for scholars? Hadn't he done just exactly what he accused all the other groups of doing by erecting a philosophy that made his own group out to be the best and only one to lead society? Mannheim was swallowing his own tail. At that moment, I stood on the brink and looked over the edge to oblivion. We were all going round in circles.

But I was a professor, earning my living by teaching ideas. Although my discovery shook me, I locked it away somewhere where it wouldn't bother me in my day-to-day work.

Unlearning: Beyond Thinking and Ideas

Fifteen years ago, I took some of these threads out of the closet and looked at them again. I perhaps was impelled by something that had happened to me in my personal life. (I never could keep my personal search separate from my scholarship as I was supposed to. I always had my grocery list on the back of my lecture notes.) For the first time, at the age of 40, I had found a happy love relationship. It profoundly changed my life and made me keenly aware that inner peace, joy, and all those unreachable items were indeed on the menu, if one knew how to order them. Other experiences had also given me the confidence to break with my scholarly tradition. Over the years, working in different universities and colleges, I had discovered that my learned colleagues were frequently very cowardly and untruthful. To my enormous surprise, I found that I had a little more courage than most of them. Here, too, was something my students were asking about—not just "How can you be happy?" but also "How do you retain your honor?"

It was at this point that I decided to take a few years off, if need be, to see whether religious mysticism might not hold the keys to what I was searching for. I began reading Eastern philosophy. The first thing I learned was that the Buddhist and Hindu philosophers insist that you really can't understand them on an intellectual level alone, that you have to do a thing called practice: You have to meditate, to seek the realm beyond words and beyond even thought. So I began to practice. It was all very undramatic. Not much happened at first. Yet, the deeper I went into this new area, the clearer it became to me that I had discovered a thought system about human life that was far more sophisticated and far more practical than anything I had learned so far. As I studied the Eastern masters, I began to remember and understand portions of the Christian Bible for the first time. They began to make sense, and it became evident that there was much in common between these seemingly disparate religious traditions.

I was particularly struck by one characteristic of the traditions I was now exploring: that the teachings insisted that "physician, heal thyself" had to be the real test. Those who called themselves masters of this mystical art were, indeed, people with very special personalities. True masters are very rare, but I was able to hear and take classes with a few who were obviously real. It made me feel better just to be in their presence. They seemed to radiate something we might call love, yet they were also fierce and direct, seeing into the lives of their students with a startling clarity. What they seemed to be saying was, "Who you are is important, not what you know." Knowledge might be a trap. Krishnamurti (1969), one of these true masters, has even given us a book called *Freedom From the Known.*

In sociology, we studied a process called socialization, the process by which the human child learns the rules and definitions of his or her culture. We looked on this process as a benign one, without which the human being would remain an animal, unable to live in society. But the Eastern philosophers looked at this socialization process through different eyes. In *Zen Mind, Beginner's Mind*, Suzuki (1970) says, "If your mind is empty, it is always ready for anything; it is open to everything. In the beginner's mind there are many possibilities; in the expert's mind there are few" (p. 21). To become enlightened, one had to unlearn one's culture and reconnect with the beginner's mind. Eastern philosophy reminded us that, as little children, we enjoyed a much more vivid experience of the world. Christianity, too, had advised us to become like little children again. The healing power of inner silence was a key to this unlearning—a break in the inward chatter that keeps our definitions alive. It did not mean that we would forget which fork to eat with at a formal dinner. You could know the rules and conform to them outwardly when you chose to do so, but it did speak of being inwardly free from the rules.

They told us that we never see the world as it really is. A gray veil of definition and admonition has been drawn between us and reality. We do not see a dance; we see sin. We do not see the human being; we see a Jew or a Black or a Republican. We react, not directly but through categories. When we make love, we do not just make love; we worry about whether it will improve or hinder our social status. We choose a life's work from similar considerations, never noticing until it is too late that we do not actually like the day-to-day routine it involves. Our marriages go sour because we never see our partner directly but only through a distorting prism of wishful thinking. We are caught inside our minds in repetitive circles that go round and round but never offer a way out. We are, in short, caught in illusion, and this illusion is learned from our culture. It can become so great that people commit suicide because they have lost their social position or march obediently into fire because they are loyal to an idea—the idea of their nation.

Even the very words we use to understand reality can obscure that reality. If you want to investigate the power of words over your thinking, try, for a month, to substitute the word *massacre* for the word *war* whenever you come across it in spoken or written communication. Now we have "World Massacre I" and "World Massacre II" and "The Civil Massacre;" we buy our children massacre toys. Changing this one word can alter your whole understanding of the phenomenon we call war.

While society trains us in its particular set of ideas, it also teaches us that without these ideas we would be monsters of immorality. Yet if one thinks over the list of atrocities committed in our century, they all seem to stem directly from belief systems, not from any absence of such systems.

If liberation lies in the direction of unlearning one's culture, then how can we get anywhere with this in college? College is, after all, a continuation of our indoctrination. If we don't watch it, it will not only fill our heads with a surfeit of ideas, but it will also teach us that we are better than other people who didn't go to college, part of a privileged elite. It is so tempting to become arrogant about your knowledge. *It is so simple to become an expert.* How can we pick our way among these boulders and find something liberating in this wilderness?

The very first admonition I would lay on you is that you should never separate yourself, who you are and how you experience life, from your studies. The key question to ask of any subject matter is, "What can it teach me about myself?" A related question is, "How does this apply to the way life is structured on this campus?"

Pursuing Wisdom in the Academy

In Chapter 9, we point out concrete ways for you to enhance that very special form of knowledge we call wisdom. We suggest ways in which you can make your search for wisdom count as part of your course load. In particular, we will explore the following:

- Using the college ambience (sort of like "global traveling" in it) to make contact with selves different from your own.
- Searching for wisdom in the curriculum.
- Seeking direct experience of the world.

Having said that the academy offers a great deal of knowledge, but little wisdom, I will nevertheless point out to you ways in which you can use your undergraduate years to enhance that very experiential form of knowledge we call wisdom. In college, you have two great advantages. First, most of you aren't working the full-time 40- to 60-hour week, which means that you have more time at your disposal than you may ever have again. The problem here is simply to make your search for wisdom count as part of your course load. I suggest ways in which you can do this. Second, you have at your disposal more cultural resources than you may ever have again. In this chapter, I talk about how you can use these to the maximum.

Using the College Ambience

Just as the best way to learn about your country is to travel to a different one, so the best way to learn about yourself is to make contact frequently with selves different from your own. This is why I have suggested that you seek out the nonconformist professors. Even more important is to seek contact with fellow students who differ from you in some important regard. *Students always learn more from each other than from their professors.* If you come from a White, middle-class home, hang around a bit with minority students, foreign students, students with disabilities, gay students, radical students, or any other group that is present on your campus. If these groups are organized, join one that holds a point of view different from your own. You can tell them you are just exploring. Groups are generally glad to attract new members on any terms.

The transition from high school to college forcefully introduces you to a much larger sphere of personalities, cultures, and sexualities. To hold strictly to your preconceived notions of personality types ("jocks," "nerds," "druggies") from high school is to do yourself an injustice by clouding your view and disallowing any social learning. While you will still find people who fit these isolated types if you focus narrowly enough, the truth is that most college students are rounded out by the experience of going through college with so many varied people. Allow yourself some freedom from judgment and view people as they are, not as you expect them to be. You may not even be sure where you fit in, so allow yourself some freedom in your own roles as well.

I am suggesting that you throw your net for friendship and acquaintance wider than just the cozy few with whom you feel most comfortable. Of course, you want these folks around, too, but they will only reinforce your current view of the world. You see, you cannot even know that you have a peculiar view of the world until you come in contact with differing views. (This is also, by the way, the classical liberal arts justification for requiring you to take a foreign language—a route for you to discover that you have, all along, been speaking your own peculiar language.) Without this, you will just assume that your version is the only possible one, or you may know that yours is only one point of view in a very general sense but without the specific little insights that create usable knowledge. Hence, your map of reality will necessarily remain narrow, and you will be blocked from many moves that you could make. Personal contact here is worth dozens of books or courses for stretching your mind and soul.

To make the most of your human contacts, *make it your practice to become a listener.* Ours is a society in which everyone is desperately struggling for attention. This was nicely addressed in an analysis of conversation behavior titled *The Pursuit of Attention* (Derber, 1983). In it, the author describes all the ploys and gambits people habitually use to bring the subject of the conversation back to themselves and to grab and hold the floor as long as possible. I believe the constant media romancing of "celebrities" is largely responsible for this sad state. But in such an environment, the occasional listener can benefit in many different ways.

First, listening is a wonderful spiritual discipline.[1] Listening forces you to lay the demanding "me me me" aside for a while. Thus, you deflate that overblown

---

[1]I must explain how I use the term *spiritual.* Christian doctrine separates the human being into flesh and spirit, and Western psychology and medicine adopted this division, calling it body and mind. This distinction is purely imaginary and conceptual. In the real world, we have only the human being, in whom what we call body and mind are inextricably intertwined. There is, in fact, no separation. I use the term *spiritual* to mean the whole person: body and mind and perhaps something that goes beyond the concepts of psychology and posits that there is, in the human being, a capacity to rise beyond the external circumstances—to live triumphantly, rather than merely be "well-adjusted."

attention-craving ego that gives you so much grief. At the same time, you attract people to yourself because everybody loves a sympathetic audience.

Most important, listening will enable you to learn a great deal. The talkers only repeat their tired old ideas over and over again to any audience, but the listener is constantly picking up new perspectives. Perhaps you will discover that other people's grief, fears, and embarrassments are very similar to your own. Perhaps you will be surprised to discover that some people operate very differently from yourself. In this arena, it is not the generalizations that matter but the vivid detail. It is the detail that catches you unaware and makes you say, "Aha! Maybe I don't need to be sexually jealous of my girlfriend—here is someone who isn't that way at all" or "Aha! Here is someone who is just as anxious about talking in class as I am, but she has found a way to nerve herself up to it."

So that you can make the most of listening, let me pass on a few techniques I learned from sociological fieldwork. First, shift your preconceptions and categories into neutral. You can always pick them up again when the experience is over, but, for the moment, listen to the categories your acquaintance is using—try to "feel" along with this person when he or she is angry, hurt, and so forth. In short, listen so attentively that you can, for the moment, stand in the other person's shoes and know how the world looks and feels to this person. To check on the accuracy of your understanding, play back what you think you heard: "You mean that you have never felt comfortable on this campus because it is a White outfit?"

In doing research, I also found that, to keep people talking, I did need to offer an occasional experience or view of my own because, as people reveal themselves to you, they become uncomfortable if they don't also know something about you. Therefore, you must occasionally respond with an "I had that experience too once," or "I know just how you feel. I felt that way myself." Only a little reassurance will keep the conversation going. Let every contact become an opportunity to voyage beyond the narrow self.

To forget the self, it is sometimes necessary to first explore the troublesome aspects of ourselves. We need to know ourselves, our weaknesses, and our confusions. Most colleges and universities offer psychiatric services to students. Take advantage of this. In later years, the same help will cost you a great deal. If you are troubled or perplexed about yourself, see a therapist. Most clinics permit you to change therapists if the first one doesn't suit you. They usually have a variety of people available. Getting a good, objective outsider's perspective on your problems can only help. Never feel that by going to the clinic you are admitting that you are flaky or weird. A very high percentage of students use these services, and it is by no means the sickest who seek the service out. Not only does it take a little confidence and energy to make an appointment but it also takes a little sense of humor about yourself. We are all a little crazy—it is just a matter of degree. Someone once said, "Normal is what people are until you get to know them."

If you don't feel you need individual help, consider joining a therapy group run by the clinic or perhaps a consciousness-raising group run by the women's center or some similar campus group or agency. Therapy groups (or encounter groups—they go by many different names) are absolutely wonderful because they enable you to observe other people with their masks off. Even though we know that we ourselves wear masks, we somehow believe the masks of others. Thus, we often think we are the only ones afraid or nervous—even though everyone in the room feels that way. We misperceive the world because we experience our own insides, but we only see other people's outsides. A group enables you to look behind the scenes, and this experience can greatly extend your capacity for sympathy with your fellow human beings. Ultimately, this will turn into sympathy for yourself—something almost everybody could use more of. Of course, you can also use the group as a sounding board for your own feelings, but be assured you can almost always avoid doing so if you don't want to. In most groups, there is a lot of competition for the floor. You can usually lie low as long as it suits you.

So go over to your counseling center and see which groups or workshops are offered. Jump into a few. Psychodrama is a particularly good method. Again, as with professors, try to find out the reputation of the various group and workshop leaders. The usefulness of groups depends heavily on having a good leader, though I have been in some very good groups that operated completely without professional leadership.

Wisdom in the Curriculum

Now, let us take a look at ways in which you can seek wisdom within the curriculum requirements of your school, remembering that wisdom consists both of self-knowledge and of a lively "feel" for the world in which this self lives and moves. Cultural anthropology is almost always conducive to developing wisdom about how your culture molds your personality. As you study and compare societies very different from your own, you will have many "Aha!" experiences: "Well, so every culture isn't as afraid of touching as ours;" "By comparison with this group, how little human solidarity we have to live with;" and so on. Cultural anthropology is usually a popular course and for good reason. Avoid it only if it has a bad reputation among students on your campus.

Psychology courses, particularly clinical psychology and social psychology, can also make you wiser to your own functioning. These courses may come under a variety of headings, like "Social Psychology," "Theories of Personality," "Abnormal Psychology," "Psychology of Small Groups," and "Self and Society." Sociology can prove a fruitful field. Sociology also offers courses in social psychology and small group behavior. (Look out! These sometimes can be highly quantitative, in which case they will not serve our purposes.) Sociology also offers classes on the structure of society: for example, "Class Stratification," "Race Relations," "Complex Organizations," "The Media," and so on. At their best, such studies can offer you a map of the society in which you must travel all your life. It helps to know where the brick walls are, so you won't run into them. They will also, it is hoped, extend your sympathy for your fellow human beings.

If you are fortunate enough to be on a campus with minority centers offering courses on Black, Hispanic, Asian American, and other minority groups, take a few and expose yourself to classes in which there will be a very different student group and different atmosphere from the rest of the campus. If there is no special center for such courses, they may be offered in the regular curriculum. These courses are often best when offered by professors who are themselves members of a minority group (though this aspect is, of course, no guarantee as to the quality of the course).

If you wish to explore your ethnic heritage, but find that there aren't any courses on your own ethnic background, you might consider taking a course in the history, literature, or culture of the country from which your forebears came. Area studies are worth checking for this. Of course, you could zero in on the American phase of your background by designing an independent study on your group's sojourn here.

The fields of political science and economics are also fertile domains to explore, though sometimes they can be more conservative than the fields of sociology and psychology. They are closer to the realms of power because they train many students to go into government or corporate service, and sometimes their faculties tend to have closer ties in these quarters. Yet you may find economics departments giving a course on the economics of Marxism, giving you a glimpse of a usually "forbidden" heresy. In political science—also in sociology, history, and economics—look for "comparative" courses, such as "Comparative Revolutionary Movements," "Comparative Analysis of Industrial Democracies," or "Comparative Socialist Societies." A comparative course is good for getting the broader picture.

Many great fiction writers were wise people, so there is real wisdom to be garnered in the area of literature. The difficulty lies in the fact that many literature professors are more interested in form than in content, that is, in the writer's skill with words rather than in his or her wisdom. My friends in literature tell me that looking at the form of a novel is looking at it as art, as a thing of beauty. They say that beauty and truth are one. Yet I must argue back that artistic talent does not necessarily go with the kind of wisdom needed to live one's life. Artistic ability occurs in people of the most diverse personality styles. There are happy painters and suicidal painters, joyful writers and psychotic writers. Certainly, their artistry must have been the best part of some of these sad lives, but it was not enough to heal them.

To me, the most troublesome aspect of Western fiction is that by constantly describing to us the character's emotions and thoughts, the authors imply that the noisy, storm-torn mind is the inevitable state of human consciousness. If you can find a literature professor who is willing to argue some of these issues with you, you might just have a lot of fun.

All of the applied arts—music, dance, drama, creative writing, painting, sculpture, glass blowing, weaving, and so on—can be fun and a welcome break from your other courses. Sports can also function this way. Try to work such a course into every semester, if you can. Courses in literature or in the history of art or in music theory are likely to involve more of the usual reading and writing but may be worth taking if they are well taught. Experience with a sport or art can greatly increase your enjoyment of professional performances, even if you are not particularly talented yourself. If you are, they can provide you with a satisfying hobby.

Wherever you can find a natural science course (or professor) that preserves and honors science's connection to human life and inquiry, it will prove most interesting. The problem here is that most science departments design their introductory courses to serve only their own future majors, rather than offering courses broad enough to be of interest to nonmajors. You are fortunate, for example, if your campus offers courses in the history of science or technology for nonmajors.

It always puzzles me that in a society that revolves so heavily around science, we seem to garner so little wisdom from our scientific knowledge. To see ourselves in the perspective of evolutionary time, or geological time, or even the immense time of the astronomers should surely help us to assess our importance in the scheme of things. Yet scientists seldom draw such connections between their specialties and the culture in which we live. If you can find such a science professor, he or she would be well worth your while.

Languages, if you enjoy them, are interesting because they are windows into another culture. When you travel, you will also find that it is a far more exciting experience when you know even a little of the language.

Philosophy and religion departments may offer courses such as "Individual Morality and Social Justice" or "Man, Nature, and Society in Western Literature," for example, which explore problems we confront in our own lives. A course in Marxism would be good. Courses in existentialism may also be of interest. Existentialism has a lot in common with Eastern thought. I used to tell my students that Buddhism is just existentialism without the "Oy, veh!"

Courses in Eastern thought or in mysticism may be offered by philosophy or religion departments. These courses may be so academic as to be nearly useless for your purposes. Check the readings. If they stress a history of ideas approach, with lots of dates, names, and the history of various schools of thought, you should avoid them. The useful course will offer readings that speak to you directly about your life. But we must be cautious here because Eastern thought is difficult to understand at first, even when it is the real thing, because such books invite you to observe the workings of your mind, and this is difficult for the mind to grasp. The English language, with its Western cultural connotations, is also a difficult language in which to express the insights of Eastern thought. A measure of difficulty must, therefore, be expected.

Most large campuses will also have some organizations that teach Buddhism, yoga, or meditation. These would be worth exploring. One college professor who recently reviewed this book made the following very valuable observation:

> Meditation is understood by most of my students as a weird, freaky, bizarre activity for cultists. Something reserved for strange out-group types— definitely not for them. Therefore, it would be helpful to give an example or two of some important person who regularly uses some form of meditation for strictly practical purposes, such as better achievement in sports or greater stamina in arduous campaigns. For example, the former president of Costa Rica told me that he amazed his co-campaigners with his stamina, which was sustained by recurrent 10- to 15-minute moments of meditation—a technique he learned in India on a trip with his friend Vincent Hardin (who was one of Dr. Martin Luther King's close advisors). It's like the "siesta" that students think is for the lazy, when in fact a half-hour siesta is what allows many of the world's inhabitants to get through 17-hour workdays. I dwell on this topic because simple, practical forms of meditation are one of the most concrete

and valuable things students can take away with them and use to their advantage throughout the rest of their lives.

To line up your courses, curl up with your institution's catalogue one evening and really explore the offerings. When looking for courses to take, remember my advice in Chapter 5, and choose by the professor's reputation rather than by the subject. Go to a lecture by the professor you are considering the semester before you would sign up for the course. This will give you a feel for the professor's teaching. If you can, strike up a conversation with a student in the class and see what he or she says about the professor's teaching methods.

Ask the professor to give you a reading list, and spend a few hours in the bookstore or the library looking at the material to see whether it interests you.

Watch also for interdisciplinary courses or courses that are different, new, or experimental. Professors and students alike are usually up for such courses just because they are out of the ordinary. If your school offers semesters abroad or exchanges with other American schools, take advantage of these, if at all possible. Travel to new environments is invariably enlightening.

Seeking Direct Experience of the World

Now, let us turn our attention to ways in which you can garner wisdom outside of the ready-made courses we have been discussing. Because direct experience and human contacts are so crucial to the development of wisdom, choose fieldwork over library research whenever that option is offered in any course. Even if the option is not specifically offered, professors may give you special permission to do fieldwork in place of library research if you go to them with a convincing project. Fieldwork projects will also ease the heavy reading requirements you always face in college.

Let us say, for example, that you are taking "America Since 1900." A fieldwork project here might be to interview older people about the changes they have lived through. Your town's senior center or a minister could probably provide you with names of respondents. This is oral history, a perfectly legitimate aspect of the historian's craft. Or, for a trip to the library that is a little more fun than the usual, take an event that interests you—perhaps the freedom rides of 1961 or the Cuban missile crisis—and look up the contemporary coverage of the event in old newspapers and magazines. You must take a very specific situation because there is so much coverage available. Old newspapers are a bit more difficult to explore because they are usually on microfilm, but old magazines are in the original and can give you a real feeling for the look and texture of another historical period.

Let us say you are taking a course in social stratification. Here you have many fieldwork possibilities. You could take two churches or two elementary schools in different income neighborhoods and visit each. Attend church services and smaller meetings and interview the minister. In the schools, ask to watch several classes and observe playground behavior. A session of sitting in the teachers' coffee room can also be very enlightening. In each case, contact the principal or minister ahead of time, preferably with a letter from your professor on school stationery vouching for your earnest purpose. It is a good move to offer the institution a copy of your final paper, in the hope that your findings may be of some use.

If you are interested in city planning, do a survey of recreational facilities and parks available in different income areas. Students of mine have investigated hospital emergency rooms, massage parlors, clothing stores, restaurants, and many other neighborhood features in this way.

With a little imagination, you can think up unusual projects for many classes. When you approach the professor, you should be able to present a good reason for wishing to engage in your project: "I would like to work with older people when I become a social worker" or "I am planning to be an elementary school teacher, so I would like to observe class differences in schools."

Perhaps you can mention that you have become interested in this particular phenomenon through personal experience or through some previous course work. If you are going to do interviews, have a first draft of a questionnaire ready to show the professor. If you are going to observe, have a well-considered list of things you plan to watch for and make notes of. Ask your professor to suggest a relevant existing study or two.

Your very best opportunity to design your own education lies in independent study courses. Most campuses offer these, but relatively few students take advantage of them. All it takes is a professor who will sponsor you. Let us say, for example, that you are planning to be a teacher and have gotten yourself a job helping part-time in a school; it may be a volunteer job or it may pay a little. Let us also suppose that you are working in a predominantly minority school. Find yourself a professor of sociology—whoever teaches sociology of education would be a good bet—and tell him or her about your job. Suggest that you enlarge your understanding of the things you will be encountering in your job by interviewing teachers, principals, and board of education members about the problems of the district. (You may be mainly interested in minority children, but it is wiser not to announce this specifically to school authorities, as they may be particularly touchy in this area. Of course, let the professor in on your true interest.)

Gather together a few books pertinent to the subject, and ask the professor to suggest others to you. When approaching a professor about fieldwork independent study, it is wise to include some reading in your plan. Because professors generally believe it is their duty to get the maximum of reading and writing out of the student, you don't want to give the impression that you are trying to get out of this requirement. You will, of course, usually have to write a paper about your findings.

You may have found yourself a paying or volunteer job with your local senior center. You will learn a great deal in this setting, but you can enhance your learning and garner academic credits by arranging an independent study in which you can write up your experiences, together with doing some reading in the field of gerontology. A sociologist who gives classes on aging, the life cycle, or urban problems would be a good sponsor for this project.

These two projects can provide excellent support on your applications for graduate school or for jobs in teaching or working with older people, especially if your independent study director gives you a good letter of reference. Both the experience in the field and your initiative in designing such an independent study will make your application stand out.

A student of mine who had a very ordinary summer job at Big Sur did an excellent independent study analyzing the social groups making up that resort area and their interactions with and opinions about the tourists with whom they dealt. Another student, who was wrestling with his homosexual feelings and trying to explore the gay world at a local gay bar, did a brilliant analysis of the various types of gayness, which gays themselves recognize and distinguish. Another student turned a trip to Scandinavia into an independent study by visiting elementary schools in Sweden and the United States and doing a comparison between the two school systems. The project enriched her experience in Scandinavia and looked very good on her application to a graduate school of education. Another student, who was planning to go into architecture, did a study of the way campus space was used by formal and informal groups. He focused on where people hung out, where they studied, made love, or even did drugs. His report took the form of a large map with several overlays depicting various types of use.

Perhaps you are wondering whether you would become a conscientious objector and refuse to be drafted. Although you have been taught the dates and names of all our wars over and over again during your schooling, none of it has given you the slightest idea of what actual combat is like. All media falsify this subject, and combat veterans usually keep silent because the experience is so utterly alien to everyday life that they fear people wouldn't understand. Yet you may find that, if you talk with relatives and friends who have been in combat, they will tell you the truth. Such an interview study would also fit into classes in history and sociology.

There are many ways to explore different occupations that interest you. A very good way is to do an interview study of people who have been successful in a particular occupation: successful lawyers, teachers, legal secretaries, and so forth. You can get a good feel for what the job is like and what people love or hate about it. There will usually also be some published research available on such occupations. Some institutions may permit you to become an intern or just observe the work environment. This type of experience can easily develop into an independent study project and can greatly help you decide on a future occupation.

Let us say that you have been elected to chair your local feminist group, and you would like to get some credits for the time you will put in. Here, you might plan an independent study project in which you will prepare, for your written report, a handbook for future chairwomen of the group, recording everything that will be of use to them. Is your group having trouble getting enough members? Do an interview study of a sample of women students to see whether they are aware of your group, why they do not join, and what would draw them in.

Perhaps you would like to make an independent study project out of an attempt to bring about social change in a nearby community. One of the most dramatic ways I know to change the whole atmosphere of a retirement home, reform school, prison, or children's group in an inner city neighborhood is to get people gardening: vegetables mainly, but also some flowers. The National Gardening Association (http://www.garden.org) sponsors such projects with support money and gardening supplies. In many areas, they also teach gardening and how to develop community gardens. Nothing is more therapeutic than gardening. Of course, you could start a community garden on your campus, too. If your independent study project is in sociology, part of your project would consist of assessing the changes in individual behavior and group morale brought about by the garden.

On some campuses, professors are only willing to take a small number of independent study students each semester. Therefore, you must set your course up during the preceding semester. This will also give you time to pursue several teachers until you find one who is willing to take you. If, after making a timely and well-prepared effort, you cannot get anyone to take you on, you have cause to complain. If your school doesn't offer independent study, you also have good cause to complain. Sometimes such a complaint may get you some action.

Independent studies are excellent ways to get at least one or two professors to know you well enough to write an informed recommendation when you need it. Once you have set up a study, you should put forth your very best effort. *Remember that the trick lies not in getting out of as much work as possible but in designing work that really interests you and then doing it well.* Students sometimes fall down on independent studies because their other courses seem more immediately pressing. It is best, therefore, to schedule a number of meetings with your professor and to set up a schedule of the work you will complete for each meeting.

The key to a good field research paper is keeping notes regularly, day by day. After each interview session, sit right down and type out your notes. After each visit to the school or church, write out your impressions. You will lose 50% of the important details if you wait two days and 80% if you wait until the end of the semester. Take notes whenever the situation allows you to do so without disrupting what is going on or destroying the rapport with the people you study. These notes will necessarily be brief. This is why you have to expand on them right after the contact is over. It is best to write or type them onto half sheets or cards, with one respondent and one subject per card. These may later be easily sorted.

One final word about fieldwork: Unfortunately, our government's economic policies have created abject poverty in most of our inner cities. These areas have become the scene of much violent crime. You must, therefore, enter these areas with caution. I hope you will enter them because our ignorance of this disaster is catastrophic for our society, but you must also be realistic. Before you undertake a project in such areas, talk to people on the faculty who know them. You might also approach the area through a church or social agency. They will know the ropes well enough to clue you in. Never go alone at night. If at all possible, it is better to work in such areas in pairs.

Finally, if your campus permits you to design your own major, this is an excellent opportunity for you to think through exactly what you would like to get out of your college education. It also enables you to combine two or more fields that interest you, and you may be able to omit required courses you wish to avoid in any one field.

A good reason for designing your own major is that degree requirements and the curriculum generally have not really been designed with undergraduates in mind. Rather, they directly reflect what your professors had to study in their PhD programs. They are therefore directly applicable only to students who plan to get PhDs—a tiny minority.[2] For example, if you are planning to be a social worker, it makes little sense for you to take all the requirements for the major in sociology or in psychology. The "History of Sociological Theory" will not help you much: neither will courses in learning theory in the psychology department. What you need is a combination of courses chosen from both fields, with courses at any available minority studies centers thrown in.

Many campuses offer joint majors, which allow the student to combine and revise the requirements of two related disciplines. If your college doesn't let you design your own major, a joint major may offer some of the same advantages.

In this section, I tried to start you thinking of ways in which you can make your education more directly experiential and thus more conducive to wisdom. In doing so, you will be counteracting what I call the maximum learning blockage of higher education. By this I mean the recent historical arrangement by which 18-year-olds with little knowledge of the world are locked away for 4 years with others similarly inexperienced and usually from the same background: the suburban middle class. Where possible, all these folks are put together in dormitories. Then, they are assigned so much reading and writing that they can rarely leave the campus. Though this arrangement has been shifting in the past decade, it still remains the primary structure of college. If one were to design a method for making the future professionals and business leaders ignorant of the world, one could hardly come up with a better trick. It is unfortunate enough to do this with science or arts students, but to do so with students of social science appears to be quite lunatic. In addition, field and laboratory experience is always offered in science but only rarely offered in social sciences. No geology department would dream of teaching only from books. Society really wants good geologists; it doesn't want good sociologists.

Where one sees a lunatic pattern applied almost universally, one must perforce ask the question, "Is this done intentionally?" Such a suspicion gains force when one considers the hostility with which the academic establishment met the demands for the admission of more minority students and students from low-income groups during the struggles of the 1960s. It was felt that such students would harm "academic standards" and could easily become "disruptive." Education, it seems, should be a matter for the elite, and one certainly does build in-group loyalties with that elite by these methods.

Indeed, *many within the academy would say that any de-emphasis on reading and writing is anti-intellectual.* On this score, I would like to say that attaining the wisdom to lead one's life is no more an anti-intellectual undertaking than learning to play the flute. You cannot learn to play by reading and writing about it, though you may wish to study some written texts on the instrument. To play the flute, you must educate the ear, the hands, and the mouth, in addition to developing certain aspects of the intellect. Attaining wisdom is very similar. It requires the education of the body, the senses, and what we sometimes call the heart. An overemphasis on reading and writing—as in the case of the flute—can get in the way.

---

[2]Often what gets included in an academic discipline is the result of historical accident. The social science and humanities fields are not governed by the strict internal necessities that govern more natural science fields.

Traveling Abroad

Traveling abroad, whether it is for leisure, business, or for academic purposes, can truly be an enlightening experience. It will not only enable you to develop new perspectives on foreign cultures and lifestyles, but it can also influence your existing domestic views.

You must not, however, merely *travel* abroad; instead, allow for immersion in the different culture(s). This can be achieved by living in the chosen society for a substantial amount of time. Living abroad (if your budget permits), rather than being a tourist, is the most effective method for this life-enriching, unforgettable experience.

Being a tourist means that you are giving yourself a label that says to others that you are foreign or different. The purpose of living abroad is to incorporate yourself as much as possible with the locals, to truly give yourself a sense of the cultural and societal similarities and differences, and to ultimately give you a better understanding of yourself.

Living abroad will definitely enhance your life. However, if you can only be a tourist, you can still enrich yourself historically and socially by visiting the sites and interacting with people as much as possible—it is imperative that you have conversations with "the natives" and always leave your familiar home group as much as possible. It is truly amazing to be able to see firsthand the places you once read and learned about in your history books. The interaction will allow you to delve into the culture more deeply, and it helps to alleviate or destroy possible cultural barriers.

Most colleges have programs with various foreign colleges throughout the world. If travel to a particular country or program is not available through your campus, other local colleges may offer it, and your academic counselors can usually arrange to have classes and credits transferred. These programs range from academic classes to internships and work opportunities. Independent studies in one's field can also be organized. Almost any kind of program is available, including a semester at sea. In addition to the vast choices in countries and types of programs available, the length of the program also varies. Depending on your preference, a summer, quarter, semester, or even a year or more can be spent on your adventure abroad.

For most college students, going abroad is very appealing, but only a small number take full advantage of the opportunity. The cost is one of the major setbacks and concerns for people. What many people do not know is that financial aid and scholarships are available. One's college years are the prime time for such an opportunity, and some people have even taken loans to help finance the trip. I will not tell you that it is not expensive, but I will tell you that it is *well* worth it.

Yet another concern of people who are interested in going abroad, especially to a foreign country, is that they may feel awkward and uncomfortable in an environment where the people, languages, food, customs, and places are all different. We all have felt awkward entering a new school, starting a new job, or moving into a new neighborhood, but as time passed, we became accustomed to our surroundings and eventually found our comfort zone. Traveling abroad is similar. To truly benefit from living abroad, one must consistently practice an open mind and cultivate an attitude of inquiry. Naturally, things will be different. That is one of the main reasons for going!

One of the greatest advantages of going abroad is freedom. Studying abroad will, of course, not completely free you academically, but it will allow you to be free in other unexpected and unforeseeable ways. It frees you from parents, siblings, roommates, bosses, and other constraints or obligations, though temporarily. If you have never lived away from home, it will teach you in a very accelerated way to become independent and a more self-sufficient person. If it is not your first time away from home, travel will undoubtedly give you time to grow as a person and gain a better understanding of yourself.

Studying abroad allows you free time to reflect, to both directly experience and analyze views of the world and where you and others fit in it. It opens your eyes to what you have accomplished and what you have yet to accomplish. It opens avenues for future opportunities—and it looks great on your resume!

Since I am from the University of California (UC) system, let me discuss how that is set up: There are a number of different Education Abroad Programs (EAP) that work quite conveniently with the regular course curriculum. The UC system works through and with different schools in the United States and internationally to give students the opportunity to enhance their college careers. The student generally has a wide selection of classes from which to choose, and those classes transfer directly as credit toward their intended degree.

For the most part, these programs give the student the opportunity to interact with other students from the host country and to experience the culture firsthand. Also, because these programs encompass the entire UC system, the students have a bit of security, in case they start feeling homesick. In my experience, I got the chance to meet other students from my school and even my hometown.

It really felt great to come back to school and see a few more familiar faces. I sometimes would stop and think that if I hadn't attended the program, these people would be just some more of the faces in the crowd whom I would not know and would just walk by. There are a few other people who live a bit farther away and whom I cannot see on a regular basis, yet still I stay in touch and network with them, either on the phone or through e-mail.

Programs that include working, volunteering, or interning are generally considered nonacademic and are part of the International Opportunities Program (IOP). The countries that have EAP opportunities generally also have programs through which IOP opportunities can be arranged; however, because IOP is a nonacademic program, EAP grants and other financial aid are not available. There are, however, special scholarships and loans specifically for the participants in these programs.

Going abroad taught me that there is an infinite wealth of knowledge in the world. I once read, "The more I know, the more I realize how much I do not know." So for me, the more I learn, the more I realize how much I want to learn. I was in an EAP summer program at Pembroke College in Cambridge, England. I took two classes, "The World Economy Today," which counted toward my economics major, and "The Glories of Venetian Art and Painting." Both classes interested me, but I was fascinated by the professors' stories and knowledge.

Part of the reason for my fascination was the more intimate size of the class; the professors knew everyone's name. (This was something I was not accustomed to at the University of California, Irvine, where my classes were mainly in large lecture halls.) Also, the professors were multifaceted, very personable, and they ate lunch with the students almost every day, addressing any concerns that became evident during the program. It was also memorable to see the buildings with amazing architecture that housed numerous scholars.

I cannot stress enough the value of such an opportunity. The fear of missing family, friends, a boyfriend/girlfriend, or other activities while you will be gone should not hinder you. Upon returning, you will find that not much has changed since you left, except yourself. Also, modern technology enables easy communication, and absence does make the heart grow fonder.

I hope that I have stirred up thoughts of going abroad. I encourage you to explore further the vast number of opportunities available. Of course, use the Web, but the best resource for this is your school's international academic affairs department, which will have interesting pictures of places and information about programs abroad as well as scholarship and financial aid information. There are many catalogues about the programs, schools, and the host countries. There are even lists of participant students who can be contacted for recommendations about their respective programs. You will also generally find enthusiastic people working there who have probably gone abroad themselves and will be happy to address any questions or concerns that you may have. You can also pick up a few interesting and informative brochures to read and to show your parents. Once you have run out of excuses, you can start making arrangements for your trip. It requires some paperwork, and deadlines are fast approaching!

—Lynette Albovias

Thus far, we have talked mainly about observing the world. You will, of course, also gather self-knowledge during these encounters. In Chapter 10, I will introduce you to some of the ways in which you can zero in more directly on the problem of the self by sharing with you some of the ways in which I tried to combine Buddhist philosophy with behavioral science to help students explore their inner landscape.

Adventures in Desocialization

Am I me, or am I society? In Chapter 10, we explore a variety of ways in which to make fish become aware of water and even, at times, to leap up out of it. In particular, we will explore the following:

- "The Self: Reality or Illusion?"
- An exercise to illuminate "Self/No Self."
- A look at the "Ideal Self/Real Self" dichotomy, only perhaps to find they are both illusions.
- An exercise called "The Critical Voice," which involves trying to name that voice inside our heads that generates so much of our misery and suffering.
- An exercise called "Roots," which explores where ancestors end and self begins.
- An exercise called "Slowing Down," which plays with eliminating from our life "time" and "stress."
- Looking at our "Maximizing and Minimizing" and finding, rather, the golden mean.
- Looking at our beloved "Daydreams" and "Great Expectations" and considering, rather, ways of paying attention to the present moment.
- Resources for a "Desocialization Course."

When I was teaching, I tried to use sociology to make students aware of the ways in which society has trained them to look at the world and at themselves. The object was to free people from the influence of society, that is, to begin to undo the indoctrination each of us has undergone growing up in this particular society. I believed that as we became conscious of the many specific ways in which our inner experience of reality had been conditioned, we might throw off this conditioning and create greater inner freedom for ourselves. In line with this, I developed a course called "Adventures in Desocialization."

Socialization is the name sociologists give to the process by which children are inculcated with the beliefs of their culture. Sociologists study this process in great detail, demonstrating how we are, completely, creatures of our culture. However, they never seem to step beyond this stage and actually try to free us from social conditioning, nor do they even point out that this freedom is possible.[1] Yet their studies of resocialization during adulthood—when someone goes into prison or into the army, for example—demonstrate that we are capable of changing enormously if our environment changes. We know that it is possible to resocialize people, but is it possible to desocialize without taking on any new set of beliefs and pressures? The Buddhists say yes, that this, in fact, is the path to enlightenment.

In this chapter, I offer you a series of exercises that were successful in helping students to begin to free themselves from conditioning. Of course, the exercises are only a first step, but they can introduce you to new ways of observing the world and yourself. They are the initial wedge entering between you and your internalized beliefs and habits. I suggest that you do each exercise before reading about the way my students responded so that you will have your own experience first, before you see what you have in common with, or how you differ from, others.

The Self: Reality or Illusion?

I have said that *wisdom consists of self-knowledge.* We have to look at this in greater detail. None of us is very fond of people who constantly think about themselves, analyze themselves, and talk about themselves. All of us like somebody whose "self" doesn't intrude very much, in the sense that such a person has plenty of attention and energy available for people and things outside. These people probably engage in relatively little self-criticism and self-laceration. We sense that, somehow or other, their self is not a problem. So perhaps what we wish to eliminate is something we might call the problematic self, the one that gives us problems.

It may help us to look at the way *self* has been conceptualized in more than one culture. We can compare our view of self with that of a radically different cultural system, that of Zen Buddhism. The New Testament strongly advised people not to take the self seriously. Are you worried about how you are dressed? The New Testament tells us to be like the lilies, which never worry about how they look but are nevertheless beautiful. It warns us not to inflate the self through the possession of wealth, power, or fame. It even advises us to "lose ourselves" to attain salvation: not in the hereafter, but in the sense that we may find refuge from all worry right here in this life. These messages accord closely with Zen Buddhism, which goes so far as to call the self an illusion that has been implanted in us by society: a sort of bogeyman who scares us but, when we look, is not there at all. Unfortunately, over the centuries, European Christianity perverted the meaning of the Scriptures. *Selflessness* came to mean self-condemnation. We were supposed to despise the flesh as sinful and to engage in all sorts of self-laceration to drive the devil out

---

[1]For an exception, see Wrong (1967).

of ourselves. Thus, subtly perverted, the message became one of paying constant and fearful attention to ourselves, lest we fall from grace through a wrongful feeling or thought. The self, far from being dropped as an illusion, became the center stage on which the drama of salvation and damnation was played out. In addition to our troublesome earthly self, we now had an eternal self to worry about, and because the afterlife was fraught with terrible hells, our anxieties increased accordingly.

A reaction to a bad system is, all too frequently, another bad system, which really is the mirror image of the first. During the 19th century, American mainstream culture began to throw off the idea of sin and hell, salvation and damnation. Yet, we were not to become lighthearted, as the Scriptures suggested; self remained the central concern, only now salvation meant the worldly success of the self, and damnation meant poverty and failure. These changes in the culture paralleled the dissolution of family and communal bonds, which actually left the individual very much alone. For the first time in history, most of us human beings must now reckon with the fact that no group will accompany us from birth through death. We will move through many groups, even several nuclear families. Essentially, we will be alone on our journey. This socially isolated self became psychologically isolated because, as the old bonds dissolved, competition came to take their place.

Today, we even have a magazine titled *Self*. We are constantly bombarded with images of celebrities whose lives consist of nothing but self-adornment, self-glorification, and self-seeking competition. Such folk are our heroes and role models. As in the perverted version of Christianity, the self remains at the center of the stage, and we all have stage fright.

Now let us return to the Buddhist idea of the self as illusion. Actually, this idea accords rather closely with the sociologist's view of self because both regard the self as a socially learned construct, even though sociology does not go as far as Buddhism in asserting that we might get rid of the illusion. At first, this may seem preposterous. Our self seems to be the one most solid, unavoidable thing with which we are in direct touch. In what sense can it be illusion? To approach this question, I would like you to do a little exercise I do with my students. Take a piece of paper and list on it all of the aspects of the self you can think of, beginning with such obvious items as "my reputation," "my clothes," "my grades," and so on. When you finish your list, come back to the book and see how it corresponds with one I have compiled from various student lists (see Exercise 10.1).

Exercise 10.1 Components of the Self

MY:	MY:	MY:
reputation	hobbies	physical space
clothes	future	youth
grades	past	writing
body	life story	hates
sex appeal	family	dislikes
friends	ethnicity	spiritual development
lovers	status	peak experiences

(Continued)

Exercise 10.1 (Continued)

MY:	MY:	MY:
acquaintances	prestige	security
opinions	neuroses	religion
tastes	career	competitive position
image	style	grudges
ideal self	sense of humor	regrets
real self	dreams	self-accusations
talents	daydreams	desires
virtues	role models	credentials
vices	ideals	personality
habits	knowledge	titles
accomplishments	skills	privileges
fears	beliefs	uniqueness
wishes	credit	honor
ambition	ancestors	name
goals	looks	sins
IQ	life	bank balance
memory	moods	

As you look over the list in Exercise 10.1, you will notice that it is very long. No wonder the self is problematic. It is a huge, overblown contraption. You will also notice that the items on the list are, indeed, items we have learned from our culture. Even "my body," which would seem to be a given, existing prior to culture, is socially learned in the sense that how we regard it (too fat, beautiful, clumsy, etc.) is learned from our culture. Even the way we relate to our body, for example, whether or not we are sensitive to its aches, depends on cultural conditioning.

But surely some of the items on this list are worth collecting. "Knowledge" and "opinions," for instance, are in very high repute in the academy. You are here to gather these, and your professors are paid for having lots and lots of them. Buddhism speaks to us very clearly on this point. The scholar's type of knowledge is considered one of the greatest hindrances to enlightenment. In *Freedom From the Known*, the great spiritual teacher Krishnamurti (1969) critically observed that an expert is somebody who knows so much that he can't learn anything more. Buddhism tells us that if we wish to attain wisdom, we must come with beginner's mind—we must come with an empty cup, otherwise nothing new can be poured into it.

Even the habit of intellectual speculation gets in the way. Krishnamurti (1967) tells a delightful story about a drive he took in the country with two scholars who had come to learn from him. Unfortunately, the driver of the car wasn't looking and ran over a goat. The two scholars in the backseat didn't notice it because they were so busy discussing awareness.

In studying people's ideologies, it is easy to see how our assumptions blind us utterly to the reality we are living through. Two men can go into combat in war, and one will come out a convinced pacifist, while the man next to him will come out a confirmed and aggressive patriot who believes we must be constantly ready for war. They lived through the same experience, but it was only the same outwardly. Just so, you can take a group of students to see a terribly poor inner city neighborhood. The left-wingers will see pure evidence of economic oppression, while the right-wingers will see confirmation of their belief that poor people are just lazy, dirty, and vicious.

To keep reality from intruding and upsetting our ideas, our brains keep up a constant babble. Above all, this babble is designed to keep the illusion of self alive. We are constantly rehearsing something we need to do next week or going over an argument we had yesterday, trying to improve on the line we took. We daydream about improving ourselves or adding luster to our name. This stream of ideas not only keeps the illusion of self ever alive, it also comes between us and our bodies so that people can strain themselves until their heart or their stomach lining gives way without ever having heard the warning signals of impending disaster. *They are too busy thinking to listen to their bodies or to see the world around them. They are self-absorbed in the sense that they are constantly working on the illusory self.*

Surely we cannot just throw all knowledge out the window. How could we live? Krishnamurti (1970) again comes to our aid in differentiating *psychological thinking* from *technical thinking.*

The latter is the knowledge we need to lead our lives, from knowing our address to knowing how to cook. The knowledge you need to carry out your job also falls into this category, although this can become complex when your job seems to require opinions. It is clear, however, that most of the daily thinking we do, the thinking that makes us uncomfortable, is just the sort of rehearsing and rehashing described previously. Thinking about the self is psychological thinking, and it takes up most of our time and emotional energy.

Exercise: Self/No Self

Now, let us do two exercises on the self/no self. First, we will do a meditation on the self. Allow about 15 minutes. Sit up straight in a comfortable position and close your eyes. Now, review as many of the aspects of the self as come to your mind, concentrating on those especially troublesome to you. As you bring up each item, imagine it turning into a heavy weight that you must hold and carry. Each time, tense the muscles holding the items. You may pile these up in your arms, pile some on your head, lay some on your lap and on your feet, and so on. Gradually increase the tensions in every part of your body that must bear the weights. Then, when you have built up maximum tension, imagine all of the weights lifting away from you and simply floating off. Relax all muscular tension and stay in the sitting position, eyes closed for several more minutes, enjoying the feeling of lightness and relaxation that comes from letting go of the self.

For the second exercise, find a friend to join you. Both of you write down four items you regard as important aspects of your "ideal self" and four that you believe describe your "real self." Make these lists separately. Now, compare notes. Do you think your friend's version of his or her "real self" is correct? Does your friend think your list is realistic? After discussing this, go over the list for the real self and see if you can remember how each item was inculcated in you by the adults around you when you were growing up.

If no friend is handy, at least jot down four items for your real and ideal self before reading on.

Ideal Self, Real Self: Both Illusions

Most people show a disastrous gap between their real and ideal selves. The ideal is usually confident, successful, energetic, and friendly, and the real is often fat, lazy, shy, and incompetent. Right away, we see why such a self is highly troublesome. Most students assume that their ideal self is a kind of daydream, but their real self is just a straight report of the facts. Actually, both versions are pure fantasy without the slightest substance. If you had a tough parent, for example, you may think that your real self is pretty awful. The same biological you, having had loving, self-confident parents, would feel much more self-approval even though this second person had the same looks, brains, or energy level. It all depends on who held up the mirror to us as we were growing up.

Buddhism tells us that to get rid of the problematic self we need not change any aspect of it. We only need to accept what is there. Of course, to truly accept, we need to know what is there. A person who cannot admit that he or she is afraid cannot accept fear; hence, this person will be constantly wrestling with it and will remain tense and anxious. The suppression of laziness is a good example of this. Our culture demands much difficult effort from us from early childhood. It disapproves most strongly of laziness. In school, lazy and stupid are about the worst things you can be. Vicious and cruel would be mild condemnations by comparison. This means that to get approval, we had to deny all our urges to rest. As we deny them, they collect and grow bigger. It takes constant effort to keep this huge pile of laziness under cover. Simply everybody suspects themselves of laziness. Had we grown up in a different culture, the accusation might never have entered our minds.

A note of caution: Don't interpret letting go of the self to mean that you should ignore your feelings. On the contrary, as we sweep away concern with the problematic self, it leaves the mind more available to stay in touch with our body, its physical sensations, and feeling states or emotions. Mind should look after body/feelings the way a good parent looks after a child. There is a saying in Buddhism, "When you are tired, lie down." I often think this should be engraved over the entrance of all college dormitories.

Exercise: The Critical Voice

Here is an exercise designed to make you more aware of how your insides function. Take paper and pencil and begin by giving your particular inner critical voice a name. Students come up with a wonderful variety of such names: the clobberer (a mean one), the nag (slightly less mean), the cold-eyed commentator, the nudge, the judge, the accuser, the perfectionist, the mother, the father, the quibbler, and so on. Freud called it the superego; some call it conscience. Most people have to cope with some form of critic; only a small number of lucky people don't.

Now, write out a list of the most frequent criticisms you hear from this voice. It is important to get your inner workings on paper where you can get a different perspective on them than if you only go over them in your head. One tricky aspect of this task is that in many people, the criticisms are not consciously heard. All that is conscious is the self-justification and self-defense about something: "I do spend my money wisely. I saved by not buying that dress last week" or "I do well in many of my classes; the ones that are important—I never mess those up." The unheard or subconscious part is "You are a spendthrift" or "You mess up in all your classes." Whenever you defend yourself like this, you know there is a silent accusation afoot. For your list, you may infer these accusations.

Now, go over your list and rate the correctness of each criticism. Then, give an overall assessment to the critical voice: right 50% of the time, 90%, 10%, and so forth. If you have a friend who will join you in this exercise, put your heads together over each list and see what your friend thinks about the accuracy of your critical voice. In the next step of the exercise, let the critical voice (always address yours by the name you've given it) justify itself: Make a list of justifications. Let the voice claim various benefits it brings you—perhaps it will claim that you couldn't function without it. Now assess the believability of the defense: very believable, barely believable, not too believable, or utterly wrong.

Although there are a wide variety of forms taken by the voice in different individuals, the accusations are usually rather similar: too lazy, too fat, not nice enough to parents, procrastinator on schoolwork, and so on. You can easily see that the content of the accusation is learned from the attitudes of the people around you as you grew up. Had you been born a Trobriand Islander, for example, you might have criticized yourself severely for any playful or slightly intimate interaction with your brother or sister.

The severity or even the presence of such an element of personality depends on culture, specifically on the severity with which children are treated during their upbringing. In a study of Polynesian culture (Malinowski, 1985), the author tells us that when he asked people whether there was anything the individual wanted to change about himself, he usually found that the respondent couldn't think of anything at all.

How people rate their critical voice on believability seems to vary greatly, but the rating appears to have no correlation to the individual's talents or personality. Some really wonderful people believe the worst accusations about themselves. This, again, is related to childhood experiences.

You have to see the critical voice as a saboteur who constantly undermines and rattles you, while claiming to be your friend. The voice makes you dread failure, and fear of failure is one of the most common causes of failure. In many years of teaching, I learned that very few low-scoring students were failing because of lack of intelligence. Rather, self-confidence is the major ingredient in success. When you are confident, you procrastinate less. We all hate to spend time at something that makes us feel bad. The confident student talks more in class and learns more by asking questions. He or she is likely to be more adventurous and creative. In short, whatever destroys your faith in yourself undercuts your performance. Learn to see the critical voice for the enemy that it is.

This doesn't mean that you are unable to see and correct errors in your work. You have to be able to see objectively where you are wrong; that is a necessary part of the process of learning. But that is quite different from the voice. You can see your error in a flash—your understanding is that quick. The nagging and inner backbiting of the voice comes on top of this quick knowing. It drags the whole affair out and makes you a culprit for having been wrong. If you knew everything already, why should you get an education?

Next time you have a severe attack of self-criticism (it may also feel like depression), take it as a perfect occasion for catching the critic. Sit right down and make a list of the accusations—get them out into the daylight. Read them to yourself out loud. Share them with a friend.

When working on the critical voice, notice that this part of your brain is very agile. When it sees you coming after it, it may quickly switch sides and join in the new game by criticizing you for being self-critical. It is perfectly capable of such treachery. What you have to learn to recognize is not so much what it says but the tone of the criticism and the way that tone makes you feel.

The critical voice is tremendously subjective. It is, in fact, incapable of objective, fair judgment. For example, it will blame you for things it would never criticize in another person. In fact, if you criticized your friends so severely, you probably wouldn't have any friends. To strengthen your capacity for cool, unbiased self-judgment, try the following exercise: At various moments during the day, whenever you think to do it, just observe what you are doing—not what you are thinking or feeling—briefly and quite unemotionally and without judgment: "I am walking to my math class," "I am watching a movie," "I am reading an assignment," "I am having coffee and a chat with a friend." This exercise should be done over a period of at least 3 weeks, catching yourself about once or twice a day—don't overdo. If you forget easily, wear something unusual to remind yourself occasionally of the exercise. Everyone will obtain his or her own result from this exercise, and I won't spell out what your result might be. Try it and see. After 3 weeks, go back and look at your list of accusations and your assessment of their correctness. See whether your feelings toward the critical voice have changed.

Exercise: Roots

Before you can let go of this troublesome self of yours, you will have to explore it, study it, and understand it. (Don't use what I am saying to think about yourself incessantly. Watch instead. The understanding I am talking about comes as a flash of insight, not as the result of endless rumination.)

To a much larger extent than our culture lets on, we are still the products of quite distinct subcultures. In my course, my students researched their ancestry as far back as they could go. They interviewed relatives and wrote letters to all the older members of their families whom they could find. Then we had a come-as-you-were party: Come as your grandfather or great-grandfather or one of your parents. As we exchanged family histories, we began to get a strange sensation of how much of a melting pot this society really is.

Here is a third-generation German Jewish immigrant whose grandparents fled from Hitler in the 1930s. Here is a Chicano student whose family has lived in a Chicano neighborhood near the Mexican border for generations. They were former landowners, pushed out when the Anglos grabbed California and reduced the family to the poverty of farm laborers. Here is a Black student, whose grandparents made it out to California from Arkansas to work in the shipyards during World War II and whose parents made it up to the level of skilled blue-collar workers. Here is an individual whose family of Presbyterian New England farmers has been in America for many generations. Here is a young woman who was born in Taiwan and whose parents had an arranged marriage. She tells us that it seemed to work about as well as most marriages she sees around her in the United States. Here is a young man whose ancestors were queens of Hawaii. Had we gone back two generations, we would have spoken in a babble of tongues; we would have come from rags and riches. We would have exchanged passionate enmities; in no sense would we have been members of a common enough culture so that we could easily understand one another.

We tend to be fooled by externals. All of these disparate people now look pretty much alike. Not only do we dress the same, *we organize our faces similarly.* We wear the same expressions; our body language signals the same reserved friendliness, the same underlying disapproval of our bodies. On the surface, we are indeed alike, but it is amazing how the old ethnicity hangs on. If we look at any trait, from people's politics to the way they discipline their children, we will always find that differences in ethnic and social class origins still show up.

I put ethnicity and class position into the same bag because they come combined in patterns that reflect the historical circumstances under which each group came to be part of the United States. Black people came in chains, and African ethnicity is still correlated with lower-than-average class position. The Italian immigrants came without money or urban skills, primarily during the years 1880 to 1920. They began at the bottom but were only partially blocked by racism and hence managed to get into better paid working-class positions and into the lower middle class. The wave of Jewish immigrants who came in the 1930s was mostly middle class and came into our economy at that level, and thus it goes. The patterns vary from family to family. Some families moved up fast; others remained in the same economic position for generations.

There are so many subtle aspects to this heritage of ours. I was the first-generation American child of Austrian Jewish parents who fled from Hitler. By a fluke, my family moved to Southern California, away from the other immigrants who stayed on the East Coast. Luckily, there wasn't much anti-Semitism among my young schoolmates in Claremont, California, and I grew up feeling totally

"American." Yet one day I found myself majoring in sociology in graduate school at the University of California at Berkeley. I looked around me in seminar and realized that 80% of my classmates and professors were Jewish. "Isn't it strange that I ended up in this group?" I thought, and then I began to put it together. My father had been a socialist and had raised me as one. Many of the sociologists at Berkeley at that time were socialists or ex-socialists of some stripe or persuasion. They had gravitated naturally to sociology because it was the newest and most militant social science, and it counted Karl Marx as one of its most influential intellectual parents. Jews have historically often been political radicals because they lived for so many centuries as outcasts within the Christian nation-states of Europe.

I married twice, both men with backgrounds completely different from my own. Neither marriage lasted. And then I found Ted and a kind of immediate understanding, as though for the first 40 years of our lives we had thought roughly the same thoughts and found the same comedians funny. There was something even more subtle afoot. The way he played with me and teased me reminded me very much of my father. Ted's mother was thoroughly American, but he is a throwback to two Russian-Jewish grandfathers with whom he lived during his childhood and who teased him and played with him in the same way my Austrian Jewish father had played with me. One of them was a labor organizer and a radical.

Another thing we discovered at our come-as-you-were party was that some people had large, cohesive, happy families with lots of positive ties and common sociability, while other people came from tiny fragments of once-extended families in which bad feelings had eaten like acid into the old kinship ties. Happiness seems to run through generations and so does unhappiness. Don't take this as an edict from fate; human beings can remake their family situations during their lifetime, at least up to a point. You cannot will a warm, extended family into being, but you can create a small, happy family on the strength of your own wisdom. In fact, it is quite possible to learn as much from bad examples as from good ones, as long as you are clear about which is bad and good.

Many of the interviews and letters from relatives turned out to be wonderful. Perhaps it was just a chance for young folks to talk with the old folks and find out about old times. That used to happen naturally because people lived near each other and weren't segregated so sharply by generations. I once read a study in which it was found that children who have close ties with grandparents feel more optimistic about life and about getting old than children who are cut off from those ties. The Roots exercise was a way to bring a little of this contact about.

Research your own roots. Perhaps you could do it as a half-credit independent study or in connection with a course. There are many interesting books, fiction and nonfiction, on just about any ethnic group. A sociologist should be able to help you find resources. Or organize a come-as-you-were party among a group of friends who are willing to put a little time into it. You will find clues to your own identity and broaden your sympathies toward others from different origins.

Exercise: Slowing Down

Time is our modern nemesis. We are slaves of our wristwatches in a social system in which 5 minutes is considered a significant interval (i.e., the difference between being on time or late to class). Imagine living in a society whose smallest unit of discussible time is the time it takes to boil rice—and not instant rice, either. It is ironic that although previous cultures had far fewer labor-saving mechanisms, they possessed a feeling of plenty of time, whereas we, with all our labor-saving devices, feel chronically time poor.

Evans-Pritchard (1940) describes an African herding people, the Nuer, as follows:

> The Nuer have no expression equivalent to time in our language, and they cannot, therefore, as we can, speak of time as though it were something actual, which passes, can be wasted, can be saved, and so forth. I do not think that they ever experience the same feeling of fighting against time or of having to coordinate activities with an abstract passage of time because their points of reference are mainly the activities themselves, which are generally of a leisurely character. Events follow a logical order, but they are not controlled by an abstract system, there being no autonomous points of reference to which activities have to conform with precision. Nuer are fortunate. (p. 47)

One of the reasons we have to time everything so carefully is that we must coordinate our actions with a highly complex system of activities, and we must do this alone. You don't move from class to class to luncheon date with any single group. You are generally entirely on your own, and the structure sets up unyielding demands. Another reason our machines don't make life leisurely is that our society is so competitive. Having your own jet doesn't put you safely ahead of other executives who also have private airplanes. Having a calculator in math class doesn't put you ahead of other students similarly equipped. As soon as everybody has a labor-saving device, nobody is benefited by it. Forty years ago, social scientists were predicting that the coming of the computer would shorten everybody's workweek. We got unemployment instead, and there hasn't been a decrease in the workweek since World War II.

The sense of urgency that fills our days has been turned into a virtue by the folks who lead our institutions. A number of years ago, I decided to try enlightening my faculty colleagues at Pitzer College by sending out a brief questionnaire that simply asked whether the individual felt he or she had plenty of time, just enough time, or was short of time, in connection with work at the college. As I expected, most people checked *short of time*. I had planned to make this situation known to the faculty to see what we might do about it. I was stopped short by the marginal comments that graced at least half of the questionnaires. Next to the box *short of time*, people had penciled, "I am glad about this; it keeps me going," "Short of time—of course—what professional is not?" and so on. In other words, they celebrated the shortage. This is not really surprising in a society where the answer to "How are you?" is frequently "Keeping busy," which means the same as "Well, thank you."

Slowing Down

I spent the majority of my academic career employing a Pavlovian response to bells. Indoctrinated to serve the clock and adhere to a hierarchical paradigm of time, the sound of the bell indicated both a mental and physical shift. I'd depart from my classroom chair in one academic environment in exchange for another awaiting my arrival. Within minutes, my brain would reprogram itself to the next subject, the rules of the subsequent teacher, and quietly, I would acquiesce to my assigned seat. Although the rules changed slightly in college, the punctuality standard remained a barometer for academic sincerity. The chiming sound that had once demarcated classes was replaced by an internal structure. Without the herd-like conformity of grade school, every student became personally responsible to uphold the structure. I found that my time management in college closely mirrored that of my early childhood education. I demonstrated respect for instructors through punctuality and my physical and mental engagement. Consequently, my concept of time was inextricably connected to the duration of the class and the specified objectives that were to be accomplished. While there certainly appeared to exist more freedoms within a university environment, I realized that my general understanding of the time-student relationship stood relatively unchanged. I still operated within the model that dichotomized time as either free or structured. My attitudes toward experiences were contingent upon the socialized definition of which time category they took up in my life.

It wasn't until I took a sociology course that I was pushed to view time with more fluidity. I began to see myself as the common denominator of my experiences, rather than the categorical attitudes of time that I had previously adhered to. One of the simplest and simultaneously challenging experiments of the Sociology of Meditation and Mindfulness course was reprogramming my response to bells. Historically, they symbolized a tardiness alert, classroom change, or shift from academic to free time. However, within a Vietnamese Buddhist milieu, I was encouraged to use the chime of a bell to return to my most inner self. In direct opposition to the anxiety and action previously associated with the sound, our class was challenged to pause. Upon the chiming of a bell, we were to take three deep breaths and look inward to a peaceful place of self-recognition. That foreign experiment marked one of the first times in my life that a bell offered a completely peaceful reformation of time and pace. That small exercise turned out to be one of my most powerfully experienced lessons. It showed me how conditioned I was to comply and thus how detached I truly was from how I was thinking or feeling in any given moment. Being forced to stand still amidst a sea of hurried students eager to take their seats forced me to view just how programmed our society has become. Something clicked within me while I experienced the sad reality of my discomfort with simply being. It felt abnormal to stop and think about what I was doing, instead of robotically blending in with my cohorts. Initially, the act of being generated a heightened sense of internal and physical angst. I found it impossible to clear my head and detach from the overstimulation that surrounded me. My body tensed as I worried what people thought when their sprint across campus was interrupted by my short meditation. Those three deep breaths during the chiming of the bell tower were just long enough to cathartically allow me to redefine my understanding of time. I began to appreciate those moments during my day when I was allowed to escape the socially imposed droning rhythm and instead plug into my own. Throughout the course, I learned to see daily rituals as an opportunity to be mindful of my position in society. Mundane and ubiquitous activities such as sitting, eating, and walking were transformed into powerful experiences. At the core of everything was my breath, which encouraged a cognizance that was previously absent. By completing everyday movements with purpose, I developed a significant understanding of how I had been raised and how society had shaped my attitudes. I am grateful that I had the opportunity to explore such a distinct approach to life and learn in the process how to slowly reshape my programmed attitudes. Traveling within myself revealed a new set of eyes as well as a deeper social understanding. The redefinition of the bell provided me with a foundation to deconstruct previous social standards and work toward discovering a meaningful convergence of my academic environment with myself.

—*Rebecca Silver Fisher*

There is probably no single cause of tension greater than this chronic feeling of time nipping at our heels. As one surveys this scene, there is a feeling that we are caught in a social structure much larger than ourselves—a structure whose wheels just revolve too fast for our comfort. But we can change these feelings for ourselves and do so without becoming incompetent. You may begin to see this by trying the following daylong exercise.

Get up 20 minutes earlier tomorrow and do 20 minutes of the "slow walk" before starting your day; that is, for 20 minutes, walk around your room as slowly as you possibly can without losing your balance.[2] It may take you 10 minutes to cross the room. Just concentrate on the body feelings of walking slowly. Don't do anything special with your mind—let it relax and go along for the ride.

Now, for the rest of the day, do all your accustomed tasks at about 50% of your normal speed—even less, when it seems possible. Walk to class slowly, take notes slowly, eat your lunch slowly, do your assignments slowly, go out on your date slowly, and so forth. Another way of getting into the feel of this exercise is to think of each separate activity as a time frame. Our usual habit is to lean forward into the next time frame; that is, as we walk to class we are already thinking about class; as we shower, we are already dreaming about seeing our date. This time, try

---

[2] I learned the "slow walk" at the Nyingma Institute in Berkeley, California. This is a Tibetan Buddhist institute founded by Tarthang Tulku Rinpoche. Although the founder is in retreat, the teachers he trained are running the institute, which offers many workshops, classes, and an academically accredited program in certain subject areas.

leaning back into your present time frame. Say to yourself, "How nice, I have a 5-minute walk now. I hope it lasts a long time, so I can settle into it comfortably." With practice, you can even learn to lean back into quite short time frames.

At the end of the day, for your own records, jot down your impressions. Try to see what you have learned about yourself, other people, institutions, and so on. Do this before reading on.

Students generally come back from this exercise astounded about something. Perhaps they sense for the first time how much they habitually rush. "I don't usually taste my food, I eat so fast," says one student; "I never realized how fast everybody dashes around," says another. But the greatest surprise is, "I got everything done just about as well as usual" or "I actually got more done than usual because I felt so sane" and "I wish I could do that every day." Well, why not? It is possible to change one's inner experience of time. Nobody need be the wiser. You won't look that different from the outside. Experiment has shown that runners actually make better time when instructed to run at just 80% of their normal speed. When tension decreases, we actually become more efficient.

Of course, this exercise, like all consciousness-changing exercises, requires much practice. You spent 20 years learning to feel hurried. It will take time and practice to undo that. A problem with such practice is that you forget to do it once the novelty wears off. One way to help yourself is to wear or carry something unusual, which will remind you to do the practice. You may wear an unaccustomed bracelet, or change the arm on which you wear your watch, or carry a bright notebook cover, and so on. The slow walk, by the way, is a very nice meditation you can use at any time to calm down. I would recommend you look at Thich Nhat Hanh's *A Guide to Walking Meditation* (1985). The activity of the mind is tied to the physical body. *When you slow the body down, the mind also slows down.*

Desocializing doesn't have to be as severe as it sounds. Although escaping reality can be a form of removing yourself from socialization (and society in the process), desocialization may be much softer. Desocialization is more like drifting to the edge of the fish bowl we're all in, rather than jumping out. Once you are at the edge, it is possible to view everyone in the middle with less biased lenses. Try this: At some point during the day, when you have a break between classes that's longer than 10 minutes, go to a quiet spot on the campus. It may be the park in the center of the school or just a quiet block along the main street. Put your stuff down and sit quietly or walk slowly. Allow your mind to wander away from the stresses of school. Do this until a feeling of calmness comes over you. If you can achieve this peacefulness, you will be able to, at least temporarily, remove yourself from the routine pressures of school. Do this every so often and you should start to see these pressures in a different light.

Maximizing and Minimizing

One of the basic, underlying styles of our culture is the tendency to maximize and minimize everything: to push everything as far as possible in a given direction and always expand to the limits of endurance. We have seen how we do this with time. We are always making the best use of our time; we can never allow ourselves to waste time. If we get an extra piece of time thrown our way, we immediately find something to fill it—something that had not been pressing before suddenly becomes pressing. Thus, we seldom allow ourselves a leisurely sense of time.

We see this tendency most dramatically in our attitudes toward spending money. Average Americans spend to the limits of their capacity. When we get a raise, we immediately increase our purchases accordingly. Thus, we are always financially uncomfortable, no matter how much we make. We could feel rich if we simply stayed at our present spending level when we get a raise, but we just cannot do this because we are surrounded by appeals to spend.

Just as surely as we maximize our spending of time and money or our attainment of sexual satisfaction, we minimize in other directions. Many of us are constantly on a diet, minimizing our food intake; at home, we minimize our housework; at school, we must minimize our errors. We don't follow the golden mean of the ancient Greeks or the middle way of the Buddhists. The inevitable accompaniment of this style is strain. Ask anybody on campus whether they feel strained by time, by finances, by sexual needs, and you will usually find a strainer. At the same time, the culture demands that we maximize "happiness." To be less than happy is to be somehow in disgrace. Yet happiness just cannot be found in this basic mode. The demand is a cruel contradiction in terms.

I know of no way to break through this pervasive pattern except by pulling yourself up short when you are about to maximize or minimize some situation and asking yourself, "Would it not be better to find the golden mean, the middle way? Suppose I don't try to write the longest paper for glory or the shortest paper to minimize the discomfort of research? Suppose I write a paper of middle length? Suppose I hit for the medium price range in my purchases? Suppose I settle for being slightly overweight? Suppose I don't change my spending patterns when I get the raise? Suppose I don't rush through every country in Europe so I won't miss anything?" It will, perhaps, seem inglorious to you, but it is certainly more comfortable. You may still choose to maximize some area of activity, but don't let the culture rush you into doing so every time. Be aware of this tendency and use your awareness to increase your freedom.

Thursday, August 6: The Day I Broke Free

Thursday, August 6, 2009. Today has been the best day in my entire life. So far today, I've gone to two classes, contributed to the discussions, and I've made a salad. I left one class early and came back in sunglasses.

Sounds routine. Apart from the early departure. But they have everything to do with why today has been the greatest day of my life.

I'll start at the beginning: I woke up. My seminars did not begin for another several hours, so I had plenty of time to get all of my required reading done. I went to my first seminar, which is an English class about comic books. I already have decent knowledge in this realm, but having read all the required reading as well, I was in top form. I talked more than any other student. My ideas were fresh and intellectual; I apologize for the arrogance, but they were. The professor was complimenting me. Other students were staring at me—some in awe, others in curiosity, and perhaps some in jealousy (once again, I apologize for the arrogance). And this being only the second day of class, the professor and the students only knew the names of a couple of students. Everybody knew my name. I felt awesome.

But this isn't why today was the greatest day in my life. There were three presentations by three students on three different comic books. The last student to go was a girl who had decided to do a presentation on the comic book "Watchmen," which is a book we have to read, but it was assigned for a later week. She had read ahead of schedule (good for her). However, because nobody else in the class had read the book, she was going to use only specific pages. She said to turn to Chapter 12, and then she said (while everyone was turning pages) that she felt awful because she was about to ruin the book. I had been thinking the same thing; I was turning the pages with angst because I had been looking forward to reading this comic. The professor laughed and mentioned that it was no big deal: "We weren't reading for fun; we were reading to deconstruct." I, however, see no reason why the two are considered mutually exclusive.

That's not a knock against my professor. He's an easygoing guy. When people ask if they may be excused to go to the restroom, he tells us to just get up and go; we're adults and don't have to ask permission. He doesn't pussyfoot around. And he loves literature. I know he reads for fun because on the first day of class he wanted to know everybody's favorite books. And he could engage almost every student in excited conversation about a book he or she had mentioned. It seemed like the statement was one that appealed to the students. Most students don't read for fun. They read because they have to.

So, back to the final presentation. Jamie was about to start her presentation, and I got up, looked her straight in the eye, and said, "Sorry, Jamie. I'm looking forward to reading this book." And I walked out of the classroom, nodding to my professor, who was obviously in good spirits and laughing raucously.

The students were stunned. I had already been getting stares when I dominated the class discussion, but now every single eye was trained on me walking out the door.

I walked out the door and it was the happiest I have ever been. I had momentarily thought about not getting up and enduring what would amount to the inevitable ruination of my future reading experience. What would the other students think? That would be so embarrassing. Should I ask if I can leave? What if the teacher said no? Do I want him to say no? Would he say no? No! I knew he was laid back. Should I pretend that I need to go to the restroom? No.

The truth shall set you free!

And it did. For years, I've been a prisoner in my own mind. I've been hacking away at the bars for years, making progress, but never completely breaking free from society's tyranny over me. This was the last hack that did it. I had conquered society, rather than the other way around. I went outside and looked at the trees and foliage. Everything was so beautiful. My subconscious disc jockey put on a song I had not listened to in years: "Desperado." In full strength, my mind reproduced a verse from that song: "And freedom, oh freedom, well, that's just some people talkin'. Your prison is walking through this world all alone."

I knew I was free, and I began to cry. I have never been so happy in my entire life—proof physically manifested in my tears. I had rarely ever cried in pain or sorrow and definitely never in happiness. I walked outside and reveled in the glory of my freedom. UCLA campus had never looked so beautiful in my entire life.

After walking around for about half an hour, I realized that my first seminar was about to end. I entered the classroom while the professor was making his closing remarks about logistics for the class. I returned to my seat with a huge grin on my face. I didn't care that everyone was staring at me. I was smart for getting out; I was going to enjoy the book later. The attention didn't bother me. The professor was jovial on my return. I chatted nonchalantly about it. My confidence was magnetic, and this made me happy. Instead of fighting against society—which I had been doing for my entire life—I was working with it to be happy. The roles had been reversed. What a glorious day!

—Kevin O'Hara

Daydreams and Great Expectations

Zen Buddhism has a very simple recipe for enlightenment: attention to the present moment. At first, it may seem to us that, of course, we pay attention to the moment. We don't, after all, fall downstairs or run into trees very often. We couldn't survive if we paid no attention. As we begin to observe the workings of our mind, we find that the attention we pay is usually minimal. Most of the time, we are relying on habit and an occasional glance to get us through the environment. As we dress, brush our teeth, walk to class, or drive into town, our heads are usually filled with thoughts about ourselves. We see ourselves as heroes and heroines of many a dramatic fantasy. In short, we daydream.

If you want to see for yourself what happens to your attention during habitual tasks, try this simple experiment. Next time you are washing and getting dressed, try keeping your mind firmly glued to the present moment by describing each little action to yourself: "I am walking into the bathroom," "I am washing my face," "I am drying my face," "I am putting the towel back," and so on. You may be surprised by what you find.

Over the years, I have been impressed by the stubbornness with which students defend their right to daydream. "But I don't want to stop daydreaming" is a frequent response to the stricture of Buddhism to remain in the present moment. Daydreaming is enjoyable; it seems to fulfill some great inner need, and, anyway, the ordinary world seems repetitive and boring much of the time. In view of this resistance by my students, I had to ask myself, "What is wrong with daydreaming? What is the price we pay for daydreaming?"

One clear price we pay is that daydreaming stirs up our emotions when we could be perfectly calm. Even though we are only walking down a quiet street, our body chemistry is responding to our thoughts of adventure, danger, revenge, triumph, and so on. Hence, we are seldom as serene and inwardly quiet as we could be if we were only responding to our environment. Thus, we tend to be either "up" or "down." We do not find our inner center and cannot respond to the happenings of the day from this center. Rather, the day's problems flow into the daydreaming, and we really cannot separate and deal with the real problems realistically. There is a kind of clean simplicity and innocence in our experience during those rare times when we are "just" in the physical environment.

Our daydreams are very frequently dreams of fulfilling our every wish. Our thoughts run so far ahead of our real acquisitions that we feel forever in need of more goodies about which we have fantasized. The daydreams make us dissatisfied with what we really have.

Daydreams can also deprive the real happenings in our life of the luster they would have if we came upon them innocent of expectation. Indeed, expectation is the great enemy of satisfaction. When we begin a flirtation with someone, our mind immediately rushes ahead to what it could be like to make love to this person, to travel with her, to be wonderfully flattered and complimented by her. By the time a real relationship develops, we are primed for disappointment. It will never be anything like our daydream. Perhaps we will never see the potential for new experience with this other person because we are looking through the old stuff of our daydreams.

In reality, our daydreams are old and repetitive and hackneyed. It is reality that is ever new and continually amazing and challenging, but we live so little in this reality that it doesn't penetrate to us. We blunt its impact. One day in class, I remarked on the beautiful and fragrant citrus tree by our classroom door. I discovered that most students had not seen or smelled it. Daydreamers are like people who spend nearly all their time watching movies. Perhaps they are really in a splendid natural scene and surrounded by interesting people, but they only take a few minutes between movies. During those few minutes, the last movie is still so much in their mind that nothing in the real scene penetrates their emotions. Immersion in the media is a good analogy to immersion in daydreams. The media are the stuff that feeds our dreams, and our constant exposure to media helps to make daydreamers of us.

In *Great Expectations*, Dickens (1982) relates the story of a woman who was jilted on her wedding day. Refusing utterly to face the reality of this, she spends the rest of her life dressed in her wedding gown, sitting at the banquet table that was to have been her wedding feast. When she is very old, she upsets a candelabra and sets her finery, herself, and the whole house on fire. Her great expectation consumed her entire life.

Ted and I had some interesting experiences with expectations as we began to plan for our early retirement. Ted's dream since childhood had always been to go to the South Seas. He thought that, perhaps, he might even want to live there. So we set out on a 6-month tour of the South Sea Islands. Having always centered my travel interests on Europe, I had never even thought about going to the South Pacific.

During our tour, we had our good and bad times, as one always does when traveling. The worst thing was that it rained much more than usual and spoiled a lot of our planned outdoor activities. An unexpected delight, on the other hand, was the marvelous diversity and beauty of the art, music, and dance of the peoples of Melanesia and Polynesia.

Our responses to the trip were very different. I experienced the journey as a great pleasure. Every new, unexpected facet of the area surprised and delighted me. At the same time, I took the bad weather rather philosophically. Ted, on the other hand, found the trip unexpectedly depressing. It did not meet his lifelong expectations, and, whenever it fell short, he suffered a real sense of loss.

Some years later, when we decided to settle in Northern California, we bought three acres that had been a beautiful garden but was long neglected. Gardening had always been my passion. I had always been land hungry on my little city lots. During all the years in which lack of space constrained me, I avidly read gardening books and magazines and seed catalogues. The media are specialists in promoting unrealistic daydreams. Just as the houses shown in home magazines are generally only affordable to millionaires, so the garden magazines contained doctored photographs of perennial borders made beautiful by the last-minute addition of hidden pots of flowers grown in greenhouses. How many such perennial borders had I planted in my mind (while skipping the chapters called "Pests" and "Diseases")? Ted, on the other hand, had no expectations of the garden. He didn't even know whether he would enjoy gardening. He just sort of went along with me in picking this particular acreage.

Of course, the results were predictable. As I began to face the real difficulties of getting three acres under control, I suffered a good deal. While I had pictured myself working 6 or 7 hours a day in my dream garden, I discovered that, at 53 years of age, working even 4 hours is very likely to give you a tennis elbow. All in all, the garden quickly became my nemesis. In the meanwhile, Ted innocently began to prune the trees and found that he hugely enjoyed the activity. He was able to take pleasure in the garden just as it was at any given moment, while I always saw weeds and other errors crying out for correction. We both learned about the influence of expectations the hard way. Luckily, reality is always there to wake us up. As I bow to the realities of my garden, I find that the garden is reshaping me quite as much as the other way around.

Often, our daydreams seem to function as rehearsals, and we have convinced ourselves that rehearsals are useful. Without them, we might not be prepared to meet various situations. That this is an error you can substantiate for yourself. Observe whether or not an encounter for which you have rehearsed ever comes off the way you expected. In my experience, real encounters are always grossly different from rehearsals. In fact, if we didn't quickly drop the rehearsed material, we would be incapable of dealing with the real situation. The very best way to meet any difficult encounter—whether an oral examination or a painful dialogue with a friend—is to go into it with a calm, quiet mind, primed to be totally alert and open to the situation as it develops.

If you want to get a handle on your own daydreaming, carry paper and pencil around with you for one day and make a tally for every time you catch yourself daydreaming. You can also make a quick note of the subject of each daydream. At the end of the day, you can take a look at what goes on in your mind.

That is Exercise 1. For Exercise 2, wait until some event is coming up from which you expect either pleasure or pain. When such an event appears on your horizon, make it your practice to forego absolutely any kind of daydreaming about that particular occasion. Of course, you may do some necessary preparation for the occasion. But this is different from daydreaming. Pick just one event at a time because this is difficult and will take energy to carry out. Be absolutely ruthless about this one event. Whenever you catch your mind wandering even near it, strike at the roots swiftly, as if you were wielding a very sharp sword. If you discover that you are in the middle of such thoughts, drop them immediately. (Don't prolong it by berating yourself.) Then, when the real event happens, see if there is any difference in your experience of it.

Desocialization Course Resources

This is a list of books I used in the desocialization course. Most of these books are available from Amazon (http://www.amazon.com).

Cohen, S., & Taylor, L. (1976). *Escape attempts.* Middlesex, UK: Penguin.

Fischer, L. (1963). *The essential Gandhi.* New York, NY: Random House.

Fromm, E., Suzuki, D. T., & De Martino, R. (1960). *Zen Buddhism and psychoanalysis.* New York, NY: Harper & Row.

Herrigel, E. (1971). *Zen in the art of archery.* New York, NY: Vintage, Random House.

Krishnamurti, J. (1969). *Freedom from the known.* New York, NY: Harper & Row.

Maslow, A. (1962). *Toward a psychology of being.* Princeton, NJ: Van Nostrand.

Matthiesen, P. (1978). *The snow leopard.* New York, NY: Bantam.

Powell, R. (1961). *Zen and reality.* Middlesex, UK: Penguin.

Putney, S., & Putney, G. (1964). *The adjusted American: Normal neuroses in the individual and society.* New York, NY: Harper & Row.

Stevens, B. (1970). *Don't push the river.* Moab, UT: Real People.

Suzuki, S. (1970). *Zen mind, beginner's mind.* New York, NY: Weatherhill.

Trungpa, C. (1969). *Meditation in action.* Berkeley, CA: Shambhala.

Watts, A. W. (1961). *Psychotherapy east and west.* New York, NY: Ballantine.

CHAPTER 11

Media Me

> Where does television end and my self begin? Why has television become our "third parent?" We are socialized throughout our lives by the mass media. The average adult American actually watches TV 4 hours a day, children more. This indoctrination is even more powerful than the school system because it comes to us in the form of "freely chosen" entertainment—a fun, fluffy, cuddly sheep hiding an insidious, addicting, parasite wolf. In Chapter 11, we attempt to do the following:
>
> - Get behind the "Media Curtain" like Dorothy did in *The Wizard of Oz* or Nemo did in *The Matrix*.
> - Use an exercise in contrasting real people with television people, aka "celebrities."
> - Explore the unsettling mind, self, and media interconnections dominating our culture.

We are socialized throughout our lives by the mass media. This agency of indoctrination is even more powerful than the school system because it comes in the form of entertainment and hence doesn't arouse the inner opposition that school, thank heaven, always arouses in the hapless pupil. The folks who do media spend many dollars and hire many experts to find out exactly what forms of entertainment will grab you. Their object is to get your absolute attention when the ads come on. That is why there is so much violence in media. It is part of our animal heritage that we become wide awake when there is any physical danger around us. Research shows that when incidents of violence are pictured on the screen, a milder form of this instinctive reaction goes into effect: We pay attention.

Getting Behind the Media Curtain

Media culture is a culture that has been invented to sell soap. There is precious little wisdom in it. Yet we are all deeply influenced by media versions of reality. Indeed, we depend on media and on schools for nearly all the knowledge we have of the world that lies beyond what we can immediately see and experience. Ask yourself, for a moment, how you "know" what China is like, how you "know" what sort of people politicians are, or how you "know" what your hometown was like a hundred years ago. If you are honest, you will see that, conceivably, you could have been lied to about all these things.[1]

Who controls what comes to you in TV, films, or newspapers? Almost without exception these forms of the mass media are owned by giant, multinational conglomerates that are interrelated in many different ways with the whole network of huge corporations that dominate the American economy. What do rich people want you to know about Cuba? South American revolutionaries have a nasty habit of nationalizing American corporate property in their countries. The United Fruit Company stands to lose every time a Castro appears on the scene. Will they tell you that under Castro, Cuba has developed the best medical care system in Latin America? What will they tell you about the nature and reality of war or when it may be necessary for you to be drafted to fight a war for rubber in Asia or for oil in Iraq or Venezuela? These are questions you must learn to ask yourself. In fact, you should become suspicious of all information you do not get firsthand. The source and the bias of the source must always be considered when getting information second-hand. You must also consider whether your source had access to good information. During Vietnam, for example, very few Americans in Vietnam spoke the language. This meant they could only speak with Western-educated Vietnamese in the cities. No wonder they didn't know what was going on in the much larger countryside.

On those rare occasions when the media cover something we know about first-hand, we are usually amazed to see how distorted the picture is. But we seldom generalize from these occasions because it is pretty difficult to admit that we don't know as much as we thought we did. It may help you to keep in mind that realizing how little one knows is the inevitable beginning of wisdom.

Media work on us in much more subtle ways than just misinforming us. Media inculcate general attitudes toward life, love, pleasure, and pain. What do the media want you to know about the real nature of love if their object is to sell you hairspray? What do they want you to know about contentment if the object is to sell you linoleum? How do they want you to feel about yourself if they are softening you up to rush out and buy the latest designer jeans? Advertisers are well aware that it isn't effective to break into an honest story about human life with an ad that tries to tell you that happiness lies in the right choice of shampoo, so the programming must be brought down to the simplest level that serves this manipulative advertising.

Media mediate between us and events in and beyond our immediate world by influencing us to define and see that world in a certain way. In the final analysis, media get right inside your personality and mediate between you and yourself. Take the critical voice, which says "too fat," for example. Isn't your ideal of the proper body form taken mainly from media? Look around next time you are at the swimming pool. See what the real range of human shapes looks like.

---

[1]If you would like to see whether your schooling thus far has misrepresented American history, read Howard Zinn's (1980) *A People's History of the United States* and James Loewen's (1996) *Lies My Teacher Told Me: Everything Your American History Textbook Got Wrong.*

Exercise: Developing Specific Insight

Generalized suspicion of media information is not enough. Rather, we need to develop very specific insights. I would like to suggest to you an exercise to start you on your way in this direction.

Sample 4 hours of television programming, picking a variety of media forms: soap operas, evening weeklies, old movies, talk shows, and so on. Pick programs that present types of human beings. For this purpose, skip sports, news, and documentaries. Concentrate on media fiction or on programs that present those media creatures we call celebrities. Take detailed notes as you watch. List the major characters and describe them in some detail: How are the characters dressed? What sort of bodies and faces do they have? What sort of posture? What do they do for a living? Are they rich, poor, or middle class? What is their ethnicity? How do they talk to each other? How old are they?

After the first 2 hours of observation, take 2 hours for real-life observation. Pick two spots in quite different neighborhoods. Choose places where you can watch people easily. Self-service laundries are very good for this, as are public parks, bus terminals, airports, and so on. Pick several people to watch and make the same observations that you made about your media characters.

Now, go back for 2 more hours of media watching. You may add new categories for observation if they occur to you during your first set of observations. Follow this with 2 more hours of real-people watching. Then, just for your own information, look over your notes and start drawing some comparisons between media people and real people. Can you see the direction in which media are distorting? Can you assess the effect of these distortions on your own attitudes toward other people—toward yourself? If you do this exercise thoroughly, I believe it will forever change the way you perceive both media and real people. I won't tell you any results on this one. I will let you find out for yourself.

If you happen to have a class or independent study in which you could use these observations for a project, one good way to present your findings is by making a visual presentation for the class. If you don't have a camera, you might try comparing people in magazine advertisements to magazine pictures of real people. (You will find real people rather hard to find in most magazines. This itself is an eye opener.) In preparing visual programs, I found that it was nearly impossible to find pictures of real blue-collar workers in magazines. I also discovered that my pictures of real people were mainly in black and white, while the advertisement people were mainly in color. How subtly such a difference acts on our intelligence, making the advertisement pictures somehow more vivid and real than actual people.

If you have a camera and don't mind taking pictures of people or can do so inconspicuously, you can use presentation software to prepare slides of real people and compare them with slides made from magazine advertising. There are many possible variations on this theme. For example, you might compare just people over 65 years of age in media and reality, or you might use teenagers or non-Whites. Take any aspect particularly interesting to you.

I hope that in this chapter I have given you the idea that knowledge can be acquired playfully. It is when we play that we are most imaginative and also the most open to new ideas. Perhaps you can design some exercises of your own to explore some dimension of experience that fascinates or frustrates you.

Mind, Self, and Media

The media have become so all pervasive in our society that it is no longer easy to determine whether the media are an extension of our culture or whether our culture has become merely an extension of the media. Although there is certainly enough in this issue alone to write a very lengthy (and probably very dry) book, I would just like you to consider for a moment that this is not an issue that should be of concern only to bespectacled professors and social philosophers. This is an issue that strikes at the very root of your experience of college and, indeed, may strike at the very root of what it means to live in this society.

To start with, I would like you to consider the idea that we are not born knowing what it means to be human. We are not born with an instinctual framework or the hard wiring that allows us to unerringly relate to others. We do not come into the world with some ingrained, prescribed set of roles and rules for interactions between ourselves and with ourselves. Unlike a bee or an ant, which seems to be born already capable of acting perfectly within the role given to it, we are born with a largely undetermined way of being. Instead, we are born into a culture, and this culture, in large part, determines what it means to be human and how we are to express this humanity in and through ourselves. Our culture, in large part, determines who we are; it determines our identity.

Considering the role that mass media play in our culture and the role that culture plays in shaping our identity, it is imperative that we begin to look critically at our personal relationship to the media and, probably more important, how this relationship affects our experience of the world.

If we stop for a second to consider where we get most of our information about the world outside of our direct experience, it becomes obvious that most information is delivered and filtered through one of two sources, either the media or educational institutions. Fortunately, our educational institutions are structured in such a way that there is some involvement in the process; it is possible to engage in healthy questioning and dialogue concerning what we are being told. Information from the media, on the other hand, is presented in such a way that we are passive, usually sitting in our living rooms or dorms while the images and words are played in front of us. The result is that we are given a view of the world that is exactly what someone else wishes us to see. This should raise some concern when we think about what the possible motivations are for presenting exactly what we are shown. Rather than listing what some of these motives might be, I think it would be helpful to let you engage in this questioning exercise yourself.

It is not only through news programs that the media shape our perceptions of the world. On a much broader and more insidious level, media shape our experience of the world through television, radio programs, and advertisements. Media culture depends on selling products for its survival, and most of its vast machinery is geared with this end in mind.

There is something that is required for the realization of this end, however. It is impossible to sell an endless line of products to people who are basically content with who they are. The survival of media culture depends first on us seeing ourselves as always lacking in some fundamental aspect. This is why the images of people given to us through most television programs and magazines are nothing like representative samples of the public. Quite simply, the media culture could not survive if it allowed itself to show us images that are closely related to what we really are. Instead, we are given an image of humanity that is very narrow, to say the least. We tend to take these images as what we are supposed to be, internalizing those images as some sort of true picture of reality. But, of course, most of us are nothing like these images.

Media culture creates, for us, an identity based not on who we actually are but rather on what we are not. We are not inherently attractive, so we need makeup and hairspray to closer approximate the image of feminine beauty given in the latest prime-time sitcom. Our bodies are not shaped properly, so we need the latest fad food supplement. And then, when it seems that we are actually catching up and have the latest fashions and the fastest computers, corporations come out with a new line that makes what we currently have obsolete.

Think for a moment about why there are new high-fashion lines presented at least yearly or why car manufacturers come out with new product changes every few years. We are told that it is to bring the consumer the latest, greatest achievements of the industry. The real reason is very different. The simple fact is that our consumer-driven media culture cannot ever allow us to think that what we have is enough. Nothing ever will be enough, so long as we internalize that critical voice of the media, which says "not thin enough" when we look into the mirror. We are never whole and complete exactly as we are.

There is a very subtle philosophical principle that the media understand and use very well. The principle is that human beings tend to use the world as a mirror of themselves. We tend to define ourselves by our experience of the world. What is cruel in the media culture's manipulation of this is that the media ensure that we are constantly inundated with images that are literally impossible to attain. The actual models in magazine advertisements can't even match the images of themselves! After the model sits through hours of makeup and uncomfortable posing, the photographs are modified and enhanced by computer imaging.

This all leaves you in a position that would seem comical if it weren't so deadly serious in its effects. We look to the world to see what it means to be a human and are given images of humanity that are complete fabrications. We tend to take the images provided by the media as some sort of ideal humanity, a model of ourselves that is somehow a perfection to be attained. We are put in a position of seeing who we really are as someone who is lacking. What is tragic, and at the same time comic if you can free yourself from it, is that these images are not only not authentically ideal, they are not even human. We are left trying to attain some grotesque characterization of humanness while ignoring that to be human means to be exactly what we are, right now.

In short, media not only mediate between ourselves and the outside world, but they also make immediate experience of who we are very difficult. Look at your own criticisms of yourself and especially of your body. Whose voice is it that is really doing the criticizing? Look at your relationship to where you live and the material things that surround you. Do you spend much time really appreciating any of it, or are you always looking for something more, something better? Look at the career you might be currently considering. Are you considering it because you really think you will find some self-expression in it, or are you looking for the power to buy more material things? When those are gained, will they be enough, or is something different needed for true contentment?

I would like you to consider one last thing in this section: the idea that real contentment is not a matter of having or owning certain things but is rather about freedom. I would like you to consider the possibility that there is a sense of the word *freedom* that we have very little acquaintance with and that we should get much closer to. Freedom, in this sense, is not the outside freedom that we usually talk about when we use the word. It is not freedom of speech or expression or anything along those lines, no matter how noble these ideas of freedom are. It is certainly not the sense of freedom that media culture gives us, freedom to get more and more, to merely own whatever it is we want at this moment.

This other type of freedom is much more radical. It is an inner freedom that isn't about how we act or what we do. This freedom is concerned with who we are. In this view, freedom isn't about being able to do, or own, what we want when we want. Instead, this freedom is about being something beyond what we have been told we are and what we tell ourselves we are. It is about being something beyond our culturally conditioned identity. It is a sort of radical self-determination, a freedom to not be limited by what you think you are or are not.

We are sort of conditioned to view freedom as the ability to do what we want, yet we rarely consider that what we want is often determined by others. In our media-driven culture, this is especially true. This sense of freedom is actually a very confined space. The radical sense of freedom, however, is very different. It is the freedom to allow ourselves not to want, to allow ourselves to simply be what we are, a freedom to be complete. Most of us don't see ourselves as simply what we are. Instead, we see ourselves as not yet thin enough, rich enough, kind enough, you-name-it enough. A large part of this is a direct result of growing up in the sea of media. Another part of this freedom is the freedom to let the world, and especially other people, be exactly what they are in our experience of them. All too often, we experience the world through the filter of the media. Instead of experiencing our apartment as what it is, we experience it as not big enough. Our families may not be loving enough; that stranger is not attractive enough or not as approachable as we want him or her to be. This freedom is also about giving freedom to others to be exactly what they are.

But this freedom is not something that can really be sensed by talking about it. It must be experienced, so there are listed here a couple of experiments to help give you a taste of that freedom. It is my hope that you will experience a little bit of breathing space through these exercises. I always find these little tastes of freedom to be satisfying in the same manner that a good afternoon nap is satisfying. You may find yourself returning to these exercises again and again.

First, look at yourself nude in the mirror, briefly, and write down the judgments that you make about the image in the mirror.

Now, as in the previous exercise, sample 2 hours of television programming, taking detailed notes on how characters are dressed, what sort of bodies they have, their posture, and the manner in which they relate to each other. Do this on a fresh sheet of paper. Are they rich, poor, or middle class? What do they do for a living? What is their ethnicity? How old are they? For this exercise, skip news programs, sports, and documentaries. Focus instead on fiction programs and especially on any programs that highlight media celebrities.

After doing this, take 2 hours and observe people in real life. Try doing an hour each at two spots in quite different neighborhoods, both in places where it is easy to observe a large number of people, such as self-service laundries, shopping malls, airports, and so on. Take the same type of notes that you did in the first part, but this time add another category. This time, *list also the judgments that you make about the people you see.* Do you see them as attractive, unattractive, fat, thin, rich, poor, and so on?

Then go back and do another hour of media watching and another hour of real-life observation and look back over your notes. Draw comparisons between the images portrayed in media and the people seen in real life. In what direction do the media distort images of people? Pay particular attention to the judgments you wrote down.

Now, compare those judgments to the judgments you wrote down about yourself. To make those judgments, what are you comparing yourself and others to? Do the judgments about yourself make sense when compared with observation of people in real life? Do those judgments arise from a comparison to the real world or to something else? Are the judgments even valid in comparison to the real world? Finally, is that critical, judging voice even you, or can you identify that voice with how the media would like you to see the world?

As a final step, go back to the mirror, nude, and listen carefully to that judging voice and, as far as possible, do not do anything about it. Don't try to squelch it or identify yourself with it or change it. Stand in front of the mirror for at least 15 minutes and simply observe your image and the judging voice. What happens to both?

—*Rick Hartman*

PART III

Survival Strategies

Survival Skills

In Chapter 12, we deal with college experientially—as an altered state of being. Specifically we address the following:

- Our intimate relationship with time.
- Work tips and techniques for juggling and keeping balanced in an unbalanced world.
- Relationships, looking in particular at how not only do one's relationships change but one's very understanding of what relationships are will also change.
- Learning disabilities and how to relate to them.
- Partying and social life; namely, how should partying, drugs, and alcohol be a part of your college experience.
- Sadness, madness, anxiety, and trouble: working with the mental and emotional disorders that often arise in early adulthood.

College is different. No matter how old—or how young—you are, no matter your life experience, it *will* be different. All of your relationships will change because you will change. Whatever your expectations are, your set of life skills will be challenged, and they will grow.

You may think you know what will happen to you in college, but the understanding is in the living. Life is not a list of things to check off, a paint by numbers experience in which you know how things will end, or a predictable sitcom in which all problems disappear in a half hour. Life is an evolving process centered on the beauty of human interactions and change. College is a wonderful microcosm of life. Prepare to break away from your preconceived notions and learn a whole new set of survival skills.

College Should Be . . .

Going to college should be about parties, playing the field, and meeting tons of new people, or at least that is what I thought. Three years after entering college, I realized how much that mentality stunted my growth. I met my boyfriend the summer before entering college, at orientation. He was a junior when I was a freshman, and in a way, I deeply resented that he wanted to date me when it was only my first year at school. I mean, I thought, "I can't have a boyfriend; I should be dating the field. Why should I limit myself?"

Coming from an all-girl Catholic high school, I was a boy-crazy girl who just wanted to meet tons of new people and date around. I wanted the "ideal" college life—you know, the whole frat-party-getting-drunk kind of life. I honestly thought that was what college was about. I pushed my boyfriend away for a long time while I was adjusting to living away from home, trying to find a major, and finding my niche in school. I pushed him farther away with my mentality that college was about dating the field. I broke up with him several times to date the field and wound up going back to him because deep down, I knew that he was someone I could see a future with. I lived by the "college should be . . ." mentality given to me by the media and society instead of listening to myself.

Now, I'm not saying that you should go get a boyfriend and stick with him for your entire college career. What I am saying is that there is no standard college experience. Everyone's college experience is different. We all experience different majors, classes, and relationships, so how can there really be a "standard" experience? Looking back, I regret that I pushed my boyfriend away so hard for such a dumb reason because our relationship could have been stronger and healthier had I known that there is no standard "ideal" college experience. Three years into college, I finally learned to just enjoy college as it is and go with the flow. I learned not to get stuck on the "shoulds" because it might stunt my growth as a person, a student, and even as a friend.

—*Christina Le*

Making Decisions Alone

A tough question I had to ask myself after entering college was am I happy with the decisions I am making? This question took on a different meaning from when I asked myself this in high school. In high school, the decisions I made were affected by parents, counselors, friends, coaches, and mentors. College has brought a feeling of indescribable loneliness. I don't live with my parents, counselors are hard to come by, I have a whole new set of friends who don't really know me, I don't play a sport anymore, and I have yet to find someone I can really confide in here.

The decisions I make seem to be more individualized and unguided than ever. So how do I know that I'm making the right ones? My parents have given up on their dreams of making me their little doctor. I've switched majors, picked up new hobbies, and made friends that are polar opposites of friends I had in high school. This has been the biggest handle I've had on the decision-making process of my entire life. When I was a kid, choosing what flavor ice cream I wanted from the store was hard enough. Chocolate or mint chocolate? Decisions, decisions, decisions!

These days, my decisions are much tougher than choosing ice cream. The hardest and most conflicted decision for me is choosing a major and deciding what I want to do when I graduate from college. It's a constant battle between practicality and passion. I'm continually reversing the choices I make—one minute I'm an English major with a Political Science minor, the next minute I'm a Political Science major with an English minor. The routes continue to intertwine—I'm not exactly sure which path I'm even on anymore.

Or is a path even necessary? Often, I wonder why it is that I can't just take classes that sound interesting, whether they are psychology classes, political science classes, math classes, or English classes. Someone suggested that I become a Liberal Arts major, and that didn't seem like such a bad idea.

Then my cell phone rings, and I get into a long discussion with my parents about "The Future." Dum, da, dum! Their new path for me, law school, looms menacingly in front of me. Perhaps law school will provide the comfortable life my parents want to ensure for me. Perhaps when it comes closer to graduation that is the decision I will make.

For now, I've decided college has become a place for me to partake in activities that I want to partake in because it's my life. And following my heart has always brought better results than following my head or someone else's heart. I've decided to major in Creative Writing, seen as a wholly impractical decision by some but a wholly inspiring decision for me. I've never felt happier and more secure in my life because, in the end, the decisions I've made have been the most fulfilling for me.

And that is the lesson I've learned since entering college. College has empowered me to be able to answer my own questions, make my own decisions, and carve my own path in life. That path, titled "Dreams," will be the path I choose to follow for the rest of my life.

—*Jasleen Ahuja*

Our Intimate Relationship With Time

Our sensed experience of time tells us that time is not real. An hour spent jet-lagged is not the same hour spent in a leisurely afternoon of pleasure reading, and it's not the same hour spent in a big boring lecture hall, and it's not the same hour spent watching television. Yet, somehow we imagine them to be the same increasingly precious hour. College will fine-tune your sense of time, usually teaching you to parcel it out very carefully and sustain the ever faster pace of the modern world.

Take a Bite Out of Time

You may balk at considering our conception of time to be a socialized idea. After all, the sun does set every night as it rises every morning. The seasons change, and the moon waxes and wanes like clockwork. But consider first that different cultures have different conceptions of time. While the Western tradition views time as linear, a progression from past to present to future, Eastern philosophy has typically seen it as a cyclical affair—dynasties will rise and dynasties will fall, just as people will be born and people will die. Most would feel humbled imagining themselves as tiny parts of this ever-churning cycle.

But this is not our world. Ours is one of breakneck schedules and all-nighters, back-to-back midterms and precariously managed social lives. When you graduate from college, you will trade all of this for PDAs, coffee breaks, 6:00 a.m. mornings, and casual Fridays. We're not quite living in the present but always worrying maniacally about the imminent future.

Have you ever given yourself a stomachache by eating too fast or "on the go" to satisfy a schedule demand? Have you given yourself an ulcer by stressing yourself out? Surely you know someone who has. Have you ever weaved in and out of traffic hoping to get to your destination on time—only to have shaved, at most, 30 seconds off? Perhaps you've failed to recognize a good friend you've passed while hurrying to class.

Try this the next time you're hurrying to class and you feel you will most certainly be late: Slow yourself to a crawling speed, and toss away your feelings of anxiety. Look around you. Is the sun shining? Are the clouds fluffy today? Maybe it's raining, and you were ignoring that spectacular din of spattering raindrops and that stinky smell that always comes out when it rains a little. Imagine yourself as a speck in the ever-churning cycle of life, and then imagine the ultimate consequences you will face for being 2 minutes late to class today. Pales in comparison, doesn't it?

—Andy Wang

Work

One of the most crucial life skills that you can develop is the ability to maintain a balanced life. But even the calmest, most balanced student is likely to struggle with balancing the time to study and earning the money to pay for it. Many, if not most, students will have to work, but it is possible to productively juggle both, and you may even find that your work and school lives complement and enhance each other.

When Working Is Required

We go to college so that when we get out we are ready for fast-paced high-paying jobs. So where does burger flipping come in? Many students at universities are finding tuition and board a bit much for their budgets and are resorting to minimum wage work with high scheduling demands.

Coming to college, I knew that I would have to get a job, the sooner the better. Never having been in college, I wasn't sure what to expect, so I waited 2 weeks into first quarter to begin the job search. I figured 2 weeks would be enough to get adjusted to dorm life and my study load. Little did I know that there were thousands of students who hadn't postponed their searches and had taken all the jobs I wanted. I applied to the different libraries on campus, but the only shifts they had left were in the mornings when I had class. I applied to fast food restaurants, but they were full as well.

After 2 weeks of searching, my bank account was getting low and my patience was growing thin. By then I was willing to work anywhere. Finally, during fourth week, a cashiering position opened up and I had my first interview. Dressed in a business outfit, I headed for the interview with mixed feelings and little hope of being hired for any job on campus. I was desperate as I walked into the manager's office, and she must have sensed that because she was really nice to me. I told her I was willing to work whenever she wanted and would alter my schedule second quarter to fit her needs. I told her I didn't care what was needed of me as long as I was hired—and I was hired on the spot.

My first college job! I was so excited. Finally, a paycheck. But would the long days in class followed by hours on my feet be worth $6.75 per hour? Would staying up all night, every night trying to catch up on studying be worth it? Where were all the easy jobs that would allow me to study while on the clock? I had heard about them on tours and orientation, but they seemed to be hiding. This was only my first quarter of college, and I was already feeling overwhelmed. What was I thinking? I hadn't even started the job, and I was already considering quitting in order to salvage my G.P.A. I couldn't work every Saturday and Sunday for the rest of the quarter! I couldn't squeeze 2 hours of work between two classes and then close at night.

My job required that I work 10 hours a week plus weekends. I also had to work a minimum of 2 hours per shift. My bosses didn't care whether I had midterms or finals because all the cashiers had them and I was new. So I found myself sleeping during classes, even when I was sitting in the front row. I wasn't studying as much as I needed to get the grades I wanted, and I felt trapped. I couldn't cut back on my hours, and I was losing sleep to keep up with my reading as it was. I didn't know what to do.

Three weeks after I started cashiering, I was talking to a friend about a job she found. It paid more than mine and had a very flexible schedule. She did fund-raising for the university. She said it wasn't telemarketing, but it sounded like it to me. Still, the schedule was tempting. I didn't want to leave my cashiering job for one that I wasn't sure of, so I worked at both for a whole quarter. Schedules clashed and I felt like I was being pulled in three directions. The workload from school and the time constraints of two jobs pulled and tugged until I had to choose. I chose to raise funds for the university because the schedule was better, and I have never regretted it.

Starting college presents budget constraints that may require that we get jobs. Finding one that fits your personality is key to your survival. Flexible schedules can save you during finals and make having a job seem like less of a burden.

—Shawna Wood

The Curriculum of Working and Schooling

I was raised in a wealthy family. All of that changed in 1992 during the deadly Los Angeles riots, which were sparked by the infamous verdict regarding the Rodney King beating. After that specific point in time, I grew up really fast.

My father is an entrepreneur, as is my mother. None of my grandparents had ever had more than enough money to make ends meet. Neither of my parents possesses more than an associate's degree. However, they had founded and successfully operated numerous business ventures, worked extremely hard, and had made wise business decisions for almost two decades. But the impact of the riots on my family's livelihood soon became clear. It heavily damaged revenues and made it impossible to realize value from the property. The financial burdens became heavier as arguments between my parents became louder and more frequent. After a bankruptcy, foreclosure, legal separation, massive heart attack, and finally a divorce, my family had fallen from a great height, and I was not sure whether things would ever return to how they used to be.

Then the phone rang.

It was my father. It was the man who had made it financially possible for me to be in Irvine. He asked me whether I would like to join him in a new business venture, and soon I was working 14-hour days, 7 days a week, alongside my 53-year-old father who had lost everything during the past 6 years. The restaurant became my icon for hope and rebirth. I did not make it back to school for the fall quarter. I became very efficient, yet somehow the time necessary to perform academically was seldom available. I re-enrolled

2 years later with a vengeance, and now, after a roller coaster ride of ups and downs, I'm enrolled in a full-time program at UCI, yet I also have responsibilities and research activities going on with the restaurant. Studying has become more difficult since my days as a freshman and sophomore; however, my study habits and note-taking skills have improved drastically. I believe that my rapid entry into the real world has something to do with the way I read, write, and most important, the way I analyze. I believe I am better off for having worked and studied simultaneously. I learned things that school does not, or rather, could not teach me. There are always benefits and drawbacks to dividing your focus, and the decisions you make today will shape your livelihood of tomorrow.

The world outside of academia is not the same as it is inside, and therefore you will need skills not available in academic courses in order to realize your dreams. Follow your heart, and always bite off more than you can chew. Just learn how to rise to an occasion.

—*Missak Michael Sarkissian*

Finding an Internship

One of the hardest, yet most rewarding aspects of college has been trying to juggle work and school. If I had to give only one piece of advice, it would definitely be to get a job related to your field of study. First of all, it gives you a chance to see the environment that you will potentially be working in. You may find that you love the work but despise the environment. For myself, aspects such as these really affect my decisions about the field of work I will choose. Also, by working in the field that you are interested in, you are already one step ahead of your peers. It is the best feeling to know that you are experiencing firsthand what the professor is lecturing on. The way that I see it, the theories that are discussed in lectures are very vague until you actually apply them. On the other hand, if you do not know the basics behind the work you are doing, then there is only so far that you can go with it. So by working in your field and studying the concepts in school at the same time, you're getting the best of both worlds.

Working while going to school also makes the material you learn much more interesting. It adds a dimension to your life that fills the void of wondering what you're learning all this for. Personally, before I started to work, I felt as though I was just memorizing material for no apparent reason. I could not figure out how they would apply to anything I was doing, but now I actually see the parallels between lectures and work.

Last but definitely not least, because most of us are starving college students, the income really does not hurt. Although you will probably end up working in an internship of some sort, the experience alone is worth it. You might not be making as much as your friend who is working at the mall, but with the experience that you are getting at such a young age, in the long run you'll be the one making the big bucks (at least that's what we tell ourselves).

Don't get me wrong. Working while going to school is definitely a very difficult thing to do. There is a lot of pressure on students who are planning to go to graduate school. Between juggling your hundreds of pages of reading, your next essay, your research that you're doing with a professor; volunteering at different places; building up your extracurricular activities; and studying for the GRE, MCAT, or LSAT, or whatever it may be, it is very difficult to make time for work. If you are planning to work part time, that's already 10 or 20 hours out of your week. Those 10 or 20 hours may not necessarily have been spent studying, but regardless, it is not fair to miss out on the social aspect of college, and it's hard to make time for that when there are so many other things going on. Doing all that is necessary to get into graduate school today takes a lot out of the ideal college experience and instead fills it with more pressure and stress. Everyone has his or her own road to travel. The best thing to say would be to do what works for you. You have to know yourself well enough to know your limits. No matter how important grad school may seem now, it is not worth having a mental breakdown at the age of 22.

—*Sheyda Bogosyan*

Relationships

An integral part of the college experience is developing new relationships and new understandings of relationships. College life is an altered state of being. The relationships you have going in to college will change, partly because of the passage of time, but also because of the self-altering effects of college life. You will be different, and your new relationships will be different, too. Whether you are beginning, ending, or maintaining a relationship in college, stay awake. Anything could happen.

The Single Life

You can feel the moist sand beneath your feet as you slowly stroll the beach, hand in hand with your significant other. You gaze into each other's eyes for what seems like eternity. You sigh deeply, content with just being in the presence of your better half. You feel a gentle breeze waft through your hair and the soft glow of the setting sun radiating on your skin. You shyly smile at each other, never wanting this moment to end. Everything seems so . . . perfect.

Okay, so not all relationships are blissful like this. However, it seems as if the media and society itself has glamorized the idea of relationships to the point where someone feels lonely if he or she does not have a significant other. Think about it logically. Do you really need a boyfriend or girlfriend in order to make you feel good about yourself? If so, being in a relationship may not be right for you. You need to establish your identity and understand yourself first, before bringing another person into the equation.

When my friends and I talk about the things that we regret doing in the past, topics that often come up are (1) having a boyfriend or girlfriend coming into college and (2) entering into a relationship during the freshman year. As far as the first regret is concerned, I am by no means encouraging you to dump your significant other now that you've come to college. Rather, proceed with caution because maintaining a relationship in this new stage of your life may be quite difficult, especially if you attend different schools. During my first year, I observed many late-night phone calls of exhausted floormates who still had emotional strings attached to a distant significant other. Even after a long, arduous day, my friends would make a commendable effort to catch up with their loved ones and try to find out what was going on in their lives until the wee hours of the morning. Unfortunately, despite these efforts, many of those long-distance relationships did not last. The difficulties of maintaining a healthy relationship are magnified when distance is involved, and ultimately, continuing the relationship becomes an overwhelming task.

Now as far as the second common regret is concerned, I understand that you may be on your own for the first time and are eager to explore various opportunities and relationships. This sudden surge of freedom that accompanies the entrance into this new and exciting environment can cause people to feel somewhat insecure and become dependent on a significant other to make them feel happy and confident. Yet during this first year, one should really try to make good friends, not boyfriends or girlfriends. Many people tend to cut themselves off from their close friends, or potential friends, while in a relationship. You definitely do not want to be cutting off people during your first year; rather, you should try to really get to know as many people as possible. Be social. You only get one first year, so you might as well make the most of it.

Relationships are inevitably time consuming. It may be more important for you to take some time for yourself instead of finding a significant other at this stage of your life. Hang out with friends. Join on-campus clubs and organizations. Go out and party. Study and do well in your classes. Being single gives you many opportunities and a lot of time that you may not have in the future, once you enter into a relationship.

Carpe Diem! Seize the day! Or rather, seize the time you can enjoy as a single adult. You have plenty of time in the future to date people and find the love of your life. As for now, enjoy the time you can spend with family and friends and the freedom of single life.

—Lisa Miyake

Long Distance Relationships

When I entered college, I was involved in a long distance relationship. My boyfriend Robert was in his senior year in high school in Michigan, and I was in college here in California. Most people think that long distance relationships never work out, but Robert and I have proved them wrong because regardless of the physical distance between us, our relationship, like any other "normal" relationship, continued to grow and develop into a very serious, committed, and healthy relationship.

I admit, however, that I did have some fears and doubts about us when I entered college. One of my fears was that one of us would feel resented or taken for granted by the other person. I didn't want Robert to feel like I was neglecting him or forgetting him, and I didn't want him to think that I felt neglected or forgotten either. I don't know if I ever told Robert or if I'll ever tell him, but I did sacrifice many opportunities to go clubbing, Del Taco runs, and house events just to spend time talking to him over the phone or instant messaging. Essentially, I spent a great deal of the first two quarters my freshman year just sitting around and waiting to talk to him, but I don't regret it at all.

Also, I was concerned about people talking and putting ideas and thoughts into our heads and making us doubt ourselves. Many of my housemates thought I was crazy and stupid for what I was doing. One guy even told me that I was being "played," but I didn't listen to him because I knew that if I started listening to what he was saying, I would start to doubt my faith in Robert and our relationship. I don't deny that there was a time when I almost believed what people were saying because I would wait for Robert to call me and he wouldn't call, or I would call him and his mother would say he was at the movies. Moments like this made me feel like a fool for spending so much time waiting for him while he was having fun. But the last thing I wanted to do was admit to myself that what people were saying could be true. So when I got to low points like this, I just reminded myself that I should never doubt Robert because he would never doubt me.

Another fear of mine was that Robert and I would grow distant and apart because we couldn't actually see each other or be with each other physically. We had about 2,000 miles separating us, so there wasn't any way I could drive to and back from Michigan during a weekend. I feared that because I couldn't see Robert and spend some quality time with him, our personalities and lifestyles would drift off onto different paths. To be honest, I was always afraid that the next e-mail I would read or the next phone conversation we'd have would be our last because I was afraid he might say that he didn't think it was going to work out because we were different now.

In retrospect, I realize that not only did I spend a lot of time waiting my freshman year, but I also spent a lot of time stressing over my fears and doubts. I realize today that all those fears and doubts were nothing but fears and doubts. The truth was that I had nothing to worry about because we never stopped loving each other, and that love kept our relationship together. Till this day, I still wonder whether Robert ever asked himself whether the voice on the other end of the phone, the person replying to his instant messages, the person reading his letters was the same person he last saw, touched, hugged, and kissed. I hope that others who are in long distance relationships will see that any relationship can work out if both people are committed and willing to be a part of the relationship.

—*Christie Vong*

Learning Disabilities

Fifteen million children, adolescents, and adults in the United States live with a learning disability of some sort. The National Center for Learning Disabilities says that a learning disability "is more than a difference or difficulty with learning—it is a neurological disorder that affects the brain's ability to receive, process, store, and respond to information" (http://www.ncld.org). If you suspect that you have a learning disability, visit your college's Office for Students With Disabilities (OSD) and get tested. The resources they offer can help you tremendously.

Disability

I have a learning disability called dysgraphia. This sentence has been the beginning of all of my introductions for as long as I can remember. It is the sentence I deliver to my professors after the first day of lectures every quarter. Living with dysgraphia, I have found that there is a terrible tendency to belittle, ignore, and reject anything or anyone out of the ordinary. I have had friends who, despite already knowing me and dealing with my disability, have completely disregarded the authenticity of people with ADD or ADHD. Of course, while casual grievances and ignorance of one's peers can be aggravating, when this denial comes from someone in a position of power, the consequences can be far more damning and far reaching. After experiencing countless barriers, many people understandably give up and quit fighting altogether. I strongly urge you not to give up. That can only make things worse. If someone confides in you that he or she has a disability, please treat him or her with understanding and respect because after so many rejections, it can be quite difficult to continue to reach out.

The most important thing about living with a learning disability is your willingness to ask for help and accommodations. You can't get extra time if you don't ask for it. The same thing goes for typing exams, recording lectures, getting copies of notes, or any of the other accommodations you may require. The more complicated and severe someone's symptoms are, the more that person has to fight for accommodations. Where do you go to get accommodations? Now that you are at college, your campus has a special department of counselors just for dealing with the needs of students with disabilities. If you weren't aware of this, you need to put this book down, walk over there right now, and get yourself registered. My experience with the OSD has been phenomenal. Not only was I given all of the accommodations I asked for, I was also offered additional accommodations that I'd never imagined. Still, getting accommodations at a university can be difficult. They may try to squeeze you into their one-size-fits-all accommodation package, and complicated or unusual accommodations are something you may have to fight for. It is absolutely essential that you get diagnosed if you haven't been already. It will just take a handful of tests over a couple of visits and an incredible weight will be lifted from your world.

There are two significant roadblocks that can tie your counselor's hands: department/campus policy and system-wide university policy. If your college imposes an edict on students that prevents you from receiving an accommodation, you may find yourself with a challenge. The origin of the edict is very important when you attempt to circum-navigate it. If the rule comes from your campus or academic department, theoretically they should be able to make an exception for you if you lay out a compelling case to the proper authorities through the proper channels, usually your counselors. If you are at a public school and the rule is a state policy for all public schools, you are not likely to be able to make much headway unless you have extreme circumstances. If you go to a private school, your circumstances will vary more from school to school, but as a general rule of thumb, you should have more wiggle room when it comes to the enforcement of edicts.

—Michael Creim

Partying and Social Life

It would be naïve to imagine that college is just for lectures, studying, and book learning and that good study skills would be the only skills you need to navigate the social world of college successfully. You should go to parties—you'll meet new friends and learn a lot—but keep in mind that parties also have a unique set of risks, including substance problems and sexual violence. Remember to maintain a balance in your life and keep a sane schedule.

Partying

As a little girl, I remember watching older family friends leave for college. Although I obviously knew little about the undergraduate experience, I quickly learned that two things were always associated with the infamous college years—all-night study sessions and beer. For every student who attends a university for the purpose of getting an education, another is there to have a good time.

As much as your parents want you to believe that college is purely a time for academic betterment, it's not. Much of what you will learn and remember from college will not be from the classroom. Rather, you will gain knowledge and memories from the people around you and from your own unique experiences. Although it is true that a significant portion of your time during college will be devoted to scholastic pursuits, it is also true that much of your time will not be filled with such activities. How you want to spend your free time is your choice, but for many college students, this is where beer comes in.

Fraternity parties, apartment parties, house parties, and clubs often draw bigger crowds of college students than do the classrooms. The combination of music, dancing, socializing, and alcohol is often difficult for most 18- to 22-year-olds to resist. Not only can you meet new people while spending time with friends, but you also have the chance to grab a drink and forget about school and various other stresses that are such a large part of college life. When handled responsibly, partying can be a very rewarding and worthwhile pastime.

Yet partying has a bad rap. Parents constantly worry about their inexperienced children neglecting schoolwork because of the great party scene appeal. Poor performance in school as a result of excessive partying is a notorious contributor to the college drop-out rate. Furthermore, parents and especially local law enforcement do not look favorably upon the alcohol present at most parties—especially the underage drinking. Ever since you were old enough to understand the word "alcohol," you were warned of its disadvantageous effects. Alcohol impairs judgment and is very unhealthy when consumed on a regular basis. Alcohol is a depressant and can cause many people to become belligerent. When consumed in excess, alcohol can cause illness, incoherence, and sometimes, even death. Certainly, it is difficult to deny the dangers associated with the consumption of alcohol. However, it is naïve to think that college students will not continue to participate in such activities despite warnings. College is a place where young adults want to experience things never available to them before—alcohol included.

Thus, it is helpful to distinguish between responsible partying and irresponsible partying. Yes, drinking is fun. However, getting sick because you drank too much is not fun. Having a hangover is not fun.

Passing out in a strange place is not fun. First of all, if you make the decision to drink, do so with good friends who will stay with you throughout the night and take care of you if you drink too much. Also, keep track of how much alcohol you are consuming. If you are unable to tally how much you have had to drink, it might be a good idea to stop. There is a point while consuming alcohol when you are most likely enjoying yourself and you do not need any more to have a good time. Attempt to recognize this point and cease drinking. Drinking more alcohol will not necessarily be more fun; rather, it will make you ill. Moreover, always open your drinks yourself, or watch your drinks being poured. This tip applies most to young women who (sadly enough) must make themselves aware of the threats of date rape drugs such as "roofies." It is worth noting that if you are an inexperienced drinker, it may take some time to discover your alcohol tolerance. Thus, it is all the more important to be especially cautious when drinking. Drink slowly and be aware of your surroundings. Do not put yourself in a situation that seems dangerous; try to exercise good judgment. After all, you are an intelligent college student.

Most important, you do not have to drink to party or to be social. Plenty of fun can be had without drinking. In fact, more college students than you would think actively choose to abstain from drinking because of religious, moral, or family-related reasons. And like many of their alcohol-consuming counterparts, these students successfully find activities that help make their college experiences pleasurable—whether it is going to parties or participating in various other group activities. Thus, although drinking may be prevalent in the college atmosphere, it is not necessary and therefore should never be forced upon anyone. Peer pressure may be difficult to overcome, but following your personal beliefs and goals is self-empowerment that will help guide you through any tough situation.

Even the most studious of college students does not want to devote all her time to studying. Furthermore, if one did want to study for every waking hour of the day, he or she would still find the task difficult. Anyone who has studied for extensive amounts of time will realize that it is very exhausting; studying can even wear on one's sanity. In fact, to be most productive when studying, it is helpful to maintain the balance between school and social activities. Spending time with friends, participating in group activities, or partying in your free time can act as a stress release and make the time allotted for school more productive and perhaps more enjoyable. Socializing also helps you build relationships with people who are similar to you, many of whom you will be friends with for years to come. However, this balance between academics and social activities is easier said than done. Creating a healthy balance may take some practice, but the prospect of doing well in school while also enjoying your college years is well worth the effort.

—Melissa Reggiardo

Professional Juggler

"Who is this so-called professional juggler?" you ask. Well, we all are, or at least that's the goal. As students, we are all trying to juggle school and our social lives. This issue may sound a bit trivial, but if we take a good look, we will find that if we don't juggle these two with care, grave consequences can result. Academic probation, suspension, drop in G.P.A., financial assistance revocation—all these things have rippling effects in our lives forever; therefore, it's imperative to go from a novice juggler to a professional one, and fast. The failure to do so could mean risking everything you have worked so hard for.

As we all know, college is a whole different world with new temptations awaiting us. We make friends with people from all over the United States and even around the world. Suddenly, the umbilical cord is cut and we find ourselves independent for the first time; we finally have freedom. The problem is that some of us might go a bit "freedom crazy." After all, we worked hard to get here; why not go out and have some fun; we deserve it, right? The problem is being able to recognize when partying becomes excessive. Most of the time, we won't be able to recognize it until our alarm goes off and we're too hung over to figure out where the snooze button is. "What 8:00 a.m. class?" The secret is learning how to balance both worlds: academic and social.

Balance is not an easy thing to do when you have many influences around you that are "pro partying." Friends play a huge part in "helping" you decide whether you should stay home and finish your essay or go out with the clan. As students of higher learning, we tend to see peer pressure as something that was left behind in high school; we're too smart to fall for those old tricks, aren't we? To be perfectly honest, I gave in to my friends' invitations plenty of times, even though I knew I had tons of work to do and even more to catch up on. What makes this worse is that I had done my fair share of partying prior to entering the college system, and yet I found myself going out with the "girls" every chance I got. There were new places to go and new people to meet. I found myself justifying this excessive behavior by convincing myself that I needed to go out because I'd been working too hard, or telling myself "I need to take a break from schoolwork." The prevailing mentality among college students is this is what college life is all about. Hey, we've all seen the movie *Animal House*, right?

Unfortunately, being a college student also involves making decisions, and we need to make decisions about the friends that we make and keep while in college. When it really comes down to it, birds of a feather do flock together. The circles of friends that we keep can really influence our decisions as far as school is concerned. I barely survived my junior year; I kept partying with my "girls." I know I could have done better academically, but my best friend at the time was Procrastination—you might know him, too. One of my girls really knew him; I think they were in love, and he messed her up really good. She kept putting her work on hold and went out and lived it up for the majority of her junior year. When she returned the following year (her senior year), she received a letter stating that she had been dropped from the university for not maintaining a satisfactory G.P.A. After a letter of appeal and a lot of stress, she was allowed to take a couple of courses while on academic probation. Her financial aid has been revoked, and she's still not technically a university student. That decision is dependent on her grades for these courses.

The only reason that I didn't meet the same fate was eventually I wised up. I learned that if I wanted to go out, it would have to be in moderation. I created rules for myself; I became disciplined. I decided that I would only go out on weekends and only if I had my homework for that week done. I cannot lie; occasionally I would break this rule and go out without doing my homework. However, when this happened, I would feel guilty the whole night and anxious because I knew that I had a deadline in 2 days. Believe me, this is the worst feeling to have at a club or a bar at 12:00 a.m. while everyone around you is having a blast. It's simply not worth it. Another tactic I found helpful was to lock my apartment door and actually study. Yes, it's true, studying actually helps with the whole school thing. When my friends would come by and knock, I pretended I wasn't home. Eventually, I actually learned how to say no. Believe it or not, it wasn't that hard; a simple "I can't go out tonight. I have a lot of homework; maybe next time," with a smile, can do the job.

The bottom line is we are now independent adults, and our parents are not looking over our shoulders every few seconds, so it's up to us to make wise decisions. Ultimately, every decision we make will have a negative or positive effect on our lives; we cannot blame anyone else for the choices we make. It's a simple matter of asking ourselves what is more important to us: our education or a good time. We have to remember that we can party at anytime, but how often or for how long will we be enrolled at a university? Yes, we all worked very hard to get to where we are now, but we must remember that it is possible to have both worlds; it's all a matter of balance and moderation. Anything in excess can have heavy consequences, and it's only when we realize this that we can go from a novice juggler to a professional one.

—*Veronica Fematt*

Recovery and Rehab

I don't want to write an essay about all the drugs I did, how much of a mess I eventually became, and how much better I am now that I've gotten my life together and "overcome my challenges." An essay like that would work great in an application to college. In fact, an essay that pretty much told that exact story helped me get into a great university (for which I'm very grateful). Essays like that have their place in the world. They help people see the power of the human spirit, and they give a little hope to others who might not feel like they can ever pull themselves out of a tough spot.

While an essay like that has a place in my life, I want to write a slightly different essay here. I want to talk about my experiences as an inquisitive student who sought to find enlightenment—either intellectual or spiritual—with drugs and alcohol as pathways to that enlightenment. I understand that this is not the experience of everyone who tries drugs in their youth. There are plenty of American kids who will try some pot or Adderall at a college party because of social pressures, continue to use those substances through college, and grow up to have a more or less healthy adult relationship with psychoactive chemicals. This essay is not for those people. This essay is for the loners, the music snobs, the band geeks, the science nerds, and the artists. This essay is for kids who are intelligent enough to have already decided whether or not drugs will be a part of their lives. I think it's important to write to people who are going through the choices I went through because now that I'm on the other side of those choices, I have a little bit more information about who I am and the potential roads I can go down in life. I want to give some "straight talk" of my own that seeks neither to advertise drugs nor to speak to young people as a conservative "adult" voice in an attempt to protect them from themselves. Drugs are complex and powerful substances, and the more that can be said honestly about them from people who actually have experience with them, the better.

I first got high on marijuana when I was 13, not due to peer pressure or wild older siblings but due to an interest that was sparked by the Drug Abuse Resistance Education (DARE) program. In California, we have DARE facilitators come into our classrooms to give progressively more and more specific "don't use drugs" talks as we make our way through grades 4 through 9. My freshman year of high school, the DARE educators brought a Plexiglas-encased suitcase full of drugs and paraphernalia (as well as engaging and photo-filled pamphlets) to my health class. Their job was to run damage control, extolling the virtues of drug-free living while giving us "straight talk" to counter all of the "misinformation that our friends were probably giving us." I don't think they meant to, but they introduced me to a fascinating world of stimulants, barbiturates, hallucinogens, opiates, and dissociative drugs that I had neither heard of nor was being pressured to do by any peers. This sparked a lifelong interest in altered states and counterculture living that would persist well into adulthood.

The first weed that I successfully smoked was snuck from the home of some neighbors whose cat I was assigned to feed and water while they vacationed. I was not bullied into doing anything or made to feel "less than" if I didn't try some scary substance. Rather, I alone, in my young adolescent brain, developed a complicated plot to obtain, smoke, and set aside time to enjoy intoxication in order to explore an alternative mental state. I recruited a friend and smoked the weed I had pilfered down at a beach by my house. I can't say the effects were particularly enjoyable in the first experiment, but they were interesting nonetheless. I didn't use drugs again for 2 more years.

I tried pot again when I was a junior in high school. I had a blast. I did it with a friend again, but this time the trip was euphoric. We made memories that night, and the type of silly laughs we had that night would be familiar to anyone who's had a good experience with a drug.

For the sake of time (and dramatic effect), let's skip ahead to 4 years after my high school graduation: I had achieved great grades in community college for the first 2 years of attendance, then started to progressively withdraw from more and more classes until my transcripts had nothing but W's for entire semesters. Between some personal struggles unrelated to drugs (family problems, a bad car accident) and my own explorations into the world of clandestine intoxication, I had veered away from straight A's into some dense chunks of experience with crystal meth, cocaine, dextromethorphan cough syrup, malt liquor, marijuana, and inhaled aerosols. For a while, I kept up my job at a special-needs preschool, I dated, I played guitar in some coffee shops with friends, and I kept my deepening substance addictions hidden from my family.

In the weeks before I finally submitted to a rehab program, my girlfriend's mom had become sick of me living in her daughter's bedroom; my girlfriend was wrestling with heavy substance abuse herself; I was no longer wanted at my parents' home; and I had traded a car, a college career, that great job at the special-needs preschool, a healthy music hobby, and any semblance of dignity I still had for a daily bottle of Steel Reserve malt liquor and a couple of vials of Robitussin Extra Strength Cough Gels. I was sleeping around with other people in front of my girlfriend——never using a condom—and I was skinny, sweaty, pimply, and pathetic.

Once again, for dramatic effect, let's fast forward to my life now. I am wrapping up my bachelor's degree at age 26. I am excelling in my coursework and am a favorite among my professors around campus. I'm a hot candidate for PhD programs (which I am in the process of applying to), I tutor writing and composition on campus, and to put myself through college I am a professional DJ. I have almost 4 years of sobriety in a 12-step program. I am living the dream, so to speak, and I don't always know exactly how I got from where I was before to where I am now.

But like I said at the beginning of this piece, I want to stray away from a Cinderella sobriety story format to tell you the truth about what substances were for me back when they were still working, or at least, before they almost destroyed my life.

I went to class high a lot during those first few successful years of community college. I was buying fat bags of extremely high quality marijuana from a girl in my philosophy class, to the tune of about ¼ ounce every 10 days or so. I was drinking a bit too, often with my then-girlfriend, and I was doing all right. I was a little weird in the head sometimes, a little dodgy, a little flighty, and a little forgetful. But for the most part, I didn't see any ill effects from weed at all. This went on for a few years. My favorite times to get high were at night by myself in my room, when I could concentrate on a painting and listen to a favorite band. I remember one summer I taught myself to oil paint and I immediately excelled at it. I probably painted 20 or so lifelike portraits copied from magazines, and the whole exercise was set to the soundtrack of whatever esoteric bands I was listening to at the time. I went on a lot of solo walks around the neighborhood at four o'clock in the morning. I read eastern mystical writings like Chögyam Trungpa's *Sacred Path of the Warrior* and [Lao-Tzu's] *Tao te Ching*. I scored an old rusty typewriter with sticky keys and wrote existential poetry well into the night. I felt extremely alive and deservedly independent.

Somewhere along the line, however, the pot smoking portion of my night went from being a brief prerequisite to being the central activity in my life. The paintings I made got lazier and fewer. The music I made followed the same pattern. My friends became less and less tolerant of the way I went about getting high. I never fully understood that aspect of things: Weren't these the same friends I had been smoking with just a few months before? In retrospect, I see that they became apprehensive when I started becoming more and more greedy with my drugs, when I couldn't have fun without weed or beer, and when the activity of securing drugs trumped everything else I was doing.

I never felt completely sure of where I fit in this world. After all, I was a good person, wasn't I? I was trying to be a responsible member of society by working with kids and getting an education. I knew that I wasn't a loser or a social mutant. But I couldn't stay on the same page with people to the extent that seemed to be bringing all my friends so much success in their lives and social relationships.

I see now that I had become cripplingly selfish. I got to the point where the ingestion of substances was more important than maintaining healthy relationships with people. On top of that, I had to spin and maintain a complicated system of lies to keep everyone off my back, and I was untrustworthy. Advances in science have shown that people with alcoholism and drug addiction most likely suffer from what we refer to in my sobriety group as "an allergy of the body," wherein individuals like myself don't metabolize drugs and alcohol like other people and thus can't stop taking them once we begin—even if we only take a little bit at first. It now takes continuous participation in a 12-step program to recognize the missteps I made and to avoid once again falling into the same destructive patterns of behavior.

My recovery now is entirely contingent upon my maintenance of the 12-step program I attend by choice. Twelve-step fellowships turned out to be an excellent tool for me, not just with respect to sobriety, but as a tool for living. We often joke at meetings that we wish everyone could get sober, just for the experience of character building and self-directed spiritual growth that the steps bring. I was really hesitant to get involved in 12 step in my initial months with it. The people seemed kind of quirky; people were talking about God and quitting booze and drugs forever. I wasn't entirely interested in the lifestyle they seemed to live or the weakness I believed they had. Why did they insist on a letting a "higher power" run their lives? Why couldn't they learn to integrate substances into their lives with the fluidity I was once able to pull off?

I learned that the members of my 12-step group were just like everyone else—meaning that there were some really successful people whom I admired, and there were some whom I wanted to avoid—but I eventually began to let them get to know me. I discovered that everyone in the room had something to offer. If nothing else, they knew what it was like to go too far with drugs and alcohol, and they were working on developing a life that brought them all the thrills they once sought but without using substances as an element to get to those thrills.

I have a lot of fun in sobriety, and I would refuse to participate in the sober lifestyle if my life wasn't better now than it was before I went to meetings. I think a lot of people who don't know me that well have the perception that I need to be sheltered from drugs and alcohol, that I need to say little mantras to "keep myself strong," or that I need constant therapeutic care from self-help groups. While there is sometimes a bit of truth in these things, they are mostly inaccurate. I live a life that includes plenty of partying, fun, energy, and even alcohol (although now I'm not the one drinking). My girlfriend and many of my friends use alcohol and even pot responsibly. They have a positive experience with substances, for the most part. As a party and wedding DJ, I am around alcohol on a regular basis and I don't feel tempted by it. The 12-step work that I have done helped me make an internal change that completely reprogrammed my relationship to chemicals, people, and myself.

I navigate work, school, and meetings with as much grace as I can muster. Twelve step is a therapeutic schedule, just like something I would need if I was diabetic or had to get regular kidney dialysis. To me, it is just as important, for if I miss meetings, my emotional (and, potentially, my physical) health is in danger. I maintain my individuality, my creativity, and my spiritual inquisitiveness.

If you are that student who is trying to figure out where drugs and alcohol fit into your life, it's ultimately up to you to decide what that's going to look like. I won't make too many universal statements about whether drugs and alcohol are "good" or "bad," but I will say this from my own experience: Drugs never helped me do better in school. Any class work or class attendance that was coupled with intoxication or a psychoactive change was, at its best, awkward and anxiety ridden and at its worst, entirely debilitating to the tune of dropped classes and failed assignments. I feel that my college life has drastically improved because of sobriety, but at the same time, I feel that my experiences showed me a dark but fascinating side of myself and of life. This is a very tricky thing to talk about. In no way can I recommend the scary situations I found myself in while I was on missions to score and do drugs. I interacted with people and places that I had only seen in movies, and it was thoroughly terrifying. On the other hand, I have developed inner strength and life experience as a result of my explorations and recovery.

Ultimately, I was extremely lucky. There are many, many other ways to build character and find yourself that don't include intoxication. The heftiest portions of growth and experience that I have enjoyed have all been in sobriety. The best connections I have made with my peers and my loved ones have all been drug and alcohol free. Nothing is a substitute for the pure and lasting joys of experiencing nature, love, health—and even pain and struggle—free from the clouding effects of psychoactives. The best advice I can give would be to take the path of least resistance, and I believe that a sober life is far less complicated and dangerous than the alternative. But if you do decide to tread, tread carefully. I didn't know what powerlessness looked like until I had lost my ability to tread when and where I pleased.

—*Joseph Guisti*

Rape: What They Forget to Mention About Partying

It begins as a slight tremor that runs down the entirety of her body. It seems as if she is dreaming, for she is still sound asleep. Then within seconds, the slight tremors turn into violent shakes. Her body writhes uncontrollably, snapping her to consciousness. But even though she is now fully aware of her surroundings, the violent writhing maintains possession of her body. Tears begin to flow from her eyes.

But all this is manageable.

The deep moans of an intense inner agony tear the witness apart. The moans resemble a person dying of a disease that has consumed each part of the body. The psychological pain is so intense that it captures control of her muscles, and she is reduced to a shaking, sweating body that desperately calls out for help in the form of awful wailing.

It is hard to wake up next to someone like this in the middle of the night. It is hard to see someone you love suffer from something far deeper than a physical ailment.

Indeed, victims of molestation and rape bear worse scars than mere physical maladies, for their scars rest upon the mind and upon the heart. These painful marks can never be erased, never be controlled, never be medicated. They arise at random and stay at will.

If parties on college campuses were intended to be enjoyable, it would seem that each could control himself or herself, be social, and meet new people. But as we mix alcohol, drugs, and hormones in a confined space, we create an ideal atmosphere for abuse. Take away our inhibitions, and we undergo a massive deconstruction of our socialization in seconds.

We become true human animals. Our instincts and drives become increasingly difficult to control. And people get hurt.

If the debauchery of parties confined itself to that "magical night" of the event, it would be easier to rationalize negative consequences emerging from such situations. A sexual rendezvous could at least be reasoned away: I got out of control once; it's over; let's move on.

But the emotional scars last for years, last for lifetimes.

An epidemic of heinous acts is taking control of our college campuses. As naïve students leave home for the first time, the freedom that parties offer tempts normally bright students to experiment and try new things. But when 20% to 25% of all college women report a sexual experience that meets the legal definition of rape or attempted rape, we know it is time to reconsider the merits of parties, drinking, and drugs (Centers for Disease Control and Prevention, 2008).

If we reflect on this number, what does it mean? When a woman shops with four of her friends, one of them will be carrying an immense emotional burden, a degrading secret. In an apartment of college-aged women, one of the four will likely experience sleep disturbance, an eating disorder, decreased appetite, and sexual dysfunction from the psychological trauma of an attempted rape (Centers for Disease Control and Prevention, 2008). Count four or five of your best female friends. At least one experienced a life shattering event. And perhaps it was or will be you.

Parties on college campuses are not the cause of rape. But they place young people in a situation that multiplies the chances that one will occur. The combination of alcohol; frequently dark, isolated spaces; hormones; and new-found feelings of complete freedom from parents encourages actions that have life-long implications.

Rape victims often feel encouraged to systematically repress the traumatic event. The sickness of rape and attempted rape lies in the fact that the victim tends to blame herself. She should have been more responsible; she should have resisted more; she had it coming. In fact, one of the sheer injustices of rape is that an estimated 84% go unreported to authorities (Office of Health Education, 2006). The victim blames herself and wishes not to implicate the friend who raped her.

Tragically, "friend" is the right word. The vast majority of assailants are known to the victim, more than half are friends, and about one fourth are intimate partners (Paralumun New Age Village, n.d.).

Partying is an important part of college life. The movement from youth to adulthood also offers a wonderful chance to experiment with life and to develop one's morality. So the abolition of social events surely is not a justifiable answer, although victims may disagree with this. Instead, it is important for young people to realize that there is wisdom in using caution around alcohol and drugs. There is wisdom in living moderately and consuming moderately. It is important to party with friends who can watch out for each other. And no matter how cynical and horrible it sounds, it is important to remember that friends sometimes hurt friends.

We live in a world where 40% of rape victims are under 18 and of that number, 12% are under the age of 12. And sadly, estimates suggest that the reported 27.7% of female, college rape victims is really closer to 50% (Paralumun New Age Village, n.d.).

The statistics abound, but for each fact there are thousands of stories. Stories of late night panic attacks. Stories of depression 15 years after the attempted rape. Stories of women not trusting men to be kind and sensitive. Stories of attempted suicide. Stories of victims who experienced not just the physical rape, but the more damaging psychological rape that comes as well. And so there are stories of successful suicide, too.

College students must balance idealism with awareness and safety with fun. It may be a tall order, but it is little to pay in the grand scheme.

It is a life-changing experience to wake up next to the victim of a rape during her panic attack from the stored mental trauma. The inner anguish spreads beyond the victim. No one deserves that.

—Christopher Patrick King

Sadness, Madness, Anxiety, and Trouble

For some of you, the pressures that you face in college will become unbearable. As Kristen points out below, many mental and emotional disorders first manifest in early adulthood, and the pressures of college can be what push you past your breaking point. As we've seen, college brings the pressure of new autonomy, new time management challenges, the need to juggle work and school, academic challenges, and the negotiation of an often complex social life. No wonder, then, to find out that one classmate is bipolar, another bulimic, and a third one deeply depressed. It seems to go with the territory. We close this chapter with three stories about some of the most emotionally challenging college situations and some advice on how to cope.

Stigma

In the still of a cold January night in 2002, I was jolted from my sleep by what I can only describe as an epiphany. My heart was racing as I reached for my bedside lamp, and I began to tremble. I wept for several minutes before my concerned parents entered my room. I proclaimed to them that I wanted to be a clinical psychologist. I envisioned myself speaking with psychiatric patients and offering them words of comfort and hope. Indeed, the next morning I found myself on my way to a psychiatric hospital. It was not until I noticed a paper identification bracelet around my wrist that I realized that I was not in the hospital to help patients; I was the patient.

Until my world was rocked by bipolar disorder, I, like many people, had little understanding of mental illness and was not entirely convinced of its existence. Yet after experiencing it firsthand, I am certain not only that it is real but that there is a tremendous stigma that comes with being labeled mentally ill. When I eventually returned to high school, I struggled to explain my absence to my classmates. I wished that I could simply tell them that I had come down with a virus, had undergone surgery, or had experienced any form of physical malady because such a reason would enable me to save face. Try telling someone that you are mentally ill and see what happens.

That January night was a profound moment in my life; even though I was at the height of my mania, I knew that I needed to tell my story. My healing process was a matter of mitigating my symptoms, understanding my diagnosis, and reconciling my disorder with my identity. I decided early on that I would not allow my bipolar disorder to be a dark secret hanging over me, and in time, I realized the potential I have to impact others because I have a story to tell. The fact that I can bear witness to the devastation of mental illness and have grown stronger because of it has given me the capacity to empathize with and the ambition to serve those who are faced with it. I believe that part of this task is to combat the stigmatization that comes with having a disability. Therefore, it is essential to educate people about mental illness and to give a face to an illness that cannot be seen.

Anyone, regardless of age, race, gender, class, or religion, can experience mental illness. The National Alliance on Mental Illness defines mental illness as "medical conditions that disrupt a person's thinking, feeling, mood, ability to relate to others, and daily functioning . . . that often result in a diminished capacity for coping with the ordinary demands of life" (http://www.nami.org). Many psychiatric illnesses first manifest in early adulthood, and significant risk factors associated with poor mental health are embedded in the college experience, for instance, stress, sleep deprivation, excessive alcohol consumption, and drug use. According to the National Institute of Mental Health, one in four adults has a diagnosable mental disorder in a given year (http://www.nimh.nih .gov). Therefore, it is critical to recognize that a mental illness is not a personal weakness and cannot be overcome simply by self-determination. Individuals can and do recover from mental illness by actively participating in treatment. I am a living testament. Get informed and tell your story.

Resources on mental illness and how to fight the stigma associated with it include http://www.nami.org, http://www.mpoweryouth.org, http://www.mentalhealthamerica.net/go/information/faqs, http://www.suicidepreventionlifeline.org, and the National Suicide Prevention Lifeline, 1–800–273-TALK (8255).

—Kristen Hammel

Eating Disorders

It was a one-time thing, just something to help me lose that extra couple of pounds in time for bikini season. Little did I know that those 5 minutes I spent bent over the toilet with my fingers down my throat would develop into a 2-year habit and a lifelong sickness. Of course, the media had something to do with it, but I believe that my family was really my downfall.

Most people turn to their families as their main support system, but this ordeal caused me to lose faith in my family. They constantly told me how much better I would look if I were five pounds lighter. It's easy to say, "Just ignore them, don't let them get to you." But what if those words came out of the mouths of people whom you trust and depend upon—for 5 years straight? You would break, too. One night, sometime during my sophomore year of high school, I purged for the first time. When I stepped on the scale the next morning and saw that I had lost a half pound, I was hooked. I was also egged on by my family, whose praise only grew with every pound I lost. The praise felt amazing, and so I continued. As a student trying to juggle a complex college life, it may seem easier to purge to keep off that freshman 15.

A network of social support is crucial in escaping the grip of an eating disorder. My friends helped me to pull myself out of this addiction. Escaping my family has been a milestone in shaking off the binge-purge cycle and has enabled me to find balance between school work and fun. Having a supportive group of friends in college has helped me realize that we all struggle with the same things, including stress and dissatisfaction with physical appearance. Having a support base of friends, both at home and at college, has been a blessing. With both groups of friends, I always have someone to lean on when stress levels are high. I am proud to say that I have not relapsed in college, thanks to supportive friends who listen to my problems and help me in whatever way they can.

Eating disorders are not a product of vanity, but a form of mental illness that affects 15% of women, resulting in numerous deaths every year. Odds are that you know someone who has some sort of eating disorder. Your support can make all the difference in the world.

—Anonymous

Depression and the Nontraditional Student

After my first quarter as a transfer student, I realized that serving at a restaurant where the majority of my coworkers were not attending school was going to hinder my academic performance. I had attended community college in order to save money because my undocumented status didn't grant me any financial aid. School is organized for traditional students. Because I still lived with my family, I had responsibilities that most students don't have to deal with, and I was faced with a dilemma. If I quit work, I would have no income to fund my last year, but I would enjoy my last 2 years getting involved with organizations and have a feel for what it's like to be just a student. I decided that quitting work would be the best option, as long as I had my green card and work permit.

In the middle of my first quarter, my parents and I finally got our interview with immigration to proceed with the legalization process. As soon as I found out, I put in my 2-week notice and looked forward to the day when I would finally get approved for a green card and work permit. Everything was planned. I had worked enough to pay for the rest of the academic year, and with my new legal status, work study, internships, and financial aid would pay for my next year. The day finally came, and my parents were called in for the interview first. I sat in the waiting room, excited and eager to finally get my green card. However, within 10 minutes of my parents' interview, our attorney came storming into the waiting room and said, "We have huge problems, and you may be leaving this place by yourself today." The attorney took me down to the fourth floor where my mother sat in a room wearing handcuffs. I was swiftly taken into a separate room where I was asked to put my hands on the wall and stand spread-eagled for a physical inspection. I was thoroughly patted down and my scalp was examined. I felt so humiliated, like a criminal, though all I had done was cross an invisible line that divides two countries in order to meet my dad for the first time when I was 5 years old. After several hours, they finally took my mother away, while my father and I were put into removal proceedings.

I stuck with the original choice to quit work. I was still able to pick up shifts, which I did about twice a week. My priorities became my 12-year-old brother, my father, and our home stability. Fourth on the list was school, but it was difficult to maintain my concentration. However, I became more involved with the support and advocacy organization for undocumented students. I learned to look for resources and found Counseling and Psychological Services. I felt I needed professional help to teach me coping skills for my self-esteem and various new behavioral problems, so I made an appointment. I was too overwhelmed to cope with my worries about my family, work, school, extracurricular activities, and relationships. I felt I had no control over my life. I was under chronic stress and would easily zone out of whatever I was doing. The lack of control over my life and the absence of my mother deeply saddened me. My anger toward everyone increased and my temper was insupportable. I couldn't stand being me. I told my therapist all of this and she said that I was depressed. Though there was nothing my therapist could do about my immigration issue, talking to someone and, more important, educating her about a problem many students face brought me some relief.

Life happens. Everyone, regardless of nationality, gender, political beliefs, religious beliefs, sexual orientation, education, socioeconomic status, and physical appearance faces challenges and life-changing events. I thought that because I was a student my problems would only revolve around school, but it is important to be aware of the extra-curricular complications that life can offer. Keep in mind that it's part of life, and as a student, you do have the privilege of many resources many citizens don't have. Use them. Help is there if you ask for it.

—*Fabiola Santiago*

CHAPTER 13

Love

In Chapter 13, we explore true love or, perhaps, the truth of love, namely how we are all now—in our current media driven and media dominated culture—really in love with being in love. We get high off of "being in love" and are perpetually in search of it. We will explore these issues:

- The dominant meaning of love in our culture.
- Romantic love—is there any other kind?
- Falling in and out of love—instead of "falling in love," we consider "walking in love."
- The not-to-be-missed college experience of the "Alone Again" blues.
- Love and friendship—trying to "fall in" love with a friend rather than a romantic stranger.
- Love and sex.
- Real love.
- A postscript about AIDS.

I did not yet love and I wanted to love so I sought what I might love, in love with loving.

—St. Augustine, Confessions

Love is like a faucet; it turns off and on.

—Billie Holiday

Music comes close to being the religion of your generation, and one only has to look at the titles of a few songs to see what is getting you down:

"Love Me Tender"

"When a Man Loves a Woman"

"I Need Someone to Hold Me When I Cry"

"Bad Romance"

"Your Cheatin' Heart"

"Lovesick"

"This Year's Love"

"Can't Get You Off My Mind"

"Somebody's Gonna Get Hurt Before We're Through"

"First Day of My Life"

"Chained to Your Love"

"Can't Let Go"

"After the Love Is Gone"

"Help Me Get Her Out of My Heart"

"I Can't Help Falling in Love with You"

"Stepping Stone"

"Battlefield"

Love has you wallowing in a sop-sorry miasma of negative emotion. Go down any dormitory hall and you will find most people in varying stages of the ancient American saga of boy-meets-girl, girl-meets-boy, boy-loses-girl, and the oh-God-I'm-alone-again blues. Tune in to any soap opera, go to any movie, put on any record, and there it is: good love, bad love, repetitive love, heartbreaking love, unrequited love, glorious love, and so on. In our media mythology, hardly anything else is going on. Because you are a creature of this culture, your life reflects the great obsession. In this chapter, I want to look more closely at this phenomenon to see whether it is possible to live without the pains of romantic love.

Love in Our Culture

When we are overcome by the various emotions of romantic love—longing, jealousy, desire, exuberant joy, horrible blues—we generally attribute these to the working of the powerful sexual instinct, and it seems to us that we are just putty in its hands. Actually, pure sexuality has relatively little to do with this flood of emotion. We must look at what is really going on.

Every culture embroiders the simple fabric of human sexuality in its own way. A look at other cultures quickly shows us how enormously malleable this emotion is. There are African cultures in which men take more than one wife. Not only do women feel no jealousy in this situation, but women count themselves unfortunate if their husbands can afford only one wife: "If there is only one wife, who will help me with the housework and take care of me when I give birth?" In the Trobriand Island culture, brother-sister incest is considered so likely and its attraction so overpowering that a rigidly formal code governs the interaction of even very young siblings. In Western culture, during Victorian times, it was considered perfectly possible to die of love, and people actually did. In some cultures, it is recognized that husbands and wives very occasionally develop a deep feeling of love, but this is regarded as uncommon, and people do not count on it happening to them any more than most Americans count on becoming millionaires.

For every person, love has a different meaning, but for most the first thought that comes to mind is romance. Romantic love is one thing that everyone in our culture dreams of and hopes to someday find. Romance, to most of us, is a mystery. We think we have an idea what romance is, but it seems all we have are fantasies, and it is fantasy that keeps us anxiously aroused. When will it happen, and how will it feel? The fact is most of us have love in our lives. The problem is when we are not romantically involved with someone, we think of ourselves as alone and unloved. We take for granted all other aspects of love in our lives. From the first day on this earth, we have all been loved by parents and family. We soon learn to love friends and friendships. As we grow older, we learn to love material possessions. We love our pets. For some, there is the love of knowledge, for others, the love for their calling or career.

The emotions love arouses in us are complex and varied. Most Americans cannot tell the difference between love and anxiety. This situation was parodied in an old film called *High Anxiety*, in which the hero sings that he knows that he is in love again because he once again has that old feeling of high anxiety. We also frequently take hostility to be love. In fact, some biologists have sagely assured us that the physical reactions accompanying anger are similar to those accompanying sexual arousal. Probably any physical arousal works similarly on some of our glands, but only a deep-seated cultural confusion leads us to confuse anger and love. Watch any John Wayne movie and you will see the taciturn macho man— who would really rather be in a good fistfight than make love—as he becomes the object of some "weak" woman's desire. As they move into the final clinch, you are never quite sure until the last minute whether it will be a fight, a rape, or mutual attraction.

Competitiveness is another powerful emotion we confuse with sexual attraction. The ideal romance of song and story is the Cinderella myth, in which physical love is joined by a sharp rise in social status. Most of us have at some time "fallen in love" with the most popular boy or girl in the class. Our sexual longings are really indistinguishable from our longing for popularity and wealth. On the other hand, most of the time when we are pining for a lost love, what we really have is a bruised ego, a sense that we've lost the game.

When all of these powerful emotions, which our culture fosters, are conjoined with sexuality, we do, indeed, feel ourselves in the grip of something so overwhelming that it is tempting to look at it as an instinct that has physical power over us to such an extent that it can raise us to heights of joy or fling us into the abyss of gloom.

Our Orientation Toward Love

He was a gritty man, a man who would have made Ernest Hemingway proud. He coached football, taught math, and lifted weights. His biceps bulged at 20 inches, and it seemed as though his heart was guarded by 20 more inches of muscle or rock or ice. He showed no emotion. But for the first time in his life as a father, tears began rolling down his cheeks. His baby girl was leaving for college, and it was time to let go.

His love for her was as real and intense as the secret he held within. He had just shared with his daughter that his roommate was really his lover: His homosexuality was now known by one more of a precious few people. People may never have the nerve to call him faggot, just as they never would think of questioning his love for his daughters.

All humans, and especially all children, deserve to be raised in loving environments. And love is not contingent upon one's sexual orientation.

In today's society, gays and lesbians often represent the untouchables. Fundamentalist religions tend to reject them as perverts of nature, and many more moderate groups tend to accept homosexuals only if they remain celibate. In other words, it is acceptable for married couples to engage in acts of lovemaking, yet if gays and lesbians make love, religious groups consider them sinful. In fact, many social groups in general find it difficult to accept any type of public displays of affection among gays and lesbians.

Even American society—predicated on theories of freedom and justice—tends to abhor the idea of gay and lesbian marriage. Even the most accepting people often find it strange to witness two males holding hands or kissing. But when such feelings arise, it is important for us to deconstruct our feelings and investigate their roots.

We are socialized from birth to accept that mommy and daddy kiss and hold hands. Later, in late grade school and junior high, children develop hormones and begin feeling attractions toward each other. Most often the attraction is to someone of the opposite sex. So follows the process of imitating parents, and youth begin holding hands and kissing.

But what about young people who find themselves falling in love with members of the same sex? It is often at this point that parents step in, and if parents fail in their attempts at socialization, society steps in. As sociologist Ernest Becker (1973) finds, a child's sexuality is checked for his or her own good by parents in early adolescence. Later, when faced with their attraction to members of the same sex, young lesbian women and gay men will often repress their own yearnings in order to fit in with the current social norms and thereby maintain a functional life within society. In this sense, we can define functional as meaning free from persecution, overt hatred, and misconceptions.

Social norms teach us not only what love is, but, worse, they also teach which love is acceptable. Thus, feelings of discomfort at the sight of gay men or lesbian women engaging in public displays of affection arise from a long history of socialization into the model that love and attraction are for men to enjoy with women.

Humorist David Sedaris (2000) tells a moving story in his book *Me Talk Pretty One Day*. While growing up, David knew he was "different." He did not like football and remembers that "there were names for boys who didn't like sports" (p. 5). David began learning the acceptable role of males in society. The sickness of this societal response to those who are "other" than we is such that we attempt to coerce, mold, and change people. Indeed, David spoke with a slight lisp and could not pronounce the letter s. He faced ridicule from peers when he would lisp, and he gained the label of "faggot" for having such an obvious deformity (vs. conformity). In fact, the school hired a speech therapist to "cure" David, to force him to conform to that which is normal and acceptable. Instead of conforming to something that was beyond his control, David learned to reformulate his speech.

The essay "Me Talk Pretty One Day" is an example of how far David went. He spoke in sentences that didn't contain the letter s. His vocabulary grew while his freedom shrank. The negative sanctions for being different, for being gay, forced David to re-create himself. He altered his speech and gave up his autonomy.

Most colleges offer us a chance to break through this deeply ingrained socialization. We can see and interact with people of all backgrounds. We study with Black, Asian, Hispanic, and White students. We work with people with mild mental disorders. We may even find ourselves as roommates with a gay man or lesbian woman. And it is at such moments of egalitarian interaction that we discover a fascinating truth: We all are human beings.

The Christian story of the Good Samaritan reminds us to open our hearts even to those we fear. A Jewish man walked along a path and suddenly was accosted by robbers. They took his money, beat him, and left him on the path. A rabbi eventually came along the path and saw the man, a fellow Jew. But the man was too bloody and too ragged: The rabbi walked on. The man's friends then came along, but, not recognizing their friend, they labeled him a beggar and told him to get out of their way.

Finally, a non-Jew, a Samaritan, came along the road. Seeing the helpless man, the Samaritan knelt, washed his wounds, and walked him into town. Although Jews and Samaritans believed each other to be enemies, deeper human truths united the men. Love for one's neighbor mattered more than religion. The Samaritan saw a person in need, a neighbor.

The question to us is, do we see "fags" or do we see people?

When we step outside our comfort zone and explore new relationships with new people, we find common truths about individuals. The struggles with identity and life challenges are difficult enough for college students to handle. Throw into the equation the implanted need to repress a huge part of one's nature—sexuality—and the individual's struggles multiply by a thousand.

By creating an atmosphere of open, nonjudgmental exchange, we encourage discovery in the university. The hope is that, as young leaders, we can bring this atmosphere to the rest of society. Falling in love is a wonderful, painful, and essential experience in our lives. Feelings between two women or two men ought not be degraded because they share the characteristic that all long-lasting relationships seek: mutual love.

One common argument against gays and lesbians rests on the grounds that they are somehow "perverted" by nature: They could never form a truly loving union because they are not capable of experiencing love, a result of some defect of character or some genetic flaw. As one, if not the greatest, of the world's prophets urges us, "Stop judging and you will not be judged. . . . Love your neighbor as you love yourself. Do this and you will live" (Luke 6:37, 10:27). A greater perversion exists, then, than being homosexual. This perversion is missing the point of the commandment to love all people without bounds.

Today, the media displays images of gay men—seldom do we see lesbian women, though—on shows such as Glee, Modern Family, and The Office. Although these shows create and perpetuate stereotypes of gays as effeminate, asexual (the "best friend you always wanted"), and carefree, they are an initial step toward acceptance. The crusade for homosexual rights mirrors the civil rights movement. Indeed, minorities sought some relatively positive media exposure to at least bring attention to their crusade. Minorities must fight to tell their real story and not the metaphorical one. The homosexual community hopes for a similar process. Ideally, such shows will at least show people that gays and lesbians are not "evil" and "perverted," always seeking sex in strange places. Rather, they show a human side of another oppressed group. Though images of gays as decorators may tend to pigeonhole homosexuals, for now at least we are seeing some nondefamatory exposure of a historically shunned group.

As we enter college, it is important to consider that love cuts across the sexual orientation divide. The term perverted love may more correctly apply to the parents who psychologically hinder their children through addictive behavior or through teachings that promote hate. The gay and lesbian community is a loving and accepting one. It knows degradation and marginalization only too well to fall victim to the same abuses it fights. Of course we are all human, and lesbian women and gay men have flaws, too. At the end of the day, our sexual orientations may divide us, but it is our shared orientation to love that will bring us together in understanding.

—Christopher Patrick King

Romantic Love

Romantic love as we know it developed in European culture during the 12th century. It was conceived as a relationship between an upper-class woman and her admirer. The troubadours, who went about making up songs for the entertainment of the nobility, were the carriers of this devotion. They would compose songs and poems for the object of their desire. The love, though, was seen as being essentially unrequited: The two lovers never really got together. It was just a matter of rosy romance and longing, and it always took place outside the bonds of matrimony.

The spirit of this medieval version of romance is marvelously portrayed in the tale of Tristan and Isolde. Tristan is sent by his liege, the king of Ireland, to fetch

Isolde from her homeland to become the king's bride. During the voyage, Tristan and Isolde drink some love potion by mistake and fall instantly and blindly in love. They cannot help themselves, despite the fact that they both owe loyalty to the king. There follows a series of adventures, during which it is intimated that the two "lovers" never quite manage to consummate their desires, and the whole thing ends in death. Here we have all the elements of the modern myth of romantic love: Love is most appealing when it is illegitimate and secret. The emotion is seen as so powerful that it simply sweeps the participants away, against their better judgment. The hanky panky never really gets good, and, in the end, a great tragedy is enjoyed by all. (If you want to read the whole brilliant analysis of the story, look at the first section of De Rougement's [1941] *Love in the Western World*. It is a rather complex but extremely interesting piece of writing.)

During the past 200 years, the idea of romantic love trickled down to the rising middle class and, finally, to the working class. It also took a rather sharp turn from its early origins and became associated with marriage. In the modern version, romantic love leads, after much ado and complication, to marriage and "living happily ever after," a state so boring that a good story always ends at just that point. In our media, only troubled love is considered interesting.

Knowing the origins of romantic love doesn't explain why the myth persists so vigorously in our own day and plays such a vital part in the mythology that governs our present culture. I would suggest that the myth of romantic love performs several crucial ideological functions. First, it is the great equalizer. We live in a country whose official philosophy is egalitarian but whose real social structure is grossly hierarchical. This presents a problem. Inequality has to be legitimized to a populace raised with some real, if abstract, expectations of equality. Romantic love is perfectly suited to this task. According to the myth, romance is available to everyone equally—rich and poor alike. Everybody has a right to expect the romantic love/marriage/happily ever after sequence in life, and it is only a few errant, mismatched souls who lose out. By putting the love experience at the center of life, the mythology deftly draws attention away from opportunities that are very unequally distributed, such as work satisfaction, a pleasant environment, and security in one's old age.

It seems to matter little that the myth is contradicted by reality. Evidence indicates that happy marriages are the exception rather than the rule. Marital bliss is also strongly associated with class position: The rich score higher than the poor and working class, among whom lack of money is the major source of marital friction. However, because these facts are not openly admitted, the myth can be used to persuade people that unhappiness is their own fault, that they have only themselves, not society, to blame. Average blue-collar workers whose work is frustrating, who are not respected as successes, and whose home lives are equally unsuccessful are forced to believe that their unhappiness is the result of some deep, humiliating flaw in their own makeup. Thus, they are kept from seeing that they have problems in common with millions of others and that many of these problems stem from inequalities in the class structure of society. Hope of salvation is kept alive by the persisting belief that some day they will find "true love" and live happily ever after. It is our modern secular version of the old "there'll be pie in the sky by and by" religion.

The belief in love as the great equalizer can be seen most clearly in the Cinderella theme, which I mentioned before. The poor but pretty working girl can dream of marrying her boss and becoming not only happy but also rich in the happy hereafter, though in real life it is likelier that the old man will only sleep with her and go back uptown to his wife. The poor young man can dream of marrying the boss's daughter. Love is the magic arena within which we can all become princes and princesses for an hour—and, in our dreams, forever. That this dream of upward mobility through love comes true for a small number of people keeps the myth alive.

The romantic love syndrome also lends itself perfectly to the purposes of advertising and commercially driven popular music. We are all familiar with the fact that the promise of romance is used to sell everything from cigarettes to deodorant to automobiles. How convenient for the advertisers to have delivered to them a nation of frustrated romantics who are desperately looking for any gimmick that might make this love thing work for them.

Independent Woman

The mass media, including various artists of the musical pop culture, tell us who we should be. Looking at the most popular songs on the charts right now, we can see that the depiction of women has changed drastically. As a young woman today, what do I have to be to survive?

All the women I admire are independent women. My parents always tell me, "You know you should learn to be independent; you should not depend on anyone but yourself to take care of yourself." So there is stress about getting the right job, being focused, and being independent. The popular song "Independent Woman" is all about women making their own money and being able to survive without the help of a man. Popular songs do not only continually emphasize the romantic view of love, but they also dictate the characteristics that shape our individual identities. They affect our relationships with the people around us and the expectations we have of each other and ourselves.

But where do all these contradictory statements about having a relationship come from? Could it be from the songs themselves? "The shoes on my feet, I bought it! The clothes I'm wearing, I bought it! I depend on me!" These are lyrics from Destiny's Child's "Independent Woman." Growing up in a family in which my parents were divorced, I experienced separation and sometimes had a fear that I, too, would end up just the same. It wasn't until I had my own love relationships later on that this fear, in fact, became my personal reality. The relationships I had did not work, time and time again. Was I cursed in love? My mind kept circling around one convincing statement: "Relationships do not work!" And with this statement I began to notice why songs with independent-woman themes seemed so often empowering. To hide my fears and give proof to myself of my inner statements about relationships, I cling to the importance of being independent. Of course, when I hear the lyric "All the women [being] independent!" it becomes my theme song. It reminds me of what I need to do to get away from "relationships don't work" and makes my convincing statement all the more convincing. In turn, my very convincing statement has had its good and bad effects. A good effect is giving me motivation to do things for myself. The bad effects are alienation, fear, and anxiety. When you are in a relationship, these feelings might drive you and your partner crazy. Thinking something is not going to work out before it develops is detrimental to a relationship. This negativity becomes present in one's self and distorts one's self-perception. A quote I remember from my social psychology class is W. I. Thomas's "If men define situations as real, they become real in their consequence." If you keep telling yourself and your partner that "relationships don't work," chances are it may come true.

—Katherine Ho

Falling In and Out of Love

Now that we have seen why the myth of romantic love enjoys such popularity in our media mythology, let us look at the social psychological mechanisms whereby people convince themselves that they are actually "falling in love." These are beautifully spelled out in a book I recommend to you, *The Adjusted American*, by Putney and Putney (1964). In it, the authors look at traits they regard as "normal neuroses" in our society, the foremost of which is love. Despite some of the changes brought about by the feminist movement, men and women are still taught to find different traits acceptable in themselves. Women are expected to specialize in human relationships, while men specialize in fierce job competition. In the process of teaching us how we should be, society forces us to bury our contradictory impulses. Girls quickly discover that being too smart threatens potential boyfriends. Boys discover that being too emotional makes them the butt of ridicule. Girls begin to repress their ambitions, while boys repress their emotionality and sociability. Through such repression, we alienate a piece of ourselves; that is, we push the unacceptable trait so far out of consciousness that we begin to believe we actually don't have the censored capacity anymore. At the same time, though, we also feel maimed because a piece of us is missing. When we find a member of the opposite sex who likes us, we are prone to project onto that person our own alienated capacities. The woman feels that she has found a man who is ambitious, aggressive, and bold, someone who will protect and shelter her poor, helpless self. The male, on the other hand, feels that he has found a woman who is sociable, affectionate, and emotionally responsive—qualities he longs for in himself but cannot enjoy directly as part of his own personality. Add to these projections all of the little fears by which we live. Are we lonely for friends? Here is a person who will meet all our needs for sociability. Do we regard ourselves as physically unattractive? Here is someone who finds us attractive, and suddenly we feel beautiful. Thus is generated that first "rush" we take to be "falling in love."

The very suddenness of this rush should warn us. Even a person we have only known for 24 hours can induce this high in us. Some even experience "love at first sight." It is obvious that we are not responding to another human being whom we really know—in fact, any number of people will do interchangeably and with equal suddenness. Two years down the road, we may look at our former love and wonder what we ever "saw" in the person. What is really happening is something inside ourselves. Temporarily, we have put in abeyance all the self-criticism that usually saddens us. Temporarily, we have granted ourselves the freedom to feel new feelings that we usually deny ourselves. We love ourselves because some member of the opposite sex seems to accept us. The more we have deprived ourselves of self-acceptance, the more helpless we are in the grip of this temporary alleviation and the more desperately we feel we need this new partner.

The problem is that what we see in our partner is not the real person but all of our own projections. We are just using the other as a screen. Since, in the first stages of a romance, both people are on their best behavior, these projections are allowed to stand. Neither party wants to interfere with this process. As a relationship wears on, the real people begin to emerge. Now we begin to see that the girl we thought was so wonderfully sociable is really just an obsessive talker, or the boy who seemed so strong and ambitious is really just selfish. Our old fears about ourselves also reassert themselves. They had no intention of disappearing; they only took time off. As we include the new partner in our category of "self," we also begin to project onto our partner the qualities we dislike in ourselves.

At the same time that the illusions are wearing away, we are usually beset by another problem. We aren't terribly good at being honest with other people. We have been taught to be "polite." We are also afraid to alienate the precious new find, so we swallow our anger as it arises. We begin to lie about how the other's lovemaking really affects us. We pretend satisfaction when actually there is physical discomfort or feelings of embarrassment. We persuade ourselves that it is just our own fault that we find some new habit of the other terribly annoying. We begin to carry a heavier and heavier sack of unvoiced grievances.

As the relationship becomes shaky, a new monster rears its ugly head: possessiveness. Nearly everybody confuses possessiveness with love, and there is a good dose of it in most American relationships. I remember one class discussion of this in which one young woman told us with complete sincerity that she felt nothing negative whatsoever when her boyfriend made love to somebody else. We were all fascinated and astounded by her. Despite her very commonplace physical appearance, her personality made her a completely appealing person. We all envied her obvious inner freedom, but alas, this is very rare. Our culture teaches us to be possessive about everything. It does this by making us feel needy at the very bottom of our souls because it destroys our childhood's innocent acceptance of the world and the self. To be needy is to be greedy. So we clutch our romantic partners and strangle them in the process.

Somewhere in the process of growing up, we get confused about the boundaries that separate us from other people. In some areas of life, we exaggerate our separateness, for example, in the cultural belief that we have to hide our inner fears from others because these fears are so private and peculiar. In other areas, we make the opposite error by ignoring the real separateness that limits our power over others and their power over us. Possessiveness in love relationships is just one instance of this kind of mistake. If we look further in this direction, we find a very important guideline I wish you would paste up on your mirror where you will see it every day: "You *cannot* control another person; you *can* take care of yourself."

Two ways in which we try to control other people—especially love objects—is to try to rescue and to try to reform them. Let us look at each of these in turn. The rescuer is somebody who is made so uncomfortable—indeed, is so threatened—by another's misfortune or misery that there is a compelling urge to rescue the other person from discomfort. In extreme cases, this is the kind of person who helps old ladies across the street even when they don't want to go. Rescuers all too frequently "fall in love" with deeply troubled persons whom they want to rescue. It never works. First, deeply troubled people are incapable of forming good relationships. Second, to the extent that the target person has some inner strength, he or she will resent being rescued because it is belittling. You can have compassion for others, but at the same time respect them by remembering that people's troubles are also their opportunities to grow. You have no business taking such opportunities away from other people.

The desire to rescue may stem from a fear that the troubled person will attack you if you don't get him or her out of trouble. This fear usually has its roots in childhood experience with a troubled parent who took troubles out on you. As a young child, you were thus forced into the impossible task of rescuing your own parents, in an effort to deflect the rage they might inflict on you. It is a defensive maneuver that is functional in the childhood situation but unnecessary when you are an adult, and it will get pretty tiresome if the pattern is repeated continually during adult life.

Another root of the need to rescue others is your refusal to rescue yourself, that is, to take good care of yourself. In this case, what threatens you about another person's trouble is that you have similar troubles you haven't addressed. Learn to recognize the urge to rescue. When you feel it, ask yourself immediately, "Do I need rescuing in this area myself?" If the answer is "yes," then be good to yourself; rescue yourself and, with compassion, leave others to rescue themselves. Above all, never let rescuing get mixed up with falling in love. It is a sure recipe for failure.

Akin to the rescuer is the reformer. This is somebody who develops a love relationship with someone whom they really don't completely like, in the anticipation that the unpleasant aspects of the other person's behavior can be reformed. Of course, nobody is going to be perfect in your eyes, but if you find a great deal to love in another person, you are naturally willing to adjust to the few aspects that displease you. You can live with them. If this is not the case, you have no business forming a relationship with the person. Wanting to reform someone is sort of like having a hidden agenda. It will be resented as it begins to surface, and it will be opposed by anybody with any self-respect. Therefore, it will poison the relationship and will not work.

The other side of the coin of "invading" your lover's legitimate turf by rescuing and reforming is that you lose a clear sense of the boundaries that protect you from what others can do to you. You really want to be rescued, reformed, and so on. When your lover doesn't respond the way you want him or her to, you feel that you cannot take care of yourself inside your own legitimate boundaries. "Don't hurt me like this; I cannot stand it" is then what you throw out to your lover. Now you make your lover responsible for your peace of mind, which isn't cricket and will be resented.

You cannot control another person; you can take care of yourself.

Walking in Love

Sometimes I think about the meaning of the word *falling* in the phrase *falling in love*. Let's say that a person is literally falling. Wouldn't that be considered negative? Sometimes it hurts when you fall. In fact, sometimes you experience such a sudden impact that you fall hard. Similarly, this is the way we have been conditioned in society to feel when falling in love. We experience the sudden impact of romantic love and all its tragedy and anxiety. It hits us! Is this really love?

At times, I think that the word falling in the context of love can add to the sometimes misleading ideals of romantic love. A healthy relationship does not always maintain the immediate rush that is associated with falling in love. The danger in falling is that usually when you fall hard it is difficult to get yourself up. During my childhood, mother always told me to walk because, if I didn't, I might trip and fall. What about in the context of love? Walking in love? I know that perhaps the wording does not sound as appealing as the intensity and immediacy of falling. Walking is a casual pace, not as sudden as falling, and, hey, if there is danger lurking ahead, you have the capacity to look, listen, and make decisions according to your surroundings.

Sometimes I think that walking is a better word to keep in mind in the context of relationships. When you are walking in love instead of falling, you might remember to take your relationship at a much slower pace, thereby reducing the chance of sudden trips and falls along the way. It is a much easier process than the struggle of getting up every time you fall. And of course there has to be a balance. If one person walks in love and the other chooses to fall, there can be an imbalance because one person is pulling or dragging the other to get up, which can lead to emotional fatigue. I think if you keep the idea of choosing to walk in your love relationships, then if there are some forks in the road ahead, and two people cannot agree on which fork to take, it is all right to walk separate ways instead of staying in an imprisoned emotional state.

—Katherine Ho

The "Alone Again" Blues

Beset by these problems, our new love relationship begins to suffer. It loses its vitality. It becomes commonplace. The process is somewhat similar to what happens when you buy a new outfit. For a month or two, the new garment makes you feel attractive; then the effect wears off.

It doesn't matter very much whether the two lovers are married or just living together. Sooner or later, one or the other will discover somebody new who holds out the promise of a fresh "falling in love." When this happens, the person who is left behind suffers a very bruised ego, which the person confuses with unrequited love. All the other self-doubts come flooding back. We are alone again and feel terribly sorry for ourselves until somebody else shows up and we can begin another round. We can't see the process in this light. The mythology lends enormous legitimacy to our belief that we are suffering from love and that such suffering is perfectly sensible, inevitable, and even biological. That we can suffer to music adds glamour to our plight. We sink into a quicksand of sentimentality.

Let us look at this "alone again" realistically for just a few minutes. It may help to sober us up. First, there probably are only two people in a hundred who will end up for life (happily or unhappily) with the very first person with whom they ever fell in love. This is a very good thing because the younger we are, the less experienced we are in human relationships and the less we understand ourselves. Thus, when you are 18 or 20 years old, you are in a very poor position to make a sensible choice or to develop a mature relationship. At this point, you have to practice, to get experience. Statistics indicate that the older people are when they marry, the better their chances for a lasting relationship. It is desirable and inevitable that you will move through numerous relationships from which you will learn. Ask older people whether they wish they had spent their life with their first love, and you will get a lot of resounding "no's." Most of us who have been around a while know that we could never have grown and developed if we had been stuck with our first choice for a lifetime.

It is also the case that we learn more from "losing" than from gaining relationships. In our previous scenario, in which one partner in a devitalized relationship finds somebody new, we can ask ourselves, "Which of these two is likely to benefit from the experience?" The answer is, most often, the one who is left behind. The pain this person can experience may teach the person to seek a different kind of partner next time or to make some changes in his or her way of relating to a lover. The one who runs off is just buying in for another round of the same game. That person hasn't learned anything.

Our fear of loneliness blinds us to the fact that what is much worse than loneliness is a lousy lasting relationship. I have even known couples who, after living together for several years in disharmony and mutual hostility, decide to get married in the hope of improving things. Some married folks have children out of the same motives. Obviously, each of these steps just compounds the difficulties.

In a bad relationship, we have to deny reality. We freeze. We cannot deal with our inner conflicts for fear of shaking the flimsy relationship. All emotional maturation ceases. We carry such a burden of grievances that we feel ourselves to be weaker and less able to face the world alone. Let me give you a rule of thumb: If a relationship isn't fun and rewarding at least 75% of the time, it is time to get out, even if it means being "alone again."[1] The very act of making the break will give you the energy you need to survive.

If you look at your experience in this light, it may help you get a little distance from your emotions when a relationship breaks up. Not everything that causes us pain should be avoided. When you have a cavity, you grit your teeth for an hour and take yourself to the dentist. The same goes for the pain of parting. It isn't going to kill you, and if you listen to the pain intelligently, it can teach you a great deal.

When my students tell me that they are blue because a romance has broken up and they are "alone again," I always have to repress a smile. Here they are on a campus with hundreds of other single folks their own age—all looking for sexual partners. In what sense are they alone? How long can it possibly last? If we could only join into the spirit of a German song that says "Why should I be unhappy because my old boyfriend is gone? Another one is waiting on the next corner." Why does the next corner seem so far away to us at this moment? Might it not even be better to avoid the "next corner" for a while?

One of the reasons we put so much emphasis on the romantic love relationship is that, in many ways, our society makes us lonely. We have no extended family, no small community to which we safely belong. Even the nuclear family is rapidly disintegrating. Social and geographic mobility is so great that our friendships rupture every few years. On top of this, we inherit little of our social position. Each of us has to prove ourselves as an individual in a highly competitive game.

Perhaps most poignantly, our culture offers us no acceptable "touching" relationships with other adults, except the sexual relationship. There is good evidence that indicates that our need for touching others is very great and very unmet. How far we are from earlier societies in which we could fall back on a fairly large, stable group with which we were indissolubly "in touch." Vivid in my mind is the anthropological film that shows a small tribe seeing one of its members through the ordeal of dying. The dying man is held in a bed made up of human hands. People are lined up on each side and are grasping each other's hands to make a platform on which the dying man lies. Such physical human solidarity is dramatically absent from our lives.

Even further, the meeting of our basic economic needs is organized around the ephemeral sexual bond. When a marriage breaks up, so does a household and an economic partnership. This aspect doesn't yet concern you, but it does hang over the romantic lives of your parents, and, even unconsciously, you see it coming.

There is not a lot you can do about the lack of lasting social bonds in our society. You can join a commune, but even most communes are temporary affairs. Still, if you understand how these aspects of the social structure affect you, you can take steps to minimize their effect. In the first place, don't confuse your need for friendship with your desire for romantic love. When you are in a new situation at

[1]Ninety-five percent is ideal and possible, but if you have 75%, you may have a base you can develop from.

college, make it your first order of business to forge some good friendship bonds. Nowadays, these nonsexual friendships may be with members of the opposite sex almost as often as with those of your own. Put some physical touching into these friendships. Treasure them and don't just toss them aside the moment you are in that state of temporary insanity you call love. The women's movement has done us a favor by persuading women to respect their bonds with other women—not always to break a date with friends for a date with a lover. The message also goes for men. If you are in a new situation, it may take a little while to form friendships and you may suffer some loneliness. You don't have to confuse yourself about what it is that you need. Because our attitudes toward friendship are much saner than our attitudes toward romantic love, you will not have nearly so much trouble coping with the need for friends.

Love and Friendship

Valuing friendships can help you with your love relationships in yet another way. Friendship is a much better model for what you need in a love relationship than the models paraded before you in the media mythology. These media images are so powerful that, unless we are fortunate enough to have had parents who were happily married (a rare phenomenon), we are likely to be completely confused about love when we first start out. I was in my 30s before it finally occurred to me that, if I wanted to succeed in a romantic relationship, I would have to treat it more as I treated my nonsexual friendships. I would have to look for the same kind of person whom I sought for a friend. I realized that, in my life, I had frequently entered romantic relationships with people I would have rejected out of hand as friends.

Nobody pretends that genuine friendship is very close to hate, yet our media constantly pretend that sexual love can come directly out of hate. In the average romantic movie, we can quickly tell which two people are going to fall in love at the end because they are so very hostile toward each other at the beginning.

Qualities we would reject in a friend are made to seem romantic in a lover: The mysterious stranger who is from a culture totally foreign to our own is made to seem attractive, even though in a friend we would quickly see that there were just too many points of difference; the emotionally dangerous character—the Don Juan, the temptress, the wildly jealous person—are all made to look sexually intriguing, even though a friend with these attributes would be seen as pitiable. Since Alice Faye sang "He left me and pawned all my furniture, but he's my man" to a scoundrelly Tyrone Power, the movies have sold us on the charms of masochistic love. We can cut through all this bull very quickly by applying the same criteria to the selection and propagation of romantic partners that we apply to the selection and development of friends.

Using friendship as an analogy is very important because the media seldom instruct us in the actual mechanics of the happily ever after. Even our "great" Western literature depicts unhappy and disastrous relationships much more frequently than good ones. There is a sort of unspoken assumption that happy relationships are at once uninteresting and self-evident. Nothing could be further from the truth. Really good relationships require enormous intelligence, honesty, and alertness. They never stand still but constantly evolve and change. They teach us who we are in profound, unexpected ways. But, unfortunately, our myth makers have so little experience of real love themselves that their versions are either nonexistent or patently phony, such as the "family comedies" on television. In the face of this cultural gap, our own experiences with friendship or with the love we have felt for our siblings is all we have to fall back on.[2]

Love and Sex

Why is it that the phenomenon of sex is surrounded by such a cloud of confusion? It is, very simply, *because we are heirs to a culture that has taken a totally mad view of sexuality for many, many centuries.* The sexual revolution of the 1960s only began to scratch the surface of this heritage. If we go back to the story of Tristan and Isolde and ask, "Why did they have to suffer so long and finally die of their love?" the 12th-century answer comes back loud and clear: *because sex is a sin.* If anything can prove to us that humans are infinitely malleable by their cultures, it should be the fact that Western European Christianity (both Catholic and, later, Protestant) has persuaded generations of people that this most intensely pleasurable of human experiences is something dark and sinister and wrong. It may give you some idea if I tell you that, during the Middle Ages, the Catholic Church recommended the use of a night garment so constructed that a man and wife might have sexual intercourse without touching any part of each other's naked bodies except in the immediate area of the genitals. Sexuality was only tolerated because offspring were seen as necessary to the survival of society. The staggering degree of deeply ingrained repression that it took to turn sexuality into sin twisted human beings into strange shapes, indeed. After all, Mother Nature made very sure that we would propagate the race.

Love had to be tragic because sex was wrong. Sex equaled sin and therefore also suffering. Women were especially cut out to pay for the price of sin by bearing children, legitimate or illegitimate. The persecution of prostitutes through the centuries is another aspect of this. The male customers were never prosecuted. It could also be argued that much of the present-day opposition to abortion rests on the secret desire to punish women for enjoying sexual intercourse.

The surprising amount of sadomasochistic sex that has blossomed in our society along with increasing sexual freedom also grows directly out of the sex-as-sinful attitudes. If sex is forbidden, it can only be enjoyed if one is in bondage and if one is being punished at the same moment that one is enjoying the forbidden pleasure. The reason why our pornography is artistically terrible also reflects our fear of sexuality. Pornography ranks so low with us that it only attracts the most mediocre talent.[3]

---

[2]Parent-child relationships are usually less useful as analogies because of the inequality inherent in most of them.

[3]For a delightful exception and a rare female perspective, see the Kensington Ladies' Erotica Society's *Ladies Home Erotica* (1984).

When I was a teenager growing up in the very Puritan little town of Claremont, California, a group of us once tried to vex our Girl Scout troop leader, Mrs. Lerner, by asking her a question we knew was forbidden on one level but could be asked in innocent curiosity on another. "What about sex, Mrs. Lerner?" we asked one day when that good lady was belaboring us about the sanctity of marriage. She blanched only slightly and then answered very stalwartly—I have never forgotten her phrasing—"Sex is the cement which holds the bricks of a marriage together."

For many years, I went about with this image of a rigid brick wall connected in my mind with the phenomenon of sex. It was many years before I came to realize that what we needed to hear from Mrs. Lerner was that sex is more like dancing than anything else: It is very close to the sheer, playful pleasure in physical movement; there is a leading and following, giving and taking on both sides; it is more fun with a skillful partner; it is better when done to music; you can spend the whole evening doing it; and it is greatest with somebody you really like. If sex is taken lightheartedly, like dancing, you will not feel the need to possess every partner with whom you have danced, nor will you expect them to solve all your problems.

Regarding dance, there are, let us say, two types of cultures: those whose dancing imitates and initiates sex and those whose dancing is as totally asexual as dancing can possibly be. Among the former cultures are those of the Polynesians, with their wild and beautiful hip-swinging dances, and African Americans, whose physicality influenced the dancing of White mainstream culture during the second half of the 20th century. But in Claremont in the 1940s, we were clearly in the latter category. Our dance teacher told us with a perfectly straight face that "nice girls don't move their hips when they dance." Of course, our dancing was pathetic and so, later on, was our lovemaking.

I mention my own experiences because you are only a generation or two away from such attitudes. They still run through our culture in innumerable ways. Thus, if you have trouble with sex at first, don't be too surprised; keep trying. But there is an even deeper reason why sexuality does not usually blossom fully when one is very young. Even when sexual Puritanism has been overcome, sexuality involves one's being so totally that it suffers from contagion by all our insecurities. If we have difficulty trusting others, we cannot abandon ourselves totally in their presence. If we are too competitive, we make sex into a contest of skills. If we are unconsciously vengeful toward our partner, we may use sex as a punishment. If we are too dependent on the other person, we may be unable to enjoy sex fully because we would then have more to lose. In short, to the extent that we aren't yet at home with ourselves and in the world, we will inhibit our sexual feelings.

Because sexuality involves your most personal, intimate feelings, you should never let yourself be pushed into doing anything that feels uncomfortable to you. There is no right and wrong here; there is an endless variety of personal tastes and feelings. You must be true to your own. Don't let fads, majority opinion, or the pressure of well-meaning friends and lovers cause you to override your own feelings. I don't mean that you should be totally unadventurous. In this, as in so many things, the Golden Middle Way is usually best.

Sex in the College Environment

As a woman on a college campus, going to parties, meeting new people, and leading a sexually active life, there is nothing that I feel is more important to have control over than sexuality. In an environment where it is easy to lose control—to fall behind in classes, begin drinking too much, become too wrapped up in the college scene—sex can turn into an uncontrollable, compulsive activity.

I have encountered friends forgetting to use a condom, friends allowing themselves to have sex with people they don't particularly like, friends in relationships having sex with other people—overall, friends being completely careless with this activity. What is it about the college environment that allows sex to run so rampant and be thought of as "no big deal"?

In movies like *American Pie, Van Wilder, Animal House*, and *Road Trip*, we see that sex is a huge aspect of college life. However, sex is also an unspoken aspect of college life. We know that it's going on all around us, yet we often fear to talk about it openly. Sex is a big deal. Whether you're having it with multiple partners, the love of your life, or not at all, sex is an activity with numerous benefits and repercussions.

Depending on where you're from, the frequency with which you've heard this statement may vary: "No glove, no love." For those of you confused about this statement's meaning, the "glove" refers to a condom, and "love" refers to sex. This slogan should be as ingrained in our heads as the advertisements we see on television. This should be the motto of our generation—a generation plagued with the fear of a plethora of sexually transmitted diseases (STDs). AIDS is on the rise again, for various reasons. One is because our current political administration is not strongly implementing sex education programs in school. College is no exception to this—perhaps you saw a video at your orientation discussing what you should do if you are about to have sexual intercourse with someone. The video I saw at my orientation was poorly produced and laughable. It contained metaphoric scenes and barely touched on the repercussions of intercourse. There isn't enough information, even in this modern day and age.

I continue to stress the stakes of having sexual intercourse because the stakes are quite high. Sex has physical, mental, and emotional consequences because sex is a physical, mental, and emotional activity. Once you begin having sex, you are also accepting a number of responsibilities that come with it. The most important of these responsibilities is contraceptive use. I am on birth control pills—I have made this decision to ensure that I won't get pregnant. I still use condoms because birth control pills do not protect you from STDs. I have also protected myself emotionally by abstaining from casual sex.

Sex, to me, is an activity that is meant to create a connection between people. Strangers are not people that I need to have a connection with. In addition, sex is not only a physical act; it is an emotional act as well, and to give my unrequited emotion to strangers is an impossible thing for me to do.

However, whatever decisions you make, as long as you are prepared for the consequences, it is up to you. Sex is something that should not be taken lightly, and, if handled correctly, it can be an enjoyable and fulfilling part of your life. When you are sound in your decisions and stable with your responsibilities, whether you choose to have sex or not, only then will you be happy with your actions and yourself.

Also, make sure you are informed—blind choices are dangerous. Educate yourself. Most college campuses have a health and wellness center where you can find information on things that I have not touched on—the different kinds of STDs, where you can get condoms, where you can get birth control, and so on. Most colleges also have counselors who would be happy to answer all of your questions on issues like this. College is a place where you should be learning things that will not only benefit you mentally but physically and emotionally as well.

—*Jasleen Ahuja*

Self-Acceptance and Love

What we come back to after all this is our old theme of self-acceptance. When you fully accept yourself, you will not put every potential sexual partner in a position to "choose" or "reject" you. Rather, you will sit back comfortably and wait to see whether you want to accept the other person. You will remain the judge until such time as you are sure the relationship is worth pursuing. Accepting yourself also means being very kind to yourself when a painful parting occurs. It means knowing how to make yourself as comfortable as possible during such a transition. Being kind to yourself doesn't always mean self-indulgence. It may also involve talking some sense to yourself, that is, "pulling yourself together" rather than wallowing in sentiment.

Above all, true self-acceptance does away with the projection mechanism we call "falling in love." A woman who accepts and develops her own strengths doesn't need a man to lean on. A man who knows his own emotions and isn't ashamed to cook himself a delicious dinner doesn't have to wait for a woman to rescue him from his cold, lonely apartment. Thus, self-accepting people can see potential partners. They will be relating to a real other person, not to a projection of their repressed wishes. When a parting occurs, they won't feel bad about it any longer than they really want to. I want to stress to you that you need self-acceptance much more than you need a sexual partner. Partners will always show up on your doorstep. Let that part of it be—flow with the stream. But make it your serious business to prepare yourself for sexual love by learning to love and take care of yourself.

Let me conclude this section by giving some first aid to those of my readers who are currently suffering the pangs of frustrated love. First, let's distinguish between purely sexual longing and the bruised-ego game. When sexual desire sweeps through you, it is stronger than, but closely akin to, what you feel when you are in a campground and suddenly the smell of coffee and bacon comes wafting over from the next camp. Although there is hunger in that emotion, there is also a pleasurable thrill. Your senses awaken, and you feel keenly alive for a moment. Even if you have no coffee and bacon of your own at the time, you still do not experience that emotion as painful. You also don't try to hold on to the emotion or to manipulate it—you just let it sweep through you and then pass on.

The sharp and often excruciating pain of parting from someone you love is very real and should be handled in the same way. Let it blow through you like a storm. Offer no resistance. Like a storm, it may blow a few hours or even a few days. Then it is over. These emotions, sexual desire and the pain of parting, are appropriate in certain circumstances and are, ultimately, not destructive. We can all endure the short storm.[4]

The emotion we want to become free of is the prolonged session with the bruised ego—the "alone again" era of self-pity and the internal argument over what you "could have done" or "should have done." Chronic jealousy during an ongoing relationship is in the same class of repetitive feelings that seem to hang around for months. This pain doesn't sweep through and disappear because it is not a spontaneous emotion but your mind chewing endlessly on its wounds. You have two people inside you: the accuser, who blames you for what happened and predicts further catastrophes, and the defender, answering back, "It wasn't my fault." And, frequently, even a third person can be present: "If you weren't so neurotic, you wouldn't be having these feelings." This is the accuser again, catching you unaware whenever you have self-doubts and are vulnerable. Your mind is coming and going in gloomy circles.

Our first impulse is to run away from the mess inside: Perhaps we get drunk or over-eat or try to sleep 24 hours a day. Or we try an internal manipulation to get rid of the pain, trying to argue ourselves out of it. All of this pain avoidance actually can make the hurt worse and cause it to hang on longer than would otherwise be the case.

When such pain hits you, go somewhere quiet by yourself and just sit with it. This does not mean thinking about the pain. In fact, it is best not even to give a name to your feeling, like calling it "jealousy" or "anxiety" or "frustration." These names all incorporate value judgments: "I shouldn't be jealous" or "Why, why am I anxious again?" All this does is carry you off into a train of self-punishing thought. So don't even give the pain a name; just feel it as a physical sensation. Notice where in your body the pain is centered. Some of my students have found it useful to write down on a piece of paper a detailed description of their physical symptoms. Being in touch with these symptoms is just like feeling a sprained ankle or a headache or like visiting a sick friend: You aren't going to argue with your friend about being sick. Maybe, if he or she is very sick, you don't even talk. You just sit there. Perhaps you hold your friend's hand. (You can hold your own hand, if it helps.)

When you are aware that a train of thought has carried you off the pain, bring your mind gently back to it. Absolute concentration is beyond us, so don't become critical

---

[4]If you suffer from prolonged, chronic, or extremely intense depression, you may be suffering from an inherited biochemical imbalance. There are now medications that are extremely effective in such cases. Consult a medical practitioner who specializes in antidepressive medication. Your college psychiatric clinic would be the place to start.

because thoughts carry you off. They are part of the process. Just bring the mind back to the pain whenever you become conscious of having wavered. Rather than running away from the pain, you should feel yourself moving toward it. Welcome the pain as a chance to communicate with a usually hidden part of yourself—a chance to heal an old wound, which is essentially what the pain really is. Do 30 to 60 minutes of this. Then, do half an hour of vigorous physical exercise and take a shower. Do this even if you have to force yourself. Take a firm hand.

Make it a point to use your time alone for something you really enjoy. Go to bed early with a good murder mystery and a nice snack. Go for a walk in the mountains, or look up a friend you've been wanting to see. A physical change of scene, even briefly, helps a lot.

Repeat the therapy daily as long as the pain persists.

When I first met my girlfriend, I was "on the rebound." My previous girlfriend—whom I had liked because she was skinny, hip, and neurotically creative—had decided that we would be better off as friends. I wasn't too torn up about the breakup, as we had never developed a really serious connection. A long line of ex-girlfriends preceded her, many of whom I had been "in love" with, but none of whom had sustained that "love" in me for longer than 5 or 6 months. I was the kind of guy often accused of "always being in a relationship," and I had avoided taking a long, hard look at how fitting that accusation was. I had attended three community colleges over the course of 7 years before finally transferring to a university, and each school had been full of classrooms with brand new girls who caught my eye. The skinny neurotic ex-girlfriend was one of many coeds with whom I attempted a monogamous relationship. After all, college is where a lot of people meet their spouses, right? By my account, I was auditioning wives. Neither my college curriculum nor my track record of serial monogamy, however, had shown me how self-centered that mindset had been. Being in a successful relationship isn't about finding the right person; it's about being the right kind of person.

I'm extremely lucky that the universe chose such a great person for me to learn this lesson alongside. I am now with a woman whom I find to be beautiful, talented, and funny. We have similar goals, values, and tastes. So we are, by those types of definitions, compatible. The other 98% of what determines our happiness with one another, however, is the level at which we are committed to putting each other's needs ahead of our own.

I often joke that while being of service to others comes naturally to my girlfriend, Monica, I am not quite as fortunate. I'm really bad at being present for other people. I have high ambitions to be selfless and giving, but I am an only child, and I'm not used to sharing what is mine. I'm preoccupied with fun, and when confronted with serious or boring things, I like to duck away from life and bury my attention in magazines, social networking sites, and text messages.

An interesting detail about Monica's life makes things a little easier for me, though: She was born with cystic fibrosis (CF). This means that her lungs are about half as efficient as everyone else's, she has to go to the hospital a few times a year for "tune-ups," and she has grown up with a pretty scary prognosis: People with CF have never lived to be older than middle-aged, and many die younger. For better or for worse, this has helped me to make her happiness a priority. Whenever I start to get discouraged with my life's circumstances, I am reminded that I am lucky to have life circumstances.

Whenever I feel that my time might be wasted by doing something she wants to do rather than something I'd prefer, I remember that I have the luxury of spare time. Whenever I feel that my schoolwork is so important that I can't take time away from it to be with her, I remember that she has to do all of her schoolwork, too, despite the fact that she takes weeks off at a time for hospital stays. Once I get these priorities straight, I have the emotional space to enjoy all of the activities that we love doing together. Now that we have been together for more than a year and a half, we have been through some taxing emotional moments. I have held her hand as she spent time in a hospital bed, and she has held mine as I have nervously awaited GRE scores or fretted about graduate school applications. As we pursue our respective goals, we have had to think long and hard about where we fit into each other's lives. We even broke up for a brief period. We both have challenges, shortcomings, and demons to battle. My attitude toward her health, as brave and loving as it initially was, is sometimes replaced with impatience, selfish emotionalism, or anxiety about the future. For her part, she often nags me when I'm irresponsible or questions my judgment, which can annoy me or make me feel misunderstood. The more time we spend together, the more I learn how much we differ in our opinions on certain subjects, and sometimes I go as far as to wonder whether we are really compatible at all. I have opened myself up honestly enough to know, however, that we are indeed compatible, but that within that compatibility we both have to pursue our individuality.

When I first started dating Monica, I sometimes quietly feared that I was just dating someone with CF to prove to myself that I was gallant and enlightened, but I increasingly feel that my real reward lies in getting to know another human being this intimately.

Sometimes I doubt my ability to keep up my end of our relationship, and I want only to be coddled. I'll find myself daydreaming about the adventures of dating new and exciting women. I'll long for those initial months of sweet nothings and the novelty of sex with a yet-unfamiliar body. If I dwell in these fantasies for too long, I begin to feel neglected, impatient, and dissatisfied.

I find that it's important to bring myself back to a spirit of service, however. For every moment that I spend thinking about Monica, I am temporarily relieved from thinking about myself. Every time I compromise during an argument, I feel the deep satisfaction of knowing that I am taking the actions of a mature person who treats his partner as an equal.

I hate Monica's disease because it is doing its best to end her life, but I also value the fact that it has taught me how important it is to appreciate my own life and the lives of the people around me. For me, CF has been an unexpected means to break through my own selfishness and give me perspective on my behavior in relationships. I don't have any tips on how to bring about selflessness in your romantic life, or any final answers about what "real" love looks like, but I think being with Monica has brought me a lot closer to an understanding of what really matters in a relationship between two people.

—*Joseph Guisti*

Real Love

Having trampled as hard as I could on the popular notion of romantic love, I need, now, to talk a bit about real love. (M. Scott Peck's 1978 book *The Road Less Traveled* also addresses this issue with much wisdom.) Is love possible? How do you know when you've got it? And how do you pick a partner with whom it might work? Finally, what does it feel like?

Beginning with the last question, I would say that it feels as though you are being well taken care of, you have the comfort of a real friend, and the relationship is fostering the sanest and best part of yourself while overcoming the most neurotic parts. You have found meaning on the deepest emotional level. The lovemaking, particularly, comes up to and past your highest expectations and previous experiences. Wonderful, you say—where do we start?

I think that the first thing I want to impress on you is that, in evaluating a potential or current partner, you pay attention to deeds and not to words. Words are cheap and, frequently, are in inverse proportion to real feelings. "Romantic" men or women—those good at whispering sweet, glib nothings in your ear—should be considered suspect. Rather, look at what your partner does. Does he or she keep you waiting frequently and occasionally stand you up? Or do you have the feeling that you can rely on your partner? Is he or she a comfort in a crisis? Did your partner take care of you when you were ill? Does your love keep his or her perspective when you lose yours and help you back to sanity? In the little day-to-day things, is there thoughtfulness and consideration? Does your partner go out of his or her way to fill the car with gas when you have to make a long drive? Does your love remember your favorite flavor of ice cream when he or she goes to the store? Did your partner jump in and type that paper for you when your typist was sick and you were up against a deadline? Did he or she take pains to be good to your parents when they visited? Can you count on your partner not to embarrass you or quarrel with you in front of other people? Does your love flirt like mad with others when you are in company? In short, is there kindness?

These are the sorts of things to watch for if you are wondering whether you are loved. Turned around, they are the questions you must ask yourself if you want to know whether you are able to give real love.

It will probably occur to you that it takes a considerable period of time to discover the answer to these questions. True! That is why instant love is always partly phony. It may take a year or two before you experience a crisis with which your partner might have helped. This is a lengthy process. Because we are all on our best behavior when a relationship begins, we really have to wait until this wears off to see how our partner does then. All of this means that it takes a couple of years to know another person. Your deepest commitment should never be made early.

Which brings us to the subject of commitment. I am wary of the kind of commitment people make when they marry, not because commitment itself is bad but because in marriage, we make a promise about all future time, and I am just not sure that this is possible. The danger, I think, lies in the feeling that once the marriage vows have been said, nothing more needs to be done—that the thing will take care of itself. This is never true. The best relationship requires continual readjustment. In a sense, two people who are lovers constantly negotiate their reality in what is a continual process of communication.

The basic requirement for this communication is absolute honesty. This doesn't mean that you have to discuss every little feeling. But it does mean that when you feel at all strongly about something in your relationship, you say so immediately. You don't suppress or withhold important feelings. In a very interesting study of upper-middle-class marriages in the United States, Cuber and Harroff (1966) found, through lengthy interviews, that most marriages begin as vital relationships, but the majority of marriages become "devitalized"—dull and meaningless. I am convinced that suppressing and withholding feelings is the first step toward such devitalization. This is particularly true in the area of sexual love. When this is disappointing and nothing is said or done about it, the sense of deprivation will always eat into the relationship like an acid.

In addition to communicating about your relationship, you must also communicate about what is going on around you generally. Perhaps you are off on a vacation, but you just aren't having a good time. Do you suffer in silence or let your partner know? I have often thought that one of the reasons my partner Ted and I have such a good time together is that we are always open to changes in what we are doing. We very frequently walk out on movies or workshops in Buddhist meditation or whatever else we undertake. If it isn't going well for one of us, there is always immediate communication that enables us to find out quickly when something isn't working.

Let me also give an example of renegotiating the relationship. When Ted and I started living together, we had separate incomes and kept our financial affairs separate—keeping track of what we spent for common purposes and splitting that. After some years of this, we decided to throw all our money together and stop keeping complicated records. However, we found, after a couple of years of this arrangement, that we did less communicating about how money should be spent. Sometimes a large amount was spent on a project only one of us was really interested in. This created some resentment. For example, I felt strongly about a trip to Europe to visit my aunt, whereas Ted would rather have saved the money for building a house. Yet the Europe trip just sort of developed without any explicit discussion of alternative uses for that money. As soon as we realized what was happening, we decided to go back to our previous, separate money arrangement. Things are once again going smoothly on the financial front. The neurotic part of me wanted to whisper that this was a failure in the relationship. I told it to keep quiet. As usual, that neurotic voice turned out to be dead wrong.

All of us have neurotic fears about relationships. Sometimes we are terribly afraid of losing love. At other times, we may be afraid of not being able to continue to give love ourselves. Everyone has his or her version of such fears. If *commitment* means anything, I think it means the determination to keep our sanest, best self forward and not to load our fearful neuroses on our partner. Again, I want to use an example from my own relationship since I know it best. Ted and I observed that each of us has a neurotic self. We gave them names to make it easier to communicate about them. Mine is Little Inge, the depressive, insecure self who fears loss of love almost to the point of ruining a relationship. Ted's neurotic part is called

Lionell. Lionell has a terrible temper and is mean. We discovered that we only had bad fights when we both happened to be neurotic at the same time. Lionell's temper frightens Little Inge, who starts cringing and crying. Lionell cannot stand cringing, and we are off on a fight. As long as one of us is feeling sane, we can handle the other one's neurotic side, but, when we are both crazy, Pow! We can understand all of this and communicate about it as long as we are feeling sane, but Little Inge and Lionell refuse to communicate. Over the years, we have become much better about keeping the neurotic selves on the sidelines. I dislike anger and conflict, so it was hard for me to realize that, to get over Lionell, Ted needs a sane friend who will just sit by until the anger passes. For a long time, I repressed a desire to laugh at Lionell, for fear he would become even more infuriated. When I finally started to giggle, I discovered that laughter was the best way of banishing Lionell. Ted, on the other hand, has learned how to banish Little Inge by letting her know that he couldn't stand her for long, while at the same time encouraging the saner part of me to take command. Over the years, I have gotten so much positive feedback for being a sane person and so much negative feedback for being Little Inge that Little Inge pops up less and less. This is, of course, a great relief for me. Lionell, too, is becoming rarer.

From my own experience, I believe that a good relationship can help us overcome basic neurotic patterns. We can admit our faults in this safe setting. We can also, by being very honest about our feelings, experience a sense of being accepted. Even our most foolish feelings or secret thoughts can be expressed, and, lo and behold, we are still loved! The trouble with putting up a front is that we always suspect that if anybody looked behind the wall, they would discover us to be dreadful, icky monsters. Just let those foolish ideas and fears see the light of day, and we are reassured that we are really all right.

It is a somewhat amusing fact that when we share a deep, frightful secret about our inner selves with another person, we almost always find that our disclosure seems perfectly harmless to our friend: "So that is your most secret sexual fantasy? That's okay, as long as you're enjoying yourself" or "So that is your secret fear? Well, well. I'm going to the store. Do you need anything?"

When living with another person—whether in marriage or just living together— we necessarily have to compromise to get along. Our society is so diverse that we come to such a setting with habits and expectations different from our partner's. It requires a certain openness and humor to deal with this. For example, Ted and I used to wrangle about clothes hangers. He felt that his hanger arrangements were being destroyed, while I felt he was just very picky. One day, when he was watching me put away the laundry, he began to laugh. As he watched me, he realized that we just lived in two different worlds when it came to clothes hangers.

"I see," he said, "that when you are hanging up our clothes you just reach behind you blindly into the closet for a free hanger."

"Of course," I replied. "What do you expect me to do?" It came out that, for Ted, there are three or four different types of hangers for different purposes. Wooden hangers are for coats and heavy sweaters, plastic hangers for good shirts, and wire hangers for anything else. To me, a hanger is just a hanger, and I am quite capable of hanging an old work shirt on Ted's best hanger without thinking a thing about it. We had a laugh over it when we saw it just that way. Another couple we know discovered one day, during a wrangle over cleanliness, that one of them was angry because the other never cleaned the top of the refrigerator. The culprit had never really thought about the top of the refrigerator as a place. It just didn't exist for him.

Ted and I have also found that there is a shortcut to ending fights, but you probably shouldn't try to take it if you are still having trouble expressing anger in a useful, negotiable way. The shortcut seems to lie in realizing right in the middle of some squabble how comic we are and how utterly trivial the cause of the fight is. Once, while watching ducks in a pond, we started laughing at the occasional squabbles ducks get into with each other. These usually occur when they run into each other or both go for the same morsel of food. There is a terrific moment of quacking and flapping of wings. Then, before you know it, they are off gliding along the pond again. Ted said, "Our fights are like that—just quacking ducks who have temporarily collided." Since then, we sometimes just say "quacking ducks" in the middle of a squabble and laugh it off then and there.

As you move into a relationship, try to get a feel for how the communication is going and how well you can work out differences. How to make an initially good choice is rather more difficult to say because everyone's choice is different. Luckily, no two people have the same ideal lover. I would like to make just two points. First, avoid becoming deeply involved with a partner who wants a lifestyle distinctly different from your own. You may not discover this right away and may find yourself in love in such a situation. You will have to make major and painful comprises. It is certainly better to discover this before a strong relationship develops. If your partner is very interested in a career and you want lots of children, or if your partner wants to live in the country and you love New York City, your relationship will be hard to sustain. Long-distance relationships often arise for students who are highly mobile. These are tough at best and should be avoided if you can see them coming.

Finally, avoid the person who is on the rebound from a previous love affair or, indeed, anyone who is in a temporary state of emotional collapse. Someone who is deeply disturbed is likely to grasp at any straw. If you are that straw, you may find yourself drawn into the disturbance. Or you may find that when the emotional disturbance of your partner wears off, so does his or her need for your support. Your best bet is to choose someone who seems to have his or her life together and is able to get along alone for a while between partners. Such folk have enough energy available for a successful relationship. Avoid romances with married people who are cheating on their partners. They are either confused or dishonest, both qualities that make for poor relationships.

Above all, there should be a sense of playfulness, lightness, and fun in a relationship. Friendship and kindness should be joined with the play of sexual ecstasy. In such a relationship, we are able to become children again, in the best sense. Yet, at the same time, there is sufficient emotional maturity to support the relationship through bad times as well as good. Such a love is one of the greatest joys to be had in this life. It is worth looking for and working toward. Certainly, there is always an element of luck involved in whom you meet when you are looking for a relationship. We can maximize our chances by becoming wiser people.

If the good partner is not available at the moment, spend the time learning to love yourself and your friends. That is the best foundation for loving others.

A Postscript About AIDS

Having written much of this very positive and sexually permissive chapter on love in the 1980s, before the AIDS epidemic was really upon us, I now find that I must sound a very serious, cautionary note. I didn't change the chapter because I hope that AIDS will not put our culture back where it was before the sexual revolution of the 1960s and 1970s. While I trust that we will not become Puritans once again, I realize that the chapter comes out of the life experience of someone who was fortunate enough to be sexually active in that brief hiatus between Victorianism and the AIDS epidemic.

A careful study of college campuses in 1990 found that students tested positive for HIV at the rate of 2 per 1,000. Yet, studies found that most students continued risky sexual behavior because they felt invulnerable. When I asked a class of 20 students how many had changed their sexual practices because of AIDS, every hand went up, accompanied by moans and laughter.

Two per thousand looks like a very slim chance, but remember that every time you have unsafe sex, your risk of contracting the disease increases. By the time you have exposed yourself to 10 different partners, your odds are 2 per 100. The same would be true if you were with a single partner who was having sex with other people. When it comes to a fatal disease, such a risk is unacceptable. AIDS is a leading cause of death for young adults today (see Kastenbaum, 1998).

AIDS: The Fears of a College Student

I am a college student, and I fear the unknown: I fear the places people have been and what they have done, I fear disease, and I fear the HIV virus. I fear this virus not because I am promiscuous or lead a promiscuous lifestyle; I fear getting too close to someone who might be infected. How am I supposed to ask someone I am building a relationship of trust with if there is a possibility he could be HIV positive? How do you know where they have been, who they have been with? Is it insulting to ask your partner to get an AIDS test? Is asking my partner to submit this information to me a signal that I don't trust this person? Each person I start a new relationship with has the potential to get serious, possibly lead to marriage, and certainly has the potential for sexual contact.

Sex is very much a part of the college atmosphere because young people are exploring everything they had restrictions on at home. As college students, we have accepted responsibility and taken on the challenge of higher education, so we should be responsible enough to handle sex, right? Handling sex is understanding consequences, thinking about our futures, and understanding how to protect ourselves. By the time people enter college, they have been lectured about, questioned about, and maybe even tested for HIV. Ignorance should not be the problem.

So what is the answer? AIDS is out there, but, unfortunately, it is something that is hidden. The only way to protect yourself and your partner is by having safe sex (or no sex) and good communication and trust. It is okay to ask your partner to use a condom. Safe sex is the responsibility of both partners. It is okay to ask your partner to wait for sex, if you are scared or unsure. If your partner cannot respect your choice, then maybe you should reevaluate whether this person is someone you want to be with. Keep dating fun and exciting; don't allow AIDS to scare you away from relationships and meeting new people. Let AIDS be a reminder to be safe, to be aware, and to be informed.

—Erin Cora

Trouble With Parents

The huge step away from home to college is another progression away from being parent-dependent. Next to grades and love, parents are surely the most frequent source of vexation among students. In Chapter 14, the topics we address are as follows:

- Why you can't go home again because now you are always only a visitor.
- Recognizing this culturally patterned conflict and hence choosing your battles wisely.
- Recognizing change in this situation and perhaps discovering how much your parents mature during your college years.
- Seeing neurotic family situations for what they are and realizing that just as we can't rescue our lover, we can't really rescue our parents.
- Addressing our grades and careers with our parents with clarity, kindness, and assertiveness.
- Looking into guilt about money and seeing how the culturally patterned conflict between adult children and parents is exacerbated by money.
- Listening to advice from some wise mothers: "And now, a word from our sponsor—being for a moment in their shoes."

The last time I went home, I realized that I was visiting my parents' house—not coming home. It was a sad feeling, but also a feeling of independence and maturity. I had to say good-bye to my childhood and the familiarity of my hometown, but I realized that I have a whole adult life of my own to look forward to.

—Eve McCullah (former student)

Cut Off

I left home 2 days after my high school graduation for a job at a summer camp. It was my first real job and my first time away from home. I was going to save all my money so that I would have spending cash for the next year while I was in school. I knew that college was going to be expensive, so I didn't want to ask my parents for more money than I had to. I had it all figured out. I got home about a week before I was going to start college. I had just enough time to shop for clothes, buy a new backpack and some notebooks, and get a new haircut. I couldn't wait to go shopping with my mom. Then I got the surprise of my life. She wasn't going to pay for anything. I had earned money; that's what it was for. So much for my plan to save money. Not only that, but I was now expected to buy everything on my own, everything from toothpaste and shampoo to food to cleaning supplies and laundry soap. And I was still living at home. My parents cut me off from everything without warning. I couldn't believe that I could ever feel so unwelcome in my own home. I coped, though. I've done fairly well for myself working two jobs and going to school full-time. My mother has started to resent my independence, but really it's her own fault.

—Kristin Rydberg

When I started plans for the second edition of this book, my friend and colleague Dorothy Mariner said, "You should put in something about trouble students have with their parents." As soon as she said it, I thought, "Why, of course! I've heard plenty about that subject over the years." In fact, next to grades and love, parents are surely the most frequent cause of vexation among students. So I took the opportunity to open up this subject with some classes that were using my book. The response was immediate. When I asked who was having difficulties with parents, most hands went up.

You Can't Go Home Again

One young man says, "You come home and they think you are still the same age as when you left. I've been living at school since I was 15, and my parents still treat me like they did when I was 15."[1]

---

[1]Throughout the student quotes, a new paragraph indicates a new speaker. I want, most warmly, to thank the students, colleagues, and friends whose words I have used in this chapter: Eve McCullah, Don McCullah, Theo Carrell, Barney McGrane, Ed Jamieson, Dorothy Mariner, Jane McCauley, Jim Kowalski, and Peg McBride.

A young woman chimes in, "When I go home, suddenly I'm back with having to be in before midnight, or my mother will lie awake and worry until I come home."

Another says, "How do I let them know that I don't need that much parenting anymore? I feel myself falling back into being-your-child-again, and at the same time, I witness them go through the transformation into we-are-your-parents. They never see you in any other role—when you return home, it's this weird time warp, as if you have never been away."

Another says about going home, "I was a guest, but I was also responsible once again for all the old assignments. I had to clean up my room when they wanted me to, not when I wanted to."

"A funny thing happened between me and my mom. It was my birthday and she came to the dorm to surprise me. I really resented it. I felt she was getting on my turf. We did talk about it and sort of straightened out our feelings."

Some students found they missed their parents. There is a temptation to slip back into familiar roles. "You kind of want the child role, and they want it for you. It is such a contrast to the independence at school."

"I used to just want to get out of the house and be with my friends; now I'm with friends all the time, and I like to spend time with my parents. When I go home, it's a lot better."

"When I come home, it's strange. It's as if I'm not living there anymore. I'm like a guest. My parents took everything out of our rooms, each child as we left home. It feels so weird."

Here somebody asked, "Would anyone want to go back and live at home?" A chorus of resounding "no's" follow.

At the point of leaving home, many students find parents hanging on too hard. "They ask, 'Why don't you come home and visit this Easter, Christmas, or stay all summer?' I want to spend some of that time with my friends."

"My mother raised me. She never went to college and had it hard. Every dime went to me. She lived for me. I took skating and every kind of lesson. She lived her life for me. I could feel that even when I was 10 years old. So I went away to college, and she calls me every day, sometimes three or four times a day. She is my best friend, but I wonder if it's always going to be like this. She calls her own mother that often. When I'm married, will this go on? She does treat me like I'm 15. When I go home for summer, I have a 12 o'clock curfew."

"My parents were divorced, and at first I lived with my father. Then my mother remarried, so I went to live with her. We grew amazingly close. Now I'm out here. Last year, I was in Connecticut, and she could deal with that. She really wants me to come home. Then she brings up that my private college is too expensive. I have to look her squarely in the eye and say, 'Mom, I'm too old, 20 years old.' You've got to teach your parents that the person they raised is now a young adult."

My class discussions were with students at small private residential colleges. To balance this bias, I got some feedback from a class at a community college, where most students live at home. Surprisingly, a slight majority of these students were very satisfied with their arrangements. In some cases, parents seem to have given the child adult status as he or she entered college:

"My relationship at home with my parents is good. After high school, where my grades were scrutinized by my parents, college has been totally opposite. They leave me alone about my grades. Ironically, I always end up telling them things anyway. I think our college relationship was a positive step in my maturation to adulthood."

"They basically stay out of my way. They understand that college, working, and friends can make life hard. Their main complaint is that I'm not home enough—I'm never there to talk to, to help pick up around the house, or to watch TV. I have two jobs and school, so it gets hard. All in all, I'm happy with the living arrangements at home."

In some cases, I had the impression that students who live at home are more willing to settle for a lack of autonomy because the arrangement is otherwise so useful to them. "I think my relationship with my mom is the same as it was in high school. I still have a midnight curfew, my boyfriend of two and a half years still can't come home when my mom is not home, and I still have to help around the house. It hasn't changed at all. It's a great relationship—we get along—almost never fight."

Another says, "I'm not saying our relationship is perfect, because by far it isn't, but I can tell you the more I respect them, the better it gets. So maybe kids should respect their parents more; after all, they do know a lot more than us."

Those who reported not liking life at home had many of the same complaints as those voiced by students living away from home, only in the former case, the conflicts have a greater impact on the student's life. "Living with my parents is difficult during college because they tie everything I do to my grades. Their control level is tremendous. Because they are paying for my education, everything in my life must not be private. They always nag at me to do my homework."

"They put a lot of pressure on me by trying to do family functions and continuing family togetherness. They don't understand that, as we get older, we want to be with friends."

"Living at home while going to school is very strained. I receive no financial or emotional support, and there is no location in the house to study for classes and exams."

The Most Hurtful of Loves

It is truly a simple equation. Adults choose to have children. They value their children and want them to be safe. They want the best for their children. Harm is the last thing in the world they would wish upon them. What could go wrong with this happily-ever-after picture?

Unfortunately, most young adults know that the story most certainly does not end happily. Our generation's reality is that most children are estranged from their loving parents. Alienated, can't wait to get away from them, why don't they ever get me—thoughts like these race through the minds of countless children. They feel so helpless trying to fix such a fundamental dilemma that their only reflex is to escape and avoid it, if at all possible. The parents, in all their decades of worldly wisdom, are equally as puzzled as to why they cannot connect with their own offspring. The truth, according to this author, is painfully simple.

Rarely does a single soul, in our hectic consumer-driven lives, ever take the time to stop and understand what makes each of us tick deep down inside. It is a long and tedious journey through personal issues that we tend to never give a second thought. And, in the end, we may come to realize that no one really knows the first thing about what the hell they are doing every second of every minute of every day. My wandering words are getting at the underlying point: Kids don't get why their parents give them trouble and criticism. Parents don't understand why their kids don't listen and appreciate their "guidance and advice."

A translation is desperately needed.

A strange and clearly unfortunate phenomenon seems to happen when people "grow" from child to adult to parent. They almost completely forget what it was like to be children and become maniacally egotistical about how age somehow automatically brings wisdom. They fall into a complex where they can do or say no wrong, and they take on the crusade-like duty to point out every error that their children make. Arguably, they care a great deal about their children and do not want to see them injure themselves by behaving unwisely. However, a discrepancy appears to develop like an impregnable oil spill polluting the pure lake of caregiving. They do not realize that their critical comments are destructive to the self-esteem of their developing children, far more devastating than any foolish error the children could make on their own.

The phenomenon continues and is emphasized in high-achieving immigrant families. Immigrant parents who have struggled to stand on their own feet in an alien country have no time for, or comprehension of, luxurious concepts such as happiness and satisfaction with one's life. They simply tell their children to be doctors, whether they want to or not, figuring that the stability will inevitably lead to "happiness." "What's there not to be happy about?" they think. So they yell, and the children, who have been watching their liberal American counterparts, become traumatized for life with unforeseeable consequences, without the parents ever thinking they made a single wrong move. And if you ever try to tell parents that they are doing a poor job parenting, so help you God. This little itty bitty misconception is the root cause for centuries of potentially constructive, yet tragically derailed, families.

Note to parents: Listen to what you say; take a step back. Think about it. There is no rule that says you have to become an echo of your own parent.

On the flipside, we kids are not free from all responsibility. Most of it, yes. I empirically justify that by saying babies do not know how to problem solve and should not be held accountable for the ignorance of their parents. The issue of baby ignorance unfortunately endures well into adolescence, adulthood, then ultimately parenthood—circle of life. Our job, as kids of ignorantly loving parents, ought to be situational realization. The truth is that we have very few weapons in our arsenal. Know that they mean well, remind yourself that they may not know what negativity they are bringing into your life, and, most important, learn from their mistakes so that your children will not have to suffer the same fate. More progressively, you might attempt explaining to your parents how you feel when they criticize you, but we know that in some of our families, our voices do not carry the weight of the wind. In all likelihood, you may be blown back with a "you're too young to understand," or something to that effect. Emotional expression is truly not an option for many of us. Do not feel badly; you are most certainly not alone. Certain actions you may want to avoid, however, are yelling back aggressively, slinging insults, taking up smoking or drugs for indirect attention, and so on. In the end, be smart about it by not ruining your future. Be smarter than your parents were.

They love you. You love them. Both want harmony and warm fuzzy feelings above all else. They just kind of lose their way and forget the goal in the ho-hum of typical life. This is the dear price we pay for being so ambitious monetarily while being so careless with human fundamentals. And know that no BMW will bring your family back together. Ever.

—Lawrence Lu

A Culturally Patterned Conflict

These conflicts are so common, even when relations in the family have been good, that we must look for a pervasive cultural pattern. The problem is that for 18 years, your parents protected you, felt a tremendous responsibility for you, tried to ease your path and warn you about the pitfalls of life, and now, suddenly, they have to shift gears. They have to trust the wisdom of their own childrearing, and they have to trust you to survive your own mistakes. They have to restructure the whole relationship.

At the same time, in our culture, a child is expected to leave home and become a full-fledged adult during the late teens and early 20s. Unlike the situation in many other societies, children are not supposed to remain blindly obedient to their elders. There must be a "breaking free." You all sense this and try to act accordingly. It is, indeed, difficult to go from a highly structured home situation into a very unstructured college situation.

As you meet the cultural requirements of thinking for yourself, you encounter disagreements with your parents. As one student put it, "Can you love your parents and not necessarily agree with them? If you express your disagreement, can they hear where you are coming from such that it doesn't mean that you don't love them? If I ever disagreed with my dad, it would be World War III." I asked her whether she had actually tried an open disagreement. She said she had not. I urged her to try but be sure that, for her part, the disagreement wasn't part of a desire to reject him in her turn.

Often students take some issue home from a college class in the wild hope that they might succeed in driving their parents crazy. During the civil rights movement, I taught race relations and was often amused at the delight with which students latched on to this issue because it was one on which they could feel morally superior to their parents.

Breaking away is better confronted on concrete issues of parental control: for example, when they demand that you come home by midnight or insist that you have to clean your room on time. Differences of opinion work better if you are just exploring your new ideas with your parents, rather than against them.

One slightly older student told us that he had a terrible time with his conservative Jewish relatives, who became outraged when he let them know that he was no longer keeping kosher. I asked him, "Who brings it up?" He said, "I guess I do." "So," I said, "why don't you just let sleeping dogs lie? They might feel much happier if they didn't have to argue the point with you. After all, on your own, you are free to cook however you like." This student seemed surprised when I told him that you don't really have to tell people everything that you think and feel. Choose your time and place, and choose your battles wisely.

Issues With Immigrant Families

Much of our trouble with parents stems from an organic, generational divide. Our parents grew up with a set of experiences and values that, for the most part, differ vastly from ours. Our base assumptions about life and the rules governing it are different. For those of us who are children of immigrant parents, this barrier of communication is compounded by a problem of different cultural expectations. Our parents bring with them their cherished values to a new land of opportunity, perhaps not always explicitly hoping for instant material success but at least for the rewards afforded by an abundance of opportunities. They do this as much for themselves as for their children, but one can be certain that once children do come along, everything becomes about their children.

Children of immigrant parents grow up with the perception that their parents sacrificed everything to build better lives in a new country for them, and, indeed, they practically did. I've often wondered whether I could have the inner strength and conviction to leave every childhood landmark behind and completely displace myself by moving to another country and speaking a foreign language for the rest of my days. The weight of such a sacrifice is awesome to us, and we grow up with tremendous pressure, implicit if not explicit, to succeed, in school and in a career. This kind of pressure usually prescribes a very narrow path of success, which we, as American children of individualistic freedoms, chafe under. Our parents were so careful in building a measure of material comfort; how can we take their efforts for granted and throw caution to the wind when it comes to building our own lives?

How can we possibly hope to reconcile these differences? On one hand, we owe everything to the sacrifices our parents made for us, the sacrifices they made before we were born, and the sacrifices they made for us while we were growing up. Our parents' old world values have also been instilled in us. For everything we do that makes our parents beam with pride, we also beam with pride, at first because we want to make our parents happy but then later because we realize there's a certain validity to the kinds of successes they've expected of us. At this point, we know that we are truly our parents' children—we've internalized the expectations they've always had of us, even if some of these expectations were never intended.

We then become two people in one. One sits on our left shoulder, tugging us toward emotional, intellectual, spiritual growth, while the other sits on our right shoulder, demanding practical rewards, a respectable salary, an upwardly oriented career path. When our parents chime in with their ideas on how we should plan our lives (as they want to do), we just as often become resentful of their interference. As others have stated, though, we often lend the advice of elders other than our parents more credibility than we do our own parents. The reality is that our resentment may stem from the fact that some part of our inner selves does agree with our parents, and we don't know how to deal with this conflict, as it is both an inner one and an outer one.

Before you can engage your parents in a mature, levelheaded discussion, you have to reconcile your conflicting desires, or at least realize that this will be a milestone you have to reach before you can hope to move on. Remember that a perfect solution is unlikely, but what you need perhaps most of all is room to make your own mistakes. After all, as immigrants, they took a huge gamble in coming here to the United States. It can only be fair for you to be allowed the same freedom, if not so drastic.

Ultimately, your struggle between your parents' ideas and your own ideas of how your life should be lived will help you both grow toward a mutual understanding. It's important to realize that, like you, your parents are people, not unchanging monoliths imposing themselves on you. They aren't perfect, but they're full of hope for you. They only want the best for you, and there may even come a time when they agree with your vision for your life, as long as you're happy.

Because what would all their sacrifice have been for, if you're not?

—Andy Wang

Real Love Situations

When there is real love between children and parents, the difficult transition period will pass. It is always surprising to college seniors how much their parents have matured in 4 years. A few filial relationships are so good that the struggle never happens. After listening to the class discussion for some time, one young woman said, "I am really amazed to hear all this because I still live at home with my father, but we don't have any conflict. I think he has always sort of treated me as an equal. I am very comfortable in the situation."

"I live with my dad and grandfather now. It's not like living at home. I do everything now like I would if I had an apartment. We are three independent males. We come and go as we want. We do our own laundry. I don't feel like leaving home at all."

"On my 18th birthday, my father brought home some beer, and we drank it together. It was sort of a coming-of-age ceremony. He tells me dirty jokes, and we hang out together. He seems more like a friend and advisor than a parent."

"Even when you're 30, they'll still have the chicken soup ready. But I think college is the time to branch out. My parents and I are separating, but the relationship exceeds what we had in high school."

In these healthy families, parent and child may enjoy role reversal, which the child's new adulthood makes possible. An older student said, "My daughter graduated from medical school. We were going to her home. We were her guests. She was making all the arrangements. What a feeling to have a total role reversal. My daughter worried about my son being late, and I thought, 'Oh, that's what I used to do.'"

"Since my brother and I left home, our parents, who are both teachers, are spending more money on us. They spent a lot on my brother's wedding. So now my dad wants to get a truck next year, and I'm trying to find a way to help him because they can't afford it, and I want it for him so badly. He always supported me. Now that I'm out of the house, I want to give back."

"I live with my dad but plan to move out so he can start dating by himself without my setting it up. [laughter] Has anybody here got a single mom?"

Neurotic Family Situations

Unfortunately, a great many parent-child relationships are deeply neurotic and tense. Here, the struggle to break away can be traumatic for both sides. One young woman told us, "My mother tries to bribe me to quit school and move back in with her. She keeps phoning me offering me money, clothes, and other things. It makes me feel terribly guilty because I know she is living alone now and hates it."[2]

Here I had to jump in with both feet: "You have absolutely no reason to feel guilty," I told her. "In our culture, it is up to your mother to make her own life enjoyable. She may have to learn to reach out to adults her own age, to become involved in the community. You wouldn't even be doing her a favor if you gave

---

[2]For all those who suffer guilt in their relationship with parents, there is a cure. Read the excellent *Codependent No More* (Beattie, 1987).

in and went home. You would only deepen her dependency on you when she needs badly to become independent, and you would resent it so much that your relationship with your mother would become more embittered than it is now."

A student in her late 30s joined the discussion. "I'm living with my mother now. I work and go to school, and at first she kept demanding that I spend more time with her. I just couldn't. Now she has become active in a number of things and is feeling much better about herself."

Just as we can't rescue our lovers, we can't really rescue our parents, but we can sometimes push them into accepting an adult-to-adult relationship. Unfortunately, sometimes, even that is impossible.

A young man comments, "My mother says 'I'll always be your mother; I'll always worry about you.' I'm 23, and I was on the phone and we got to talking about marriage. She knows that that's not for me, at least for a while. I'll be 28 when that happens. And she says, 'Remember, when you do decide to get married, I want to have a talk with you.' And I said, 'What would you have to tell me that I don't know already?' She just said, 'I want to talk to you.' She wouldn't say what about. I cannot think, 'Did I really miss something?'" [laughter]

In dealing with neurotic relationships, the student may be up against raw fear. When we are children, parents are all powerful for us. Their nurturance is a matter of life or death. So it may be necessary to get past this fear. One way to do this is to get some assertiveness training.

A college counselor who teaches assertiveness training states the following:

Assertiveness training is exactly for the child-parent problem. I teach adults from 18 to 70, and I find that in every class, the thing most of them want to deal with is their relationship with their parents. In assertiveness training, I teach them how to write a DESC script. [DESC stands for Describe, Express, Specify, and Consequences.] Under D, people describe the problem to their parents: "You criticize everything I do." Under E, they describe how they feel: "I still feel like a child." Under S, they specify what they want: "I would like some positive feedback." Under C, they describe how it would make them feel if parents met their wishes: "If you give me positive feedback, I would feel closer to you and would be more likely to share other plans with you."

Fear is the main problem most people are up against with their parents. We deal with that through what we call cognitive restructuring—for example, the idea that we must get parents' approval or that they are always right and we are wrong. We try to get people to challenge the idea that parents still have power over them. We get them to see that they may never get parental approval, but they don't need it: "I can live without that." Changing their thinking takes away some of the emotional power parents seem to have over them (see Ellis & Bernard, 1983).

In the group, we role-play how the situation with parents should be handled. We practice until the student feels ready. We start with small assertions of power—perhaps how to ask for attention you want in a restaurant. From small beginnings, we work up to dealing with parents. (Assertiveness training may last 2 hours or a whole semester. Probably about half the college counseling centers or reentry centers offer some assertiveness training.)

Remember that parents will treat you according to the way you react. If you throw a tantrum, that is childish behavior. You should be less reactive—communicate your feelings in a direct, open way.

We really can change the kind of relationship we have with our parents by becoming the adults we need to be for ourselves. We also have to see our parents as people with their own struggles and limitations and gear our expectations accordingly. We must see that parents are no longer the gods they were when we were children.

Grades and Careers

"My parents called the school and asked for my grades. I wanted to fight with them but they won't listen to me because 'We are your parents and that's the way it is.'"

"As an only child, there is so much pressure on me to do well."

"My parents bug me about grades, but I don't want to have to be an A or B student all the time. So I tell them, 'Lay off, I work at school full-time. That's all I can do. I know you're paying and all that, but there's a limit.' It just bounces off, but I don't bug myself about it."

"It doesn't matter what A's I get. It's never good enough. For a time, I cut myself off completely from my parents. I didn't let them know what was going on with me. They got noncommittal answers until I learned to value myself and my own achievements. Now I'm proud of my achievements, and I pay attention to myself because no one has a right to lay their criteria on their children."

"Last summer I was so worried about grades because they're spending so much money. I landed in the hospital. My dad says, 'Don't pressure her. We have the money.' My mom won't listen. She makes me sick. Literally!"

"College isn't just learning and grades; it's about managing your time, making decisions about the future, making relationships. Grades are just one aspect. My folks know that, and they're very open about it."

"Grades are the only thing your parents can evaluate you by. You're an investment, and grades are their dipstick. Sometimes it's difficult for your parents to accept mediocrity. Every parent thinks, 'My child is so smart.' I feel like saying, 'Back off.' I'm working and going to school and earning my own way."

Sometimes parents pressure students about their choices of major, career, or even extracurricular activities. "My parents had a traditional nuclear family. They grew up in a rural area. Dad was the big football player in high school, and Mom was a cheerleader. It really gets corny. I'm the first grandchild in my family, and a load of obligations come down on me. It's never said outright, 'We want you to be on the honor roll,' but it is said indirectly. When I was a kid, we moved to Southern California. My growing up here has been so different from their lives. For years, I went out for football just to please my mom. I hated every game. It took courage to quit. My dad understood, but my mom disapproved."

An older woman says, "My daughter went to medical school. Her roommate was also a medical student, but she only did it because both her parents were doctors and pressured her into it. She committed suicide."

"Why don't parents understand that—that their children have to make their own choices? I think it is because they are distant from their children. They never really see who the child is. My folks used to say, 'Whatever makes you happy.'"

When you disagree about college majors and careers, I think you must try to prevail. You cannot let yourself be put into the position of living out your parents' hopes for themselves in your own life.

It may be that your parents didn't achieve what they wanted and now load their hopes and dreams onto their children. In other cases, parents feel they were so successful in their own careers that it would be insulting if you didn't follow suit. You cannot let yourself be pushed around that way, but you have to prepare yourself for the confrontation.

I would advise you to do some thorough research about your desired major, career plan, or summer job prospect. Go to the college placement office; get a list of the kinds of jobs your desired major will lead to. If there are graduate schools involved, research these so you can make a really informed choice. Most college campuses have an office of career planning that gives vocational and aptitude tests. Take these and show the results to your parents. Thus prepared, you will have an easier time staying calm and reasonable—always the position of strength.

Guilt About Money

The culturally patterned conflict between adult children and parents is exacerbated when parents are still footing the bill. A student says, "I was the oldest and given lots more responsibility than my sister. I was the intellectual and got sent to a private college. But now my sister is making college decisions, and they tell her to go to a state school. We're having an uproar in the family. For my parents, I was a kind of savior, and it carried a lot of burden and guilt for me. I made my parents proud, but I feel guilty about my sister."

Sometimes students shoulder blame where none was intended. One young woman told us, "I feel so terribly guilty because my parents are spending so much to send me to this private college, while my other siblings went to state colleges. If they even mention a financial worry, it sets off this terrible guilt." I asked her, "Do you think they do resent it, or was this something they really wanted to do for you?" She agreed that they were, indeed, pleased that she could have this experience. "So," I told her, "tell them some of the positive things that have happened to you because they did send you here. That would be much better than wallowing in secret guilt."

A young woman says, "I've been taken care of so much, I don't know what money is. I feel guilty that I've had it so easy. I feel out of control. I don't know how to get a job and save money. It's not my money. It's theirs. It's confusing. It's very hard to define it."

Guilt over money is very common. I found this out when meeting with a class. Someone asked whether I was sorry that I had never had children. I said, "It has its advantages. That I didn't have to put kids through college enabled me to retire early." At this, a guilty moan went up from at least half the students present.

My suggestion is that, if you feel guilty about the money your parents are spending on you, you should begin by talking it over with them. Perhaps you will be surprised by their real feelings and circumstances. If you still come away feeling guilty, perhaps you should find a way to contribute to the cost of your education. Get a part-time job if you can. Look into loans you can pay off after you finish college.

The money situation can turn ugly, as this student relates, "Last spring, my stepdad comes up to me and says, 'You know, you're an investment. I'm paying so and so many thousand dollars a year, but I know that someday I'm going to have a claim on you and you're going to have to help me.' You know how girls say that some men make them feel like a piece of meat? That's how it felt. It made me feel like a piece of meat."

"I have so much respect for people who work and go to college. There are so many afternoons when I can go take a nap, but my roommate has to go to work."

"Independence for me now is impossible. I feel trapped by my parents' money." Another student says, "I haven't asked anybody for money. My dad, if I ask for money, he moans. I don't know how I'm doing it—I guess I'm charging it." [laughter]

Upward Mobility

One of the most intractable family conflict situations occurs when children are upwardly mobile, when going to college means moving up from the working class or lower middle class into the upper middle class. A young woman says, "I only go home one week a year. My father and I disagree on almost everything. I don't have any rights. Sometimes I feel that he resents me for having the chance to go to college." It is very difficult for both parties in such a situation. Parents are afraid their children will look down on them. In a certain sense, they are right. We all absorb class snobbery. Reassuring your parents that you love them is probably the best way to deal with this problem. It is also important that you don't shoulder a big load of guilt. You are not to blame. The class system is to blame. (For further thoughts on the problem of upwardly mobile children, see Chapter 15.)

As you struggle with a variety of conflicts, you must see that to work through the situation with your parents *you have to make a special effort to see them as people, rather than simply as parents.* Just as they must see you as an adult, you must see them as fellow creatures. One student says, "When you are a kid, it seems like you do all the changing, while your parents are unchanging figures. I'm now watching my parents change, and it is quite a kick." Ideally, the conflict will end with both sides letting go of their stereotypes of one another and moving on to a more authentic and better relationship.

Advice From Some Wise Mothers

Never having been a parent myself, I couldn't tell you how this whole process looks from the parents' viewpoint. So I asked mothers of my acquaintances for some words of wisdom. I will let them speak for themselves.[3]

I always looked on college as a maturing experience. Go, have a good time, meet people, broaden your interests. If you also happen to learn something, that's nice. If it contributes to your career, that is remarkable. Actually, my son's extracurricular activity, photography, is now his career.

I remember going up to see Doug every year over the Washington's Birthday weekend. I think it was the first part of an adult-to-adult relationship. He would show me around, line up good restaurants, take me to a movie, and introduce me to his friends, whom I would take out for a meal.

I think that college is really the last significant gift you can give your kids. Education in general. One should be generous and gracious about it and grateful that they have come this far.

Talking things over is the mature way to solve problems between adults. That is different from arguing about problems, fighting, or trying to get the best of your parents. The most satisfactory way to talk is to present your feelings on the problem. Try to come from this point of view: "I am just going to tell them (calmly, quietly, without heat) how I feel about the situation. Maybe then they can tell me how they feel, how it looks from their point of view. We will understand one another better. Maybe we can begin to compromise or change or ease up on it."

If you don't ordinarily talk to your parents in this kind of way, you will need some help and rehearsal before you try it. Talk it over with a friend or two, particularly the kind of person who knows how to communicate in this way. After talking it over with someone, it can be helpful to take pen in hand and write about it. Try to state clearly what the problem is that you are trying to alleviate. If you have a lot of sore issues with your parents, pick the one that is uppermost in your mind and concentrate on it. If you can make some headway on it, you can tackle the other issues later. Write how you feel. For example, in the case of the student who is being harassed about his grades, start your sentence with "I feel hurt, angry, pressured...." Write about what your ideal resolution would be. Also, write what you might reasonably expect from the discussion with your parents and where you could give a little ground to reach a compromise.

---

[3]A good book is Nancy Friday's *My Mother, My Self* (1977).

Remember, the point is you are initiating an adult-to-adult discussion. You are not going to win the battle or war. Ideally, there won't be a battle or war. They will listen to you, and you will listen to them. And one thing is for sure, no matter what the upshot, you will feel better for having said how you really feel in a rational way and for having taken the initiative in a mature way.

You might ask your parents to read this chapter as a common background for discussion.

Another mother, who is also a college professor, tells us the following:

Parents do feel a deep responsibility toward their children. That does not simply end when they become college students. Often, if you don't do well, are confused or unhappy, parents wonder where they went wrong: "What could we have done when our child was growing up to help prevent this trauma?" If parenting has been a major job, then the outcomes of their children's lives reflect on the parents' job competency.

It is also true that students both seek and take my advice, as my children do not. The respect I am accorded in my role as professor is not offered to me in my role as parent. Students seem willing, even eager, to accept professorial authority at the very same time that they resent parental authority. Are they just looking for new authority? Thus, frequently, my students receive more perceptive advice from me than my children do, and we can often have more intimate exchanges than are possible between me and my children.

Another mother says the following:

This is how we have always felt about children. Parents do not own their children. Children are very special gifts—to be loved, enjoyed, nourished, educated, guided to a recognition of moral values and to a sense of responsibility and accountability. Then follows the difficult part—a time to trust, to let go, and to hope they've done a good job. Deep inside, mothers and fathers never stop being mothers and fathers, never stop caring, but they can adjust. They can recognize maturity and can value sons and daughters as mature young men and women, capable of making good decisions. The guidelines are to listen and learn and try to understand. Anger and harsh words solve no problems. Love them, but love them with open arms, not clutching or restraining. Most important of all, believe in them—believe in their potential, their special destiny—and let them know that you believe in them and that you trust them. Try to remember how you felt when you were young—the excitement, the challenges, the frustrations, the importance of being with your own generation. Respect them, and they will be more apt to respect you.

One of the biggest hang-ups is a mother who insists on being best friends with her daughter: the tell-each-other-everything burden. We've been watching this domineering, demanding situation for many years until it finally erupted into revolt and flight. So sad and so unnecessary.

One mother wisely observes, "I think this is inevitable: I am much more concentrated on my children than they are on me. In the same way, my mother is more concentrated on me than I am on her."

Finally, this mother states the following:

No one should be surprised that parents are trouble. Conflict between parents and children starts as early as the age of 2 and continues right up to the day one or the other dies. It's just the nature of the relationship. How intense it is, how it is handled, how it is resolved is the big variable.

Any person who has a child invests so much emotion, so much love, so much longing, so much time into that relationship that it's impossible to step back and be totally objective about that child. The hardest part of being a parent is to let go, to say to a child, "You are your own person."

The step away from home to college is just another progression away from being parent-dependent. It's hard for both sides of the equation. Parents know a child leaving for college is making another major break on the way to being an adult individual. They hope they can say, "You're on your own" and mean it, and if both sides learn this fact in the usual 4-year process of college, they can end up being adult friends.

That, I think, is the ideal parent-child adult relationship: You are comfortable being adults together. You respect each other's adult persona, you love each other, but you know you are individuals with individual needs and differences.

Parents and children share too much to be completely detached. Conflicts are lifelong, just as they are in any human relationship, but the wise parent and the wise child learn to be patient with each other.

To conclude, I interviewed a woman whose specialty is working with older adolescents and their parents:

Separating from parents is a learning process for both sides. I find that it usually takes about 2 years, roughly from your freshman to junior years, though this differs greatly for different families, depending on how good communication has been all along. Children should realize that, for their parents, especially for mothers, the process can be extremely anxiety producing because the parents have to find new organizing principles for their lives. For the woman, the mother role has taken up more than 20 years of her life. In many cases, she came into maturity in this role, never having experienced her own adulthood before becoming a mother. Who is she, if she isn't your mother? Often she has had no adult models for taking an adult-to-adult role with her child because her own mother never made the transition and still treats her like a child.

The marriage, too, may need to be restructured. For 20 years the couple's relationship has revolved around parenting. They have both changed during those years. They need to renew their relationship as part of the process of separation from their child. These difficulties have nothing to do with you personally, but you need to be aware of them.

If there have not been good models for a friendship relationship with their children, they may fear that without the old parent-child relationship, there may be no relationship at all. Here, sons and daughters can help by initiating new kinds of joint activities with their parents. They can also help by not pressuring their parents to change all at once: You must bring up Mom and Dad.

This lengthy and sometimes difficult process is part of your growing into adult ways of dealing with other people. Adulthood isn't reached just by the act of going away to college. Becoming an adult involves going past egocentrism. You have to learn to step outside yourself. You have to engage your brain, instead of your emotions. If you join in a power struggle with your parents, you are stepping right back into the child role and forcing them back into the parent role. You need to study the situation your parents are in: what changes they are going through, what their fears are.

Accept your parents' right to believe as they do, however different it is from what you believe. In the same way, you have a right to what you believe. You may just disagree; it isn't a matter of right or wrong. Accepting disagreement, it is still possible to work out compromises in the area of rules.

Your parents grew up in a different time. I find that, where curfew rules are concerned, parents still feel they have to protect daughters from sexual encounters. They may even realize that society's rules with regard to sex have changed and still feel that their older values are the right ones. Perhaps they still have younger children at home and are afraid that, if they change the rules for you, they would have to change them for all the children, and they just aren't ready to do that.

I advise students to do some research. If there are older siblings, how did they handle conflict situations as they were breaking away? Seek out other adults you know who have older children, and ask them how they handled things like rule changes. You may discover that your parents are, indeed, coming from left field. Or you may find that, in their concerns, they are very much like other adults. Either way, you are acquiring a broader context: getting some distance from your particular parent-child conflict. Seeing a counselor just for the purpose of sorting out these issues is also advisable. Become solution oriented rather than just emotionally reactive.

If relations with parents have been generally good, and you wish to deal with a conflict, make an appointment with the parents when you will have ample time to discuss the issue. (Sometimes it is easier to do with just one parent, choosing the one who is more reasonable toward you. One-on-one discussions give you a better chance than a two-to-one situation.) By doing this, you are showing your parent that you are willing to take the initiative to deal with the problem. You don't need a yes or no right away. Just think about the problem together.

If your parents are very emotional and have difficulty communicating, I advise you to write a letter. Begin by affirming your love and by telling your parents that they have a right to their position. Then state your own position. Again, ask for an appointment.

If you are arguing about something like curfew rules, ask your parents to tell you when in the future they would relax the rule. How old would you have to be?

If you make this kind of effort, it is rare that you would make no headway with your parents. If that turns out to be the case, you have to make your own choices: Are you willing to put up with the situation? For how long do you want to put up with it? Is it desirable to make a break and accept the consequences? Now you are thinking like an adult. You can live without your parents' consent. It's nice to have it, but you can live without it.

Remember that, in negotiating the situation in these ways, you are learning the vital skills of adult relationships. In the process, you are becoming a mature adult.

All of this very good advice on communicating with your parents still leaves us with the unfortunately frequent case of a parent who is incapable of loving or honest communication. There are parents who never have and never will love you, not because there is anything wrong with you, but simply because there is something wrong with them. I was well into my 30s before I was one day struck with the realization that I had done my best to love my mother, but she had not been capable of loving me or, indeed, anybody. For a few moments, I had a truly sad feeling about it. When it passed, I felt a good deal lighter. Never again would I feel guilty because I didn't do enough for her. The truth was that I had done plenty, and she had never reciprocated except to demand more.

If you find yourself in such a situation, you may simply have to do what I did after my sophomore year in college: I transferred from a private college to a state university and began to support myself completely. Yes, it slowed me down a bit. I graduated one semester late. It really didn't matter. Yes, I ran up debts. I had a serious illness and a great deal of dental work. By the time I finished my degree, I owed quite a lot of money, but it was not a great burden to pay it back.

With such a parent, there does come a time to break away and support yourself. Perhaps you can go back after some time has passed and approach him or her from a new position of strength. I continued to see my mother until her death, but she no longer had any power over me.

The Painful Avenues of Upward Mobility

College will make a dominant-culture middle-class person out of you. It will help you to understand what you are up against in college if you realize that undergoing the college upward mobility assimilation trip is only in small part an intellectual matter. In Chapter 15, we discuss the following ideas:

- A model of the upwardly mobile.
- Group unity and your morale.
- Socialization versus education.
- Minority pride and majority power.
- Becoming bicultural.

Our American society tells us that we live in an "open class system," that is, one in which you need not stay in the socioeconomic class into which you were born. This system has various "avenues of upward mobility" through which the children of the poor and blue-collar classes may ascend into the ethereal realms of the middle and upper classes.

Avenues of upward mobility: It sounds so nice, so smooth and wide open—a comfortable, uncrowded highway on which the earnest and deserving may glide upward. Of course, nobody pretends that the way is without effort. Hard, competent work is required. Even a measure of competition is expected. But the person who can really perform certainly has nothing to fear on these wide, sunlit avenues. In our society, the most important avenue is the educational system. You who have made it to college have already, by definition, begun your ascent. You are the ones I want to speak to particularly in this chapter—you who belong to minority groups and you who are "upwardly mobiles" from the blue-collar or poverty classes, blessed ones in the lexicon of the capitalist system.

I need to speak to you because nobody in authority will admit to you that there has been a subtle misnaming here. The broad avenues should, more wisely, have been named the "painful ways of struggle" because, in fact—even for the most successful—these ways bring with them alienation, betrayal, and broken relationships. They involve a painful friction as you pick your way among the terribly innocent snobbery of those who just don't know that everybody wasn't born with a middle-class, White spoon in their mouths and past professors who imply that the vernacular you speak is aesthetically, if not morally, reprehensible. Finally, you must face the lack of unity with your fellow sufferers along the way, for this is a society that fears and, in fact, violently opposes the unity of the oppressed.[1] Society intends that you should, each of you, go this painful path all by yourself. It asks nothing less than that you betray your fellows—both those you have left behind in your old neighborhoods and those who are your companions on the avenue.

For most Americans, upward mobility involves a double change: a change from one economic class to another and a change from a racial or ethnic culture into the dominant culture of middle-class America. (Dominant not in the sense of numbers, for most Americans are not comfortably middle class, but dominant in the sense of power. It is middle- and upper-class power that controls all the media and all the major institutions of society, including the educational institution you are now in.) Strong racial and ethnic cultures only exist below the middle class. The process of acquiring a middle-class income necessarily involves a process of learning to appear as a White American: to speak without cultural accents or slang; to dress in generic, noncontroversial clothes; to have proper haircuts; in general, to fit a mold. Of course, these are subtle processes. Middle-class Blacks, for example, know perfectly well they are not White, but they also know that they must often appear to be culturally White. There is a painful ambivalence here. They have one foot in and one foot out—never a very comfortable position.[2]

A Model of the Upwardly Mobile

On the whole, *class is a more powerful factor than race and ethnicity.*[3] That is, minority students from middle-class backgrounds will have a somewhat easier time than nonminority Whites from poor or working-class backgrounds. This may be hard to grasp because class differences generally receive less attention than racial differences.

First, you need to identify which of the major groups you belong to. Perhaps a simple model will help you to locate yourself in this process. Like any model, this is an oversimplification, but let's get it straight before we go on to the complications. The "normals" in college are the students from the White majority whose parents are middle class or higher. For these folks, schooling has been a relatively simple

---

[1]For a history of America very different from what you were taught in high school, see Frances Fox Piven and Richard A. Cloward's (1979) *Poor People's Movements.*

[2]I would like to recommend Lisa Delpit's *Other People's Children: Cultural Conflict in the Classroom* (1995) as a great resource on this phenomenon.

[3]In this section, I am treating only minorities that are underrepresented in the middle class and on college campuses.

business because the school culture has closely matched the culture they grew up in. Their parents' values, attitudes, and beliefs are similar to those of the teachers, professors, and administrators who run these institutions. They, quite literally, speak the same language as their teachers. The other groups represent different combinations of fate: the various types of upwardly mobiles. The following paragraphs describe examples from these groups.

	From middle class or above	*From below middle class*
From racial/ethnic minority	PAUL	MARIA
From White/Anglo group	COLLEGE "NORMALS"	JOE

Maria is the opposite of the normals. Her name still has an ethnic ring to it because her parents were still wedded to another language—another cultural way. Maria's parents are blue collar and borderline poor. Her father is a semiskilled worker. Her family is cohesive, perhaps giving her enough of an emotional advantage to become upwardly mobile. Maria is also a member of a minority group, whether Black or Chicano or Puerto Rican or Native American or Asian American. Perhaps Maria was one of the lucky few whose ability was recognized, even in a ghetto school. Perhaps she was tracked early into a "gifted" section, though there are other ways she might have come this far. Maria has the hardest way to go because she must readjust *both to a new class position and to a new ethnic culture.*

Paul, on the other hand, is a Black student whose father is a well-paid civil servant and whose mother went to college. Very likely, Paul went to a racially mixed school in which Whites were the majority. His background gave him the great advantage of being able to speak his teachers' language. He was always groomed and dressed according to the dominant culture's modes. Yet the world never quite let him forget his color. There was always a measure of alienation.

Joe is the son of a coal miner. He descends from early Scottish and Irish settlers who were farmers in the West Virginia mountains before that region was taken over by coal mining. He looks just like the Whites, but his accent isn't quite right, and his clothes never seem to sit on him with the casual assurance achieved by his peers. He isn't sure whether becoming a white-collar worker is an honorable thing to do. Back home, the "pencil-pushing jackasses in the front office" weren't exactly admired, even if they were feared.[4]

Of course, the real variety of backgrounds and routes upward is much greater than this simplification. Some Marias have families who are very proud of their achievements; others have families who think they should get married and settle down and stop hanging around with a fast crowd at college "doing nothing." Some Marias attend predominantly minority schools in which they are tracked into a

---

[4]In a book I would recommend to you, Richard Sennett and Jonathan Cobb's (1971) *The Hidden Injuries of Class*, the authors interview a young man from an Italian American working-class background who is attending college and is assailed by doubts about his aspiration to a middle-class, white-collar job.

high section. Some make it all the way through a master's degree despite that, being Marias, they were early tracked into the "slow" section because they didn't do well on an English language test. Some had to go the hard road, taking a bus across town to a school in which they were the one and only minority student.

Paul may have grown up in a Black but middle-class neighborhood and attended a Black middle-class school. Or, again, Paul may have been the only Black or one of a handful of Blacks. The handful may have stuck together, or they may have stayed apart in mutual shame—afraid to call attention to their minority status. Paul may be a very light-skinned person whose parents disapproved if he went out with a girl of darker skin. On the other hand, his parents may have been militant civil rights fighters who went to jail in the 1960s and settled into unhappy political passivity in the 1970s. Joe, too, may have come by many different routes. He may have gotten his high school diploma in night school while contributing to the support of his family.

Culture Clash

I am an Indian. From India. When I came here at the age of 7, to Orange County (that beacon of "White culture," that city upon its shining white hill), I must admit that I suffered some culture shock. Friction, if you will. My clothes were different, my accent was different—hell, my skin was different. And if you think that it's easy for a little Indian boy who was surrounded by like-colored people with like-colored hair his whole little adorable life to come and try to make friends with other little adorable children who thought he was just dirty and didn't shower and probably stank of poop, which was why his skin was that color because, ewww, that's gross . . . if you think that, then you're wrong. But I doubt very many of you thought that. Immigrant children. I'm sure some of you reading this right now are first-generation immigrants. At the very least, most of you will know the awkward and devastating process of a change of city even within this country. There is isolation; there is fear and loneliness and self-doubt and hesitancy. There is inevitable sadness, and, hopefully, there is the return to a stable life. Moving from one city to another is hard enough—moving from one country to another is as close to Herculean a task can be for young boys (and girls, no doubt). I, the timid but wanting-to-be-accepted-oh-so-badly boy that I was, carefully studied the other kids—their manners, their interests, and most unfortunately, their insults. Obviously, these little boys and girls could not be wrong—this was America! Kids in India must never shower properly . . . Indians must never really clean themselves . . . what dirty filthy people . . . not like the White boys and girls who look so pristine and darling, like rosy cherubs. They were in the right when they called me names, when they laughed at me and pushed me down, down, down the social ladder past Fat Kid, and Slow Boy, and Glasses, and Mole, and Freckles until all I could do was look up. So I did what any confused young Indian boy with a penchant for assuming the guilt of crimes that were not his own would have done—I showered for hours on end. I went through bars of soap every week, just trying to scrub the God-awful filth off. Why won't it come off? What's wrong with me? Don't cry, you stupid boy—the White kids never cry. What am I doing wrong? Why won't it come off? Well, after weeks of trying, I eventually gave up and decided (after an emotional confrontation with a swollen-eyed, tearful mother and a chuckling, everything-will-be-all-right father) to embrace my "deviant self." Those kids are jerks; what do they know? Me and Glasses and Mole would get together during recess and make fun of Freckles, because honest to God, Freckles was a freak. Eventually, we all would learn, with the swelling rush that is boyhood discovery, about the wondrous adventure that was tag. And how if you tag Fat Kid you could basically sit down and still never be "it" again. And that it was okay if we didn't fit the mold because at the end of the day we were getting ice cream just like them.

—*Rohan Shamapant*

Group Unity and Your Morale

It is important for you to locate yourself on this complex map. Each background and each route upward has its advantages and its pains. Unfortunately, these differences may keep the group of upwardly mobiles in college apart because each background brings with it different reactions and different ways of handling the college situation. Some students may feel such a painful alienation from the dominant group that they want to retreat into a tight in-group of fellow sufferers. Others, feeling more confident, resent the attempt to draw them into a group that would feel limiting and isolating.

Perhaps I can illuminate the nature of the problem by contrasting the current situation with what went on in colleges during the 1960s. In that period of nationwide civil rights struggle, students from ethnic and racial minorities forcefully prevailed on colleges to give admission and financial aid to minorities and poor students. As a result, the usual small group of middle-class Blacks and Hispanics was swelled by the newcomers—the inner city kids. These students brought with them a passionate radicalism. They were enraged when they found themselves in institutions where the cost of the chandeliers could have fed a poor family for 5 years. They were aggravated beyond bearing by the middle-class pretensions in academic garb that surrounded them. They were also afraid—terrified—of failing in this strange environment that represented their only chance to get out of poverty. All these things made them outspoken. They took on their professors and their fellow students and started educating them about the bitter realities from which they came. In those days, sociology classes almost taught themselves. It was especially effective because students always learn more from each other than from teachers.

There was a lot of hostility in the air, but for the first time, it was out in the open and the minorities were on the attack.

In this atmosphere, it was relatively easy to forge a meaningful unity between those from middle-class backgrounds and those from the lower reaches of the class system. There was a common battle to be waged. Even many of the Whites joined in—some out of innate decency, some because, as Jerry Rubin, a highly publicized "hippie activist," put it, "It was more fun to be in the revolution than out of it."

The 1960s students volunteered for every kind of social work, from tutoring inner city children to visiting and helping people in prisons and mental hospitals. There was a powerful commitment to return to the ghetto and lead one's own people up and out.

However, this stimulating situation lasted only a short time. Soon the presidents of the colleges realized that the "financial aid people" were the most radical. College administrators soon set certain sociologists to work to see what kinds of students should not be admitted because they were potential troublemakers. The sociologist's studies confirmed the college presidents' suspicions. Professors wanted out of this situation, too. They didn't appreciate the "insolence" of the inner city kids, and they preferred to use financial aid money to lure high school students with the highest GPAs to their schools, rather than bringing in a "disrespectful," confrontational crowd.

Very quickly the financial aid funds from state and federal governments dried up, and colleges forgot about their commitments to minorities and the poor. Soon the inner city students were a tiny minority again, and the Black and Hispanic students from middle-class backgrounds were finding it easier to wear a white mask and to succumb and assimilate to the institution. Media were busy telling them that they were now part of the 1970s generation—more conservative, more competitive and serious, and just plain good-old-American selfish. The 1980s and 1990s continued in this vein—lean and mean.

The pain of America's minorities and blue-collar poor was neatly excluded once again from the orderly halls of knowledge. Each Maria and Paul and Joe was alone again on the painful paths of struggle.

Most campuses still have groups representing minority students. All has not been lost. The best defense you can erect against feelings of isolation or unworthiness is to band together with others from your background to fight for the rights of your group. We have seen many academically successful minority students are those who understand the system of racism but who also feel they can fight the system. As the gay and lesbian movements have so dramatically taught us, those who have feelings of unity and pride in their own background have an easier time than those who just try to lay low hoping their minority status will go unnoticed. If you are fortunate, a group or organization of people with your background already exists on your campus. If it doesn't, it may prove rewarding to start one. A good way to do this is to undertake an independent study or class project that consists of interviewing all, or a sample of, the pertinent minority students on your campus about how they feel and what they want and need. This will give you contacts and good ideas about how to start and orient your group. Another good thing is to volunteer to do tutoring or social work in a nearby minority community.

Socialization Versus Education

It will help you to understand what you are up against in college if you realize that undergoing the college upward mobility assimilation trip is only in small part an intellectual matter. Gaining intellectual skills appears to be the main game going on. But, actually, the most important part of your "training" comes in extracurricular ways—in contacts with the majority of White middle-class students; in your informal contacts with faculty; in your dormitory living arrangements; in social affairs of the college; in learning to act, speak, and dress in new ways—learning to consume in a different style. In short, college will make a dominant-culture middle-class person out of you, quite apart from what it has to teach you by way of intellectual skills and specialized knowledge.

The intensity of the effect of this extracurricular training differs greatly between institutions and may well determine your choice of an institution. Community colleges and state colleges in big cities often enroll large percentages of working class and minority students. Here you will suffer the least social isolation but will also acquire less socialization toward the White middle class. Large universities are next in line. Here you will find some fellow sufferers slugging along the difficult paths of upward mobility, but the institution will make greater demands by way of changing you into a dominant culture personality. Small liberal arts colleges provide the greatest "retraining." Here you necessarily live very intimately with majority students and faculty—all of whom are, almost by definition, middle class. This is the setting in which you will find the greatest personal and emotional difficulty and the greatest pressures to conform.

I will always remember a Black student I taught at Pitzer College. He was outstandingly bright and able and also a dedicated radical. In my class, he continually raised racial issues, to my delight—but much to the embarrassment of the other Black students in the class, who were all trying to keep a low profile. He provided an education to everyone in the class, including me. On the day before his graduation, he told me that, if he had to do it all over again, he would not choose a small college like Pitzer. "I just paid too high a price in social isolation," he said. In his case, he had been isolated not only by his color but also by his radical politics.

As college teaches you to speak differently, dress differently, and aspire to different goals, *you may find that it is hard for you to go home again.* Your old friends may begin to resent your upward mobility, which, after all, leaves them behind. Even members of your family may resent your new "airs." One of the most painful parts of upward mobility is the feeling that you have deserted, or even betrayed, your old friends and family.

Some parents bitterly resent that the college student child will begin to feel "better" than them. Most want their children to succeed, but it is difficult to deal with the cultural estrangement that interferes with the old, easy relationships. How does one take one's father or mother as a positive role model, while striving so hard to supersede them in one's own life? The strains are often just unavoidable. You may well feel yourself caught between an old environment that rejects you and a new environment in which you are not yet at ease. Such emotional pressures can make the intellectual part of your job much harder. You are fighting a battle on at least two fronts, while most of your classmates only have to apply themselves to their studies without a worry about their social standing.

Another source of strain for children of the poverty and blue-collar classes is simply lack of money. You haven't got money to spend on fancy clothes, DVDs, trips, designer drugs, and other accoutrements of middle-class lifestyles. It is often even hard to afford to buy all the very expensive books on the professors' class lists.

For Christmas, you go back to the ghetto or barrio or reservation to struggle with relations there, while your richer classmates are off to Utah to ski or to the Bahamas for a family holiday. Such differences also enter into your intellectual work. I well remember a very capable Latina student who felt less experienced and knowledgeable than her upper-middle-class peers. When she signed up for a Latin American history class, she hoped that, at least in this subject, she would have some natural advantages. What she discovered was that half the students in the class had visited or lived in Latin America while their fathers served in the diplomatic corps or headed up branches of American corporations. Even here, she had less to go on from her own background.

On the strictly academic side, one of your chief hurdles may be that, if you attended a high school in a poor neighborhood, you probably didn't get nearly as good an education as those who went to suburban or private schools. You may have to make up these deficiencies during your first years without getting any college credit for your efforts. If your school or ethnic studies center has a tutoring service, it would serve you well to use it. In this difficult situation, you will have to forgive yourself some temporary failures.

As those of you for whom English is a second language already know, language will be the most difficult stumbling block for upwardly mobile students. Subjects like math and science offer the least trouble in this area. In the humanities and social sciences, however, language is absolutely pivotal. The student to whom "good, academic English" comes easily will have an enormous advantage. Unfortunately, professors usually see it as their mission to inculcate academic English in their students. They may penalize you for having a different dialect and for using colloquial but academically improper usages. It may actually be that your own dialect is more colorful and interesting than academic English—for example, the Black dialect in the United States is far more poetic than standard English— but this will not cut any ice with your professors. The best of them realize that "a language is just a dialect with an army and a navy," but they may still feel it is their duty to instill in you the language others will expect from you in your graduate school or middle-class jobs.

Minority Pride, Majority Power

Although celebrations of cultural diversity are definitely on the increase, I still feel compelled to ask, why is it so difficult for minorities to have pride in their backgrounds? It has always seemed to me that many minorities have endured heroically and survived magnificently. If I may use the example of Blacks, with whom I am most familiar, they have survived the most terrible system of slavery in human history. The slave owners tried to eradicate African culture, but Blacks brought much of that culture with them through the struggle. Out of their great pain, they made great music and great poetry. They reinvigorated Christianity with the bright magic of their gospel singing. They created joy and celebration in the midst of absolutely brutal oppression. Urban mural art and break dancing and rap are recent examples of this creativity in the face of overwhelming odds. Yet, still it seems a constant battle to keep pride alive in the face of so much poverty—and failure is made inevitable by poverty. I believe that the basic problem that must be confronted is the worship of power and wealth in America. If power is, indeed, the primary virtue, then the powerless can never justify themselves. There is, however, a radically different way to look at power and wealth. As Hippolyte Taine, the 19th-century French critic, put it, "A man can achieve comfort by means of the efforts of his own labor—he can achieve wealth only by exploiting the labor of others." In fact, behind every great aggregation of power and wealth lies the destruction of human beings. Behind the Rockefeller fortune are the ruined competitors, the betrayed associates, the cheated consumers; behind the Astor fortune, the lives of poor immigrants who lived in the terrible slums of Manhattan from which that family made its fortune; behind the Ford money, the labor organizers beaten up by company goons; and behind the Du Ponts, the bodies of young men slaughtered in World War I with the weapons that made that family rich. Behind how many Southern fortunes are the lives of slaves working at backbreaking labor with barely enough recompense to survive? The truth is not all of us began the race from the same starting line. The race has always been fixed.

When we look at it this way, we can easily see that the slaves were better human beings than their masters. We could even see that the poor are more decent by far than the rich. We might recover the lost insight of Christianity that the lowly are blessed, that it is harder for a camel to go through the eye of a needle than for a rich man to get into heaven. Surely one Gandhi shines brighter than a dozen Genghis Khans. If we could see it this way, we might more easily believe in the oppressed groups from which we come.

Power is, in the final analysis, a matter of who has the biggest guns and the greater ruthlessness in using them. Of course, once power is established, the powerful are able to prescribe standards of physical beauty, language, table manners, and personality styles. Through their hold on schooling and mass media, it becomes easy for them to make the powerless also feel worthless. I do not mean to suggest that powerless people should accept their fate. Powerlessness is a great misfortune. All I am saying is that it should not also be seen as a disgrace.

The past 500 years have been a period of European domination throughout the entire world. But, due in part to their terrible internecine world wars, the European nations are now weakened to the point where the third world is successfully fighting back. You are a historical character in this age of the waning of European and American hegemony. In this age of the globalization of social reality, these historical forces will play themselves out in your life. To survive, you have to see your historical position and fashion your life accordingly. To flourish, you need to break frame and burst the paradigm, to access the unforeseen, creatively expect the unexpected, and intentionally create the never before imagined.

Becoming Bicultural

From a global perspective, college isn't doing you a great favor by acquainting you with middle-class, White language and cultural styles. The style is only worth learning because you will need it in your professional life. *You are becoming bicultural.* Imagine, for a moment, that you were suddenly sent to France to attend a university there. If you don't speak French, you would expect to have a difficult time. What you would actually find, though, is that your job would be considerably easier than what you are facing now. While you are learning French, everyone would realize you had to start from behind. When teaching you their social habits, the French students would not consider themselves socially superior to you. They would just be different. You would survive much more easily than in the middle-class college setting we have been talking about. Crossing countries is, in fact, much easier than crossing class lines or even crossing the street into a middle-class neighborhood. To some extent, you should look on your college experience here in a similar light. You are becoming bicultural, keeping your old culture and learning the new, not because the new one is better but because you need it to get along in this different country. Becoming bicultural doesn't take an outstanding mind; normal people will become bicultural if they are exposed to a culture different from their own. If you have made it to college, you may be completely confident in your ability to become bicultural. The only blockages are emotional.

The analogy about becoming bicultural is useful, although it leaves a major issue up in the air: Different cultures breed different types of personalities; that is, they affect what we commonly think of as people's psychological characteristics. Although nearly every psychological type can be found in any culture, still, different cultures favor the development of some psychological traits and discourage the development of others. In becoming bicultural, therefore, you are faced with some tough decisions about your values and your whole personality. Upward mobility, you see, is much more than raising your class position; it creates a new "self." Ideally, being highly conscious of what is at stake will help you to decide these issues in ways that do not damage your integrity. The following paragraphs detail some of the highly valued characteristics in middle-class America.

The model upper-middle-class personality is, first of all, highly competitive. There is little sense of solidarity with others. Although such people can be polite and friendly with their fellow students or coworkers, they generally maintain a highly individualized and isolated sense of identity. This competitiveness may take the form of backstabbing and politicking against people toward whom one is outwardly friendly. Ego's own success is the main thing that matters to these people. These traits are so highly developed at all leadership levels that the coherence of the entire social fabric is continually threatened and at risk.

When nobody is looking out for the common good, the entire community suffers. Out of such selfish motives, corporate leaders decide on technologies that are unworkable but allow a few people to get rich or make successful careers, while everybody else suffers. This same motivation leads your professors to neglect teaching for research because the latter is more beneficial to their careers. Indeed, the entire phenomenon of career revolves around such individualistic (and selfish) motives. The only reason our society continues to function at all is because most Americans are far more cooperative and selfless than their leaders.

In contrast to our upper-middle-class leaders and our strong mythology of individualism, blue-collar workers and members of ethnic minorities usually have more sense of solidarity and kinship with their fellows. Often, family ties are more highly valued in these groups; that is to say, they are actually lived rather than merely espoused and glorified. Ultimately, you have to decide how far to let yourself be pulled in the direction of selfishness. Selfishness certainly isn't the only motive for achievement. We have only to look at the lives of people like Cesar Chavez and Rosa Parks, Martin Luther King and Maya Angelou, Malcolm X and Alice Walker, and Nelson Mandela and Amy Tan to see that great deeds have sprung from loyalty and selflessness. You do have a choice here. If you need inspiration, read about the lives of some of these leaders. The following books are well worth reading: *The Autobiography of Malcolm X* (1977), Martin Luther King's *Stride Toward Freedom* (1958), Levy's *Cesar Chavez* (1966), and Fischer's *The Essential Gandhi* (1963).

A related personality trait is the acceptance of authority. Certainly, this is the best way to get ahead on the job. Those groups that suffer at the bottom of the economic ladder usually have some built-in resistance to authority. This is a fine trait because it keeps you from becoming a tool in the hands of others. The price may be rougher sailing, but you will be sailing under your own steam and direction.

The upper-middle-class personality stresses self-control. Values like strict punctuality; attention to detail; and the capacity for hard, consistent, self-directed work are essential. You may have to strengthen yourself in these areas. You may find that you have to sacrifice an easier going, more spontaneous personality style to achieve this. Only you can decide how far to push in this direction. Unhappily, the middle-class style creates a great many people who are highly successful but have long since forgotten how to have a good time. It is possible to lose too much in the process of becoming successful. I well remember a Chicana student I had who was in the process of deciding to go to law school and to aim for the grades that would get her in. She told me sadly one day that she was losing the capacity to "just veg around sometimes." She was becoming a tenser person.

Looking on the more positive side, the upper-middle-class personality is usually highly self-confident, reaching out easily—through reading and travel—to widen its scope and understanding of the world. There is usually a sense of being able to control circumstances. Self-confidence and a feeling of effectiveness in the world have been found to be highly correlated with upward mobility. If you have gotten as far as college, you have good reason to be proud of the achievement and reason to believe yourself effective in controlling the circumstances around you.

I have suggested to you a few ways in which assimilating the new culture may affect your personality. You will be able to see more for yourself. It will help you to keep in mind that traits like those I have just discussed are not just "individual" but can often be seen as cultural or class related. The more clearly you see this, the better you will be able to pick and choose what you want for yourself.

California Proposition 209: The Death of Affirmative Action?

California's Proposition 209, the antiaffirmative action measure, was passed in 1996, and the Supreme Court declined to review the measure. As a minority woman (I'm Black), how do I get ahead—or even in the game—with two strikes against me? Will my only opportunities for secondary education be limited to expensive private universities or all-minority colleges? What will the future hold for my children? Why is society taking away the little hope that I have?

Proposition 209 bars, in the state of California, all preferences in any government enterprise, including education and government contracts. California was the first state to enact this type of measure, and Ward Connerly, the most outspoken proponent, is actively endorsing similar measures in other states. What is interesting about Ward Connerly is that he is full of contradictions: a Black man advocating the end of affirmative action in the name of fairness. Similarly, affirmative action is itself a study in contradictions: Initially seeking to create opportunities for those who had suffered discrimination, it has, in fact, created unintentional discrimination against other groups.

So if affirmative action is taken away, where does that leave Paul and Maria, the two examples discussed in the beginning of this chapter? While it may be true that affirmative action did cause unintentional discrimination against certain groups, nevertheless, when I honestly look around me, I can see that life's opportunities are not equal for minorities. So we have a dilemma: How do we create racial equality without causing the very thing we are seeking to rectify—discrimination?

To know what needs to be done next, it is necessary to understand the larger problem of discrimination and how affirmative action was intended to address this problem. Further, it is equally important to understand the shortcomings of affirmative action before advocating another strategy because I believe it is only by understanding why affirmative action did not resolve racial inequality that we can devise a genuine solution.

Before affirmative action, minorities were barred from most professional and educational opportunities. Our communities usually had a lower standard of living, poor public education, and a higher crime rate. It was accepted and expected as the natural order of life. After affirmative action, minorities slowly came to be seen in every profession and to have visible access to educational institutions. Today, it does not raise much of an eyebrow for one to see a successful minority. It is now more widely accepted as, quite simply, the order of things. In this sense, affirmative action has been a great success! Affirmative action has broken the surface tension of professional and educational opportunity. Most important, it has provided a radical change in our self-image and in our estimation of our potential.

However, what are the concealed realities of affirmative action that are not often discussed? How did affirmative action fall short of its intended result?

Although affirmative action created educational and professional opportunities for a few select minorities, the vast majority of our community has not benefited. In fact, the deep structural conditions of poverty, poor opportunity, substandard education, and high crime rates remain unchanged and unchallenged by affirmative action. In essence, the program would offer educational and professional opportunities to the best and the brightest in the communities, while offering little redress for everyone else. A more cynical view might point out that affirmative action allowed the mainstream White culture to redirect the push for racial equality into a direction that failed to offer substantive changes (i.e., changes that could potentially destabilize the ruling identity, ethos, feeling, and tone of mainstream White culture). And minorities, for their part, have taken a hiatus from the march toward full-blown, authentic racial equality by treating affirmative action as a panacea.

Even those who were the direct beneficiaries of affirmative action were assumed by its very precepts to be substandard as a result of substandard education and social opportunities. But this begs the question, when would they be up to par? For society at large, affirmative action was a much cheaper solution than giving minority communities the educational resources necessary so that we might be capable to compete on a fair playing field. Also, minority students still live with the stigma of being beneficiaries of affirmative action. Therefore, even if we were up to par, we could not escape the lingering suspicion of being specially favored products of affirmative action.

This brings me back to Prop. 209, Ward Connerly, and the purpose of creating a fair playing field called *merit*. It is Connerly's belief, as well as the belief of the majority of people voting in California (which is another issue), that every individual should receive a fair chance for upward mobility without consideration of race or gender. What Connerly and the majority of people voting are not considering is that access to merit is something minorities have always striven to gain. Affirmative action helped prove that given the intentionally created opportunity to be there in the first place, we do, in fact, merit education, success, and upward mobility. What is disappointing is that Connerly, a product of affirmative action, does not relate to that struggle anymore. Hence, with the disappearance of affirmative action and the continued absence of substantive structural changes in the educational system, minorities raised in impoverished areas are at a distinct disadvantage.

What is to be done? Rather, let me ask, what are you and I to do? It is incumbent on us to go back into our communities and create systems for our people to receive a better chance early on, before being thrust into adulthood with nowhere to go but down. Simply, we need to be affirmative action ourselves: to be proactive and prevent our younger sisters and brothers from becoming enslaved educationally and economically.

I am not advocating that we as a group band together and exclude others because isn't that the very phenomenon of discrimination we are trying to change? What I advocate is that we, this generation, band together with the majority to show and teach them our true situation about where we come from and simultaneously continue to improve academically. I believe that the majority of people who voted for Prop. 209 have not really seen or really related to the true destitution of our environments and, therefore, are controlled by fabricated ideas about "minorities taking advantage of special favors." I am encouraging you to take the responsibility and use your frustration, anger, and sadness proactively to improve the larger situation we face, our future, our status. Affirmative action brought us half circle, providing a chance to a select few of us to exist in middle- and upper-class society. Therefore, we have two options: to lose what we have gained by being reactive, upset, and hostile or, better yet, to progress, drawing full circle our hopes and dreams of the plight of our people. In terms of the preciousness of our education, never forget your forefathers and mothers who fought to fund the education of Black preschool-aged children, or the "Little Rock Nine" students who first walked on to a high school campus needing to be protected by federal troops, or the 1954 Supreme Court decision in *Brown vs. Board of Education*, which was the very first battle in the domain of education for the right to be seen as more than three fourths of a person. Thus, you and I must go forward and continue to break new ground, to be affirmative and to be in action.

Will your only opportunities for post-secondary education be limited to expensive private universities or all-minority colleges? First of all, considering private universities and all-minority colleges is a good thing. You should consider what they have to offer you. You would learn more about yourself and the struggle out of which you come. You would gain momentum and inspiration to propel yourself to a higher level. But the reality is that mainstream society and the professional world seldom recognize a degree from those institutions as valid compared to the "normal" educational and professional way of doing business. Why? Well, what does mainstream society know about all-minority colleges except that they are all-minority colleges? The curriculum and degree requirements are not known and seem foreign to mainstream society. For minority colleges to be recognized as valid as, for example, USC or UCLA, the public needs to be educated. We have to actively endorse and advocate minority universities and colleges to receive the credit we need for social acceptance, acknowledgment, and upward mobility. Remember, you have to be a proponent in your cause, just like Ward Connerly is a proponent against affirmative action.

What Will the Future Hold for Our Children?

As a minority student, what I want to say to you is, simply, do not abandon your community and your culture but go back and inspire and give. As the former First Lady Hillary Clinton said, "It takes a village to raise a child," and for us to be able to be judged strictly on merit we must actively participate in the educational needs of our future generations. We know that public schools in our sectors do not and cannot prepare students for successful college careers.

Therefore, it is our opportunity as college students to actually share our experiences and to help prepare these children. What is most amazing about doing this is that you will gain and grow more than you have in your short-lived college career, which you were doing only for yourself. We can most profoundly advance our individual educations by sharing them, by giving them away to others, by being educational affirmative action.

Why Is Society Taking Away the Little Hope That We Have?

Society at large believes that we are not earning our own way or paying our dues. The truth is that this is false. We know we are paying our dues because we know where we come from and we know that it has not gotten any better. However, our situation is not going to get any better unless we continue to feel and to act hopeful. I do not want to sound Pollyannaish or trite, but you have to choose to look at the positives and realize that these struggles are a part of our life and our very existence.

Most important and most immediate, throughout your struggles in your college career you will often think about quitting and just giving up. I know because I have quit and given up—but I went back. I went back to receive and to work hard for what our forerunners set out to provide for us and to complete what I started. And, after receiving my bachelor of arts degree, I found that people now not only hear me, but they want me to speak and to write.

—Rhonda Wofford

Graduation

What They Forgot to Mention

In Chapter 16, besides the well-known pomp and circumstance, we look at the roller coaster of negative as well as positive emotions and the more traumatic feelings we vividly begin to have as graduation looms. These are, as it were, the birth pains we are undergoing as we are pushed out of the canal of our familiar 16 odd years of being in the amniotic educational, school womb. We address, in particular the following:

- Facing the big day.
- Looking realistically at life after graduation.

Life Without Homework

Life without homework: That is how I personally describe graduating from college. I am approximately 6 weeks away from receiving my degree, and I have no idea what I am going to do once I graduate. People ask me, and I have to come up with some clever answers, such as "Get a job;" "Oh yeah, I should start thinking about that;" or "I'm graduating." I avoid the question as much as I can. But I can't hide from myself when I ask that question. I went into college thinking that, when I graduate, I will be "smart." I will have skills (useful ones), I will be able to get a good job and earn money (have to pay back those loans), and, most profoundly, I will know what I want. Well, it's 4 years later and I am right back where I started from, still asking myself the same question and still lacking a definite answer!

Going to and graduating from a major university, or any college for that matter, gives one a false sense of security—that after graduation and the countless (and I do mean countless) hours of studying, there will be something out there in the "real world" that is a perfect job. I would like to mention that I don't believe that money is the most important thing in the world; happiness, health, and love are the most important, and money will come later and without stress. But I also know that I owe about $14,000 in loans, and I do want to have money to pay for things. Money is a necessity in this world (we rarely work on the barter system—or the free system).

I want a job, and money is a nice bonus, but right now I find myself struggling. I have met with the people in the career center, and they were supposed to help me, but I found out that I have few "real-world" skills, no particular field of interest, and a lot of work to do—fast! I am so confused. I feel that I am a relatively intelligent person who can problem solve or figure things out rather quickly (with the exception of rocket science and some aspects of physics) and who is very personable (or as my friend says, *je ne sais quoi*), and yet there is nothing for me. My 4 years of schooling have done very little for me, and I don't know why.

I have opened my mind in amazing ways over the past 4 years. The way I handle people is very different, and I have broadened my horizons incredibly. Schooling is wonderful yet very misleading (and quite profitable, if your name is UC Regents). Is it something to fill the time or postpone the career decision-making process for at least 4 or 5 years? I have decided to take education for what it really is and not for what the "supposed" outcome will be. Education is to open the mind to new ideas, cultures, people, and myriad things, not to provide one with a good job. The good job is just the byproduct of expanding the wrinkly gray matter. Wish me luck in finding that byproduct!

—Lauren A. Bragg

Life After School

An interesting phenomenon occurs at the moment you graduate from college. Unless you have specific plans to attend graduate school or a definite job, you begin to realize that for the first time in your life you have nowhere to go. After preschool, there was kindergarten, then elementary school, then junior high and high school. After high school, college was the logical next step. So you skipped along, following the path of each successive school environment, until one day you looked forward and saw that there was no set path any longer. You are handed a diploma (or mailed one 3 months later) and then kicked out the door. "So long, good luck!" Now it's time to find that great job with a promising future or attend the medical school of your choice or. . . . Well, what exactly should you do? Is more school the answer? It worked for the last 16 years. Should you find a job? Move back home with your parents? At this point, such questions begin to overshadow your accomplishment of finishing college. Life becomes altogether more confusing. The speed of your college years of fun slows down, and you are left with decisions and the all-too-familiar "What are your plans now?" or "What are you up to?" or "What career are you going to go into?" from family and friends. School was so much easier, it seems. Sure, there were decisions to make and studying was tedious, but at least you knew your goal was to graduate. There was no question about that. The hard part now is knowing what your goal is and how best to achieve it.

—Tatian Greenleaf

College Loans—A Fine for Becoming Educated?

The thought of graduating terrifies me. I'll parade in my gown in front of friends and family and file down a neat little line to receive my hard-earned piece of satin-covered cardboard with a little note inside reading, "The diploma's in the mail." And when the diploma comes, with it will be a friendly reminder: Don't forget that you only have 6 months to choose your career, a career that will last the rest of your life, a career that will make you a good citizen, a career that will help you repay your $80,000 college loan.

College loan? Oh yeah, that thing that covered just enough of my tuition to keep me scraping together money for books every year. That thing that caused so much tension between my parents and me that now we barely speak to each other. That thing that the institution has been holding over my head for 4 years. "Don't challenge our system," they said, "We're giving you money."

"Meet our standards. We're giving you money."

"Sacrifice your integrity. We're giving you money."

"Assimilate. We're giving you money."

When I chose my college, everyone told me that money wasn't important. They told me that I should choose a school that would interest me and challenge me and that the money would "work out." I was expected to choose carefully, even if I had to spend a year exploring to find just the right school.

Now, when I'm choosing a career, something that will likely be for the rest of my life, I only have a 6-month grace period before my decision is carved in stone. I'll either make it in some high-road profession, or I'll be trapped in loan-induced poverty because I couldn't choose the right career fast enough. A simple college loan soon becomes a fine we pay for being educated.

I guess it's no wonder that students are spending 5 or more years in college. Why not? By deferring graduation, you can defer your loans. But where does that leave us, the ambitious people, the people who are anxious to get into the working world but just want a little extra time to figure out the rest of our lives? We're stuck. Screwed by the system.

Well, maybe loan-induced hell is better than career hell. At least I'll have my integrity. And my peace of mind. I've got 6 months to think about it, though.

—Kristin Rydberg

Facing the Big Day

Graduation Day—What We Didn't Learn in School

Graduation from college is a day of celebration and rewards; it's the day that people dream about and strive to reach during their college career. For the first time, each person dressed in cap and gown is the same, regardless of race, age, and even major; for one day in our lives, we are united as college graduates. This day is a time to be selfish and to celebrate ourselves and our achievements. For me, graduation day was about feeling a sense of successful completion. I felt proud knowing that my friends and family were present to celebrate with me, to share in my special day and what I had accomplished. It was a day of growing up, waking up on that morning as a child and walking away finally an adult.

The day of graduation had been built up in my mind for the past 18 years, and I was full of emotion. The entire day was planned around the ceremony, the parties and celebrations, the time spent with family and friends. There was little time left to think. Upon my arrival at school for the ceremony that day, everywhere I looked were graduates in caps and gowns. I had feelings of anticipation and anxiousness as I checked in and had the roster searched for my name, thinking, "Please, please let it be there!" I also remember the relief felt when, after frantically searching the graduation program, I found my name, printed in black and white and spelled correctly! We lined up with excitement as we prepared our walk, socializing with our friends, our fellow graduates, waiting as our families filled the stands. As I walked out among the procession of graduates, I felt proud; I felt excited for myself. This day was all mine.

When the day eventually came to an end, I felt exhausted both physically and emotionally. After years of anticipation, this day was over, and my future would begin tomorrow. So here I am, waking up the morning after the biggest day of my life, in my family home where I grew up, sleeping in my familiar bed, thinking to myself, "What is wrong with this picture?" I look around me, wondering, "What am I doing here? How do I move on now that this whole process is complete? Today, I am supposed to be an adult, so why am I here, lying in this bed, in my parents' home?" For the first day that I can remember, I thought, "What am I supposed to do today? I have nothing to do today. What am I supposed to do tomorrow, and the next day, and the rest of my life?"

For the past 18 years, my life has revolved around an educational system of one kind or another. In fact, from the age of 5, school has been all I have known. I can remember my first day of school and how scary the whole experience seemed. I remember looking at all the unfamiliar faces that seemed just as confused as mine. I remember learning the importance of listening to rules, such as being quiet or standing in line, dictated by this person everyone called my "teacher." I think the most important lesson of all was when I realized that if I didn't conform to the rules, I would be subject to some pretty scary consequences, such as sitting in the corner for a time out or being denied recess time, punishments which, as a small child, seemed like the end of the world. From this early age, we were taught how to conform to societal structures. We learned how to fit into the mold that had been made to ensure that, if nothing else, each person would leave this system as a person acceptable to society and society's rules.

I have spent countless hours, in the past 18 years, memorizing dates from my history book, understanding formulas from my math book, reading my English books, and writing papers that would be acceptable to my teachers. I have spent most of my past agonizing about my grade point average, worrying about upcoming tests, and cramming for final exams. I now think about this time and am left wondering how much of this information, fed to me throughout the years, I have actually retained. Is it any wonder that after all these years my life revolves around thoughts of school? There is no doubt: This system has taken over my mind. So what happens then on that fateful day of graduation? Each graduate must find a way to retrain his or her mind, to begin to steer away from the ideologies of school and academics, and to move forward to find what is ahead. This is not an easy thing to do! Leaving school behind is not as easy as it seems.

Looking back, I wonder how well school has prepared me for my future. After all, I thought the point of this whole process was to provide me with stability and survival for my future. All these years of attending classes, listening to lectures, studying textbooks—did it actually teach me about my future, about goals, about a satisfying career? I never gave much thought to what I was actually supposed to do once this whole school process came to an end. To tell you the truth, I am not sure I even realized it ever would end. It sure seemed endless. I knew that a career was to follow, but what career, and exactly how was I supposed to obtain this career? This space, this gap, between school's end and life's beginning was something I neglected to prepare myself for.

I have memories of leaving high school and feeling the high of knowing that I was now an adult and would no longer be forced to succumb to parental control. I could be myself, think for myself, and make my own decisions. Even then, when I felt as though I was finally free, finally an adult, it turned out this was really only a temporary state of illusion. This feeling of excitement came to a halt when, at the end of the summer following my high school graduation, I found myself expected by society, and my parents, to walk back into a classroom that would ask much more of me: a college classroom. For me, college was the next step in my already prepared itinerary for life and certainly not an option. At some point in our lives, we all had to choose a college path. For some, college meant a big move far away to an unfamiliar place, and for others it simply meant attending a local college. I do not think many of us even knew why we were going to college. I had very few, if any, friends or acquaintances who actually had a planned course of study in mind. Personally, I had confidence in knowing that I would just enroll in the "general education" courses first, and a major would come to me later—later when the school told me it was time to choose one.

Later. Later has always been my favorite word. Everything would all be figured out later. I do not think I anticipated that later would actually ever come. After 2.5 years in a community college, where I took just about every general education course they offered, I figured out *later* was approaching. It was time to move on to a 4-year university, and, even more important, it was time to decide my major course of study. What? Decide on a major? I have no idea what I want to do with my life. How can I make such a huge decision? I am not ready. How can I decide where to continue my studies if I don't know what it is I want to study? And you expect me to decide it all now? Here I am, 21 years old and unable to decide what I want to be doing for the rest of my life. How can that be? It seems everyone has his or her life together by now, or so I thought. What I did not realize is that it was *okay to be confused*. I was not alone.

On my first day at a 4-year university, I entered a classroom full of strangers and a professor I had never heard of, and, even more scary, a full schedule of courses in a major that I knew absolutely nothing about. I looked forward to graduation when this would all be over. I looked forward to the excitement I would feel when my days of being tested and doing homework would finally be over. The oral presentations, term papers, stress over my grade point average—it would all one day stop. I could go on knowing this happiness would come in just 2 short years. I could not wait. I saw a light at the end of this tunnel. I would graduate, and finally I would be able to do what I want to do, not what my parents expected me to do, not what my professors assigned me to do. I would finally be freed from the hassles of school.

I decided I would take a full load each semester and even take interterm and summer courses to ensure that I would graduate on time. Of course, I thought by the time I hit graduation I would have the next step in life figured out: what career to choose, how to obtain this career, and how to accomplish my goals. Everything would finally be in order for me. I had confidence in my future because I would have a college degree that was supposed to guide me to a successful career. I was certain to have it all together, just as soon as I finished college.

The 2 years in my new university went quickly. These 2 years seemed different from the years past, though. Now that I had a major that I could focus on and classes that actually interested me, my perspective on school started to change. I actually enjoyed going to class: I listened to lectures, rarely dozing off, and I actually respected my professors and found what they had to say insightful and enlightening. I read what they said to read; I did the homework they assigned and used term papers as an opportunity to expand my knowledge on a topic that interested me. This whole education process actually became educational! It changed from being a chore to being my life. As I became more disciplined and my outlook changed, I began to see school in a whole new light. School became my friend and not my enemy. Now this was scary. What was happening to me? Like school? How can that be? I began to experience college as a unique and valuable opportunity; it was precious, rather than an extension of high school. School had always been my enemy, and maybe this is what had held me back for so long. Imagine what an experience this process could have been if only I had taken such pride in my education earlier. Maybe, however, if I hadn't made such a shift, I wouldn't be able to look back on my past few years with such admiration and excitement. I was so happy to have finally found a way to make sense of all of my years of education. I was excited to celebrate in my realization of what could have been learned from school all along. How exciting— after all this time, I had finally figured it out.

I now wish it hadn't taken me so many years to value this educational system. It is now time to graduate and I am disappointed, yet excited at the same time. I wish I could have spent more time enjoying my time and making my education useful. If I had actually spent the time wisely, maybe I wouldn't be so scared of what is ahead. A million thoughts are drifting in my head. Very few of these thoughts are without worry or fright. It is time to exit one door, a huge door, the only door I have ever known, and it is time to find a new door to enter. I am caught in a hallway between two lives. The in-between. Why was I never told about this? Why has graduation been portrayed only as the happiest day in a person's life? Why did everyone leave out the part where I feel scared and confused? I feel trapped, as if I am floating in a constant search for answers. I just keep hoping to wake up one day and a lightbulb will turn on in my head telling me where to go from here, telling me what it is that will make me happy and successful. Realistically, I know that I am the only one who can turn on this light.

So my question remains, "How does one choose the next door to enter?" I wonder this daily. How can such a huge accomplishment have turned itself into such a great fear? Hardly a day goes by when, in conversation with another, the topic of my graduation doesn't surface. Once surfaced, the ever-dreaded question is sure to arise: "What's next now that you have finished college?" I cringe when I hear that question, not because I am unsure of what is next or feel I am inadequate to survive in this competitive world. I cringe because it is as if the answer that I am supposed to provide should be a great big impressive goal. This goal is something I have been pursuing for years and years and now can't wait to attain. If only it were that easy!

I fear the in-between time—the time in which I am caught between doors, between the label "college graduate" and "person with a career." What if in the process of attaining future goals I forget what I am after and find myself settling for something that won't be satisfying? My biggest fear is the fear of unhappiness, the fear of "settling." There seems to be a hole in my itinerary that has yet to be filled that I must fill on my own. Please do not allow me to settle. Please do not ever let me wake up forgetting my goals and dreams in search of money or survival. Please allow me the strength to overcome obstacles and speed bumps without losing track of what is ahead.

In a conversation with my best friend, also a recent graduate, we spoke of the times in the past when we relished the idea of being a graduate. We would complain together about the work that we had due and fantasize about the day when we would no longer have this weight on our shoulders.

It was always such a great feeling during Christmas break and summer vacation when we would be free from our troubles, free from deadlines; in fact, our only worry was the countdown until school started again. I look back at these times and these conversations and I now wonder what I was actually thinking. Yes, I knew one day it would all end, but I never imagined that I would look back with admiration for what I had experienced and gained from my time and hard work. My friend and I now speak of our futures and the feeling of entrapment as we make decisions that will alter our lives. My friend just recently described to me how she feels. She said, "I feel as though a ton of bricks is being dropped on my shoulders. I have no clue how to go about figuring out what I want and what is available for me. I am getting sick to my stomach just thinking about it."

Some have chosen graduate school for their next step. For others, it is time to seek employment, to find a career that will provide experience and income for the future. For myself, I feel so excited inside, like a child right before recess. I am impatient because I am ready to move on with my life. I am ready to be a responsible, active adult. I am ready to begin my future, and I feel as though I am driving down a road and it is time to make a turn, but I don't know what corner I should choose. I am impatient because I want to be around that corner now. I cannot wait to begin this new stage in life, if only I could just get there a little faster. If only I could get there without this dead time in the interim.

For everyone, a large choice lies ahead, the first choice in the history of our lives that can solely be made by ourselves. After years of begging for the freedom to be able to make our own choices, here we are, ready to make some of the biggest decisions of our lives. We are overwhelmed with a feeling of excitement, a feeling of fear. We are left pondering the questions, "Am I ready? Can I do this?"

—Erin Cora

I Am Terrified

Two months until graduation? I am so excited. Am I? Of course I am. Don't be ridiculous. Who am I trying to kid? I am terrified. I've never been more scared or questioning of myself in my life. Am I smart? Am I capable? Can I survive out of school? Did I get the right degree? What am I going to do with my life? On one hand, I am feeling really excited and alive. I am starting a new journey, a new section of my life. Time to be what I want to be and do what I want to do. The main problem is that I have no earthly clue as to what I want to do. I finally know who I am, or at least I am beginning to understand who I am. I know what kinds of things interest me, but how do I turn that into a career? And what, if anything, does it have to do with my degree (liberal studies)? And did I choose the right course of study in the first place? Today, I caught myself looking at the class schedule for next semester! I was picking out which classes I'd want to take. OK, face it: I don't want to leave school. I love being a student. I love homework (Did I just write that?). I love writing papers. College is fun, easy, safe, and good. The job market is scary, tenuous, hard, and boring. I am terrified. And what happens to my brain if it's not being used to think, study, research, and learn? Won't my brain atrophy and turn to mush? But on the other hand, I am getting kind of sick of this school stuff. It does get kind of tedious and causes a tremendous amount of stress. On the other hand, what if the only job I can get hired for is a receptionist or a grocery checker? What good is a brain full of facts in a mindless, boring job? I want to do something intellectually stimulating, but what if "those types of employers" don't want me? And what if I'm not smart enough? I guess it all boils down to the fact that now that I have a college education, I still feel like I know nothing about what to do about this incredible thing called life. There should be a course in graduating and joining the "real world." Maybe if I'd had that I'd feel more prepared. Probably not!

—Lisa Kraft

Life After Graduation

Graduation Is Instant Unemployment

Except for the students who have already been accepted into graduate programs, most students become unemployed the moment their diploma is handed to them on stage. There is a mentality that college is a place where young people blossom from a student to a working adult. However, most of the positions that are offered require skills that college does not give us. For example, most jobs require previous experience in the field, which a lot of college students do not have. College is a place where you learn life skills, figure out who you are, and grow as an individual. This does not necessarily include job training and does not actively prepare you for the "real world" of employment. However, there are ways to better prepare yourself for this reality. One way is to plan early. Start figuring out where you want to be after graduation and find out the necessary steps to get there. You know exactly how that works; you've been doing this since you were young! Just like applying for college, getting a job requires research, understanding what the minimum requirements are for each position, and going above and beyond such requirements. Most college students start this process during their last year in college. This may be reasonable for jobs that have limited requirements, but for those who want a more technical position, it may be necessary to start understanding the requirements as early as your first year in college. Planning may include making connections. Most have heard the saying, "It's not what you know, but who you know." This especially rings true during tough economic times when jobs are only available through word of mouth. If you know individuals in many different fields, you can increase your chances of landing a job immediately after graduation. Looking into internships during your first couple of years in college may be a wise choice, both for your career and for your studies.

Though planning ahead has its advantages, a lot of recent graduates find themselves in a desolate position when their plans have fallen short. Thus, my next advice is to not plan. Not that you should not think about your future, but understand that plans can change. By realizing that there are many other options available that your plans may not include, you allow yourself to be open to more opportunities that your peers may have overlooked.

Congratulations graduate, and best of luck in the real world!

—Aggie Wong

Graduation and Life After

At a point in my life when I should be filled with joy and a sense of accomplishment, I feel an overwhelming sense of dread. I cannot shake the feeling that my life will soon be over, although I know that it's just beginning.

Maybe I feel this way because, in our society, too many people have ho-hum, dead-end jobs that they have to drag themselves to every day. That is not something that I want. I worry that I won't make enough money to pay off all my loans and get a car, an apartment, and other staples for an independent life. I don't want to have to depend on my parents for years after graduation. Don't I owe it to them to get on with my life after they educated me? Or do I? Maybe I should think about what makes me the happiest and go with that, but I don't even know what that is yet.

Staying in college would make me the happiest at this point in my life. I don't want to graduate so soon. Why can't I take 5 or 6 years like everyone else? Twenty-one years old is still fairly young to be a college graduate these days. Many of my older classmates may have the extra maturity or experience that I lack. These things keep me awake nights.

Then I ponder all of life's big questions, the kind that spring up when you begin to have doubts or question your decisions. Where will I be in 10 years? Am I prepared for rejection? Will I be able to handle it? What about my friends? Will life be too hectic to include them? Are we all going our separate ways? Am I going to have to sacrifice my family for a career? Will I do something that I really enjoy? How do I figure out what that is, and when does the big book of answers fall out of the sky—the one with all the answers to life's important questions, the one that prepares you for entrance into the big bad "real world"?

Sometimes I get a dose of reality; the child inside me is shoved aside, and I hear a voice calmly and rationally saying, "Maryanne, don't be ridiculous. You are young, bright, talented, and outgoing. All of this negative thought isn't going to do you any good. You will find a job that makes you happy. If you don't, then you simply look for another one. Your life is not set in stone with your first job. Take it for what it is—experience, a growing time, a time to place roots—and then feel free to move on. Don't let this change scare you; let it excite you. You are done with school—no more papers, finals, or tests. You can enter our society as a beneficial, contributing member of it. You'll be independent from all that held you back before. This means that you have ceased to be a child! So forge ahead, and don't look back with any regrets."

Well, okay, but I still want my mommy.

—*Maryanne Wilson*

Surviving After Graduation

Postgraduation life feels a lot like your first time seeing a naked 90-year-old walking around in the shower room of a gym; your reaction to it depends on your perspective. Certain people might find the naked body as being distasteful, some might not think anything of it, and others might even look at it as a work of art. Whatever the case may be, everyone believes that their opinion on the naked body is the correct one. Similarly, many will claim that their perspective on life after graduation is the correct one. Putting your ear close to the mouth of society, you'll constantly hear people spewing out their outlook on the "real world." One person might tell you that surviving the "real world" means one thing, while another person might tell you something entirely different. Like missionaries, these people will preach their perspectives to you, tempting you to take on their same belief system. That is where college comes into the picture. College is a life lesson that prepares you for the many challenges that you're bound to face when dealing with your future jobs, career, and family. College is even helpful for future challenges one might face while sitting alone in a room. It prepares you by allowing you to develop your very own, personalized belief system about how life is and how it should be. Depending on what belief system you eventually internalize, your idea of success will be different from that of others.

On the surface, the purpose of college is rather straightforward. Simply put, you enroll in a wide range of classes until you decide which subject you want to specialize in. During this process of specialization, the primary purpose for school becomes quite clear. Personally, I've noticed that there is a rationale to everything I've done at school. I'm now aware that most events and tasks related to school actually have a purpose. For example, through group projects I've learned how to coordinate and cooperate with others. Through writing essays, I've learned how to coherently express myself in words. Even getting a poor grade on an assignment has taught me how to adjust and be versatile. Since assignments also have due dates, I've learned to become punctual and more aware of time. Research projects have allowed me to understand the most efficient ways to gather resources and do Internet searches. Through having multiple classes and assignments, I've learned the importance of prioritizing. Even the student teacher interactions have taught me how to work with an authority figure. These are just some of the ways in which college got me ready for life after graduation.

Unfortunately, the "real world" has stricter requirements. Learning the primary lessons that school teaches you isn't enough to allow you to survive the confusing mental rigors of postgraduation life. Life after graduation can be a very confusing place indeed. You're constantly bombarded with messages that advocate different ways you should act. You're told to keep your chin up without letting your guard down. Everyone is supposed to be optimistic, yet remain realistic. Society says that you need to improve yourself, but you're also perfect just the way you are. To survive, you need to be funny and have a good sense of humor, but you can't act like a clown. Confidence is a plus, but being cocky is looked down upon. You must always live in the moment but also plan for the future. Society tells you to not be selfish, but society also says to always think about yourself too. How is a person supposed to cope with these types of mixed messages? That's why college has secondary purposes as well. Beyond the more obvious benefits that one gains from attending college, there are also other advantages. College provides the perfect environment to calibrate the many sophisticated personal parameters one might have. As for myself, I have become much better prepared for the mental aspects of life after college. I have interacted with a great deal of like-minded classmates, where I've learned how to fine tune my communication skills. Furthermore, I have used college as a platform to experiment with different styles of clothing, which has enabled me to gauge my own preferences. By having formed romantic relationships with girls I've met at school, college has helped me determine even my intimate preferences. A well-defined set of preferences has subsequently facilitated my ability to make decisions in a work environment in addition to other environments. This is because knowing what you like, what you don't like, what you're good at, and what you're lacking in allows for better decision making. I have also come across many stressful situations during my college career, allowing me to determine the best ways to prevent stress from occurring in the first place. If an unavoidable stressful situation does indeed occur, I have conditioned myself in a way to better handle such an occurrence. Again, these are only a few of the many ways in which college has helped me form a stable set of beliefs about myself, life after graduation, and the world.

All this is to say that college makes you, more or less, ready for surviving life after graduation. Going to college gives you a leg up on the competition, partly because of the invaluable knowledge and skill set you gain from it. This can then be translated into an economic gain. Thus, by going to college, you are actually investing in yourself. Besides this, college also has secondary purposes. College allows you to form your own unique set of beliefs about life. Being able to do this in a college environment shouldn't be taken for granted since many form their beliefs about the world in a much harsher arena. After some time, you begin to understand that the education system, in general, is certainly the best method to become prepared for what's to come later in life. Abraham Lincoln once said that if he had 8 hours to chop down a tree, he would spend 6 of those hours sharpening his axe. In other words, there should always be a great emphasis on preparation. In the case of surviving postgraduation life, college is that preparation. Surviving life after college is also similar to learning how to ride a bike. You could read a plethora of books about it, but it's never like experiencing the real thing. You take time to prepare for it and fall many times in the learning process, but you eventually develop your own set of beliefs about how everything should work. Soon you realize that you were indeed more prepared for this new experience than you thought. Once you slowly get the hang of this new experience, it starts to become second nature. Even once it becomes second nature to you, you're bound to still fall once in a while. When you do fall, it is your perspective that dictates what you will do next. If your perspective and belief system is adequate enough, you will disregard the falls and concentrate on the fun. At that point, it's your turn to act like a missionary and preach your own beliefs to others.

—Soheil Shahri

A Graduating Mother

Graduation! I have earned a bachelor's degree. This still seems like a fantasy. I can hardly believe it has come true. How do I feel? Amazed, astounded, flabbergasted—mere words barely sufficient to describe my feelings. I came to college with high hopes and am happy to say they have been more than fulfilled. I achieved the biggest goal of my life, and it feels fabulous.

To reach this day, I had to wade through a lot of muck. I was a single mother on welfare just 11 short years ago, and I had no intention of going back to school. I honestly thought I was too dumb to do it. But my sister talked me into a class at the local community college, and the rest is, as they say, history.

The sense of accomplishment and the memories of so many wonderful learning experiences are pure gold to me, certainly worth every ounce of effort and every minute of the 6 years it took me to reach this goal. From a position of impotence, I have been empowered to do whatever I set my mind to. This is heady stuff!

Along the way, I discovered myself and the special talents I can bring to bear in this world. I know that I can go on to apply those talents successfully in my chosen field. If I could send a message out to those who feel hopeless about their situation, it would be "Have a goal, find out what you need to do, then work as hard as you can to get there." I know it sounds corny and trite, but I have found that you really can do anything you make up your mind to do, you just have to *do* it.

I'm proud to say that I am graduating with honors, and this pleases me because I know how much I sacrificed for those grades. But the grades are not the important thing. What is important is the growth, the experience, and the self-respect I have gained, which have given me a strong foundation for a better second half of my life than the first half.

Having a goal doesn't have to mean school. It is simply what you want enough to make sacrifices for and what you are willing to work hard for. Achieving a goal that requires diligence, hard work, risk taking, and endurance will bring you special rewards that you will carry with you for the rest of your life.

—*Darra Ross*

Considering Grad School? Consider This

Only two quarters to go and I would finally be done with college! But, wait. Through all the experiences gained and lessons learned, one small detail had escaped me: What was I going to do with the rest of my life?

I liked the outdoors and being physically active. What about being a forest ranger? What? I hadn't gone through college with honors to barely get by financially. Then I realized that since my first job in high school, I had always done something related to teaching. I thought, "I love teaching, and I would have good job security, a good living, and good vacation time!" I had gone this far with my education—it was only natural that I continue, to get my PhD and become a college professor. I had it all figured out. Then I started my first year of graduate school. Surprise! Within the first couple of quarters, I realized that the life of a professor at a research university was not at all about teaching. And the idea of having vacation time seemed so naive in retrospect. Between conferences, teaching courses, advising students, and doing fieldwork for projects, which would lead to writing papers in order to survive the "publish or perish" world of academia, when would one even have a chance to breathe, let alone vacation? The thought of never really leaving work or "clocking out"—after all, there is always something more you can work on, like a grant proposal or reading or writing another article—was beginning to haunt me. I wasn't alone in my exasperation. My colleagues were having similar epiphanies, wondering why they had signed away 6 years of their life. Slowly, our incoming class began to shrink from 15 to 11. But I stayed. Now, finishing my dissertation, I can't imagine having left graduate school. Though the realities remain, the initial shock wore off, and I realized that life is what you make of it. I really enjoy doing research—I had dabbled in it as an undergraduate as well—and I still love teaching. And these do not have to be in opposition. I am glad I stayed. Not everyone's experience will be the same, and that is okay. But think about the following things before you make a decision: Don't go to grad school just because you don't know what else to do. It's a whole world apart from the undergraduate experience. Think about how you could use a master's or a PhD in your field. Different disciplines have different types of programs—some more academic, which are aimed at producing researchers, and some professional. The potential applications of a PhD in sociology are very different from that of a PhD in business. The experience will differ according to the degree (master's or PhD) as well as the field (e.g., sociology versus education). Ask your professors what they do on a regular basis. Think about what you're interested in. Is there something that you enjoy thinking, reading, and writing about? Finally, take on a research project of your own and see how you like it. Many campuses offer undergraduate research opportunities or financial support. Ultimately, whether or not you decide to go to grad school, it will work out. In a department meeting, someone once said the average person changes careers seven times in a lifetime. Seven times! So, the next time you hear someone (or yourself) say, "I don't know what to do with the rest of my life," remind them that they'll have plenty more opportunities to make that decision.

—Georgiana Bostean

Relish Your Transition

If I could step outside of my body and reassure my mind and heart, this is what I would tell myself:

Anees,

Just when the caterpillar thought the world was over, it became a butterfly. You are about to enter a transition period where you may be living with your parents. You swore to yourself that this would never happen, but you may not have a choice. You may not land your dream job, or even a job, and you might struggle to pay off student loans. You may be just as broke after college as you were during. You might rely upon your friends and family to ensure you have a roof over your head. Your 2-year relationship might not last the drastic changes going on in your own life and your partner's life. You may feel as though you are making no difference in this bizarre world.

This is a friendly reminder to breathe and to relish these experiences. This state will not last forever, although it will feel like an eternity has passed before you reach the next benchmark. Enjoy being young and vibrant. Take pride in watching yourself grow and mature throughout this transition. Relish in your evolution, because at the end of this period you will be different. You will be stronger, you will be wiser, and you will be more experienced. You will probably be something you could have never predicted. You will face opposition. People may struggle to reconcile the current you, the butterfly, with the previous you, the caterpillar. Do not allow them to prevent you from accepting who you have become and from looking forward to your next evolution.

Lots of love,

The voice in your head that is rooting for you.

—Anees Hasnain

The Career

Friend or Foe?

Why are we trained to want a career rather than a job? In Chapter 17, we explore our relationship to our work. Where does my job end and my self begin? In our society, we are all encouraged to feel, "I am my job." We look into the obsessional and pathological approaches as well as the genuine and fulfilling possibilities. We explore the following:

- When work becomes an obsession.
- I share about how I lost my career somewhere in my garden.
- We consider the options available in our attitudes between being a careerist verses being a craftsman.
- We contemplate the value of going beyond ambition and what lies outside the official system.

From the moment a person starts treating his life as a career, worry is his constant companion.

—Maccoby (1976, p. 202)

O ne of the most important reasons for being in college is to choose for yourself a way of earning your living and to get whatever college can give you by way of preparation for your future job. If you are going to college, you will probably end up in a middle-class occupation. Nowadays, this is almost equally likely for women as for men. In other words, the world expects you to have something called a career. However, *career* is much more than simply a way of earning a living. *Career* is a total life pattern, a distinct way of being in the world. It requires certain character traits and priorities and values. It invades the most intimate spheres of life, from your family life to your digestion to your very dreams.

In this chapter, I would like to explain this life pattern and compare it with a different, older pattern that is generally dying out in our modern world but that is still available to those who wish to choose it: that of the artisan. Whether you choose to be a careerist or an artisan *doesn't depend on the particular field you enter.* You can be a physician-careerist or a physician-artisan, a teacher-careerist or a teacher- artisan. *The difference lies in the way you approach your work and integrate it into the rest of your life.*

The most powerful element in the career pattern is competitive ambition. Ambition is a trait so highly valued in our society that it is difficult to even grasp that we have a choice about it. Indeed, we must have a choice about it because, although we begin by choosing careers, careers end up dominating us.

Krishnamurti (1969) has posed the disturbing question "Can an ambitious person really love?" Heavens! We all expect to be ambitious yet successful in love. Can there really be a conflict here? There can and, usually, there is. Ambition is a very intense form of self-involvement that draws much of its power from the strong social approval it is given in our society. It is not the kind of self-involvement I recommend. It is not a self-love, which takes enlightened care of you; rather, it is like a consuming vanity that may lead you to harm yourself and others in all sorts of ways. It is no secret that ambitious people frequently make themselves physically ill through excessive work and constant worry. It is less clearly understood that a career is also a psychological pathology.

In the middle class, careers are one of the major reasons for the failure of marriages. So much time and energy are taken up by the career that there just isn't enough time left for spouses and children. This increases as one moves up the hierarchy. High executives, successful doctors and lawyers, and prominent scientists all work overtime. They travel a lot. Their most powerful emotions revolve around the job, and the job offers plenty of opportunities to form emotional ties that may override the ties of family.

Take, for example, this description, which a top television executive gives of his work life:

> My day starts between 4:30 and 5:00 in the morning, at home in Winnetka. I dictate in my library until about 7:30. Then I have breakfast.... Oftentimes I continue dictating in the car on the way to the office.... I will probably have as many as 150 letters dictated by 7:30 in the morning. I have five full-time secretaries, who do nothing but work for Ward Quaal.... I get home around 6:30, 7:00 at night. After dinner with the family, I spend a minimum of two and a half hours each night going over the mail and dictating. I dictate on Saturday and Sunday. When I do this on holidays, like Christmas, New Year's, and Thanksgiving, I have to sneak a little bit, so the family doesn't know what I'm doing....
>
> I've always felt throughout my lifetime that if you have any ability at all, go for first place. That's all I'm interested in.... I had only one goal in life and that was to be president. (Terkel, 1972, p. 51)[1]

---

[1]Throughout this chapter, I use excerpts from a marvelous book called *Working: People Talk About What They Do All Day and How They Feel About What They Do,* by Studs Terkel (© 1972, 1974 by Studs Terkel. Reprinted by permission of The New Press, www.thenewpress.com). I recommend this book to anyone who is thinking about their future occupation or anyone who is curious about the nature of work in our society. The book contains more than 100 short, revealing interviews with people in every line of work, from garbage collector to executive.

Corporations often demand that the employee's spouse fit their particular bill. They move their employees around whenever it suits them or train employees in various branches of the enterprise. This may mean that the children must change schools every few years or that the wife must sacrifice her job or her community ties. The executive who refuses a promotion because his family doesn't want to move will probably never be offered another one. The joke among IBM executives is that IBM stands for "I've Been Moved."

When Work Becomes an Obsession

One of the symptoms of careerism is that people who are deeply involved become incapable of enjoying other people's company unless they can talk constantly about their work. This talk is seldom about the substance of the work but is usually a kind of gossip about who is doing what where. The real purpose of this social game is to situate oneself relative to others in the enterprise or the profession. In the course of these conversations, people score points by being one-up on the latest news or by letting others know about their accomplishments. At a gathering of serious careerists, there is never much hilarity, just a constant buzz of conversation. Frequently, the men separate from the women to pursue the one topic. Recently, at such a gathering of college personnel, I noticed one of the college maids, sitting by herself in a corner. I went over and asked, "What do you think of the party?" She said, "This is sure a peculiar party—no music, no dancing. I think I'll go home." She was the only noncareerist there.

Corporations and other large institutions love careerism because *it guarantees an endless supply of people who will sacrifice everything for the job* and never endanger their chances by questioning those in authority. Maccoby (1976) found that among the survivors in high positions, most were almost slavishly devoted to the organization in which they worked.

The quote with which I began this chapter is from a book I recommend to you. Michael Maccoby's (1976) *The Gamesman* is a study of high-ranking executives. In it, Maccoby shows us how career comes to dominate every other aspect of life. Most damning, he found that the longer a man was in a high executive position, the more he hardened his heart. Such men become incapable of ordinary morality. There is no product they will not make if making it would help their career. There is no harm to the community from which they will shrink. Values of personal loyalty, love of family, and respect for the world of nature all go down the drain. What is left is an individual who is frequently very effective and brilliant at work but who has lost his or her way, in the sense that the only end this person serves is the end of self-glorification.

As old age approaches, such people frequently feel an aching emptiness. They have gotten everything they went after, yet peace of mind, genuine self-respect, and loving relationships with others elude them. At retirement, they are likely to suffer intense feelings of deprivation. Away from their luxurious boardrooms and lecture halls and constantly ringing telephones, they feel themselves to be nothing. Because of their very success and power, they have not learned humility. Now, as physical deterioration and death confront them, they are aghast. They cannot accept the inevitable.

Income is of vital importance in most careers, not for what it can buy but because it is society's shorthand for career success. Americans often accuse themselves of being too materialistic, and it is certainly true that we spend enormous amounts of energy acquiring material possessions. In reality, most of these possessions are coveted for the physical gratification they give, not for the prestige they impart. An expensive house and a Mercedes-Benz are primarily symbols of success. Traditionally, it has been men's success that has been symbolized, while women are used as a sort of Christmas tree on which the men can hang the various baubles signifying their rank.

Far from enjoying these goods directly, we are a culture that really despises the sensual pleasures material goods offer. We are heirs to the Victorian puritans. The executive who has a business meeting in an expensive restaurant is too busy making a deal to really taste the food. We love success, not good sex or beautiful objects or a wonderful scene of nature or a delicious meal. We aren't materialists at all. There is something otherworldly in our disregard of the concrete reality around us. A minister who serves the executives of the automobile industry in Detroit says, "These men are monks—monks who've traded in their prayer books for a production line." We are so lost in symbolism that, in the words of Alan Watts (1962), "We eat the menu and miss the meal." Businessmen, alas, seldom dance by the light of the moon.

But beware the academic conceit that believes that careerism only attacks industrialists. The academy is full of careerists and so is every other professional field, from science to the ministry. Maccoby (1976) says,

> Comparing my own experience in universities, I would say that although academics consider themselves more humane than businessmen, the engineers and managers we interviewed are no more competitive and a lot more cooperative with one another than most professors. If corporate managers engaged in the nitpicking and down-putting common in universities, little would be created and produced. (p. 209)[2]

All this may seem very far away from you and the problems you have at this point. But you have already been bitten by the career bug. School is the beginning of it. If school has made you anxious, this is but a pale forerunner of career competition. You will also have begun feeling the roller coaster effect of career. This is a phenomenon that was described in an old but excellent study of upper-middle-class people called *Crestwood Heights* (Seeley, Sim, & Loosley, 1967). In it, John Seeley shows how the course of a career resembles a roller coaster: Just as you get to the top of one situation, you plunge downhill and start from the bottom of a new situation. Thus, just about the time when high school became manageable and you felt at the top of the system as a senior, you were plunged down to being a freshman in a new, more demanding college environment. Just about the time you get

---

[2]In the academy, *professionalism* is often used as a synonym for *careerism*.

on top of this, it's "whoops" again, and you are in graduate school, where you are a greenhorn and the competition is tougher. From there you careen into your first job. If you fill that one well, you will be pushed higher up to a new position, which will offer new "challenges." This will just go on and on until, just after you reach your highest position, the roller coaster plunges into the abyss of retirement. You will never be secure. I realized this painfully while I was a young professor, laboring to turn my doctoral dissertation into a publishable book. One of my friends, who was a few years ahead of me, said to me comfortingly, "You know, it's not really your first book that counts; it's your second book."

You are on the first sharp curve of the roller coaster now. If you think it is going to let up somewhere ahead, you are kidding yourself. It will never let up until you get off it. Luckily, this isn't the kind of roller coaster that kills you if you jump off. The jump may be made at any time. It doesn't even necessarily involve abandoning your job, though it could lead to that. Primarily, it is an inward change.

I Lost My Career Somewhere in My Garden

I lost my *career* one day while weeding my garden. I had been a fierce perfectionist. Throughout my schooling, I had worked tremendously hard. It was not just personal ambition, though that was certainly involved. I also had the feeling that to become a scholar was a tremendously high calling, and I stood in great awe of the important men who were my professors. But my first full-time teaching job disillusioned me. Seeing these important people at their own level, I was aghast at the personal rivalries and vanities that seemed to dominate the academic landscape. In these departments, there were people who worked together but had not been on speaking terms for 10 years because of some past rivalry or insult. They admitted to doubts about the Vietnam War but managed to evade anyone who tried to get them to support controversial antiwar action on the campus. Worst of all, they didn't seem to be particularly fascinated by their own research and frequently cared not at all about their teaching. At the first campus, where I only taught for 1 year, I had only one intellectual conversation with a colleague: It was about the style of footnoting in the *American Journal of Sociology* versus the *American Sociological Review*. My second job, at UC-Irvine, was even more disillusioning. There, almost everybody was out for Number One. They sat around discussing their image as a department as if they were advertising executives.

It was about this time that I had a garden for the first time in my life. I had long wanted to garden, and this became my way of comforting myself and assuaging the sense of loneliness I felt around my new colleagues. The hours in the garden sometimes brought me profound peace of mind. A kind of inner silence would settle in on me among the weeds and bulbs and flowers, but the old feeling of having to be a success was still in me. I still had a sinking sensation when I came across a particularly good article I felt I "should have" written. I still felt that I should be anxious to move to a "better" institution. I still felt guilty because I had spoiled my chances at a really first-rate job by letting emotional problems interfere with my graduate work for several years.

So, this one lovely Saturday as I weeded my annual border, the familiar voice inside said to me, "If you spent as much time doing research as you spend in the garden, you would be famous by now." Then a strange new voice came back loud and clear. "Yes, and you wouldn't be in the garden now . . . you'd be off at a conference, reading a paper." At that moment, the heavy mantle of *career* slipped from my shoulders. I knew that I would much rather be in the garden.

I don't mean to imply that it fell away all at once. I also found a slower way of healing myself. Whenever I felt jealousy or disappointment with my career, I just let the discomfort be and let myself feel it, sympathetically, until it vanished. I refused to let these emotions drive me to work harder. As time went on, the feelings became dimmer until, finally, they disappeared altogether. What a freedom it was when I finally knew that I would never have those feelings again. How wonderful to feel nothing but pure pleasure at the success of a colleague. Jealousy is a terrible mistress.

Being a Careerist Versus Being a Craftsman

Of course, one alternative to a successful career is to become a sloppy worker, to avoid the work more and more until you turn into a career failure. This is the wrong way out. There is real pleasure and genuine self-respect in doing your work beautifully and well. Fortunately, we can reach back a few centuries in our society's history and come upon a quite different way of relating to work, a way that highly values a job well done, but from a different perspective.

Whereas the careerist worships power and gathers up as much of it as he or she can, the artisan delights in rendering good service. This quality was beautifully expressed by the craftsmen who built the medieval cathedrals of Europe. Their rich, detailed wood and stone carvings decorated even areas on ceilings and behind pillars, which no human worshipper would ever see. For the craftsman, it was enough that God would see it.

The joy of craft seems to come most easily to people who work directly with aesthetically pleasing materials. This includes crafts that many college students might consider beneath them, such as carpentry or stonemasonry. But there are also many offbeat, middle-class occupations that give aesthetic pleasure. Consider, for example, the words of a binder of rare books and a highly skilled piano tuner:

> You roll out this design and you fill it with egg white. Then you cover it with pure gold leaf. I enjoy restoration very much. . . . You must be very clever with a binding and give it the dignity it deserves. Because the pages are so full of stunning *fantastic* things that say This is life. So what do you do with a binding like that? I don't know. You just give it a strength. If it's leather or it's cloth or it's paper, you give it strength, an indication of what is inside. . . . Keeping a four-hundred-year-old book together keeps that spirit alive. It's an alluring kind of thing, lovely. Because you know that belongs to us, because a book is a life. (Terkel, 1972, p. 412)

There is such a thing as piano tuning, piano rebuilding and antique restoration. There's such a thing as scale designing and engineering, to produce the highest sound quality possible. I'm in all of this and I enjoy every second of it. . . . If I'm working on some good Steinways my day goes so fast I don't even know where it's gone. But if I'm working on an uninteresting instrument just the time to tune it drags miserably. There's something of a stimulus in good sound. . . . I hear great big fat augmented chords that you don't hear in music today. I came home one day and said, "I just heard a diminished chord today!" (Terkel, 1972, p. 419)

Artisans are people who love their work for its own sake. Their rewards are intrinsic rather than extrinsic; that is, the process of work is directly rewarding to them. They care very little for higher salaries or more prestigious positions. They may even refuse these if it would change the nature of their work. You can find the parallel in your schoolwork: The intrinsic reward comes to you when you just plain enjoy an assigned book or find yourself truly fascinated by a research project. The extrinsic reward is the grade. The two types of rewards compete for your attention. If you care too much about the grade, you may be too tense to ever feel intrinsic pleasure from your studies. If, on the other hand, you love doing a piece of work, it may not matter nearly as much to you how your professor ranks it. Intrinsic rewards are a sort of pay-as-you-go proposition: The fun is in the process. Focusing on extrinsic rewards means focusing only at that point in the very end when you collect your grade or, later, your money or promotion. This empties out the process and concentrates all the meaning at a point outside the process.

As an extreme example of someone who empties out the intrinsic joy of work, consider these feelings expressed by George Allen, a highly successful professional football coach:

Everything we do is based on winning. I don't care how hard you work or how well organized you are, if you don't win, what good is it? It's down the drain. . . . One of the greatest things is to be in a locker room after a win. And be with the players and coaches and realize what's been accomplished, what you've gone through. . . . When you lose it's a morgue. That's the way it should be, because you've failed. . . . Some people can lose and then go out and be the life of the party. I can't. The only time you relax is when you win. If you lose, you don't relax until you win. That's the way I am. It's a state of tension almost continuously. (Terkel, 1972, p. 508)

Anyone whose work brings them in contact with other human beings can render artisanal service simply by being kind, good-humored, and supportive—replacing the hierarchy's system of subordination and superiority with a simple humaneness. Consider the words of a teacher, an occupational therapist, and a poverty lawyer as they discuss what their human contacts give them by way of work satisfaction:

He is "headmaster" and administrator of the Southern School in Uptown. It's an alternative school. . . . I knew the kids were getting in trouble around here. I simply felt I could teach them and make their troubles less. Someone offered me a storefront church which was used only on Sundays. Someone gave us desks and a couple of tables. . . . We're involved in picking up basic skills that others have neglected to teach the kids. Some of them have feelings of rage, undefined, and they're acting it out in school—dangerously. We try to calm them down. . . . The person who's sixteen realizes he has a lot of catching up to do. . . . They're reaching across and trying to touch something they've never experienced before adulthood. In a specific situation of urban life—poverty. . . . My work is everything to me. (Terkel, 1972, p. 635)

I'm an occupational therapist. For several months I worked with hemiplegics, elderly people who've had a stroke. Half their body is paralyzed. First thing in the morning I'd get to the old men's ward and I'd teach them dressing. They didn't think they could do anything, but they could dress themselves. If people can take care of themselves, they have more self-esteem. . . . Being sick can be like going through early developmental stages all over again. It can have profound growth potential for people. It's like being a child again, to be sick. People who've been seriously ill may come out much stronger, happier. . . . Some kind of learning. (Terkel, 1972, p. 644)

He is a lawyer who quit his job with a corporation to become a poverty lawyer: My clients are Appalachians, Blacks, senior citizens, people in landlord-tenant cases. We're in juvenile court. We represent inmates of the state penitentiary. . . . Every day is different. There's no boredom 'cause there's so much going on. . . . Here you're aware of the suffering of your client. You know the type of landlord he has. You know the pressure he's under. It makes you all the more committed. . . . You get to know them intimately. We're very close. . . . They're my friends. (Terkel, 1972, p. 695)

Beyond Ambition: Outside the Official System

In Terkel's (1972) book, we find the greatest satisfaction expressed by people who have managed to find jobs outside the official system: the teacher not in the school system, the lawyer not in the corporation. This is hardly surprising because the existing bureaucratic hierarchies are frustrating and dehumanizing. Yet, even those who work within the system, in areas where their official position forces them to oppress others, can mitigate the impact for those around them. One of my former students is working now in an employment office. He has to disqualify people from compensation they need, and he fears what this work will do to him as a person. Yet, when he told me that the last man he had to disqualify ended up comforting him in his distress at having to break the news, assuring him it wasn't that bad, I knew that my friend was keeping his humanity and spreading a little of it around, even in his bitter position. Most of us are victims of the huge bureaucracies in which we have to work. In this common predicament, it is service for us simply to help each other, to shield each other from the impact of the system.

If you are able to resist the blandishments of career, you are a good deal freer to find work outside the system or to make your work within the system creative for yourself and others. I have always enjoyed teaching even though teaching is not much valued in academia. But I followed my heart and spent most of my energy on teaching. I loved designing new courses, inventing all sorts of ways to open my students up to new ideas. That I didn't care about career gave me a wonderful freedom to design my own sphere of work in my own way. My craft brought me rich rewards all the time in the form of students' responses.

Craft does not have to be competitive at all. It is just a relationship between you and your work. A real artisan takes genuine pleasure in the good work of other artisans. Being a good artisan can get you through your work life very nicely.

The role of the artisan is not entirely without its attendant dangers. The bane of the artisan is perfectionism. Careerists, too, may be perfectionists, thus exposing them to a dangerous double jeopardy. The artisan is not immune. Since we were children, adults around us have encouraged us to be perfectionists. The concept "perfect" is certainly a human construct. It never occurs in nature. It implies some sort of perfect cube: straight edges, absolute angles, and absolute control—the world of nature and of our human nature is, by contrast, a totally wiggly world, random in its movements and constantly offering up the unexpected. Do yourself a favor and let the human construct of perfection fade totally from your inner vocabulary. It is as imaginary as nuclear supremacy or the idea that sex is sinful— just a human invention, and a particularly troublesome one, at that.

The perfectionist is indulging in delusions of grandeur. Perfectionists imagine themselves to be gods, capable of absolute control not only of their own actions but also of the actions of all those others on whom the outcome of the perfectionist's work usually depends. There is a failure of humility here. Let us take our cue from those marvelous Asian painters who always left or created one imperfection in every work of art, just to remind themselves and their audience that nothing is perfect.

I have often been helped by remembering the words of a very successful executive who said to me, "I usually feel that if 50% of my decisions turn out to have been correct, then I am doing well." As a judge of your own work, you should be thorough and competent but never unreasonable. Be a humble artisan, and you will avoid the pitfalls of perfectionism.

"Okay," you say, "the artisan's route sounds good to me, but how do I explain this to my parents or my peers who are going to judge me by the money I make or how high I can climb in an official hierarchy?" We have been taught all our lives to be "successful" by the world's standards, so there is a fear that if we don't go for this prize we may be shamed by others or may regret our decision later.

People who are "success" minded will, indeed, have a hard time evaluating the artisan's role. There is an old saying that when a pickpocket meets a saint, all he sees are pockets. When Coach George Allen looks around him, all he sees is winning or losing. Do you want to go through life with the eyes of a pickpocket? Your career-minded friends and parents are suffering from the illusion that there is only one game in town: the rat race. They will even call it that at the same time that they urge you to enter it. They just haven't managed to see beyond the glamorized main event to all the wonderful variety that lies outside. As one who has seen beyond, you must try to educate them.

Doing without some of the extrinsic rewards is not as bad as it sounds. People who are on the extrinsic bandwagon are insatiable. They never get enough because the extrinsic reward is really a substitute for the intrinsic satisfactions of craft. Frequently, it is also a substitute for the love the careerist missed. That is why it is usually the successful careerist who later regrets. The artisan has collected his or her reward all along.

Don't Let a Job Define You

You are not unique. In the ways that really matter, you are just like everyone else.

This momentous realization hit me when I was in my mid-twenties, holding down a job that I wasn't particularly happy with and wondering why my life didn't seem more grand. In the back of my mind, I'd always assumed that I was destined for an impressive, influential career. I graduated in the top 5% of my high school class and received my bachelor's degree *summa cum laude* when I was only 20 years old. My professors, my family, and my friends all believed that I would go on to do great things. But after a few years in the workforce, I understood that I wasn't doing anything extraordinary or grand. In fact, my life was starting to resemble something I never thought that it would: the life of an ordinary person.

For members of my generation, an ordinary life is not good enough. From a very young age, we are told that we are special, that we can succeed at anything we put our minds to, that we can be anything we want to be. And so we simply *expect* to succeed—which, notably, means finding a job that not only pays well, but is intellectually stimulating and emotionally fulfilling. (In contrast, previous generations were taught that if they worked hard, with a bit of luck, their diligence might pay off). For most of us, this dream job fails to materialize, and we are sorely disappointed. Some become bitter, feeling that the world owes them something that it has failed to deliver. Some blame themselves, wondering, "Where did I go wrong?" Others learn to rethink their definitions, recognizing that a job can be just that: a job. It is not the totality of your existence; it does not tell the world "who you are." It just shows the world something you're good at.

I think it's these "others" who are happiest. They seem to realize that we are all complex, multidimensional beings who love many things; we do not necessarily need to get paid to do them. If you love basketball, play basketball—you do not need to be in the NBA to do what you love. If you are passionate about social justice, do something that contributes to it—it does not need to be your primary source of income. The best career advice I ever received was not "do what you love," but "find something you're good at, and do it." Of course, it would be nice if one's career and one's interests matched up perfectly—and a few of us may be lucky enough to see that happen. But the truth is that there aren't enough dream jobs for all the dreamers. And even those lucky few must give things up and make sacrifices for their careers.

> I see now that my job wasn't what was making me unhappy. I was unhappy because I thought my job was what defined me. But I am also a partner and a lover, a gardener and a baker, a friend and a daughter, a student, a mentor, and a citizen—in other words, an ordinary person trying to figure it all out. So today, when people ask me what I do for a living, I tell them: "Oh, it's nothing special—just an ordinary job." And then I tell them about the things that I really love.
>
> *—Elisabeth Wilder*

So you don't get to *the top*. The top isn't a terribly comfortable place. It is ceaselessly glamorized in our media. On the screen, it fairly seems to glitter. When you look at it close up, though, you see that the top is full of ferociously ambitious folks who are all afraid of each other. The tensions are sharper here, the rewards of success and failure more dramatic and gripping. The person at the top has to be on his or her guard every moment. When you think about it, only a powerful mythology could make people want to be celebrities—never really free to just move around and live. As one student of mine put it, "All your life you've been looking at these people on TV and thinking, 'Oh wow!'"

Ambition, so highly valued in our culture, usually arises out of a fierce dissatisfaction with oneself. The lonely man becomes the ambitious man. The cartoonist Jules Pfeiffer said that when he was a kid he was very small and often bullied by bigger kids, so he thought to himself, "Someday I'm going to get big enough to beat everybody up." When he finally realized that he would never be that big, he thought, "Someday I am going to be rich enough to fire everybody." Of course, not everybody who is famous is ambitious. The great operatic tenor Luciano Pavarotti was asked in an interview, "How does it feel to be a superstar?" He said, "My ordinary self doesn't know about it."

Ambition is something that grabs you when you have lost a part of yourself. Schools are brutal to little kids precisely because they mean to take away part of you to offer it back on condition. Sometimes parents begin the process even earlier by offering children only conditional love: "Mother loves you only when you are good." The child who has been trained in this way easily transfers the game to the teacher: "Teacher loves you when you are smart." Pretty soon, children cannot grant themselves approval; they have to get it from the outside, and then they are hooked. This is how society controls us. Once the hook is in, anybody can pull the string and we dance.

The cure for this is self-approval. Our culture is rather suspicious of self-love. The usual misinterpretation of Christianity pits self-love and love of others against each other, as if they were two mutually contradictory qualities. Quite the opposite is true. You always take basically the same attitude toward others as you take toward yourself. Merciless perfectionists are hard on themselves and equally hard on others, but the people who take good, sensible care of themselves are also capable of giving good, sensible care to other people. Love is love, whether directed inward or outward. If you can't direct any love inward, you won't really be able to direct genuine love outward. You may have hefty crushes and wrenching "love affairs," but none of these is love.

One final word: If you lose your ambitions—or if reading this chapter has just made you aware that you aren't really ambitious—don't broadcast this fact, particularly to your teachers or employers. They think ambition is good, and they would just be affronted. They would probably also dismiss you as not a "serious person."

It is amazing, but inner freedom doesn't show on the outside, except to people who have similar freedom. They recognize it because they are attuned to it. The ambitious ones are too busy projecting their own motives on everybody else to notice people who don't fit their projections. This is very convenient. It means that you can go incognito. If, in addition, you find an area in which you can enjoy being an artisan, you need not fear for yourself. You will be able to make a good living and have energy left over for living your life.

> *Is it not possible to live in this world without ambition, just being what you are? If you begin to understand what you are without trying to change it, then what you are undergoes a transformation. I think one can live in this world anonymously, completely unknown, without being famous, ambitious, cruel. One can live very happily when no importance is given to the self; and this also is part of right education.*

> —Krishnamurti (1970)

Directing Your Own Development

In Chapter 18, we address the need for a vital skill-set that relates to an issue that comes up so very frequently at this stage of life, "How do I make decisions?" In particular, we explore the following:

- The concrete skills and specific strategies to apply in making decisions.
- A tool called "bidding" that is helpful in making decisions for two.
- Moving toward the periphery when we notice how dangerous our culture is.
- How to make changes in yourself.
- The search for enlightenment.
- A meditation and two blessings.

Making Decisions

When speaking with classes that have been using my book, I have been surprised, but also delighted, to find that students are still asking many of the same questions they were asking when I first began teaching during the 1950s. After all, things do not change as rapidly as the media would have us believe. One question, in particular, struck me because I so clearly remember a group of students who were trying to ask me the same question years ago at UC-Irvine. I say "trying" because I was still teaching conventional sociology then, and it took me a little while to grasp that what they were asking me was urgent and personal: *How do you make decisions?*

This is a very understandable question. Most of you did not have to make major decisions until you got to college, and now, suddenly, you are supposed to decide where to live, what to major in, what career to choose, and whom to love and perhaps even marry. It seems a fitting conclusion to discuss this issue with you.

The first point is that in this domain, every decision is revocable and amendable. Indeed, you really cannot know all these answers at this point in your life. You may not yet know which major will delight you or dismay you; you can't yet understand what kind of preparation and work a given career entails; you cannot yet be completely wise about relationships. In all of these areas, you are like a beetle finding its way through the grass. You have a couple of feelers out, so you can tell what is happening a few inches in front of you. If you have ever watched a beetle, you will know that it constantly redirects its path according to what those feelers encounter. It will climb up many a wrong blade before it finds what it is looking for. But one thing the beetle isn't foolish enough to do is to make an early decision and stick to it, come what may. Only human beings do that. We tend to confuse inflexibility with strength of character. If changing your major costs you an extra semester, so what? It has not been decreed by the Almighty that your education must take 4 years. It is a rather ridiculous idea forced on us by bureaucrats who like to make everything mechanical and schematized.

The spiritual teacher Krishnamurti advises that as long as there is a "decision" to make, you aren't yet ready to act. At some point you will just know; there will not be any "choice." This suggests that if you still face a difficult choice, you haven't explored the alternatives far enough. For example, if you are torn between two possible college majors, maybe you need to contact some seniors who have majored in each of the two areas and find out how satisfied they were with their choices. You can get the names of seniors from your academic advisor, department secretary, or registrar's office. If you are uncertain about the job possibilities a given course of action will lead to, spend time at your college placement office or contact some personnel departments in the industry in question. If you are wondering whether to transfer to another campus, perhaps you need to make a trip to the proposed institution and spend a few days there. The admissions office there will be glad to see that you meet some students and have the chance to sit in on a few classes.

If you have explored as far as possible and are still facing a difficult choice, it will help if you find a friend and ask him or her to listen first to all the arguments for Decision A and then all the arguments for Decision B. In the process of verbalizing the pros and cons, you may discover that one side has the better arguments. Or, your friend may say, "You certainly don't sound too happy about Decision A." If there is nobody to talk to, try verbalizing the pros and cons out loud (this is important) or try writing them down. You will find it helpful to pull the issue out of the area of thought where it can chase around forever without enlightening you.

Sometimes during these verbalizations a third alternative develops. For example, shortly after I met Ted, I had the opportunity to attend a conference in Hawaii. Because I had never been there, and because my way would be paid, I really wanted to go, but I was torn because I also wanted to spend the time with my newly discovered friend. On my commute from school, I talked out both sides of the question. As I completed the two arguments, a new thought popped into my head, "Why not persuade Ted to come with me?" I did, and we had a wonderful time. Be open to new developments.

In this process of decision making, you will encounter what the world calls "failure" or "mistake." It would be well for you to banish these man-made concepts from your private emotional vocabulary. What the world calls failure or mistake is, for you, an invaluable piece of feedback: "Well, I see that math is just not the right major for me." Finding that out is every bit as valuable as finding out that you like or do well in something. It is all part of a process of elimination to find the most congenial path. It would be better to call these discoveries "negative feedback" and to forget "failure" with its unrealistic assumptions about the process by which people find their way. Remember that in your search for a career, as in love, you only have to succeed once.

In the same vein, keep your mind open to learning what you don't know. This is another piece of negative feedback and is really just as important as knowing that you do know something. For example, I know enough about mushrooms to know that I would need to know a great deal more before I could safely pick them in the forest to eat: absolutely crucial information. Discovering that you don't know something important opens the opportunity for learning and keeps you from making premature decisions.

One day, one of my students charged into my office in a panic. She had to decide between spending the next semester in Europe or spending it at a high-toned Ivy League college.

"Well," I said, "it seems to me that you would have a great time whichever alternative you choose." This thought came as a surprise to her. It didn't make her decision for her, but it took off some of the heat. When we are faced with choices, we too often think that there is a "right" choice. If we make it, we will be perfectly satisfied, whereas if we make the "wrong" choice, we will be perfectly miserable.[1] This is never the case. There will be good and bad in every alternative. Perhaps this type of thinking is still a reflection of the heaven-hell dichotomy in traditional Christianity. It will help us all to remember that we will always end up with a mixed bag. Of course, we want to choose the better path, but nothing is either perfect or irrevocable.

Making Decisions for Two

When two people are involved in making a decision, I recommend a process that I call "bidding" because of its similarity to bidding in bridge. In the first round, each person lays on the table exactly what he or she would most like to do. If, on this round, there is a difference of opinion, in the second round both people indicate how strongly they feel about their choice. At this point, you may find that one person feels much more strongly about his or her choice than the other, and you may decide, as we often do, to go the route desired by the person with the strongest feelings, on the assumption that when things are next the other way around the

---

[1] In line with our cultural attitudes toward "mistakes" are our attitudes toward "winning" and "losing." When television covers the Olympic Games, all it focuses on is who will win. Very often, when announcers ask the athletes to express their feelings, they flatly contradict this emphasis. They are well aware that the difference between a gold medal and a runner-up position is infinitesimal compared with the difference in skill between all the Olympic contestants and the average person. If athletes were actually as hung up on winning as are the television announcers, they would have a hard time performing at all.

partner with the weaker desire will give way, in turn. It isn't fair always to claim strong feelings just to get your way; there have to be trade-offs here.

Suppose, however, that the partners both feel strongly about their choice. In round three, attempt to find a new solution to the problem. Here, try to be inventive. Perhaps you can compromise by doing a little of each or synergize and come up with a third alternative that will please you both. For example, when Ted and I were choosing wallpaper for our house, we found that we often disagreed. So our practice was simply to keep looking until we found a pattern that appealed to us both. Try not to make a decision until such a solution presents itself.

The whole trick in this method is for each partner to ask what he or she wants and to lay it clearly on the table. Do not guess what the other person might want and try to go along with it. Only direct statements about one's own position are allowed. It also isn't fair to ask the other partner, "Are you sure you want to go to England?" rather than saying, "I really want to go to France" because this would be an indirect way of stating your own preference.

Some of the techniques discussed under individual decisions can also be applied here. For example, if you are in really deep water, you might go to a neutral third party and lay your case before him or her.

Moving Toward the Periphery

If, while reading this book, you have become aware that you live in a dangerous culture, you have gotten the point. Our culture is dangerous because it is based on false values that, if you live by them, can easily destroy your life. As another agent of socialization, college can become a part of this danger, although I hope I have shown you how to move upstream, using whatever currents are available. Here, I want to say a few words about your future life and how you can direct your own development.

Because this culture is dangerous, it is well to move to the periphery of it wherever possible. I have already hinted to you that the geographical periphery—that is, the rural areas that exist on the edges of this overwhelmingly urban society—are often much nicer places to live than is the megalopolis.

In the same vein, wilderness—what little remains to us—has a tremendous healing force. Nature, in any of her guises, has this capacity. If you grow your own vegetables, hike in the mountains, take care of animals, or collect rocks, you will be touching the hem of Mother Nature's splendid robes. Whenever I am in the wilderness, I always clean up whatever trash I see (unless it is just too overwhelming). To me, it is like combing the hair of a goddess. She will reward you with a keener appreciation of her wonders. People who have marveled at the complex beauty of a forest floor will never grind their cigarette butts into the duff.

I have spoken to you at length about political radicalism because the radical position is a highly critical one and therefore enables you to see society very sharply and clearly. You should at least expose yourself to some critical viewpoints. The perspectives of minority groups belong in the same category. I have advised minority students to hang on to their subcultures because these are healthier, in many ways, than the dominant culture. Majority students can pick up some of this by taking courses on minorities and by joining groups who work on behalf of oppressed minorities. *The oppressed always see society more clearly than their oppressors.* They have to, to survive.

All of the great religions enjoin us to practice charity. There are people going hungry and cold in the city in which you live, down the street from you. The clergy at almost any church or synagogue can tell you which churches are feeding the hungry or serving the poor in other ways. To take part in this work, even with small contributions of money or time, will do great things for your self-esteem. It has this added advantage: In becoming aware of poverty and giving of your own resources, you will ensure that you will never feel poor. If, on the other hand, you constantly and enviously look up—toward the richer and more famous—you will always feel poor by comparison.

In America, we have a counterculture that is particularly well represented on college campuses. Although the counterculture reached its greatest influence in recent history during the 1960s, it has always existed in some guise. Ethnically speaking, the counterculture contains an overrepresentation of Jews, non-Whites, Hispanics, and people from ethnic groups who came to this country between 1880 and 1920, the years of greatest immigration from southern and eastern Europe. The majority culture, also sometimes called the straight culture, is heavily dominated by the oldest ethnic stocks, from England and a few other countries of northern Europe. In terms of occupation, the majority culture is business oriented, whereas the counterculture is strong in certain professions, including the academic profession and the arts. If you are from a majority culture background, it would pay you to take a peek at the counterculture organizations on your campus, and vice versa.

If, however, you are already a member of the counterculture, either by upbringing or by your own early choice, I must warn you of this: The counterculture is also another culture. Its belief system is prone to all of the exaggeration and wish fulfillment that distorts any group's belief system. You can become dogmatic and closed-minded in the counterculture almost as easily as in the straight culture. For example, many counterculture folks believe that only holistic medicine should ever be used and all traditional medicine is utterly wrong. This is taking the useful insights of holistic medicine and running away with them to a place where you might deny yourself necessary medical help. The individual who values his or her health will be aware of both medical systems and use both.

Another example of counterculture madness was the violent political rhetoric that developed during the radical era from 1959–1974. Although the movement never really did much violence, the rhetoric caused it to lose supporters and was used to justify the police violence against the movement. It also made possible the work of government agents—provocateurs who pushed some movement groups to violence. At the height of this era, radical students even convinced themselves that they could overthrow the existing elite by violent means. Of course, there was never the tiniest chance of that, but believing it led people into many foolish words and wrong actions.

If you think that you may be a dupe to the counterculture, expose yourself to other points of view. I once did considerable research on right-wing belief systems and organizations. It didn't make a conservative of me, but it opened my eyes to many things, particularly to the realization that right-wingers are also a mixed bag of human beings—some good, some bad, most just people doing their best by their own lights. One of the interesting things I discovered was that the right and left ends of the political spectrum see eye to eye on more matters than the members of either group suspect. This is not surprising, as both oppose the same power structure.

How to Make Changes in Yourself

Sociologists have done much research to show that the individual human being is a very weak reed, indeed. People need groups to reinforce their beliefs and to support them in the adoption of new values or ways of life.[2] The phenomenal success of groups like Alcoholics Anonymous and Weight Watchers testifies to the power of the group over the individual. We don't like to hear this because it insults our illusion that we are free agents. But, if we are intelligent about it, this insight can guide us when we want to make changes in our lives. *When you want to change yourself, find a group that will support you.* When you join a group, you come in contact with a new set of expectations, and the expectations of others govern our behavior to an amazing extent (and, often, subliminally). The strength of this influence increases as your emotional ties to people in the group become deeper and stronger. (By the same token, if you want to rid yourself of influences that pull you in an undesirable direction, you must cut your ties to the people who pull you in that direction.) It is very hard to disappoint people to whom we feel close and on whom we depend for moral support. The interesting thing about this process is that it works even if you are fully conscious of how it works, just as surely as an apple will fall on a physicist's head even though he knows the law of gravity. If you want to inspire yourself to exercise regularly, take a yoga or physical education course. If you want to meditate regularly, find a group that meets regularly for meditation. If you want to explore the wilderness, join the Sierra Club or the hiking club on your campus. These people will not only encourage you, they will show you the ropes. If you would like to kick your emotional dependence on grades, it might be an interesting independent study to investigate how Alcoholics Anonymous and Weight Watchers work (go to meetings). Then see whether you can organize a "Praise Junkies Anonymous" group on your campus.

Luckily, a large campus offers a tremendous variety of group experiences, although it is also very salutary to get off the campus for some of your group contacts. Just about any change you want to make in yourself will correspond with some group already in existence. If you want to find out what groups are available on your campus, search the school's Web site for student associations, groups, and organizations, or contact the Dean of Students Office. If you want to explore what is available in your city or town, you might begin with a Google search. In some

---

[2]To convince yourself of the power of groups, see the experiments of Solomon Asch and Muzafer Sherif in Eleanor Maccoby's (1958) *Readings in Social Psychology.*

cases, you may have to organize a group yourself, a very educational experience. If you are new on campus, by all means join a group. Groups, if they are functioning at all well (not all groups do), usually welcome members and provide you with a place to meet congenial people.

Changing the World by Changing Yourself

In my experience at the undergrad level, I have found that in order to make any kind of difference or meaningful impact, the changes you desire to see need to take place within yourself first. Specifically, the challenges we face within the next years in dealing with environmental issues are daunting. The earth currently bears 7 billion people, with the population slated to reach 10 billion within the next decade. Our earth does not have the resources to support 10 billion people at the rate we are consuming. We are running out of oil and depleting our fresh water sources, while also deforesting at record setting rates. Most alarming is the fact that global warming is very real and has the capacity to start natural feedback loops that, once begun, cannot be reversed.

When I was first introduced to these issues in one of my sociology courses, I was beyond overwhelmed. I felt like I was looking at an impending apocalypse or something, like a "Day After Tomorrow" type scenario. I left class every session discouraged and unsure of what I could possibly do to help. We watched several documentaries and read articles in class about people who were researching solutions and suggesting ways to slow and possibly curb the consequences of global warming. I am not a bioengineer, nor a political activist. I hadn't even studied any kind of earth science in college. I felt inadequate and helpless.

However, toward the second half of the course we began analyzing solutions and it occurred to me that none of the large scale solutions that had been proposed could be effective if no one *knew that they existed*, and especially not if people are *unaware* that there even *is a problem*. I started talking to peers and friends and family about what I was learning in the course. I challenged my mom to take shorter showers and get a water filter instead of buying bottled water. I discussed overpopulation and adoption with my boyfriend, asked him questions, and challenged him to eat less meat and consider vegetarianism. I asked my roommates to consider hanging their laundry out to dry instead of using the dryer to conserve energy. At the same time that I was inciting these discussions, I was also making these changes for myself. I hung my laundry, took 5 minute showers, turned off all the lights and electronics when I left a room, opted for fans instead of using our AC, and so on.

I realized that the more changes I made in my own lifestyle, the easier it became to bring up global environmental issues with others. The more aware I am and the more diligent and active I am in addressing the issue in my own personal, day to day life, the more of an impact I can make on those around me. I may not have saved the earth from impending doom yet, but my friends and I carpool almost everywhere, one of us will soon have a gasless electric car, and my roommates still continue to keep the AC turned off.

Changes are not made overnight, and global issues cannot be solved by just one passionate, undergraduate student. Yet, if you want to see anything happen, no matter how big or how small, you have to jump-start change by jump-starting yourself.

—Erika Martin

Building a Community of Heroes

On September 22, 2009, an army of 4,300 UCLA freshmen and transfer students swarmed into various sites in Los Angeles: not to fight a war, but to do community service. Funded by a grant from Hollywood's Entertainment Industry Foundation, UCLA Volunteer Day was the largest-ever volunteer day of any university in the nation. From beach cleanup in Malibu, to trail repair at Griffith Park, to beautification of various Los Angeles middle schools, this large-scale community service day built upon President Obama's call for increased national service initiatives.

I was in charge of leading the 70 or so freshmen and transfer students on my dormitory floor to paint the decaying walls of Gompers Middle School. Los Angeles Mayor Antonio Villaraigosa, along with UCLA Chancellor Gene Block, paid a visit to the school and did a bit of painting. I was truly moved by how many eager students were willing to wake up at 7:00 a.m. to do volunteer work, and as a result, I'm motivated to do even more community service work myself.

I would argue that a college student doesn't have to be a student at UCLA to discover the joy and value of engaging in community service. Any college student in the nation has the choice to give back to the community by participating in meaningful service. From UCLA Web sites (e.g., http://volunteer.ucla.edu/) to national Web sites (e.g., http://www.volunteermatch.org/, http://www.serve.gov/), there are countless opportunities for all students in the United States to search for ways to be involved. As college students living in a globalized world, we are tremendously privileged to have access to higher education, an opportunity that most young people in the world do not have. There is much more to college than just getting good grades or partying until 2:00 a.m. on Thursday nights, as inevitable as those are to the college experience. We have a responsibility as global citizens to help those who are less fortunate, and volunteering is one of the most meaningful ways to do so.

—Draco Chu

Finding Who You Are: The Time Is Now

You often hear people say, "What you get out of something depends on how much you put into it," and that's precisely the college experience in a nutshell. Whether you realize it or not, there is nothing worse than spending 4 or more years only studying and socializing. Believe it or not, college is not just about education; it's an incredible opportunity to expand yourself, and that only happens if you take a few detours on your way from class to dorm to frat house. Many students seek employment and internships to start preparing for the postgrad life. Other students may take part in campus sports. There are countless other ways to get the most of the college experience, but what I want to encourage students to do is become active on campus—whether for a cause unrelated to campus life or something like student government, to improve conditions for students, professors, and the school at large. I guarantee there is nothing more fulfilling than knowing you have helped make a positive impact or, as corny as it sounds, graduating having made your college, or even the world, a slightly better place.

During my sophomore year, I was introduced to a club called Student Coalition for Marriage Equality (SCME), founded to help lead the effort in legalizing marriage for same-sex couples. I became a regular member, attending weekly general meetings and their annual same-sex wedding on campus. I moved up to a board position, as treasurer, by my junior year. Then, lo and behold, I became president of the club by my senior year.

Never in a million years did I think I'd be president of anything, leading any type of organization. I was always very shy and reserved, with low confidence in being able to carry out big responsibilities like planning events and working on election campaigns. Yet, during the first couple years I was involved, it really sparked something substantial within me. I paid attention to how things were done, how they were run, who did what. There is quite a lot that goes into running an organization and planning events. Being a board member (or a very active member) of such organizations is almost like having a part-time job. It demands a great deal of time and nudges you to become more coordinated, organized, outgoing, responsible, and even social. You learn to navigate school bureaucracy. Securing a venue, sound, food permits, or any of a million other things; planning, designing, and executing events; seeking funding from a variety of sources (trust me, wherever there is money, you will be looking); promoting and advertising your club and events; and building coalitions and relationships as well as networking with other people and organizations are all skills that you will use at one point or another in your life after college.

So, when it came time for me to step in as the leader, I knew event planning and school bureaucracy like the back of my hand. And although the countless hours per week focused on the club did take a toll, it was easily the most rewarding experience of my life because not only was I making a difference in other people's lives and the community but I really learned a great deal about myself and developed skills and qualities I did not know I had. In addition, joining this club opened up so many other opportunities for me. Through my involvement in the club's activity, I became more aware of campus politics and more willing and eager to not only learn how to but actually implement change. I also became connected with several off-campus organizations related to this cause I had become so passionate for, and I started volunteering—a path that can often lead you to new professional or career interests and opportunities you otherwise would never have stumbled upon.

I understand that a lot of students may have no clue what they are really passionate about and may be intimidated by most of what I have been talking about. To those students, I say start looking, start searching. There will never be a better time to take advantage of exploring anything and everything.

Students have such limitless power. They really do. Think back to the sixties. The social movement that shaped the America we know today was run on student fuel. You can demand change or you can create it yourself—either way, don't forget that the power resides within you. Whether it's truly an apathetic attitude our generation has or a stronger influence over society that the media and social elites now hold, complacency has taken the majority. Don't blow out the flame. Keep fighting. Lead the next student revolution. It's all in your hands—it always has been.

—*Raffi Sarkissian*

On Religious Beliefs (or Lack Thereof): Learning to Own Them

In college, most people, whether they desire to or not, end up facing the cracks in the architecture of their religious beliefs. This deliberation and self-reflection can result from direct confrontation over these beliefs with peers or perceived pressure and persecution from peers and professors who dwell in the pretentious world of academia where the only things worth believing in are things you can prove or understand. This might not apply to the experience of all first years, but it is certainly the experience I had. I grew up in the Evangelical church and became a Christian around the beginning of my high school career. After graduating from high school, I was told multiple times that my beliefs would be challenged—by other people and myself—once I entered college. I intended to stay strong in my beliefs and entered college intending to be an agent of change and influence, not a subject of it. However, knowing that my beliefs would be challenged and intending to stay strong didn't prepare me for what was to come. During my freshman year in college, I encountered the usual doubts and challenges that one suspects he or she will run into: Social issues such as abortion, LGBT rights, the abuse of drugs and sex, and scientific issues such as the Big Bang and evolution were thrown at me during the first quarter of college. Although these issues can be greatly polarizing and are often hotly debated, they weren't what shook my faith. After all, these issues aren't issues only college students encounter; they are issues most people have come across and resolved at some earlier point in their life. What shook my faith was realizing my lack of autonomy. In college, I encountered people who had strong passions for their beliefs and philosophies, which they seemed to have arrived at as a result of their own deliberation. I looked at my own beliefs and philosophies and asked myself whether I independently, purposefully chose them or whether they were merely a product of the environment I grew up in. Not for one second did I doubt the existence and power of God. What I doubted was the legitimacy of my belief and whether it was something I actually chose. If my beliefs and philosophies were nothing but products of the environment I grew up in, I wanted to throw them away and start fresh, and today I encourage this mentality. Whatever you believe in, it is important that you arrived at that belief through your own reasoning and conscious choosing. This is what makes that belief your belief and your opinion, not the church's opinion, not your parents' opinion, and not your friends' opinion. A coworker I met in college told me that you must learn to own your complete self—the good and the bad. I was in the process of learning how to own my faith. My first year definitely had its ups and downs and its experimentation. Through this journey on a convoluted, twisted path that wasn't necessarily the right one or the wisest one, I was actually able to come back to the narrow path I walked on before and know that I was walking on that path because I chose to do so, and I don't regret it. No matter what religious creed or philosophy you follow (or lack thereof), various tenets of your belief will come under fire once you enter college. But the most daunting challenge you will face will be a challenge to the authenticity of your belief. I encourage you to face this challenge and work your way through it, knowing that a more confident and self-owned you will arise from the ash heap of confusion and doubt.

—Andrew Quan

The Search for Enlightenment

In this book, I have talked a good deal about Eastern philosophy and practices like meditation. Reading and practice are valuable, but you should be warned that *if you really wish to pursue enlightenment in the classic Eastern sense, you need to find a teacher and a community of persons who are working together toward this highest of human states.* You need a teacher because you need individual attention. A spiritual teacher can see exactly where you are and which way you have to move. Such a teacher can zero in on the needs of your particular being, something a book can never do. A teacher can also safeguard you against spiritual materialism,[3] making another illusion out of the teachings of liberation.

---

[3] A priceless book on this subject is Chogyam Trungpa's (1973) *Cutting Through Spiritual Materialism.*

Working with undergraduates on the practices of Eastern philosophy, I have become aware that very few people of college age are ready for such a commitment. Most of you do not yet feel the need because you have not yet experienced the severest suffering of life. Enlightenment is, above all, a way to end the suffering that accompanies our usual approach to life. I have, therefore, felt that all I can really do for most of you is to let you know that this path exists. Maybe there will come a time when you wish to take that path, and, at least, you will have some idea where to look.

In the meantime, you must find "teachers" wherever you can. A deep friendship or love relationship can be a very real teacher. The right group can be a teacher. Even a college professor will, at times, be a teacher. Finally, the situations of life, with all their positive and negative feedback, can also be your teachers. Try to remain open to all these possibilities. Don't be afraid to hear criticism. The saddest sight in life is an old person who has been too stubborn and oversensitive all his or her life to listen to criticism or to take advice. Such people can never learn. As the weight of the years piles up, their personalities become more dense and impervious, and they are, more and more, lost inside a cage of their own making.

There are two opposite kinds of development in people's lives. Some people learn from life and become happier as the years pass; some learn nothing and become ever sadder. Of course, people are complex. They may be growing in some directions, while woefully stuck in others. Be one of the learners. Learners are not afraid of "mistakes." They are humble enough to accept criticism. They approach each day with an empty cup that may be filled with new experience.

A Meditation and Two Blessings

I think that one reason I always wanted to make learning fun for my students was that I was very lucky to have a father who was a very intelligent and wise man. Schools had not cut him down to size because he was self-educated. He taught me so much about the world and also about life. In his teaching, there was no judgment, no evaluation, no competition, only love. I would like to pass on one piece of his advice, which has been a blessing to me. He said, "Do something that delights you every single day." Do something, however small, even if it is only a 10-minute walk to some lovely spot on your campus or 15 minutes listening to some music you love. I would like to pass on to you my favorite meditation. It is a wonderful one for getting in touch with your body and your feelings.[4]

Sit comfortably, either on the floor, cross-legged, or in a straight-backed chair with your feet on the floor. In either position, make sure the spine is straight from the base of the spine to the top of the head. Remove glasses, if you wear them.

Begin by getting in touch with the way the top of your head feels. It may take a few minutes before you get feedback from there. Your feedback may come in the form of a cool or warm feeling, a tension, itching, pricking, whirring, contraction,

---

[4]My thanks to our wonderful yoga teacher, Jane Evans, for this meditation.

expansion, or simply feeling your hair on your head. Proceed, bit by bit, to your forehead, eyes, nose, cheeks, ears, chin, and throat. Then go down the back of your head and neck. Now, work down your right arm from the shoulder to the upper arm, elbow, lower arm, and hand. Sometimes what you may feel is the material of your shirt next to your body or the arm of the chair as it touches you. Work down the left arm, then down the front and back of your torso, and down each leg to your feet.

When you have finished, spend what remains of your 20 minutes just watching your breath as it moves in and out of your body. Do not try to change your breathing in any way, just observe it. Be aware of your breath, whether it is a long breath or a short breath.

In the course of this meditation, you may, at times, get feedback from an area of your body other than the one you are concentrating on. Just feel that new sensation for a moment, then return to your systematic coverage. You will also find your mind wandering from the exercise. This is inevitable and should not bother you. When you notice that you have drifted off, just bring yourself gently back to the exercise. If you can't remember where you were, start again at the top of the head. Be patient with yourself but persistent. Whatever feelings occur, be a witness or observer, not a critic or judge. Rather, be a scientist and observe whatever is occurring for you at the moment.

Finish your meditation or exercises by repeating this blessing from the Hindu meditation master S. Goenka:

May all beings be peaceful

May all beings be harmonious

May all beings be happy

References

Babbie, E. (1998). *Plagiarism*. Retrieved September 1, 2004, from www.csubak.edu/ssric/ Modules/Other/plagiarism.htm

Beattie, M. (1987). *Codependent no more*. San Francisco, CA: Harper/Hazelden.

Becker, E. (1973). *The denial of death*. Boston, MA: The Free Press.

Carroll, L. (1960). *Alice's adventures in wonderland*. New York, NY: Signet. (Original work published 1865)

Centers for Disease Control and Prevention. (2008). *Sexual violence facts at a glance*. Retrieved from http://www.cdc.gov/violenceprevention/pdf/SV-DataSheet-a.pdf

Cohen, S., & Taylor, L. (1976). *Escape attempts*. Middlesex, UK: Penguin.

Cuber, J. F., & Harroff, P. B. (1966). *Sex and the significant Americans*. Baltimore, MD: Penguin.

Delpit, L. (1995). *Other people's children: Cultural conflict in the classroom*. New York, NY: The New Press.

Derber, C. (1983). *The pursuit of attention: Power and individualism in everyday life*. London, UK: Oxford University Press.

De Rougement, D. (1941). *Love in the western world*. New York, NY: Harcourt Brace.

Dickens, C. (1982). *Great expectations*. New York, NY: Penguin.

Domhoff, W. G. (1975). *The Bohemian grove and other retreats: A study in ruling-class cohesiveness*. New York, NY: Harper & Row.

Ellis, A., & Bernard, M. (Eds.). (1983). *Rational-emotive approaches to the problems of childhood*. New York, NY: Plenum.

Ellis, D. (1984). *Becoming a master student* (4th ed.). New York, NY: College Survival.

Evans-Pritchard, E. E. (1940). *The Nuer: A description of the modes of livelihood and political institutions of a Nilotic people*. London, UK: Oxford University Press.

Fischer, L. (1963). *The essential Gandhi*. New York, NY: Random House.

Freire, P. (1970). *Pedagogy of the oppressed*. New York, NY: Continuum.

Fried, R. (1995). *The passionate teacher*. Boston, MA: Beacon Press.

Fried, R. (2001). *The passionate learner*. Boston, MA: Beacon Press.

Fried, R. (2005). *The game of school: Why we all play it, how it hurts kids, and what it will take to change it*. San Francisco, CA: Jossey-Bass.

Friday, N. (1977). *My mother, my self*. New York, NY: Delacorte.

Fromm, E., Suzuki, D. T., & De Martino, R. (1960). *Zen Buddhism and psychoanalysis*. New York, NY: Harper & Row.

Gardner, J., & Jewler, J. (1992). *College is only the beginning*. Belmont, CA: Wadsworth/ITP.

Goldberg, N. (1986). *Writing down the bones: Freeing the writer within*. Boston, MA: Shambhala.

Herrigel, E. (1971). *Zen in the art of archery.* New York, NY: Vintage, Random House.

Holt, J. (1982). *How children fail.* New York, NY: Delacorte.

Kastenbaum, R. (1998). *Death, society and human experience.* Needham Heights, MA: Allyn & Bacon.

Kensington Ladies' Erotica Society. (1984). *Ladies' home erotica.* Berkeley, CA: Ten Speed Press.

King, M. L. (1958). *Stride toward freedom.* New York, NY: Harper & Row.

Kohn, A. (1986, September). How to succeed without even trying. *Psychology Today,* 22–28.

Kohn, A. (1993). *Punished by rewards: The trouble with gold stars, incentive plans, A's, praise, and other bribes.* New York, NY: Houghton Mifflin.

Krishnamurti, J. (1967). Fourth public dialogue, 5th August, 1967. *Talks and dialogues Saanen, 1967* (JKO Serial No. 152). Bramdean, UK: Krishnamurti Foundation Trust.

Krishnamurti, J. (1969). *Freedom from the known.* New York, NY: Harper & Row.

Krishnamurti, J. (1970). The mechanical activity of thought. *Impossible question Part I, Chapter 6. Sixth public talk Saanen, 28th July, 1970.* Bramdean, UK: Krishnamurti Foundation Trust.

Levy, J. (1966). *Cesar Chavez.* New York, NY: W. W. Norton.

Loewen, J. (1996). *Lies my teacher told me: Everything your American history textbook got wrong.* New York, NY: Touchstone.

Maccoby, E. (1958). *Readings in social psychology* (3rd ed.). New York, NY: Holt, Rinehart & Winston.

Maccoby, M. (1976). *The gamesman.* New York, NY: Simon & Schuster.

Malinowski, B. (1985). *Sex and repression in savage society.* Chicago, IL: University of Chicago Press. (Original work published 1927)

Mannheim, K. (1936). *Ideology and utopia: An introduction to the sociology of knowledge.* New York, NY: Harcourt Brace.

Maslow, A. (1962). *Toward a psychology of being.* Princeton, NJ: Van Nostrand.

Matthiesen, P. (1978). *The snow leopard.* New York, NY: Bantam.

McGrane, B., & Gunderson, J. (2010). *Watching TV is not required.* New York, NY: Routledge.

Mills, C. W. (1959). *The sociological imagination.* Oxford, UK: Oxford University Press.

Nhat Hanh, T. (1985). *A guide to walking meditation.* Nyack, NY: Fellowship.

Office of Health Education. (2006). *Rape and sexual assault.* Retrieved from http://www.vpul.upenn.edu/ohe/library/violence/rape-assault.htm

Paralumun New Age Village. (n.d.). *American rape statistics.* Retrieved from http://www.paralumun.com/issuesrapestats.htm

Parsons, T. (1951). *The social system.* Glencoe, IL: The Free Press.

Peck, M. S. (1978). *The road less traveled.* New York, NY: Simon & Schuster.

Piven, F. F., & Cloward, R. A. (1979). *Poor people's movements.* New York, NY: Vintage.

Powell, R. (1961). *Zen and reality.* Middlesex, UK: Penguin.

Putney, S., & Putney, G. (1964). *The adjusted American: Normal neuroses in the individual and society.* New York, NY: Harper & Row.

Rico, G. L. (1983). *Writing the natural way.* Los Angeles, CA: Jeremy P. Tarcher.

Rock, D. (2009). *Your brain at work.* New York, NY: HarperCollins.

Salzman, J. (1993). *If you can talk, you can write.* New York, NY: Warner.

Schiller, D. (1994). *The little Zen companion.* New York, NY: Workman.

Schopenhauer, A. (1960). *The art of literature.* Ann Arbor, MI: University of Michigan Press.

Sedaris, D. (2000). *Me talk pretty one day.* New York, NY: Little, Brown and Company.

Seeley, J. R., Sim, R. A., & Loosley, E. W. (1967). *Crestwood Heights.* New York, NY: Wiley.

Sennett, R., & Cobb, J. (1971). *The hidden injuries of class.* New York, NY: Vintage.

Smith, D. N. (1974). *Who rules the universities?* New York, NY: Monthly Review Press.

Stevens, B. (1970). *Don't push the river.* Moab, UT: Real People.

Suzuki, S. (1970). *Zen mind, beginner's mind.* New York, NY: Weatherhill.

Sykes, C. J. (1989). *PROFSCAM: Professors and the demise of higher education.* Washington, DC: Regnery Gateway.

Terkel, S. (1972). *Working.* New York, NY: Random House.

Trungpa, C. (1969). *Meditation in action.* Berkeley, CA: Shambhala.

Trungpa, C. (1973). *Cutting through spiritual materialism.* Berkeley, CA: Shambhala.

Turkle, S. (2012). *Sherry Turkle: Connected, but alone?* Retrieved from http://www.ted.com/talks/sherry_turkle_alone_together.html

Turkle, S. (2011). *Alone Together.* New York, NY: Basic Books.

Watts, A. W. (1961). *Psychotherapy east and west.* New York, NY: Ballantine.

Watts, A. W. (1962). *The way of Zen.* London, UK: Penguin Arkana.

Watts, A. W. (1966). *The book: On the taboo against knowing who you are.* New York, NY: Pantheon.

Wrong, D. (1967). The oversocialized conception of man in modern sociology. In P. I. Rose (Ed.), *The study of society: An integrated anthology* (pp. 136–146). New York, NY: Random House.

Wylie-Kellerman, B. (Ed.). (1994). *A keeper of the word: Selected writings of William Stringfellow.* Grand Rapids, MI: W.B. Eerdmans.

X, M. (1977). *The autobiography of Malcolm X.* New York, NY: Ballantine.

Zinn, H. (1980). *A people's history of the United States.* New York, NY: Harper Colophon.

Index

About the Authors

Inge Bell, emeritus professor of sociology at Pitzer College, close friend and colleague, died April 29, 1996. Born in 1930 in Austria, Inge and her family escaped from the Nazis, emigrating to the United States in the 1940s. She grew up in Claremont, California, just blocks from Pitzer's campus, which in 1968 was to become her academic home, within which she would shape the bulk of her distinguished academic career.

Inge earned her PhD at the University of California at Berkeley during the 1960s, a decade that expressed and clarified the values and sensibilities that would subsequently inform her lifelong perspective on teaching and scholarship. At Berkeley, Inge was heavily involved in the Civil Rights Movement, contributing especially to the organization and functioning of the first Berkeley/Oakland chapter of the Congress of Racial Equality (C.O.R.E.). Her work with C.O.R.E. soon became a central research interest, resulting eventually in the publication of her first book, *C.O.R.E.: The Strategy of Nonviolence* (Random House, 1968).

Inge's capacity to join her personal and civic commitments to her professional activities was in evidence early in her academic career. She refused to compartmentalize her life. For example, following Inge's personal explorations into the meditations of Zen Buddhism, she fleshed out the humanism embedded in its practice and theory, themes she went on to weave into her 1979 classic essay "Buddhist Sociology."

Inge took early retirement from Pitzer College in 1982 in order, as she put it, "to think, to write, and, most important, to tend to my garden." And she did all three with much zeal and enthusiasm. She continued her conversations with colleagues, exchanging ideas, information, and insights. Inge also wrote and published the enormously influential *This Book Is Not Required* (The Small Press, 1985) during her retirement. The book gained widespread circulation and adoption, winning praise and admiration from colleagues in all academic disciplines. Written as an undergraduate "survival manual," *This Book Is Not Required* is a humane repository of wise sociologically informed observations; it has taught and will continue to teach countless students how to flourish during their college years. And, we would add, Inge's garden became the envy of many in and around Fort Bragg, California, where she retired with her husband, Ted Hoffman.

Inge lived her life as a warm, loving, and wise human being. She was an incredible *listener,* capable of transcending her own concerns and making herself available to those in need of a sympathetic ear. Scores of colleagues and friends and a multitude of students benefited from Inge's understanding and wisdom over the years. Inge Bell enriched the lives of everyone she touched, and she enriched our discipline of sociology with her humanistic voice and vision. Although we are thankful that her voice and vision will continue in print and memory, Inge herself will be sorely missed.

Glenn A. Goodwin
Al Schwartz
Professors Emeritus, Pitzer College

Bernard McGrane received a PhD from New York University. He has taught at a wide variety of universities—Vermont College, Colby College in Maine, Cuesta Community College, UCLA, UCI, and Pitzer College. He currently teaches at Chapman University. He has studied Tibetan Buddhism under Chögyam Trungpa Rinpoche and transformative education with Landmark Education. He is the author of *Beyond Anthropology: Society and the Other* (Columbia University Press, 1989), *The Un-TV and the 10 MPH Car—Experiments in Personal Freedom and Everyday Life* (Small Press, 1994), and *Watching TV Is Not Required* (Routledge, 2009). He is also featured in two educational videos created by the late Harold Boihem: *The Ad and the Id: Sex, Death, and Subliminal Advertising* and *The Ad and the Ego: Advertising and Identity.*

John Gunderson received his PhD from Claremont Graduate University. He has taught at the secondary and university level for many years. He currently teaches at Dana Hills High School in South Orange County and at Chapman University. His work is grounded in the belief that passionate teaching and learning can transform education and the lives of individuals. He is the coauthor of *This Book Is Not Required* (3rd ed.; Pine Forge Press, 2004) and *Watching TV Is Not Required* (Routledge, 2009), both with Barney McGrane, and the author of *Flow and Effective Teaching: A Study* (Verlag, 2009).

Terri L. Anderson (PhD, Sociology, UCLA) teaches Sociology at various Southern California colleges and universities, including UCLA, Occidental College, Pitzer College, and Loyola Marymount University. Her research concerns include the self, technology, arts and culture, pedagogy, and gender and power. She is also the creator and executive director of AMP, the Artists' Meeting Place and Resource Collective, an international arts community. She proudly parents Charlotte and Rose, two vibrant Dalmatians.

About the Contributors

Team Bell

The student team came together to approach the task of revising Inge Bell's book in the wake of her death.

The team was a dynamic collection of individual perspectives, a gathering of strengths. Each person responded to a different facet of the book. One person commented that it is a book about diversity. Another remembered that Dr. Bell spoke of minorities leaving their families behind. A few members of the group were in transition: graduating, getting married, moving, applying to graduate schools. They heard Bell addressing the emancipation quandary. Fittingly, Bell wrote in metaphors, extending in different directions. What emerged was a multifaceted whole.

The team as a group shared a common task: to preserve Bell's message and make it more accessible to others. All agreed that a first step could be to modernize the language. We are in a new millennium. How does this impact the readers? Several members of the team had something new to contribute, as an expansion of Bell's philosophy. Each brought a new segment, to be distilled by the group as a whole.

Regarding the process of revision, the team agreed to first work together to distill Bell's original text and then to contribute individual voices to the whole. It was important to first step into Bell's world. As with a historic building, the job was to preserve and to renovate.

The question at issue was how to maintain the integrity of Bell's voice—its intensity and impact—while updating language and references. The team agreed that the function of updating was to enhance the field and range of relevance and reader responsiveness.

In the end, the voice that speaks is the new entity: the collective voice of Bell, her readers, and those who want to continue her legacy. The team spoke of making the book an organic event, an open conversation, by allowing for ongoing new contributions and enhancements. Several spoke of having a moral obligation to find the language to continue giving Bell's message to contemporary student readers.

—Patricia Harriman

Jasleen Ahuja is an undergrad at the University of California, Los Angeles, is 20 years old, and is still figuring out what decisions she needs to make to have the "perfect life" she's always dreamed about. Those decisions are tough but have resulted in an English major, political science minor, and, ideally, law school in the near future. Choosing an educational route may be a tough decision, but it is one of the most rewarding.

Lynette Albovias graduated from University of California at Irvine with a bachelor's degree in economics and a minor in management. Her plans include obtaining work experience in marketing and, ultimately, a master's degree in business administration. Lynette believes that the dynamic ideas of Bell's book are powerful because they reveal a truth specific to each reader. Contrary to Bell's title, Lynette believes that Bell's book should be required in a student education course to allow the truth to come through. It was both an honor and a privilege to be part of a team working to update Bell's ideas so that they can continue to speak their truth to students.

Paula Apodaca

Sheyda Bogosyan was born in Istanbul, Turkey, to Armenian parents. At the age of 7, she was told that her family was moving to Los Angeles, so she packed her bags and stepped into the land of opportunity. She attended a private Armenian school from 1st through 12th grade, so naturally it had a big influence on her personality. She attended UCI and graduated with a degree in psychology. She currently works as a behavioral therapist for autistic children and plans to pursue a career in special education. She is extremely grateful to be given the opportunity to contribute to this book because it made such a big impact on her life when she first read it. She hopes her contribution to this book will help make a few students' college lives just a bit easier, or at least seem a bit more normal.

Georgiana Bostean: When Georgiana isn't hard at work setting up camp all over Catalina Island, snowboarding, or training in the art of capoeira, she finds some time to do research and churn out journal articles. She passionately pursues her research on immigrant health and complementary and alternative medicine and will be finishing her doctorate soon. A student of life, she believes learning exists everywhere and is a lifelong journey. She hopes to bring this message to students and to continue her own learning through teaching.

Lauren A. Bragg, from Lake Tahoe, California, believes in saving the earth, protecting wonderful creatures from extinction, and achieving peace and harmony for all. She has her beliefs, which nobody can take away—ever. She believes that one day, one moment, one person can change your life forever. Carpe diem and no regrets!

Daniel Bulone graduated from Chapman University with a BFA in creative writing and went on to earn his teaching credential. He currently teaches English/Language Arts at a middle school in Monterey County, surrounded by the same fields and mountains that inspired much of John Steinbeck's fiction. He is a published author of horror and science fiction and can frequently be seen jogging at evening twilight with (or away from) other crepuscular creatures.

Rose DeLeon Carter: Proud Mom to Trevor, Ryan, and Jared who have helped me learn that it IS all about the quality and the experiences of the journey that truly matter and not just the destination.

Kenneth W. Chow Jr. grew up in the small town of Caruthers, where he could stand on his rooftop staring toward the horizon and see nothing but grapevines. He is in his fourth year at UCLA and sees nothing but pollution in the sky, with the occasional star here and there. He found this book enticing because everyone can relate to it, and the issues involved are important for a well-balanced life. Kenneth plans to become a business consultant, to help those who want to simplify their lives and fulfill their dreams. He dedicates this book to everyone in search of the truth and, most of all, to his lovely parents for providing him the opportunity to be who he is today.

Draco Chu: I am a work in progress, currently in my fourth and final year at UCLA. Majoring in global studies, I have been working on a four-year fieldwork research project involving a comparative case study of globalization's effects on higher education in the U.S. and China, specifically with regard to students' views of global citizenship and the field of student affairs. As a two-year RA with the UCLA Office of Residential Life, I have been fortunate enough to be able to directly mentor 112 college students each year, and I hope that I've inspired them in some way to be a global citizen and contribute to our global community.

John Chuidian: John was born in San Francisco and brought up all around East and Southeast Asia. As a diplomat's kid, he quickly learned that he really doesn't know what to say when someone asks him, "Where are you from?" Typically, he just says, "I live down the street." A Third Culture Kid by definition and rascal prince by practice, he believes that after reading his contributions to this book, people will have no excuse for the trouble they get into, for they are now duly warned, just like when their parents told them not to touch the burning stove moments before they did. His family and his friends all love him to death—emphasis on the latter part. The feeling is mutual.

Erin Cora was born and raised in Southern California and has survived a school system that she spent years rejecting. In the end, she found relief and, more important, blessings and appreciation for her journey. A Chapman University graduate, she is now pondering the next journey in her life. At present, she is searching for a career that can incorporate the knowledge and wisdom she has gained and provide her with the opportunity for personal growth. She is pursuing a life of completeness, blending a self-fulfilling career, love, fun, and happiness.

Andrea Crane is a Chapman University sociology student who has studied in both the United States and Australia. She plans to attend graduate school in California to further her studies in the field of sociology, particularly gender studies. Apart from sociological endeavors, Andrea is also a published poet and art student.

Michael Creim: I am a psychology major at UCLA in the Class of 2012 and am a 2008 graduate of La Canada High School. At UCLA, I am a member of the Alumni Scholars Club and the College Honors Program. Upon graduation I intend to earn a master's degree in education before pursuing a career in law.

Lorraine Feldman

Veronica Fematt has walked many different paths throughout life, some very rocky, others serene. Her life story could be summarized by the following equation: immigrant parents + the American dream = upper-middle-class life + divorce = poverty—basically, your average hardship novel. Veronica came to UCLA as a transfer student, even though all bets were against her. She is most thankful for having so many different and challenging life experiences, allowing her to see the world through multiple lenses, which she believes is key to actually making a real difference in the world. Her ultimate goals are to do social research, publish a few books, and become a professor at a university. She thanks her mom, Rosaura Lavenant—her inspiration to succeed—for always challenging her and her sisters to set high aspirations. Watching her mom jump all the hurdles and triumph makes it impossible for Veronica to call anything difficult. Gracias.

Rebecca Silver Fisher was born and raised in Los Angeles. She graduated with degrees in sociology and gender studies from the University of California, Los Angeles, in 2008. Rebecca currently resides in New York, where she works for a nonprofit health organization and enjoys yoga, live music, traveling, and exploring Brooklyn.

Daniella Reynoso Graves: Born in the small southern California town of Fillmore, she graduated from UCLA in the winter of 2005 with a major in sociology. She continued to fuel her passion for the field by enrolling as a master's student at CSUN. In the summer of 2008, she completed her thesis on tattoos and identity. She hopes to continue her education in sociology and is currently considering a few different PhD programs. She is much honored to be a part of the new edition of this book.

Tatian Greenleaf grew up in Berkeley, California, and graduated from UCI in 1997 with a bachelor's degree in sociology and a minor in computer science. As a member of the orientation staff there, he helped prepare incoming students for university life. As an undergraduate, Tatian worked as a teaching assistant, leading discussion sections in "Sociology of the Media" and "The Social Psychology of Higher Education." Tatian also served as the editor-in-chief of the UCI yearbook, an award-winning publication. He now works for a test prep company, coordinating and teaching courses for high school and college students, and plans to pursue a master's degree in education and continue to teach.

Joseph Guisti: I am a 26-year-old undergraduate, and I'm okay with that. I just celebrated four years of sobriety, the birth of a baby sister (my first sibling ever!), and the completion of my second-to-last quarter at UCLA. I am currently DJ-ing all over Los Angeles, studying for the GRE, and applying to a bevy of graduate programs in medical sociology and science and technology studies.

Kristen Hammel graduated from UCLA in 2008 with a bachelor's degree in psychology and is currently pursuing a doctorate in clinical psychology at the Rosemead School of Psychology. She hopes that this book will continue to serve undergraduates by helping them navigate the university system and by opening their eyes to the potential for personal growth that takes place when they are empowered to participate in and shape their education. Kristen praises God for the blessings he continues to pour into her life, especially her family, friends, and memories.

Rick Hartman, 24 years old and currently a salesman and student-in-waiting, is on a seven-year degree program with a major in philosophy. His major area of interest and driving passion is an exploration of the space where language, identity, and the world somehow come together and, at the same time, generate each other in some strange form of dependent origination. He is committed to transforming the boundaries of what is possible for human beings to think through a change in their relationship to language. More important, he is the proud new companion of a German shepherd puppy.

Anees Hasnain is a recent graduate from the University of California, Los Angeles, with a bachelor's degree in sociology and minors in education studies, LGBT studies, and political science. She is not sure what she wants to do with her life, but knows that it should involve having moonshot goals and challenging social structures. When she is not running around in an owl suit or finding mustache accessories, she can be found reading everything from scholarly journals to trashy-but-she-reads-them-anyways beach novels with her cockatiel perched on her shoulder. She hopes that the thoughts, memories, and advice shared in this book will help others navigate the rather bizarre and often ridiculous aspects of college and life.

Christine Hazy: I am a mother of four and finishing my undergraduate degree after 25 years. I find Professor Anderson's classes at UCLA extraordinary and have been fortunate enough to be part of five of her classes: "Sociology of the Family," "Sociology of Mental Illness," "Sociology of Mass Communications," "Sociology of Art Worlds," and "Social Psychology." Sociology is everywhere around us and fascinating to find through my work in nonprofit organizations and fundraising.

Katherine Ho attended UCI, majoring in music performance and sociology. Coming from a very culturally diverse background and family, she finds that culture and the complex ways we all carry ourselves within our close relationships continue to be the creative drive in one's educational career and life. A man named Michael Bartel once said, "Happiness is a conscious choice, not an automatic response." She hopes that this book will help people to see that in this world you have a choice, in your education and any other aspect in life.

Sara Kalawi was born in Montreal, Canada, and is the product of a Lebanese father and a French-Canadian mother. For this reason, she has always felt that she relates well to diverse people. When she first read this book, Sara was intrigued by the diversity of topics covered and touched by the number of students who shared their words. She has found the book to be a useful tool in terms of college emotional survival and only wishes she could have found it earlier in her adolescent life. She takes pleasure and honor in contributing to this book and hopes her thoughts are appreciated and useful.

Eric Kim received his BA in sociology at UCLA in the spring of 2010 and is planning to pursue a master's and PhD in sociology. He is passionate about street photography and is seeking to combine the disciplines of sociology and photography in the field of "visual sociology." Through his experiences and random acts of kindness, he realizes the power of the individual within society: Although an individual might feel small in the overbearing sphere of society, he or she can still become "the change [he or she] wishes to see in the world." He wishes others to realize that they can make a meaningful impact in the world and that they should not become jaded by the overbearing presence of society. He also hopes that individuals who read his piece will truly pursue their passions.

Moo Young Kim grew up in Burbank, California. She completed her undergraduate work at University of California, Los Angeles, where she graduated with a BA in sociology. Kim has recently completed the Summer Institute in Global Affairs at New York University. She hopes to focus her career on public health—especially in the area of health education and policy. She lives in New York City.

Christopher Patrick King: We are students in the Class of Life. We are individual, walking experiments. The power of our humanity is that we can teach each other, while still learning what life is all about for ourselves. May all the students hear the love with which we write and know they are not alone. May they see the world as one endless chance to grow and mature. And may the students, empowered with a heart-filled passion, then become teachers in love and in life. Thanks to all of you for teaching me.

Lisa Kraft

Christina Le

Roberta Lessor

Lawrence Lu is someone who simply wishes to be a kid again and forever. He longs to look at the world with the wide-eyed optimism that plagues the youthful and feel the comfort of being part of a loving, genuine family. "Getting real" and "growing up" are not among his chosen hobbies. As a graduate of UCLA with a degree in psychology, he believes that everyone, at some point in life, is truly happy and that there is not a thing in the world more important than trying to find your way back, even for just a moment, even if it takes a lifetime.

Erika Martin: "We ourselves feel that what we are doing is just a drop in the ocean. But the ocean would be less because of that missing drop" (Mother Teresa). I believe in acting for what you believe in even if no one else will ever notice; *even if the only change that ever occurs is a change in you.*

Lisa Miyake was born in Tokyo and was raised in Orange County, California. Lisa is a second-year mass communications and Japanese double major at UCLA. She enjoys making the most of her years as an undergraduate by being involved with on-campus organizations, and she plans to work as a coordinator for international relations with the Japan Exchange and Teaching Programme after graduation. Her plans include going to law school, working in the field of international relations, and making the world a better place.

Sarah J. Morando is a graduate student in the sociology department at UCLA. Her research focuses on international migration, employment, and the sociology of law. She works as a Teaching Assistant in the sociology department and has led discussion sections in "Introductory Sociology" and "Social Psychology." She graduated from UC San Diego in 2006 with a bachelor of arts in sociology and a minor in Italian studies. She studied abroad during her junior year of college at the Università di Bologna in Bologna, Italy.

Sarah Nagy is 19 and a student at UCLA. She is majoring in business economics but has been interested in sociology, also a social science, since taking a general education course. She is honored to have been invited to contribute to this book as a part of Team Bell. Her hobbies include composing, directing and producing small films, and golfing. She lives in Los Angeles and after graduation will move to New York in early 2010.

Nkemdilim Nwosu is a graduate of UCLA, where she obtained a bachelor of arts in sociology with a specialization in communication studies. As an undergraduate, she worked as the editor-in-chief for UCLA's *Nommo* newsmagazine during the 2002–2003 school year. Her talent is writing, and she is currently working toward becoming a major TV script- and screenwriter.

Kevin O'Hara: I used to major in chemical engineering, but I changed to English. I love basketball, passion, thrill, joy, reading, writing, and music. Music wasn't important to me in the past, but I now listen to it daily and I constantly seek fresh melodies for my brain. I often find myself vacillating between contempt and amusement when I reflect on the nature of society. I enjoy life more when I'm arrogant instead of humble. I don't know how to properly conclude an autobiography, so I'll end with a couplet in the efforts of abandoning tradition with grace. My Muse advises me to be cryptic here: I'm not just a cog, but am I a gear?

Neil Poria: I'm a fifth-year UCLA anthropology student and am currently working as a part-time DJ in greater L.A. I'm originally from Corona, California, and have lived there since 1993. I enjoy music, a good wine, avocado on my sandwiches, and basketball, not in any particular order. I plan to pursue a master's degree and then apply to medical school.

Andrew Quan is currently a second-year undergraduate studying sociology at UCLA. He works for the student union, the associated students of UCLA, and participates in the Christian fellowship In Christ Alone and the Marina Del Rey Middle School mentoring program Bruin Partners. Besides observing and studying human behavior, he enjoys playing the guitar, photography, and running. His current plan for the future is to obtain a master's degree in social work and to pursue a career working with foster youth as a social worker.

Melissa Reggiardo graduated from UCLA in 2005. After graduation, she took a year off from academics to pursue a few of life's other pleasures: rest, work, and travel. Graduate school is in the future, but the specifics are currently undecided; such details will undoubtedly fall into place when the time is right.

Darra Ross

Kristin Rydberg is an overworked and underpaid college student who, upon first reading Inge Bell's book, discovered that she was an unassuming victim of a stagnant educational system. Now she aspires to become an educator who is willing to move beyond the institution of education and challenge students to pursue true knowledge and wisdom. She hopes that her contribution to this book will inspire you to do the same.

Gagendeep Sandhu graduated from UCI with a BA in psychology and sociology. Gagendeep has worked as a rape crisis counselor with a nonprofit organization and just received a master's in psychology.

Fabiola Santiago was born in Oaxaca, Mexico, but has lived in the U.S. since the age of five. Earning a BA in sociology from UCLA in 2009, she was the first in her family to graduate from college, and for that she is grateful to her family, friends, support system, and God/supernatural higher powers/angels/etc. who bless her life. Currently, she is still working as a restaurant server, waiting to hear what will happen with her immigration status, and applying to MPH programs. She is prepared to journey on to the public health field, where she will practice social justice by decreasing health disparities. However, the future—and life in general—is uncertain; therefore, she is taking everything lightly but optimistically.

Missak Michael Sarkissian

Raffi Sarkissian was born and raised in Southern California. As a recent graduate from UCLA, with degrees in both communication studies and sociology, he plans to pursue his interests in media studies at the graduate level en route to researching, teaching, and giving back to the environment that shaped his interests most—the university. Also an activist for LGBT rights, Raffi continues to lend his efforts in the fight for equality all across the nation.

Soheil Shahri was only six years old when the government decided to ruthlessly bind him to a reality of continuous education that extended into his late teens. While this may be true for almost every student in America, the government was oblivious to the fact that Mr. Shahri actually loves to learn and gain knowledge. Thus, he decided to pursue higher education. During his undergraduate career, he balanced his work life and social life with his numerous science and sociology courses at UCLA, where he eventually graduated summa cum laude in 2012. His driving force today is his strong desire for understanding people and social dynamics, which can only be overshadowed by his passion to help individuals directly. He is currently in the process of applying to dental schools.

Rohan Shamapant is a third-year international developmental studies/international economics UCLA student. Twenty years without a clue.

Fred Smoller

Samantha St. Laurent

Steffany Strain, UCLA sociology undergraduate: "For in much wisdom is much grief, And he who increases knowledge increases sorrow" (New King James Version, Eccles. 1:18).

Allison Taka graduated in 2010 from UCLA with a degree in sociology and a minor in education. She is a four-year member of the UCLA women's basketball team as well as a part of Athletes in Action and the Asian American Christian Fellowship on the UCLA campus. A fourth-generation Japanese American and UCLA Bruin since birth, she thanks God every day for blessing her with the opportunity to be a part of both the athletic and educational worlds at the best university in the nation.

Steven Truong is a graduate from UCLA with a degree in sociology and a minor in Asian American studies. Driven by his passion for love, life, and justice, he currently works as a paralegal in commercial real estate law and securities litigation and spends his off time as an activist for the Asian American LGBT community.

Christie Vong was born in Thailand and was raised in Southern California. She pursued a BA in sociology and social science at UCI. As cliché as it sounds, she hopes that in the future she can make a difference in the world, if only in touching one person's life.

Andy Wang, barely more than 21 years old, is a Los Angeles native and the son of immigrants from Taiwan. Andy is a typical college student, reaching the brink of his education: that edge where we fall off into the much-vaunted real world. But having learned his way off the road, overworn with unwilling travelers, he has confidence that he can navigate the wild world on his own terms. If he has learned anything in college, it's that we are to prepare ourselves to take on the world, not to mold ourselves into what the world expects us to be. He's ready—send him off!

Elisabeth Wilder received her bachelor's degree in political science from Pennsylvania State University before moving to Los Angeles, where she spent four years as an elementary school teacher. Her love of nature took her to the Pacific Northwest, where she completed her master's degree in sociology. Currently a doctoral student at Northeastern University, her broad areas of interest include environmental justice, globalization, stratification, and sustainability. She plans to build on her master's thesis and investigate the social impacts of transnational pipelines on vulnerable communities using an environmental justice framework. She enjoys hiking, camping, stargazing, and crafting and is learning to play the banjo.

Maryanne Wilson

Rhonda Wofford was born in California's Los Angeles County and resides in Santa Clara County. She is a graduate of Chapman University with a bachelor's degree, the first in her family to have graduated from college. She is currently employed at Intel and is applying to master's degree programs. She has crossed the boundaries and thrived in an atmosphere of racism and sexism. A Black woman with the desire for success, she has confronted and amended her substandard primary education. A Black woman who desires to just be recognized as an outstanding citizen, she knows that the word *Black* will always come before the word *citizen.*

Aggie Wong was born in Hong Kong, raised in Macau, grew up in San Francisco, fell in love with Los Angeles, and is now in search of a place to call home. She is a graduate of UCLA with a degree in psychology and sociology. As a first-generation college graduate, she finds herself mystified by all that life has to offer. She is grateful for all the opportunities that have been presented to her and is looking forward to living her life to the fullest, wherever she may be.

Shawna Wood is a second-year English major at UCLA who hopes to pursue a career in writing. With this book, she strives to help those like her who felt that getting straight A's was less important than learning to achieve real success in college, not just the kind that shines on transcripts. She also wants to thank all the people who have given her the ability to recognize what is worth fighting for in life.

SAGE research**methods**

The essential online tool for researchers from the world's leading methods publisher

Find exactly what you are looking for, from basic explanations to advanced discussion

More content and new features added this year!

"I have never really seen anything like this product before, and I think it really valuable."

John Creswell, University of Nebraska–Lincoln

Discover **Methods Lists**—methods readings suggested by other users

Watch video interviews with leading methodologists

Explore the **Methods Map** to discover links between methods

Search a custom-designed taxonomy with more than 1,400 qualitative, quantitative, and mixed methods terms

Uncover more than 120,000 pages of book, journal, and reference content to support your learning

out more at
w.sageresearchmethods.com